AFRICAN AMERICAN FAMILY LIFE

Duke Series in Child Development and Public Policy

Kenneth A. Dodge and Martha Putallaz, *Editors*

Aggression, Antisocial Behavior, and Violence among Girls:
A Developmental Perspective
Martha Putallaz and *Karen L. Bierman*

Enhancing Early Attachments:
Theory, Research, Intervention, and Policy
Lisa J. Berlin, Yair Ziv, Lisa Amaya-Jackson, and *Mark T. Greenberg*

African American Family Life:
Ecological and Cultural Diversity
Vonnie C. McLoyd, Nancy E. Hill, and *Kenneth A. Dodge*

African American Family Life

Ecological and Cultural Diversity

Edited by
VONNIE C. McLOYD
NANCY E. HILL
KENNETH A. DODGE

THE GUILFORD PRESS
NEW YORK   LONDON

© 2005 The Guilford Press
A Division of Guilford Publications, Inc.
72 Spring Street, New York, NY 10012
www.guilford.com

Printed in the United States of America

This book is printed on acid-free paper.

Last digit is print number: 9 8 7 6 5 4 3 2 1

Library of Congress Cataloging-in-Publication Data

African American family life : ecological and cultural diversity /
edited by Vonnie C. McLoyd, Nancy E. Hill, Kenneth A. Dodge.
       p. cm. — (Duke series in child development and public policy)
   Includes bibliographical references and index.
   ISBN 1-57230-995-4 (hardcover : alk. paper)
   1. African American families.   2. African Americans—Social
conditions.   3. African Americans—Socialization.   4. Community life—
United States.   I. McLoyd, Vonnie C.   II. Hill, Nancy E.   III. Dodge,
Kenneth A.   IV. Series.
   E185.86.D585 2005
   306.85′089′96073—dc22

                                                        2005006715

About the Editors

Vonnie C. McLoyd, PhD, is Professor of Psychology and Research Scientist at the Center for Developmental Science at the University of North Carolina at Chapel Hill. Her scholarly work focuses on the impact of economic disadvantage and employment-related transitions on family life and child development, the mediators and moderators of these impacts, and the implications of research on these issues for both practice and policy. Dr. McLoyd also has a long-standing interest in how race, ethnicity, and culture shape child socialization and development. She is director of a training program at UNC in research on Black child development, funded by the National Institute of Child Health and Human Development. Dr. McLoyd's work has been published in several journals. She is coeditor of *Economic Stress: Effects on Family Life and Child Development* (1990, Jossey Bass); *Studying Minority Adolescents: Conceptual, Methodological, and Theoretical Issues* (1998, Erlbaum); and two special issues of the journal *Child Development*.

Dr. McLoyd is the recipient of several awards, including the Ruben Hill Award from the National Council on Family Relations, the William T. Grant Faculty Scholars Award in Child Mental Health, the MacArthur Fellow Award, and the 2003 Distinguished Career Contributions to Research Award from Division 45 (Society for the Psychological Study of Ethnic Minority Issues) of the American Psychological Association. She is president-elect of the Society for Research on Adolescence and a member of the Research Network on Transitions to Adulthood and Public Policy, supported by the John D. and Catherine T. MacArthur Foundation.

Nancy E. Hill, PhD, is Associate Professor of Psychology at Duke University and Research Associate Professor of Psychology and Faculty Affiliate of the Center for Developmental Science at the University of

North Carolina at Chapel Hill. She is one of the founders of the Study
Group on Race, Culture, and Ethnicity, an interdisciplinary group of scientists brought together to develop theory and methodology for defining
and understanding cultural contexts within diverse families. Dr. Hill is
interested in how cultural, economic, and community contexts influence
family dynamics and family socialization patterns and in turn shape children's developmental outcomes. Her research focuses on how parenting
and family socialization vary across ethnicity and socioeconomic status,
and demographic variations in the relationship between family dynamics
and children's developmental outcomes, especially among African American and Latino families. Dr. Hill is the Principal Investigator for Project
PASS (Promoting Academic Success for Students), a longitudinal study
examining demographic variations in family-related predictors of children's early school performance, and ACTION/ACCIONES, a multiethnic,
longitudinal study of parental involvement in education at the transition
between elementary and middle school.

Kenneth A. Dodge, PhD, is the William McDougall Professor of Public
Policy Studies and Professor of Psychology at Duke University. He di-
rects the Duke Center for Child and Family Policy, which is devoted to
finding solutions to problems facing children in contemporary society
through research, policy engagement, service, and education. Dr. Dodge
is interested in how problem behaviors such as chronic violence, school
failure, drug use, and child abuse develop across the lifespan; how they
can be prevented; and how communities can implement policies to
prevent these outcomes and instead promote children's optimal development. He has teamed up with colleagues to create, implement, and evaluate the Fast Track Program to prevent chronic violence in high-risk
children, and he is now leading the Durham Family Initiative to prevent
child abuse in Durham, North Carolina. Dr. Dodge has been honored
with the Distinguished Scientific Contribution Award from the American
Psychological Association, the Boyd McCandless Award, and the Senior
Scientist Award from the National Institutes of Health. He is a Fellow of
the American Association for the Advancement of Science, the Academy
of Experimental Criminology, the American Psychological Society, and
the American Psychological Association.

Contributors

Valerie D. Anderson, MA, Department of Psychology, Duke University, Durham, North Carolina

Oscar A. Barbarin, PhD, School of Social Work, University of North Carolina, Chapel Hill, North Carolina

Chalandra M. Bryant, PhD, Department of Human Development and Family Studies, College of Health and Human Development, Pennsylvania State University, University Park, Pennsylvania

Linda M. Burton, PhD, Center for Human Development and Family Research in Diverse Contexts, Pennsylvania State University, University Park, Pennsylvania

Sherri Lawson Clark, PhD, Population Research Institute, Pennsylvania State University, University Park, Pennsylvania

Stephanie I. Coard, PhD, Center for Child and Family Policy, Duke University, Durham, North Carolina

Cheri Coleman, MSW, Frank Porter Graham Child Development Institute, University of North Carolina, Chapel Hill, North Carolina

William Darity, Jr., PhD, Department of Economics, University of North Carolina, Chapel Hill, North Carolina

Peggye Dilworth-Anderson, PhD, School of Public Health and Institute on Aging, University of North Carolina, Chapel Hill, North Carolina

Kenneth A. Dodge, PhD, Department of Psychology and Center for Child and Family Policy, Duke University, Durham, North Carolina

Noemí Enchautegui-de-Jesús, PhD, Department of Psychology, Syracuse University, Syracuse, New York

Paula Y. Goodwin, PhD, Department of Child Development and Family Studies, Purdue University, West Lafayette, Indiana

Brenda Jones Harden, PhD, Department of Human Development, University of Maryland, College Park, Maryland

Nancy E. Hill, PhD, Department of Psychology, Duke University, Durham, North Carolina

Angela D. James, PhD, Department of Psychiatry and Biobehavioral Sciences, University of California, Los Angeles, California

Vicki L. Lamb, PhD, Center for Demographic Studies, Duke University, Durham, North Carolina

Kenneth C. Land, PhD, Department of Sociology and Center for Demographic Studies, Duke University, Durham, North Carolina

Jennifer E. Lansford, PhD, Center for Child and Family Policy, Duke University, Durham, North Carolina

Jacqueline S. Mattis, PhD, Department of Applied Psychology, Steinhardt School of Education, New York University, New York, New York

Terry McCandies, PhD, Frank Porter Graham Child Development Institute, University of North Carolina, Chapel Hill, North Carolina

Vonnie C. McLoyd, PhD, Department of Psychology, University of North Carolina, Chapel Hill, North Carolina

Sarah O. Meadows, MA, Department of Sociology, Duke University, Durham, North Carolina

Velma McBride Murry, PhD, Department of Child and Family Development, University of Georgia, Athens, Georgia

Melba J. Nicholson, PhD, The Family Institute, Evanston, Illinois

Ellen E. Pinderhughes, PhD, Department of Child Development, Tufts University, Medford, Massachusetts

Robert M. Sellers, PhD, Department of Psychology, University of Michigan, Ann Arbor, Michigan

Howard C. Stevenson, PhD, Graduate School of Education, University of Pennsylvania, Philadelphia, Pennsylvania

Fasaha Traylor, MA, Foundation for Child Development, New York, New York

M. Belinda Tucker, PhD, Department of Psychiatry and Biobehavioral
Sciences and Center for Culture and Health, University of
California, Los Angeles, California

Chanequa Walker-Barnes, PhD, private practice, Raleigh, North
Carolina

K. A. S. Wickrama, PhD, Department of Human Development and
Family Studies, Institute for Social and Behavioral Research, Iowa
State University, Ames, Iowa

Donna-Marie Winn, PhD, Center for Child and Family Policy, Duke
University, Durham, North Carolina

Series Editors' Note

This volume is the third in the *Duke Series in Child Development and Public Policy*, an ongoing collection of edited volumes that address the translation of research in child development to contemporary issues in public policy. The goal of the series is to bring cutting-edge research and theory in the vibrant field of child development to bear on problems facing children and families in contemporary society.

This series grew out of interactions among faculty members at the Duke Center for Child and Family Policy in the Terry Sanford Institute of Public Policy and the Duke Department of Psychology: Social and Health Sciences. With generous support from the Duke Provost's Initiative in the Social Sciences, we began to plan an annual series of working conferences, each of which would lead to an edited volume.

Each conference brings together scholars from diverse disciplines, along with a participant audience of over 100 scientists, students, policymakers, and practitioners, who wrestle with a problem in contemporary society. Because each conference is defined by a broad current problem or issue, scholars are forced to depart from their silos of disciplinary-based theories and methods in order to address the practice and policy issues that are germane to a particular problem. The solutions to vexing contemporary problems require the best efforts of multiple disciplines working together.

The first volume in the series—*Aggression, Antisocial Behavior, and Violence among Girls*, edited by Martha Putallaz and Karen L. Bierman— challenges myths about girls' aggressive behavior, provides important new findings, and guides future research as well as policy. The second volume—*Enhancing Early Attachments*, edited by Lisa J. Berlin, Yair Ziv, Lisa Amaya-Jackson, and Mark T. Greenberg—addresses interventions for problems in the parent–infant attachment relationship. Practitioners, developmental scientists, and policymakers have recently recognized the importance of the early parent–infant relationship in future outcomes for children. Interventions have proliferated to address this relationship, some with remarkable success but others with well-publicized disastrous outcomes. The volume provides a concise overview of attachment theory, the empirical evidence regarding effectiveness of interventions in real-world settings, and the policy issues that must be navigated to bring these interventions to standard practice in the community.

The current volume brings multiple disciplinary perspectives to bear on important issues facing African American families in the 21st century. It emphasizes family strengths in growing wealth, religiosity, family relationships, and rich cultural traditions. It also addresses important challenges that African American families face, ranging from children's academic development to balancing family needs and employment.

Future conferences and volumes will focus on the prevention of depression in adolescence, the problem of deviant peer contagion in adolescent groups and interventions, and cultural influences on parenting practices.

KENNETH A. DODGE, PhD
MARTHA PUTALLAZ, PhD

Acknowledgments

Completion of this book would not have been possible without the generosity of the Provost and Deans of Duke University, the Duke Center for Child and Family Policy, and Susan Roth, PhD, Chair of the Duke Department of Psychology: Social and Health Sciences. With their support, a multidisciplinary group of scholars was able to meet to share research findings, debate theories, and formulate crucial questions pertaining to African American families. The group's activities culminated in a 2-day conference held at Duke's Sanford Institute of Public Policy on May 15–16, 2003, attended by 125 scholars, students, and public leaders. The lively discussion and penetrating analyses that emerged during that conference led to this book.

The contributors also wish to thank the following people for their insightful reviews of early drafts of the chapters: Dalton Conley, Martha Crowther, Christina Gibson-Davis, Algea Harrison-Hale, Hayward Derrick Horton, Diane Hughes, Beth Kurtz-Costes, Ruth McRoy, Scott South, and Lorraine Taylor. Their constructive critiques and intellectual generosity greatly enhanced the quality of our work. In addition, we are very grateful for the assistance of Lynda Harrison and Barbara Pollock of the Duke Center for Child and Family Policy.

Contents

AFRICAN AMERICAN FAMILY LIFE

PART I

EMERGENT ISSUES, THEMES, AND CONCEPTUALIZATIONS

CHAPTER I

Introduction

Ecological and Cultural Diversity in African American Family Life

Vonnie C. McLoyd, Nancy E. Hill, *and* Kenneth A. Dodge

Few would dispute that the family is the basic social unit in the organization of human society and a primary context for the development and socialization of society's children (Hill, 1993). These axioms undergird efforts to modify family processes and understand factors that protect, strengthen, threaten, or otherwise affect these processes. They also stoke acrimonious debate about the legitimacy of particular family forms and practices, particularly those thought to have either direct or indirect influences on children's development and well-being. African American families, especially those at the lower end of the income distribution, often have been at the center of these debates, owing to their differences from "mainstream" American families in terms of family structure, living arrangements, and childrearing practices. Some of these differences have been purportedly linked to poor child functioning (e.g., Bracey, Meier, & Rudwick, 1971; Kelley, 1997; Moynihan, 1971; Peters, 1978; Quadagno, 1994; Tulkin, 1972).

This volume, informed partly by these controversies, focuses attention on emerging issues in numerous facets of African American family life, including family formation, marital relations, childrearing, care of the elderly, employment, and religious practices. Special attention is given to recent contributions to our understanding of how African American families accommodate, subvert, transform, and otherwise

adapt to contextual factors and the nature of their transactions with societal subsystems and institutions such as schools, churches, the workplace, the child welfare system, and social service agencies. In addition to
providing rich descriptions of the contexts within which African American family life is situated, the authors of the various chapters detail
within-race differences as well as racial disparities in these contexts.
They also explicate and pose queries about how African American culture intervenes in and is itself influenced by these processes.

Our overarching goal extends beyond highlighting emergent issues
and recent contributions to our knowledge base. We also seek to advance research and theory. Hence, we identify critical substantive, theoretical, and methodological issues and gaps in extant work and set forth
new directions for research and theory. Finally, we hope to shape conversations about strategies to support and strengthen African American
families by offering critiques of current policies and institutional practices and setting forth recommendations in these domains. Toward these
ends, the chapters are purposefully broad in their treatment of the focal
issues at hand—the authors highlight their own work but give discerning
attention to the contributions of other scholars and the overall state of
knowledge within a particular domain of study.

Traditionally, the study of African American family life has been the
bailiwick of sociologists and historians, but with the proliferation of
African American scholars with doctorates in psychology and human development beginning in the early 1970s, psychological and developmental perspectives—with a special focus on child development—although
evident in earlier work, became more prominent in research focusing on
African American family life. These perspectives are heavily represented
in this book, in keeping with the fact that most contributors were
trained in psychology and human development. As theory and research
designed to understand African American families, historically, was
based in multiple disciplines, so too is this book (i.e., human development, psychology, sociology, economics). Understanding strengths, resilience, and challenges confronting African American families is best
achieved through multidisciplinary discussions and collaborations.

EMERGENT ISSUES, THEMES, AND CONCEPTUALIZATIONS

We introduce this book by highlighting demographic markers of the
contexts within which contemporary African American family life is sit
uated because of their implications for family functioning and well-being.
Both variations among African Americans and differences between Afri-

can Americans and non-Hispanic White Americans (e.g., family structure, children's living arrangements, family size, geographic location, and a range of economic indicators) are important to consider. It is undeniable that African Americans lag behind European Americans on numerous indicators of well-being, but several points bear mention to lend perspective to this portrait of inequality. First, as Hill, Murry, and Anderson (Chapter 2, this volume) so well document, tremendous heterogeneity exists within the African American population on myriad dimensions, appreciation of which has often been a casualty of debates about this population. Further, there is evidence of substantial narrowing of racial disparities on numerous economic indicators during the past several decades (Myers, 2004), across-time improvement among African American children on several markers of well-being, and growing similarities in cultural practices across American ethnic groups (Hill et al., Chapter 2, this volume). Lamb, Land, Meadows, and Traylor (Chapter 3, this volume) assemble indicators of child well-being from numerous archived databases to show the gains that African American children have made in the past 25 years in education, health, and well-being, and identify factors that apparently have contributed to these gains.

Race differences in family structure have long existed, and they continue to be substantial. The importance of family structure derives partly from its strong link to income and poverty status, both of which are related to child and family functioning (Duncan & Brooks-Gunn, 1997). In 2002 nearly one half (48%) of all African American families were married-couple families, as compared with 82% of non-Hispanic White families. Forty-three percent of African American families were maintained by women with no spouse present, and 9% were maintained by men with no spouse present, whereas the corresponding figures for non-Hispanic White families were 13% and 5% (Fields, 2003). During this period, almost half (48%) of African American children were living with a single mother. When those living with a single father (5%) are included, more than half (53%) of African American children were living with a single parent. This contrasts with 16% of non-Hispanic White children living with a single mother and 4% living with a single father (Fields, 2003).

It is difficult to discern the true effects of these race differences in single- and two-parent families because of the greater prevalence of extended family households among African Americans. African American families on average are larger than non-Hispanic White families. In 2002, among married-couple African American families, 33% had two members and 20% had five or more members; the corresponding figures for non-Hispanic White families were 47% and 12%. Among families maintained by women with no spouse present, 40% of African American families had two members and 11% had five or more members, as compared with 55% and 5% of non-Hispanic White families, respectively. African American children are more likely than non-Hispanic White children to live with a grandparent. In 2002, 12% of African American children ages 17 and younger were living in households with a grandparent present, as compared with 5% of non-Hispanic White children—a disparity that partly reflects African Americans' greater economic fragility. Three fourths (75%) of African American children living with a grandparent lived in their grandparents' household, as compared with 69% of non-Hispanic White children. Grandparents are assumed to be *providing* assistance if they are the householders, whereas they are believed to be *receiving* assistance when they are living in their child's or someone else's household (Fields, 2003).

Geographic location also distinguishes African Americans from non-Hispanic Whites, with a greater concentration of African Americans residing in central cities. Whereas 52% of African Americans lived in a central city within a metropolitan area in 2002, only 21% of non-Hispanic Whites did so. In contrast, 57% of non-Hispanic Whites lived outside the central city but within the metropolitan area, as compared with 36% of African Americans. In light of evidence that residence in low-income neighborhoods is linked to less positive development in children (e.g., cognitive functioning, school dropout, adolescent childbearing), independent of personal and family background characteristics (Leventhal & Brooks-Gunn, 2000), the economic character of neighborhoods where families reside is perhaps of greater significance for child and family well-being than whether families live outside versus inside the central city per se. Here, too, race differences are seen.

During the 1970s and 1980s, poor African Americans were far more likely than poor non-Hispanic Whites to live in high-poverty inner-city communities (i.e., those in which at least 40% of the residents were poor) where jobs, high-quality public and private services (e.g., child-care, schools, parks, community centers, youth organizations), and informal social supports are less accessible (Duncan, 1991; Shinn & Gillespie, 1994; Wilson, 1987). This pattern has persisted, though the disparities appear to have narrowed in the past decade. The 1990s brought both declines in the concentration of poverty (the share of the metropolitan poor who lived in high-poverty census tracts—those with poverty rates of 40% or more—dropped from 17% in the 1980s to 12% in 2000) and changes in the composition of concentrated poverty by race. In particular, the share of all high-poverty tracts with predominantly (more than 60%) African American populations declined from 48% in 1980 to 39% in 2000, with compensating increases occurring in the shares that were predominantly Hispanic (Kingsley & Pettit, 2003).

In 2000, about 54% of African American children who were officially poor lived in high-poverty neighborhoods (as assessed in 1989), as compared with 47% of poor non-Hispanic White children (U.S. Department of Health and Human Services, 2002).

Economic resources are significant determinants of a wide range of quality-of-life indicators; hence, racial disparities in this domain assume special significance. Because African Americans, as compared with non-Hispanic Whites, have lower levels of education attainment (in 2002, 17% of all African Americans held at least a bachelor's degree, as compared with 29% of non-Hispanic Whites) and experience higher rates of unemployment (in 2002, 11% vs. 5%, respectively) and poverty (in 2002, 23% vs. 8%, respectively), racial disparities in income are hardly surprising (McKinnon, 2003). Income is an important indicator of economic well-being because it measures the ability of families to purchase food, shelter, clothing, childcare, and other basic goods and services required for the survival and sustenance of family members. In 2001, the median money income of African American families with related children under age 18 was about $30,000, about 50% of the median income of comparable non-Hispanic White families. Controlling for family structure does not eliminate the racial disparity. In 2001, for example, the median income of African American married couple families with children was about 78% of the median income of comparable non-Hispanic White families ($55,734 vs. $71,102, respectively), and that of African American mother-only families with children was about 75% of the median income of comparable non-Hispanic White families ($19,086 vs. $25,455) (U.S. Department of Health and Human Services, 2002).

As Darity and Nicholson (Chapter 4, this volume) point out, analyses of wealth reveal an even deeper racial divide. Wealth refers to a family's or individual's net value of economic assets—including money in the bank, real estate, ownership of stock, business ownership—less debt held at any one time. Whereas, for most families, income provides the necessities of life, wealth "represents a kind of 'surplus' resource available for improving life chances, providing further opportunities, securing prestige, passing status along to one's family, and influencing the political process" (Oliver & Shapiro, 1995, p. 32). Furthermore, wealth provides an "insurance backup" that buffers families in times of emergency and enables families to aspire to greatness in times of comfort. The lack of financial backup may account for the inability of some families to rebound from stressful times.

Many of the racial disparities cited here are legacies of institutionalized racism in education, employment, and housing that were embodied and codified in government policies. Indeed, U.S. history is replete with social policies guided by a race-conscious framework that assumed the fundamental inferiority and "unworthiness" of African Americans and other persons of non-European descent. The intertwining of race and welfare policy is a case in point (Schram, Soss, & Fording, 2003). In the debate over the Social Security Act of 1935, congressmen from southern states successfully excluded domestic and agricultural workers from social insurance coverage, "effectively channeling people of color into public assistance programs controlled at the state level" (Soss, Schram, Vartanian, & O'Brien, 2004, p. 11). New opportunities for racial bias in U.S. welfare policy were created in the 1990s as federal welfare reform shifted control over several aspects of welfare down to the state level. Analyses indicate that states where African American recipients make up a higher percentage of the caseload have lower cash benefits and are more likely to adopt strict time limits and family caps (i.e., excluding from assistance children born to families already receiving welfare), even when other relevant state-level factors are taken into account (Soss, Schram, Vartanian, & O'Brien, 2001, 2004).

In other examples of racial discrimination at the policy level, African Americans were systematically excluded from more than a century of asset-building policies in the United States, which included the Homestead Act of 1862 and the mortgage system of both the Federal Housing Authority (FHA), established in 1934, and the Veterans Administration. Restrictive covenants based on race and social class and discrimination in mortgage lending relegated African Americans to inner cities in disproportionate numbers and locked them out of opportunities for wealth accumulation. This egregious historical treatment has translated into staggering racial differences in wealth and inheritance to this day. These differences are further compounded by current racial disparities in access to mortgage loans and housing markets and by segregated housing that lowers the demand for, and hence the value of, homes owned by African Americans, on one hand, and increases the price African Americans pay for goods and services on the other (Oliver & Shapiro, 1995; Williams & Rucker, 1996).

The statistics presented here make the point that, on average, African Americans and European Americans transact their family lives in substantially different multilevel contexts. Hill and colleagues (Chapter 2, this volume) provide an overview of these contexts, wrestle with their influence on African American culture, and pose challenges for the scholarly inquiry of cultural effects. Tucker and James (Chapter 5, this volume) analyze how contextual and cultural factors have shaped the structure and function of African American families. They present a historical and anthropological perspective on current and emerging conceptualizations of family, as well as broader societal trends that impinge on contemporary African American family life and distinguish it from that of previous eras.

CONTINUITIES AND DISCONTINUITIES IN THE STUDY AND APPRAISAL OF AFRICAN AMERICAN FAMILY LIFE

This book builds on the seminal work of Du Bois (1909), Billingsley (1968, 1992), Frazier (1939), Hill (1971), McAdoo (1978, 1982), and Staples (1985), among others. It continues a tradition of bringing together writings about African American family life that spotlight the research contributions of the authors and draw attention to advances and limitations in knowledge, as well as emergent issues (Clark, 1975; McAdoo, 1981, 2002; Peters, 1978; Staples, 1994; Taylor, Jackson, & Chatters, 1997). Its link to early work on African American family life is especially salient with respect to the attention given to contextual influences. Prominently woven throughout the rich and venerable history of the study of African American family life is the notion that family organization and dynamics are, to a major extent, adaptations to the broader context within which the family is situated. Indeed, throughout its 17-year run, the first publication outlet for the systematic study of African Americans—the highly esteemed Atlanta University Monograph series established in 1898 by W. E. B. Du Bois—was devoted principally to detailed examinations of the social context of the Black experience (Conyers, 1970).

For example, Du Bois's *The Negro American Family,* published in 1909 as one of the monographs in the series, encompassed analyses of how economic demands shaped intimate relations between African American males and females though their impact on marriage formation and skewed sex ratios—salient themes to this day (Tucker & Kernan-Mitchell, 1995). Du Bois observed that "low wages and a rising economic standard is [*sic*] postponing marriage to an age dangerously late for a folk in the Negro's present moral development . . . present economic demand draws the Negro woman to the city and keeps the men in the country, causing a dangerous disproportion of the sexes" (Du Bois, 1909, p. 36).

E. Franklin Frazier (1939), whose work stands as an unrivaled benchmark of stellar and influential, if controversial, sociological scholarship on African American family life, accorded even more functional significance to social context than did Du Bois. Unlike Du Bois, he discounted the notion that African culture influenced the development, organization, and functioning of African American families, maintaining that the social characteristics of African American families could be understood solely in terms of the social conditions in the United States that shaped them. Nonetheless, Frazier lamented and was highly critical of some of the ways that African American families adapted to racism and subjugation and their attendant negative social conditions (e.g., mother-headed families, out-of-wedlock births). Although he saw only a minimal role for government to play in transforming the conditions of African American life, he expected that positive economic and social changes in the broader society would operate to strengthen African American families (Glazer, 1966).

The 1950s and 1960s saw the assertion of a different emphasis in the analysis of African American family life, one that did not disavow categorically the influence of social context, but gave analytic preeminence to the notion of African American families as a significant force in the creation of social conditions and social structure (Glazer, 1966). Social and economic disadvantage were seen primarily as products of problematic organization and functioning in African American families maintained intergenerationally through families' socialization of values, personality, and social character deemed ill suited for upward mobility (e.g., Kardiner & Ovesey, 1951). This dualistic framing of issues in terms of whether African American families are principally a product of or the creator of social conditions has proven extraordinarily resilient, with the contrasting positions posing radically different implications for social policies intended to support and strengthen African American families. Those scholars and advocates who regard African American families as products of social conditions tend to champion strategies that remove economic and social barriers. Advocates of the alternative view, predictably, tend to give priority to changing internal family dynamics (e.g., childrearing) and psychological functioning, as these factors are seen as underlying economic and social disadvantage. This task typically is regarded as a rather arduous one, on the grounds that these dimensions of functioning are obdurate cultural patterns established though decades of intergenerational transmission. This debate continues to be played out in the popular press and among public leaders every day—witness the controversy surrounding comments by cultural icon Bill Cosby.

As many readers will recall, precisely this issue was at the heart of the controversy that erupted in the 1960s among social scientists about Oscar Lewis's (1966) "culture of poverty" notion. Maintaining that poverty is more than a mere lack of economic resources, Lewis identified an array of psychological orientations and behaviors that he believed characterized the poor and rendered poverty self-perpetuating (e.g., lack of impulse control, present-time orientation, minimal ability to defer gratification and plan for the future). Echoing this perspective, Moynihan (1971), in his acrimoniously debated treatise, contended that the "tangle of pathology" found in many African American families—marked by a matriarchal family structure, low levels of education, and high rates of marital dissolution, out-of-wedlock births, unemployment, and poverty—"is capable of perpetuating itself without assistance from the white world" (p. 158) and that "unless this damage is repaired, all the effort to end discrimination and poverty and injustice will come to little" (p. 126). Related notions of "cultural disadvantage" and "cultural deficit" also made their appearance in the child development literature during this era (Tulkin, 1972), the term "cultural" implicitly contrasting with "genetic" to underscore the environment as a determinant of behavior seen as inferior and undesirable (Condry, 1983). These concepts provided the conceptual scaffolding for remediation policies and interventions. Most were focused on children directly (e.g., early childhood education) or indirectly through their parents (e.g., parenting programs), based on the notion that social and economic disadvantage results from an intergenerational cycle that can best be broken during the victim's childhood (de Lone, 1979).

Critics decried analyses that invoked these "culture concepts" as explanations for disproportionately high rates of poverty among African Americans, intergenerational poverty, the existence of an "underclass," and race differences in children's intellectual and school performance that favored European American children. They questioned both the veracity and interpretation of evidence cited by proponents of these perspectives, arguing that these conceptualizations of culture decontextualized the social and economic problems experienced by racial and ethnic minorities, gave short shrift to institutionalized racism and other historical and political factors that undergird these phenomena, and were founded on invidious comparisons that disparaged non-European American, middle-class cultures (Cole & Bruner, 1971; Corcoran, Duncan, Gurin, & Gurin, 1985; Labov, 1970; Tulkin, 1972). The race comparative paradigm came under scathing attack on these conceptual grounds, but also because research procedures and instruments were egregiously biased against African Americans (McLoyd & Randolph, 1985). To a considerable degree, these skirmishes brought disrepute to the culture concept as a tool for understanding the effects of poverty and racism (Sullivan, 1989) and, more generally, induced apprehension among scholars about its value in explaining race differences in children's socialization and development.

These tensions in psychology bore similarities to competing ideological perspectives on African American family life that existed during this era in sociology and family studies (Peters, 1978). In his now classic paper, Allen (1978) noted that researchers who favored the *cultural-deviant* perspective tended to view qualities of African American families that deviated from those of European American middle-class families as evidence of dysfunction and pathology. In contrast, those researchers who endorsed the more ecologically oriented *cultural-variant* perspective viewed differences between African American and non-Hispanic White families as "outgrowths of their respective sociocultural contexts," acknowledging that "while family functions are more or less universal, situational constraints vary and therefore dictate the adoption of culturally distinct styles of organization and interaction" (pp. 125–126). A third perspective—the *cultural-equivalent* perspective—was characterized by a tendency to deemphasize distinctive qualities of African American families and highlight qualities shared in common with European American families.

Allen's analysis was perhaps even more valuable for its explicit framing of these ideological perspectives as orthogonal to conceptual approaches to the study of Black family research within sociology during this era (i.e., structural-functional, interactional-situational, developmental—life course). The two dimensions have often been conflated. As Allen pointed out, researchers might concur as to the general validity of terminology, definitions, and assumptions about the set of conditions believed to be most crucial to understanding family phenomena (conceptual approach), but disagree about the essential character and functioning of Black family life (ideological perspective). Allen endorsed the cultural-variant perspective as most appropriate for the study of most facets of African American family life. However, he cautioned against the view "that any aspect of black family life which exists, no matter how perverse or harmful, must serve a useful function," on the grounds that "such radically functionalist reasoning . . . undermines societal commitment toward assisting black families in coping with devastating problems, not necessarily of their own creation" (p. 126).

As these brief historical notes illustrate, there have long been proponents of the notion that African American families must be understood within the context of extant environmental demands and circumstances. However, not until Bronfenbrenner's and Ogbu's luminous, well-developed, and tightly argued analyses did a wide swath of scholars in human development explicitly embrace this general perspective as an analytic tool for understanding aspects of African American family functioning and the socialization and development of African American children. Bronfenbrenner (1986) argued persuasively that children's development is influenced not only by the family system, but also by systems well removed from the family's control—among them, parents' workplaces, neighborhoods, schools, available health and daycare services—and macroeconomic forces that result in stressors such as parental unemployment and job and income loss. He exhorted researchers to take seriously the potency of the family's ecology by undertaking multilayered, contextual, and more process-oriented analyses of family relations and children's development. Ogbu (1981), focusing specifically on poor African American children and families living in urban settings, articulated a cultural-ecological model that underscored the potency of extrafamilial forces on parenting goals, child socialization practices, and child development.

AFRICAN AMERICAN FAMILIES IN COMMUNITY CONTEXTS

A prominent theme of this book is how cultural factors such as religiosity, family and kin support systems, childrearing values and practices, racial socialization, racial identity, and attitudes about maternal employment and women's responsibility as economic providers, influence the nature of these adaptation processes and are themselves shaped by contextual factors. These cultural factors are important resources and strengths that shield African American individuals and families from some of the negative consequences of exposure to stressors and help account for paradoxes such as the lower rates of psychiatric disorder among African Americans as compared with non-Hispanic Whites (Harrison-Hale, McLoyd, & Smedley, 2004; Williams, 2004).

Contributors to this edited volume eschew the cultural-deficit ideological perspective. Their analyses of factors that protect, strengthen, and threaten African American families are more in keeping with the cultural-variant perspective in that differences between African American and non-Hispanic White families are seen largely as the result of differing sociocultural contexts. However, the contributors do not hew to any single conceptual approach delineated in Allen's (1978) typology. Rather, their collective work is guided by multiple approaches, and some authors incorporate elements from multiple conceptual frameworks in their work. Elements of the structural-functional approach—defined by its emphasis on the origins and evolution of families through cross-historical comparisons and families' interactions and interdependencies with other societal subsystems—are readily apparent in Tucker and James's (Chapter 5, this volume) analysis. They discuss changes in African American family structure and dynamics within the context of broad societal trends and historical events such as migration, increased geographic dispersion, decreased ability of young adults to secure jobs that permit economic independence, increased reliance on women's economic contributions, and relatedly, the reconstruction of gender role expectations.

This perspective is also evident in Burton and Clark's (Chapter 8, this volume) ethnographic study of the significance of "homeplace" in the day-to-day lives of low-income urban African American families. The homeplace, defined by the authors as a multilayered and nuanced family process anchored in a defined physical space, has been instrumental in families' ability to construct social and cultural identity, to procure privacy, power, and control, and to develop and maintain family routines and legacies. The authors highlight some of the ways in which federally assisted housing programs that disperse low-income families to low poverty areas (e.g., Moving to Opportunity) hinder fulfillment of these functions and the strategies families use vis-à-vis these housing programs to both maximize their housing options and meet the critical functions of homeplace. Several of the chapters exemplify elements of the interactional-situational approach, distinguished by its emphasis on interpersonal relationships in the family and how community and institutional contexts affect these relationships. Bryant and Wickrama (Chapter 6, this volume) examine the relation of community characteristics (e.g., concentration of poverty, residential instability, percentage of minorities, informal and formal community social support) to marital quality and the extent to which perceptions of adversity in the community mediate these relations. Dilworth-Anderson and Goodwin (Chapter 10, this volume) provide insight into the adaptation processes that extended families adopt in order to provide a system of care for noninstitutionalized dependent, functionally or cognitively impaired elderly family members. They detail the structure and extrafamilial context of caregiving, but also the role strain, emotional distress, and physical health problems that caregivers often experience as a result of caring for dependent elderly family members.

McLoyd and Enchautegui-de-Jesús (Chapter 7, this volume) set a particular societal subsystem and context—the workplace—in the foreground of their analyses, exploring the implications of African Americans' employment status and work life for family and marital functioning, parenting, and African American children's development. Mattis (Chapter 9, this volume) starts with the almost ubiquitous reality of religion in the daily lives of African American families by noting that 90% of all African Americans self-identify as religious. She weaves a complicated texture of reciprocal relations between the institution of religion and family life by noting how each influences the other. Religion provides support in troubled times but also affects the very fabric of African American family life.

SOCIALIZATION PROCESSES
IN AFRICAN AMERICAN FAMILIES

How best to contextualize ethnic differences in parenting and other socialization practices is another hotly debated issue. Whereas previous research has typically found that African American families are more likely to endorse authoritarian practices or "no-nonsense" socialization strategies, including high levels of control, the debate often pertains to the extent to which the relation between parenting practices and child outcomes generalizes across ethnicity (Baumrind, 1972; Brody & Flor, 1998; McLoyd, 1990). Theory and research acknowledging culturally based variations in parenting goals and values have begun to explain variations in family dynamics and socialization process (Billingsley, 1974; Garcia Coll, Meyer, & Brillon, 1995; McAdoo, 1991; Taylor, Chatters, Tucker, & Lewish, 1990; Willis, 1992). The history and cultural context of contemporary African American families present particular opportunities and challenges in raising children. African American parents attempt to nurture their children's strengths in order that they become productive and contributing members of society, but they are faced with unique obstacles and challenges. Several authors identify distinctive family socialization practices, contextualize ethnic differences in parenting practices within the sociocultural context of African American families, and examine processes that lead to within-group heterogeneity in African American family socialization practices.

Drawing from a wide body of research literature on children from prekindergarten to high school, Barbarin, McCandies, Coleman, and Hill (Chapter 11, this volume) present a systematic account of how and why various aspects of family life (e.g., family structure, parenting practices, home learning experiences, socioemotional climate within the family, ethnic and religious socialization, parental academic expectations, and home–school relationships) relate significantly to the academic success of African American children. They conclude that parents exert a powerful influence on children's academic achievement through multi-level efforts that involve activities direct and indirect, witting and unwitting. In light of evidence that African American students lag behind European American and Asian American students on most indicators of academic achievement, beginning with school readiness at kindergarten and early achievement in elementary school and continuing through to differential rates of high school and college graduation, Barbarin and colleagues call for more research detailing the impediments African American parents experience in exploiting these strategies fully to their children's advantage.

Dodge, McLoyd, and Lansford (Chapter 12, this volume) discuss the parental task of disciplining children. Use of corporal punishment is a discipline practice that, on average, differentiates African American families from European American families, although this difference appears to be shrinking across time. Dodge and colleagues identify cultural and contextual factors that may underlie not only this difference, but also corresponding race differences in the endorsement of corporal punishment and, most importantly, race differences in the effects of physical discipline on children's development. A number of studies have found that corporal punishment is positively associated with externalizing behavior problems in European American children, but not African American children. Dodge and colleagues conclude that the cultural context of corporal punishment, including its endorsement and whether it occurs in a warm parent–child relationship, alters the meaning that it conveys to the child and hence modifies its impact on development.

Coard and Sellers (Chapter 13, this volume) focus on the nature and consequences of family-level racial socialization, defined as the process by which messages are transmitted inter- and intragenerationally regarding the significance and meaning of race and ethnicity. They begin with the premise that despite enormous diversity within the African American community, one commonality is that African Americans must make psychological sense of the dominant culture's openly disparaging view of them and negotiate racial barriers in an environment that marginalizes them. Coard and Sellers critically analyze research about African American families' use of racial socialization as a strategy to prepare, buffer, and insulate their children against these forces (e.g., content, modes of transmission, sources of differences among families) and to foster a positive and functional group identity. They discuss the policy implications of this research and offer suggestions for the future study of racial socialization.

African American children have a higher likelihood than European American children of residing in homes without the presence of their birth parents. Pinderhughes and Harden (Chapter 14, this volume) offer a thoughtful analysis of the unique psychosocial and developmental challenges that confront African American children and their caregivers in the most common alternative caregiving arrangements, specifically kinship care, nonkinship foster care, and adoption (including transracial foster placement and adoption). They assess research about the characteristics of these caregivers and the effects of these caregiving arrangements on children's cognitive and socioemotional development and elucidate thorny methodological and interpretational complexities in this field of study. As their analysis suggests, the policies and laws regulating these placements are as controversial as they are daunting to implement.

Finally, Stevenson, Winn, Walker-Barnes, and Coard (Chapter 15, this volume) provide a framework for professional interventions with African American families. They explain why it is important to incorporate cultural worldviews into psychological practice and posit a number of reasons for the lack of progress in the development of culturally relevant interventions. Advancing toward remediation of this problem,

Stevenson and colleagues outline specific constructs, practices, and policies that are fundamental to culturally relevant clinical practice and identify several modes of behavioral expression whose integration into prevention and intervention efforts with African American children, youth, and families would likely maximize their effectiveness.

In sum, each chapter in this volume is grounded in previous theory and research describing African American family life as it influences and is influenced by economic, community, and cultural contexts. Simultaneously, each chapter outlines substantive issues, themes, and gaps in our current knowledge and suggests ways to render theory, research, and practice more culturally sensitive. Ethnic and cultural diversity within the United States as a whole, and among African American families in particular, is increasing at an incredible pace. To enhance the likelihood that children reach their full potential, research and policies affecting families must build on common strengths across ethnicities, while capitalizing on the heterogeneity of family forms and functions.

REFERENCES

Allen, W. R. (1978). The search for applicable theories of Black family life. *Journal of Marriage and the Family, 40* (1), 117–129.

Baumrind, D. (1972). An exploratory study of socialization effects on Black children: Some Black–White comparisions. *Child Development, 42,* 261–267.

Billingsley, A. (1968). *Black families in white America.* Englewood Cliffs, NJ: Prentice-Hall.

Billingsley, A. (1974). *Black families and the struggle for survival: Teaching our children to walk tall.* New York: Friendship Press.

Billingsley, A. (1992). *Climbing Jacob's ladder: The enduring legacy of African American families.* New York: Simon & Schuster.

Bracey, J., Meier, A., & Rudwick, E. (Eds.). (1971). *Black matriarchy: Myth or reality?* Belmont, CA: Wadsworth.

Brody, G., & Flor, D. (1998). Maternal resources, parenting practices, and child competence in rural, single-parent African American families. *Child Development, 69,* 803–816.

Bronfenbrenner, U. (1986). Ecology of the family as a context for human development: Research perspectives. *Developmental Psychology, 22,* 723–742.

Clark, J. H. (Ed.). (1975). Black families in the American economy [Special issue]. *Journal of Afro-American Issues, 3,* 3–4.

Cole, M., & Bruner, J. (1971).Cultural differences and inferences about psychological processes. *American Psychologist, 26,* 867–876.

Condry, S. (1983). History and background of preschool intervention programs and the Consortium for Longitudinal Studies. In Consortium for Longitudinal Studies (Ed.), *As the twig is bent: Lasting effects of preschool programs* (pp. 1–31). Hillsdale, NJ: Erlbaum.

Conyers, J. E. (1970). Introduction. In W. E. B. Dubois, *The Negro American family* (pp. xi–xv). Cambridge, MA: MIT Press.

Corcoran, M., Duncan, G., Gurin, G., & Gurin, P. (1985). Myth and reality: The causes and persistence of poverty. *Journal of Policy Analysis and Management, 4*, 516–536.

de Lone, R. (1979). *Small futures: Children, inequality, and the limits of liberal reform.* New York: Harcourt, Brace Jovanovich.

Dubois, W. E. B. (1909). *The Negro American family.* Atlanta, GA: Atlanta University.

Duncan, G. (1991). The economic environment of childhood. In A. Huston (Ed.), *Children in poverty: Child development and public policy* (pp. 23–50). New York: Cambridge University Press.

Duncan, G., & Brooks-Gunn, J. (Eds.). (1997). *Consequences of growing up poor.* New York: Russell Sage Foundation.

Fields, J. (2003). Children's living arrangements and characteristics: March 2002. (*Current Population Reports*, Series P20-547). Washington, DC: U.S. Bureau of the Census.

Frazier, E. F. (1939). *The Negro family in the United States.* Chicago: University of Chicago Press.

Garcia Coll, C., Meyer, E., & Brillon, L.(1995). Ethnic and minority parenting. In M. H. Bornstein (Ed.), *Handbook of parenting: Vol. 2. Biology and ecology of parenting* (pp. 189–210). Mahwah, NJ: Erlbaum.

Glazer, N. (1966). Foreword. In E. F. Frazier, *The Negro family in the United States* (pp. vii–xvii). Chicago: University of Chicago Press.

Harrison-Hale, A., McLoyd, V. C., & Smedley, B. (2004). Racial and ethnic status: Risk and protective processes among African American families. In K. Maton, C. Schellenbach, B. Leadbeater, & A. Solarz (Eds.), *Investing in children, youth, families, and communities: Strengths-based research and policy* (pp. 269–283). Washington, DC: American Psychological Association.

Hill, R. (1971). *The strengths of black families.* New York: Emerson Hall.

Hill, R. (1993). *Research on the African-American family: A holistic perspective.* Westport, CT: Auburn House.

Kardiner, A., & Ovesey, L. (1951). *The mark of oppression.* New York: Norton.

Kelley, R. D. (1997). *Yo' mama's disfunktional! Fighting the culture wars in urban America.* Boston: Beacon Press.

Kingsley, G. T., & Pettit, K. (2003). *Concentrated poverty: A change in course* (The Neighborhood Change in Urban America Series, Brief 2). Washington, DC: Urban Institute.

Labov, W. (1970). The logic of non-standard English. In F. Williams (Ed.), *Language and poverty.* Chicago: Markham.

Leventhal, T., & Brooks-Gunn, J. (2000). The neighborhoods they live in: The effects of neighborhood residence on child and adolescent outcomes. *Psychological Bulletin, 126*(2), 309–337.

Lewis, O. (1966, October). The culture of poverty. *Scientific American, 215*, 19–25.

McAdoo, H. P. (1978). Factors related to stability in upwardly mobile Black families. *Journal of Marriage and the Family, 40*(4), 761-776.

McAdoo, H. P. (Ed.). (1981). *Black families.* Beverly Hills: Sage.

McAdoo, H. P. (1982). Stress absorbing systems in Black families. *Family Relations, 31*(4), 479–488.

McAdoo, H. P. (1991). Family values and outcomes for children. *Journal of Negro Education, 60,* 361–365.

McAdoo, H. P. (Ed.). (2002). *Black children: Social, education, and parental environments.* Thousand Oaks, CA: Sage.

McKinnon, J. (2003). The Black population in the United States: March 2002. (*Current Population Reports,* Series P20-541). Washington, DC: U.S. Bureau of the Census.

McLoyd, V. C. (1990). The impact of economic hardship on Black families and children: Psychological distress, parenting and socioemotional development. *Child Development, 61,* 311–346.

McLoyd, V. C., & Randolph, S. M. (1985). Secular trends in the study of Afro-American children: A review of child development 1936–1980. In A. Smuts & J. Hagen (Eds.), *Monographs of the Society for Research in Child Development,* 50(4-5, Serial No. 211), 78–92.

Moynihan, D. P. (1971). The Negro family: The case for national action. In J. Bracey, A. Meier, & E. Rudwick (Eds.), *Black matriarchy: Myth or reality?* (pp. 126–159). Belmont, CA: Wadsworth.

Myers, S. (2004). African-American economic well-being during the boom and bust. In L. Daniels (Ed.), *The state of Black America* (pp. 53–69). New York: National Urban League.

Ogbu, J. (1981). Origins of human competence: A cultural-ecological perspective. *Child Development, 52,* 413–429.

Oliver, M. L., & Shapiro, T. (1995). *Black wealth/white wealth: A new perspective on racial inequality.* New York: Routledge.

Peters, M. (1978). Notes from the guest editor [Special issue]. *Journal of Marriage and the Family, 40*(4), 655–658.

Quadagno, J. (1994). *The color of welfare: How racism undermined the war on poverty.* New York: Oxford University Press.

Schram, S., Soss, J., & Fording, R. (Eds.). (2003). *Race and the politics of welfare reform.* Ann Arbor: University of Michigan Press.

Shinn, M., & Gillespie, C. (1994). The roles of housing and poverty in the origins of homelessness. *American Behavioral Scientist, 37,* 505–521.

Soss, J., Schram, S., Vartanian, T., & O'Brien, E. (2001). Setting the terms of relief: Explaining state policy choices in the devolution revolution. *American Journal of Political Science, 45*(2), 378–396.

Soss, J., Schram, S., Vartanian, T., & O'Brien, E. (2004). Welfare policy choices in the states: Does the hard line follow the color line? *Focus, 23*(1), 9–15.

Staples, R. (1985). Changes in black family structure: The conflict between family ideology and structural conditions. *Journal of Marriage and the Family, 47,* 1005–1015.

Staples, R. (Ed.). (1994). *The Black family: Essays and studies* (5th ed.). Belmont, CA: Wadsworth.

Sullivan, M. (1989). Absent fathers in the inner city. *Annals of the American Academy of Political and Social Sciences, 501,* 48–58.

Taylor, R. J., Chatters, L. M., Tucker, M. B., & Lewis, E. (1990). Developments in research on black families: A decade review. *Journal of Marriage and the Family, 52,* 993–1014.

Taylor, R. J., Jackson, J., & Chatters, L. (Eds.). (1997). *Family life in Black America.* Thousand Oaks, CA: Sage.

Tucker, M. B., & Kernan-Mitchell, C. (Eds.). (1995). *The decline of marriage among African Americans: Causes, consequences, and policy implications.* New York: Russell Sage Foundation.

Tulkin, S. R. (1972). An analysis of the concept of cultural deprivation. *Developmental Psychology, 6,* 326–339.

U.S. Department of Health and Human Services. (2002). *Trends in the well-being of America's children and youth.* Washington, DC: Office of the Assistant Secretary for Planning and Evaluation.

Williams, D. R. (2004). Health and the quality of life among African Americans. In L. Daniels (Ed.), *The state of Black America* (pp. 115–138). New York: National Urban League.

Williams, D. R., & Rucker, T. (1996). Socioeconomic status and the health of racial minority populations. In P. Kato & T. Mann (Eds.), *Handbook of diversity issues in health psychology* (pp. 407–423). New York: Plenum Press.

Willis, W. (1992). Families with African American roots. In E. W. Lynch & M. J. Hanson (Eds.), *Developing cross-cultural competence: A guide for working with young children and their families* (pp. 121–150). Baltimore: Brookes.

Wilson, W. J. (1987). *The truly disadvantaged: The inner city, the underclass, and public policy.* Chicago: University of Chicago Press.

CHAPTER 2

Sociocultural Contexts
of African American Families

Nancy E. Hill, Velma McBride Murry,
and Valerie D. Anderson

Early classic studies of the African American community highlighted variations among African American families, describing these families as adaptive, resilient, deviant, pathological, and culturally distinctive (Drake & Cayton, 1945; Du Bois, 1908). The heterogeneity of Black family life, with regard to value systems, lifestyles, and social class structure, makes it impossible to characterize a single type of African American family (Murry, 2000). Such diversity implores consideration of how circumstances emerging from exosystemic and macrosystem-level factors affect the daily life experiences of African Americans—that is, a sociocultural perspective (Dilworth-Anderson, Burton, & Johnson, 1993). Unfortunately, previous research has not fully captured the range of sociocultural contexts that have an impact on African American family life.

Sociocultural contexts, including social, political, and economic features, in which families reside, have strong implications for family functioning and dynamics and how families raise their children. Considering the complexity of the sociocultural context, we have identified three emerging issues that build on previous research and influence the next generation of scholarship on African American families: (1) how the terms "race," "ethnicity," and "culture" influence our understanding of and approach to studying African American family life, culture, and context; (2) the increase in diversity among African American families in the last century; and (3) identifying African American culture and the role of minority status in defining culture. Addressing these issues will lead to a reevaluation and an enhanced understanding of the centrality of cultural values and ethnicity to human behavior and family processes in all populations.

TERMINOLOGY INFLUENCES REALITY

Increased globalization and the effects of mass media, in which a "universal" or general culture (albeit largely Western and European American) is promoted, could predict increased cultural enmeshment and decreased importance of ethnic distinctions. However, increased similarity in cultural practices across ethnic groups is not associated with a reduction in the salience of ethnic identity (Barth, 1969). Humans seem to need an identity with a group that is larger than their family (Glazer, 1975). Although there are theoretical and methodological challenges for conceptualization and operationalization, "race," "ethnicity," and "culture" represent a multifaceted conceptual paradigm for understanding human diversity. These terms have come to represent minority status, lower socioeconomic status, and immigrant status to many people, although these factors influence the lives of all families (Cohen, 1974). Race, ethnicity, and culture represent unique but interrelated constructs, and their resulting categorization shapes the study of African American families; their economic, political, and social positions; and our understanding of how within-group variations reflect or represent culture. Although the debate about the definitions and use of the terms "race," "ethnicity," and "culture" is longstanding and politically charged, the first emerging issue is developing a consensus on terms and definitions and understanding how their use influences our research and knowledge.

"Race" most often represents biological/genetic differences in groups of people, although these biological differences are increasingly difficult to distinguish and social scientists rarely assess race biologically. More often in the social sciences, "race" represents assumed shared genetic heritage based on external physical characteristics such as facial features, skin color, and hair texture (Thomas & Sillen, 1972). These phenotypic distinctions maintain importance largely because, in its origin, "race" did not reflect phenotypic characteristics but political distinctions that were "legislated to be hereditary, innate, and immutable" (Sollors, 1996, p. xxxv). That is, "biological differences provide a symbol around which social differences are defined and evaluated" (Warner & Lunt, 1942, p. 73). Because of the social constructions associated with these phenotypic characteristics, they reflect an important sociocultural context for

African American families (Cavalli-Sforza, Menozzi, & Piazza, 1994; Johnson, 1990; Landrine & Klonoff, 1994; Phinney, 1996; Yee, Fairchild, Weizmann, & Wyatt, 1993). Although "race" does not necessarily represent cultural values or practices, its importance in understanding African American family life remains as long as racial groups continue to view one another as inherently "different," because this prescribed difference results in the need to maintain group identity for political clout and representation with or without cultural connections (Gans, 1979).

"Ethnicity," derived from the Greek terms *ethnos* (meaning nation or tribe) and *ethnikos* (meaning nationality; Betancourt & Lopez, 1993), was coined to be a euphemism for "race," a term sullied by its association with racism (Sollors, 1996). It is most often as a euphemism for "race" that the term "ethnicity" has been used in research on African American families. However, "ethnicity" is distinguished from "race" in that it implies common values, beliefs, and practices based on nationality, common ancestry, and/or common immigration experiences, and not phenotypic characteristics (Sollors, 1996). Distinguishing the study of race from ethnicity allows for the examination of why racial differences remain while cultural practices across groups are becoming increasingly similar. Moreover, the distinction will free up the concept of ethnicity as it relates to African Americans so that researchers can begin to examine ethnicity *within* the African American population (Omi & Winant, 1986). With increased immigration, Black Americans draw national and cultural affiliations from many countries around the world, in addition to regional variations in historical and cultural practices and migration patterns within the United States. These variations may indeed reflect ethnic differences *within* the African American population. With increasing diversity among African Americans, within-group ethnic variation is sorely understudied and, thus, an emerging issue.

When research suggests ethnic or racial group differences in family processes, researchers often look to underlying values and beliefs associated with the culture of the ethnic group for explanations. Barth (1969) characterizes "ethnic groups as culture-bearing units" (p. 12). *Culture* is a dynamic variable that includes family roles and values, communication patterns, affective styles, and interpersonal interaction patterns. It reflects learned behavior patterns and a way of life that a particular group of people share, including social norms, roles, beliefs, and values that are transmitted from one generation to the next (Rohner, 1984). Constructed through human social interactions and the ways in which people process their experiences, culture is continuous, cumulative, and dynamic (Valsiner & Litvinovic, 1996). People construct and transform their cultures in relation to their experiential frameworks. Even among American ethnic groups that are largely similar, relatively minor variations across groups are often perceived as major cultural differences (Sollors, 1996). In addition to culture as derived from ethnic group identification, experiencing discrimination and perceiving oneself as having minority status relative to a dominant culture have been linked to variations in ethnic identification and acculturation (Phinney, 1996; Trimble, 1990; Williams, 1996) and often result in a unique culture. Mutual experiences of discrimination and common coping strategies can draw people together and lead them to identify with each other, thereby creating a shared cultural experience. Social scientists have largely ignored African American cultural values and practices. Much of what has been documented about African American culture is in the humanities (Dilworth-Anderson et al., 1993). Linking this knowledge to our scientific understanding of the relation between African American cultural practices and family dynamics would significantly increase our understanding of African American family life.

AFRICAN AMERICANS: AN INCREASINGLY DIVERSE GROUP

Although African Americans are often considered a homogeneous group, scholars (e.g., Boykin & Toms, 1985; Guthrie, 1991) have cautioned against envisioning a single African American experience. Although there is a shared history and common bonds, there is also great diversity among African Americans. This diversity reflects divergent realities brought about by variations in immigration experiences, regional residence, political views, and phenotypic characteristics, in addition to socioeconomic variations, religious beliefs and practices, and marital and family constellations. To reflect a second emerging issue in the sociocultural context of African American families (i.e., within-group diversity), we focus on immigration experiences, regional residence, political views, and skin tone. Other chapters in this book deal with socioeconomic variation (Darity & Nicholson, Chapter 4), diverse religious beliefs and practices (Mattis, Chapter 9), and diverse marital and family formation (Tucker & James, Chapter 5; Bryant & Wickrama, Chapter 6).

Who Are African Americans in the United States?

A snapshot of the African American population reveals that African Americans comprise 13% (35.5 million; 48% male, 52% female) of the total U.S. population, and this proportion is projected to increase to 14% of the total population by 2025 (U.S. Bureau of the Census, 2003).

African Americans are slightly younger than the U.S. population as a whole (median ages are 30.4 years and 35.5 years, respectively). In 2000, half of African Americans (54%) lived in the South, resulting from both historical trends and more recent remigration to the South (Stack, 1997). In contrast, only 8% reside in the West, and the Northeast and Midwest are each home to 19%. On average, about half (53%) of all African Americans live in central cities and metropolitan areas. Although half of the African American population resides outside of major metropolitan areas, very little research has examined the lives of rural and suburban African Americans. With the growth of immigrant populations (e.g., Mexicans and Asians), African Americans will no longer be the largest ethnic minority group in the United States by the year 2025.

Immigration and Cultural Pluralism

Increased immigration to the United States is a significant sociocultural factor affecting African Americans. As of 2002, the nation's foreign-born population totaled almost 12% (32.5 million; Schmidley, 2003), the highest proportion since 1930 and roughly equal in size to the African American population. Almost half of the nation's foreign-born population is from Latin America (mainly Mexico, followed by Cuba, the Dominican Republic, and El Salvador), whereas one fourth is from Asia (the Philippines, China, Vietnam, and India are top countries of origin), and about 20% is from Europe (U.S. Bureau of the Census, 2002).

The increased influx of immigrants occurs in the context of lagging economic prospects for African Americans, which may result in perceived competition. Perception of group competition for resources is a reliable predictor of attitudes toward immigration and immigrants (Esses, Dovidio, Jackson, & Armstrong, 2001). Although African Americans generally support the ideals of global interdependence through immigration; they also may perceive increased rates of immigration as a threat (Esses et al., 2001). Such perceived threats often result in a heightened sense of ethnic group distinctiveness and stronger ingroup/outgroup distinctions (Barth, 1969; Tuner, Hogg, Oakes, Reicher, & Wetherell, 1987). Careful analyses of the *actual* effects of immigration on African Americans' educational and labor market opportunities and its impact of African American family dynamics and socialization practices are needed.

Research on African Americans' attitudes toward immigration and immigrants must acknowledge regional variations in immigration patterns and outcomes. Although nationally representative polls indicate that African Americans favor immigration more than other American racial or ethnic groups, such polls include rural African Americans, who do not experience immigration in the same way that those in the major immigrant magnet cities do (Nissimov, 2002). Research must also consider the sources of tensions and conflicts between African Americans and immigrants, including perceived judgments of inferiority or superiority and income or educational differences between the two groups. For example, African immigrants are more highly educated on average than African Americans (47% college graduates as compared with 13%). This difference in resources, combined with stereotypes that each group may hold, might pave the way for intergroup conflicts, which may be especially heightened among African immigrants groups and African Americans, who are often perceived as members of the same race group (i.e., Black Americans).

Finally, the influx of immigrant groups has consequences for how policy issues relevant to African Americans are framed, such as whether affirmative action policies should apply to immigrants who are members of a racial or ethnic minority group. The original purpose of affirmative action was to ameliorate social and economic conditions that were brought about by racial discrimination against African Americans. However, the Immigration Reform and Control Act of 1986 made it illegal to bar immigrants from affirmative action programs. Because of affirmative action, some immigrants have been given preference in hiring, minority contract set-asides, and municipal jobs (Robb, 1995), which may add validity to the perception that immigrants are directly competing with African Americans for economic resources and livelihood. Investigations of the interplay between African Americans and immigrants must be informed by the immigration pattern specific to the geographic region under study, including the history of immigration and the racial or ethnic background of the immigrants.

Regional Residence

In contrast to the largely rural, Southern, and racially homogeneous residential patterns that marked mid-20th century African American family life, today African American families live in increasingly diverse locations and regions. African American culture reflects such variations in experiences. Relative to other U.S. regions, which are becoming more similar to one another, Southern culture remains distinct in religious and moral values, conservative attitudes about race and gender, and political conservatism (Hurlbert, 1989). Consistent with the notion of a distinct Southern culture, some differences between African Americans and European Americans disappear when residency in the South is taken into account (Jones & Lui, 1999), suggesting that regional differences are at least as, if not more, important for understanding family values and beliefs as racial background. Because recent research suggests that the South maintains a distinct culture, apart from race or ethnicity, it is important to study the cultural values, practices, and family dynamics of African American populations both within and outside of the South.

Another distinct change in the regional residence of African American families is that more families are living in urban or suburban areas rather than in a rural context. Much of the research on African American families has been conducted with urban samples. Research on rural African American family life within and outside the South suggests that collective socialization is a salient factor that affects family life and child outcomes. Collective socialization processes are inversely associated with children's affiliation with deviant peers (Brody, Murry, Kim, & Brown, 2002). In addition, the benefit of collective socialization processes is stronger for children living in more disadvantaged surroundings. Thus, in many rural African American communities, the "village" continues to raise the children (Brody et al., 2002, 2003).

At a microlevel, neighborhood characteristics and the "sense of community" that African Americans share are a strong part of the culture. Length of residence, residential stability, spatial configurations of neighborhoods, and psychological distance between African Americans can affect culture and family dynamics, especially among ethnic groups in multiethnic neighborhoods (Hutchinson, Rodriguez, & Hagan, 1996). Considerable tension across socioeconomic status among African Americans has reduced the social and cultural resources, employment opportunities, and positive role models available in many urban communities, resulting in the deterioration of urban neighborhoods and the impoverishment of the residents who remain (Pattillo-McCoy, 1999, 2000; Wilson, 1996). The increased social distance experienced by those of higher socioeconomic status who are more integrated into the mainstream society reduces their sense of collective group identification and limits interaction, while increasing psychological distance and tensions across socioeconomic statuses (Allen, Dawson, & Brown, 1989; Broman, Neighbors, & Jackson, 1988; Hall & Allen, 1989; Harris, 1995; Tatum, 1987; Thornton, Tran, & Taylor, 1997).

Related to, but distinct from, the issue of neighborhood context is the issue of community among African Americans. "Community" implies shared geographic and psychological space, indicating shared interests, social characteristics, and social interaction (Warren, 1978). But it takes more than close physical proximity to create community (Hutchinson et al., 1996). Even as African American families do not often reside in close proximity, there is a sense of community at an abstract level, a collective understanding of cohesion and belonging among African Americans despite differences in ethnicity or cultural practices. It is a sense of community that comes from common political and social experiences and goals (Weber, 1922). Although much has been written about the sense of community in literature, our current measures of community and neighborhood characteristics are not sensitive to assessing this issue.

Diverging Political Views: Fiscal Conservatives and Liberal Social Policies

Ethnicity and race are intertwined with political action, views, and clout. Feelings of a common ethnicity or cultural group are linked to differences in economic and political circumstances as much as similarities in customs and practices (Weber, 1922). Based on this perspective, studies of African Americans' political activity reflect homogeneity in political views, such that African Americans in general support policies that ensure equal treatment and protection from discrimination; enhance self-help opportunities through college scholarships and tax benefits for minority-owned businesses; and endorse preferential hiring, promotion, and college admission (Krysan, 2000).

Consistent with the growing social and economic heterogeneity among African Americans, however, divergent political views have been documented since the 1970s (Bolce & Gray, 1979). Although endorsement of liberal political views is considered the norm, African Americans tend to endorse conservative views on issues such as abortion, stricter law enforcement, prayer in the classroom, and homosexual rights (Gilliam, 1986; Seltzer & Smith, 1985), which influence how parents socialize their children. Endorsement of conservative or liberal views tends to vary across socioeconomic backgrounds. For example, middle-class African Americans are more supportive of social welfare programs than are African Americans of lower social class. In contrast, middle-class African Americans hold conservative views on welfare spending, but liberal views on health and education funding (Welch & Foster, 1987).

Aside from the ubiquitous obstacles of racism, discrimination, and other barriers, there are socioeconomic variations in African Americans' political and ideological perspectives (Cose, 1993). Working-class and impoverished African Americans tend to focus on more immediate economic and social interests by addressing the material realities of their everyday lives, such as by advocating for higher wages, more funding for local schools, and quality housing (Marable & Mullings, 1994). Middle-class African Americans tend to concentrate more on implementing strategies that combat systematic racist practices ingrained in social institutions. An emerging issue for understanding African American families in their sociocultural context is examining how diverse political perspectives and perspectives on racism influence ethnic and racial socialization within families.

Skin Tone: A Racial Construct

Diversity in African American skin tone and facial features runs the gamut from unmixed African Blacks to people who appear to be White (Davis, 1991). As was true in the postslavery era and continues to be true today, the delineation between "Black" and "not Black" is not as clear-cut as it may seem to be, and informal barometers of Blackness (e.g., appearance, speech, political ideology, etc.) have governed this distinction rather than formally developed codes. Further complicating this issue is the reality that phenotypic variations are not equally valued either within or outside of the African American population. Variations in phenotypic characteristics, such as skin tone, predict adult socioeconomic status, such that those with lighter skin tone report higher education, income, and occupational status than do those with darker skin (M. E. Hill, 2000; Hughes & Hertel, 1990; Keith & Herring, 1991). This correlation has held across the 20th century. In the early 1900s, lighter-skinned African Americans had greater opportunities, were perceived to have greater intelligence, and were accorded higher status than "full-blooded Negroes" (Rueter, 1918, p. 379). At mid-century, lighter skin tone was found to be associated with material advantage among African Americans (Dollard, 1937; Drake & Cayton, 1945; Frazier, 1940; Freeman, Armor, Ross, & Pettigrew, 1966). Moreover, contemporary research demonstrates social and economic advantages among lighter-skinned African Americans beyond the effects of parents' socioeconomic status (Hughes & Hertel, 1990; Keith & Herring, 1991; Seltzer & Smith, 1991). The social contextual processes through which bias based on skin tone influences African Americans' life chances need to be better clarified (M. E. Hill, 2000). Because members of the same family may exhibit variations in skin tone and messages given to children vary by skin tone (M. E. Hill, 2000), future studies should examine whether variations in development, adjustment, and achievement are associated with skin color across siblings.

Immigration patterns, regional residence, political views, and variations in phenotypic characteristics are just some of the ways in which African Americans are diverse. Each of these factors affects African American cultural experiences and contributes to the development and maintenance of African American cultural diversity.

AFRICAN AMERICAN CULTURE: A MOVING TARGET?

Although previous research on culture often has characterized it as a static construct or even as reflecting a consensus among group members, scientists need to understand the dynamic and developing nature of culture (Wainryb, 2004)—a moving target. Culture is not a bounded or static unit tied to a geographical location (Gjerde, 2004), it is continually created and recreated. To begin to account for culture as a dynamic, and not static, variable, continuities between the past and present need to be outlined, along with an understanding of how people make sense of the values, traditions, and practices that are passed from generation to generation. Although there are similarities across generations and between African and African American cultures, each generation's historical experiences recreate and shape African American culture.

African American Culture across Generations

Generational and historical experiences have shaped and diversified African American culture. Influenced by ongoing sociohistorical events and patterns (Elder & Johnson, 2002), African American culture can be said to be a "moving target." The changing demographics and social, political, and economic indicators of African Americans over the past decades have influenced African American culture. Because of the improvements and gains over the past century, there are a number of generational differences in African American culture. The first involves the definition and manifestation of community. A sense of coherent identity and cultural values and practices was facilitated for older African Americans by residential integration of African Americans from diverse economic backgrounds (Jaynes & Williams, 1989). In prior generations, African Americans met at the same cultural institutions, used the same doctors, lawyers and ministers, and occupied a shared, albeit limited, social space (Bracey, Maier, & Elliot, 1971). Furthermore, residential segregation kept African Americans concentrated in localized neighborhoods, which facilitated the maintenance and development of culture and the role of extended family and fictive kin networks in childrearing.

In contrast, in contemporary society, owing in large part to advocacy designed to reduce practices of discrimination in areas such as housing, education, and occupational attainment, African Americans are less likely to live and interact in racially homogeneous community settings (Iceland, 2004; Iceland, Weinberg, & Steinmetz, 2002). This change has been accompanied by a trend toward reduced racial segregation of schools. Unlike those of prior generations, today's African American children are more likely to attend racially diverse schools, though this trend depends to some extent on geographical location and urbanicity (U.S. Department of Education, 2002). Such patterns are in stark contrast to the cultural milieu that defined life in the mid 20th century. Indeed, even the cultural outlets for various forms of art, entertainment, and recreation have undergone substantial revolution. Whereas about two generations ago, African American art and cultural outlets flourished in "Black-only" venues, contemporary society has witnessed a pronounced endorsement of African American art and entertainment forms by the majority population (Jaynes & Williams, 1989).

Gender roles and attitudes constitute an additional area in which there are continuities and changes in African American culture across generations. Although working outside the home has been part of African American women's experiences throughout history, today's African American woman is even *more* likely to work outside of the home (U.S. Bureau of the Census, 2000). Because of the longstanding tradition as well as economic necessity, African Americans (both men and women) are less critical of maternal employment than European Americans and often consider maternal employment to be compatible with the role of wife/mother (Bielby & Bielby, 1984; Blee & Tickameyer, 1986, 1995; Hill Collins, 1990). Even though African American women's employment is long-standing, African American women have become even more likely to experience gender inequality in employment (Hill Collins, 1990) and difficulty in finding full-time work than their European American counterparts (Amott & Matthaei, 1991). Because of the tendency to conceptualize maternal employment as a "choice" in much of the literature, which is less applicable to African American women, much of the research on maternal employment, family dynamics, and child outcomes is not readily generalizable. Understanding how decisions about maternal employment are negotiated and resolved within families requires exploration of African Americans' cultural conceptualizations of the role of mothers, cultural models of optimal parenting, and ethnotheories of children's development (e.g., Holden & Edwards, 1989).

Cultural niches (i.e., African American, American, and minority) are commonalities that unite African American generations and have implications for family processes and childrearing. Still, within the shared experience of cultural heritage and ethnic minority status, there are generational differences. African American parents during the slavery era and the civil rights era had to, and in today's era still must, make sense of their race, as perceived by the African American community and by the dominant society. But each generation of parents has experienced a unique type of oppression and received distinct messages concerning the value of cultural diversity. Furthermore, unlike the discourse in previous eras in which "race relations" was traditionally framed largely as a "Black/White issue," contemporary discussions of race relations are more centered on the reality of a burgeoning multicultural society.

Accordingly, research in this area must examine the messages—both explicit and implicit—that all parents (i.e., ethnic minorities and members of the majority population) convey to their children regarding the meaning and significance of race, ethnicity, culture, and minority status.

Continuities from African to African American Culture

Although it is often assumed that African American culture reflects some African cultural heritage, such cultural influences are seldom enumerated. African cultural heritage represented in contemporary African American society includes those practices that may have been handed down through socialization processes and active attempts by African Americans to connect with their African cultural heritage (Mitchell, 1975). The West African belief system, characterized by a positive life view, belief in the spiritual realm, and a powerful and compassionate God, is apparent in African American culture today, especially in religious practices. Trusting that God will provide for one's needs and praising God even while in challenging circumstances is characteristic of virtually all West African traditional religions and characterizes the African American slaves' striving for freedom, as well as today's resilient African American families living in the most challenging neighborhoods and economic conditions (Mitchell, 1975). Other enduring "Africanisms" in contemporary American and African American culture include vestiges of African language in African American English and African spiritual styles of worship that are reflected in African American religion (Asante, 1988). Moreover, communalism, a West African ethos reflecting an emphasis on collective unity, destiny, and social interdependence (Boykin, 1997; Nobles, 1991), has manifestations in African American family life and patterns of social development (Boykin, 1983; Foster, 1983). Contemporary manifestations of communalism include strong kinship values and collective struggle and destiny. Other elements of this ethos include spirituality, harmony, expressiveness, expressive individualism, and oral tradition (Boykin, 1983).

IS IT "AFRICAN AMERICAN CULTURE" OR "MINORITY STATUS"?

Commonalities and Distinctions among Minority Groups

Because many ethnic and racial minority groups within the United States share common experiences of being an "out-group," including experiencing discrimination and a higher probability of economic disadvantage, there may be similar reactions and adaptations to such experiences that result in common features among the cultures of ethnic and racial minorities. Based on experiences of African Americans and Puerto Ricans, who have historically been disadvantaged in the United States, an integrative model for studying minority children (Garcia Coll et al., 1996) points to cultural similarities across ethnic and racial minority groups by considering how factors such as social position, social stratification, racism, and segregation lead to the development of an "adaptive culture," which, in turn, affects family dynamics and child development. This model does not distinguish the unique cultures or histories of African Americans, Puerto Ricans, or other ethnic minority groups, but reflects a "culture" based on minority status and the associated disadvantage.

The common experiences of racism, discrimination, and social disadvantage often promote within-group solidarity and cohesion as much as commonalities in cultural practices and values based in ethnic identity (Gans, 1979; Weber, 1922). When studying the influences of culture and ethnicity on family life, how do we distinguish influences that are due to a common cultural, historical background from those that are due to commonalities based on "out-group" experiences relative to the mainstream American population? In fact, ethnicity in America is often conceived as a deviation from the norm (Sollors, 1996). The cohesion or collective identity among minority groups may be due both to forces within the group and to barriers that are erected by the majority group to limit the interaction with and participation in the larger majority society, also known as "caste stratification" (Ogbu & Stern, 2001). The perpetuation of racial and ethnic groups is dependent on maintaining the boundaries between groups (Barth, 1969). Even as the cultural practices across American ethnic groups have become increasingly similar, especially among families of higher socioeconomic statuses, the salience of ethnic identity and distinctions across groups remains, often because of shared political interests (Sollors, 1996).

Consistent with the premise of a "minority culture," research on culture among minority populations shows similar values across groups. For example, Asian American, African American, Native American, and Hispanic cultures have each been purported to value interdependence and extended family, values associated with particular parenting practices (Garcia Coll, Meyer, & Brillon, 1995). Moreover, similar parenting strategies, (i.e., authoritarian/directive parenting practices) often result from these values and are associated with positive outcomes for minority children (Brody & Flor, 1998; Chao, 1994, 2001; Hill, Bush, & Roosa, 2003). These authoritarian parenting practices, often deemed as based within particular cultural values, are also associated with positive out-comes for those residing in low-income (Hoff-Ginsburg & Tardiff, 1995; Pinderhughes, Dodge, Pettit, & Zelli, 2000) and high-risk neighbor-hoods (Baldwin, Baldwin, & Cole, 1990; Brody et al., 2001; Fursten-burg et al., 1993; Sampson & Groves, 1989). Others suggest that these values, which seem to reflect cultural perspectives, actually develop in the context of common experiences due to immigration, poverty, dis-crimination, and social disadvantage (Bean, Berg, & van Hook, 1996; Selby, Murphy, & Lorenzen, 1990).

Because much of the research confounds cultural or ethnic back-ground with other sociodemographic factors such as socioeconomic sta-tus, community of residence, and minority status, it becomes difficult to determine how cultural practices affect family dynamics. Much of the literature on African American families has been conducted on low-income, urban samples (Murry, Bynum, et al., 2001; Roosa, Morgan-Lopez, Cree, & Specter, 2002). Moreover, much of the best research on African Americans has been reactive—to refute stereotypes and reinter-pret data from a culturally variant perspective and not a culturally devi-ant perspective (Allen, 1978; McAdoo, 1997; McLoyd, 2004). For example, the characterization of African American families as a "tangled web of pathology" (Moynihan, 1965) generated a tremendous amount of research to identify the strengths of African American families living in high-risk contexts (Billingsley, 1992). To date, little research has been conducted with middle-class African American families or African American families from diverse socioeconomic backgrounds (see Hill, 1997, 2001; Smelana, Campione-Barr, & Daddis, 2004, as exceptions). Because of the restricted focus, we know relatively little about how Afri-can American cultural values relate to family processes or child out-comes across socioeconomic status groups.

Although some scholars have attempted to delineate African Ameri-can culture (Boykin, 1997; Nobles, 1991), others, such as Hutnik (1991), argue that African Americans do not have a unique culture and that it is only shared experiences of social disadvantage that draw Afri-can Americans together and maintain a coherent identity. Some African Americans actively seek to preserve African cultural values by incorpo-rating African cultural traditions into African American family life, through using African names, the wearing of African dress, and the dis-play of African art, literature, music, and drama. The African culture–based holiday Kwanzaa and African-centered schools are deliberate attempts to embrace African principles of togetherness and collective support, prepare youth for future leadership, and preserve African American culture.

We have not studied, as a social science, African American families and communities in a way that identifies cultural values and practices and links them to African American family life. Much of the research has been comparative and restricted to a subset of the population. One of the emerging issues in understanding the sociocultural context of African American families is to conduct within-group studies of African Americans from diverse backgrounds to identify common cultural experiences and values that are not linked to social disadvantage or coping with social disadvantage.

To move beyond understanding culture as an ethnic group variable in comparative research, Cauce (2002) identified acculturation (i.e., adaptation to a host culture), enculturation (i.e., learning about one's own culture), and ethnic minority socialization (i.e., learning about the unique experiences of being in a "minority group") as three measurable ways to begin to assess culture. Used together, they can shed light on individual differences and within-group variations. Similarly, Gjerde (2004) called for understanding culture by beginning with individuals and determining what they have in common with other individuals. Rather than attempting to identify an "objective," "distant" culture that shapes individuals, one should determine how individuals shape and create cultures within families and communities. Identifying potentially universal concepts and family processes; determining how these concepts are manifested commonly and uniquely across cultures, while considering who is involved the lives of families; and identifying the goals, values, and beliefs surrounding family activities, and the common communication patterns, are other ways to understand cultural practices and cultural variation (Cooper, Jackson, Azmitia, & Lopez, 1998).

Distinguishing Culture and Poverty

Distinguishing African American culture from minority group experiences begins with disentangling ethnicity and race from socioeconomic status, because parenting and family dynamics are codetermined by socioeconomic factors (Hoff-Ginsburg & Tardiff, 1995) and culture (Garcia Coll et al., 1995). Unfortunately, the literature has not systematically examined ethnicity apart from socioeconomic factors. Attempts to tease apart poverty, community factors, and culture as they relate to parenting and family dynamics, using samples of multiple ethnic groups residing in the same neighborhoods, has found many more similarities than differences, suggesting that neighborhood or socioeconomic factors may be more salient than cultural values for understanding family dynamics and child outcomes.

Low-income African American and European American adolescents who reside in the same neighborhoods expressed similar types of goals and perceived similar types of barriers to reaching their goals (Hill, Ramirez, et al., 2003). Moreover, African American adolescents in the study did not identify discrimination among barriers or point to cultural values when discussing their career goals and family support. It is likely that common experiences of long-term poverty and community context result in similarities between low-income African American and low-income European American families. Similarly, in another study of low-income families residing in the same neighborhood, the influence of parenting on mental health was found to be largely similar across ethnicity (Hill, Bush, et al., 2003).

Consistent with Hill's work, impoverished African American and European American families were found to be similar in endorsement of the importance of instilling a work ethic in their children—more similar than each group is to its higher socioeconomic ethnic counterpart, suggesting that poverty is distinct from minority experiences (Jones & Lui, 1999). However, the relations between socioeconomic indicators and parenting *within* African American and European American families show some ethnic differences. For European Americans, higher socioeconomic status is associated with more maternal warmth and fewer hostile parenting practices, whereas there are no such relations for African Americans (Hill & Adams, 2005). Among African Americans, it was only when lower socioeconomic status was coupled with high levels of other family risk indicators that lower socioeconomic status was associated with maladaptive parenting practices (Hill & Adams, 2005).

METHODOLOGICAL ISSUES

Although there has been a considerable amount of research on African American families, there are a number of limitations that preclude our ability to draw firm conclusions from research. Many of these issues are not new, but they still persist. First, although this chapter and other work (e.g., Hill, Bush, et al., 2003; Hill, Ramirez, et al., 2003) have begun to disentangle race, ethnicity, and culture, measuring these constructs in a way that is both meaningful and accurate in light of their dynamic and reciprocal nature is an enduring issue. Second, measures that are used to assess parenting, family dynamics, and mental health often have not been validated or developed for use with ethnic minority populations (Knight & Hill, 1998). Using measures that are not equivalent across groups may lead to mismeasurement of the construct under study and cause erroneous results and conclusions.

Third, much of the research on ethnic minority families has confounded ethnicity with socioeconomic status and neighborhood social context (Cauce, Coronado, & Watson, 1998; Roosa et al., 2002). For example, low-income ethnic minority families or families residing in disadvantaged neighborhoods are often compared with European American families from middle-class backgrounds and advantaged community contexts. Based on such comparisons, group differences are often attributed to ethnicity. However, much of this research cannot disentangle the influences of ethnicity, culture, socioeconomic status, and community context as possible alternative explanations of results. Distinguishing how group differences may be due to cultural/ethnic background, community context, or family socioeconomic status (SES) has explicit implications for developing the most appropriate prevention/intervention programs and policies to enhance children's development. Some studies that compare across ethnic groups using samples that differ on economic and community demographic factors statistically control for these factors in their analyses. Although this practice alleviates some of the problem, it often results in a restriction of range within each group. If there are few or no low-SES European Americans or few or no middle-income African Americans in the sample, then statements made about African Americans and European Americans are based on data that do not represent the full range of the population for each group. Similarly, what aspect of social class or socioeconomic status drives the relation between SES and particular outcomes? Examining the effect of each of these factors on outcomes may shed light on the specific factors and processes driving outcomes.

Fourth, examining the influence of ethnicity draws one to make comparisons across groups. Making comparisons often highlights between-group differences while failing to attend to within-group differences (Hunter & Johnson, in press). As we have already outlined, within-group variations may be just as large and important for understanding normative developmental trajectories as comparative, between-group findings.

Finally, research on African American children and families often focuses on mean-level differences in parenting practices or child outcomes instead of variations in the influence of parenting on child outcomes (Hill & Bush, 2001; Hill, Bush, et al., 2003). Because of differences in parenting context, similar parenting strategies may have different meanings and influences on children's development, as discussed in this book by Dodge, McLoyd, and Lansford (Chapter 12). Determining whether particular parenting strategies have the same impact on child outcomes is often more important than knowledge about mean differences.

The sociocultural contexts in which African American families find themselves are ever changing and complex. Studying sociocultural contexts highlights the increasing heterogeneity of African American family life that has heretofore been neglected. Understanding the diversity and influence of social, political, and economic contexts that constitute the sociocultural contexts of African American families is central to developing appropriate and useful programs and policies and identifying the developmental trajectory of the African American and American cultures.

REFERENCES

Allen, R. L., Dawson, M. C., & Brown, R. E. (1989). A schema-based approach to modeling an African American racial belief system. *American Political Science Review, 83*, 421–441.

Allen, W. (1978). The search for applicable theories of black family life. *Journal of Marriage and the Family, 40,* 117–131.

Amott, T., & Matthaei, J. (1991). *Race, gender and work.* Boston: South End.

Asante, M. (1988). *Afrocentricity.* Trenton, NJ: Africa World Press.

Baldwin, A. L., Baldwin, C., & Cole, R. E. (1990). Stress-resistant families and stress-resistant children. In J. Rolf, A. S. Masten, D. Cicchetti, K. H. Nuechterlein, & S. Weintraub (Eds.), *Risk and protective factors in the development of psychopathology* (pp. 257–280). Cambridge, UK: Cambridge University Press

Barth, F. (1969). *Ethnic groups and boundaries: The social organization of culture difference* (pp. 9–38). Boston: Little, Brown.

Bean, F. D., Berg, R. R., & van Hook, J. V. W. (1996). Socioeconomic and cultural incorporation and marital disruption among Mexican Americans. *Social Forces, 75,* 593–617.

Betancourt, H., & Lopez, S. R. 1993. The study of culture, ethnicity and race in American psychology. *American Psychologist, 48,* 629–637.

Bielby, D., & Bielby, W. (1984). Work commitment, sex-role attitudes and women's employment. *American Sociological Review, 49,* 234–247.

Billingsley, A. (1992). *Climbing Jacob's ladder: The enduring legacy of African American families.* New York: Simon & Schuster.

Blee, K., & Tickameyer, A. (1986). Black–White differences in mother-to-daughter transmission of sex-role attitudes. *Sociological Quarterly, 28,* 205–222.

Blee, K., & Tickameyer, A. (1995). Racial differences in men's attitudes about gender roles. *Journal of Marriage and the Family, 57,* 21–30.

Bolce, L., & Gray, S. (1979). Blacks, Whites, and race politics. *Public Interest, 53,* 61–75.

Boykin, A. W. (1983). The academic performance of Afro-American children. In J. Spence (Ed.), *Achievement and achievement motives* (pp. 321–371). San Francisco: Freeman.

Boykin, A. W., Jagers, R., Ellison, C., & Albury, A. (1997). Communalism: Conceptualization and measurement of an Afrocultural social orientation. *Journal of Black Studies, 27,* 409–418.

Boykin, A. W., & Toms, F. (1985). Black child socialization: A conceptual framework. In H. P. McAdoo & J. L. McAdoo (Eds.), *Black children: Social, educational, and parental environments* (pp. 33–51). Thousand Oaks, CA: Sage.

Bracey, J., Maier, A., & Elliot, M. R. (1971). *Black workers and organized labor.* Belmont, CA: Wadsworth.

Brody, G. H., & Flor, D. L. (1998). Maternal resources, parenting practices, and child competence in rural, single-parent African American families. *Child Development, 69,* 803–816.

Brody, G. H., Ge, X., Conger, R., Gibbons, F. X., Murry, V. M., Gerrard, M., & Simons, R. L. (2001). The influence of neighborhood disadvantage, collective socialization, and parenting on African American children's affiliation with deviant peers. *Child Development, 72,* 1231–1246.

Brody, G. H., Ge, X., Kim, S. Y., Murry, V. M., Simons, R. L., Gibbons, F. X., et al. (2003). Neighborhood disadvantage moderates associations of parenting and older sibling problem attitudes and behavior with conduct disorders in African American children. *Journal of Consulting and Clinical Psychology, 71,* 211–223.

Brody, G. H., Murry, V. M., Kim, S., & Brown, A. C. (2002). Longitudinal pathways to competence and psychological adjustment among African American children living in rural single-parent households. *Child Development, 73,* 1505–1516.

Broman, C. L., Neighbors, H., & Jackson, J. S. (1988). Racial group identification among Black adults. *Social Forces, 67,* 146–158.

Cauce, A. M. (2002). Examining culture within a quantitative empirical research framework. *Human Development, 45,* 294–298.

Cauce, A. M., Coronado, N., & Watson, J. (1998). Conceptual, methodological, and statistical issues in culturally competent research. In M. Hernandez & M. R. Isaacs (Eds.), *Promoting cultural competence in children's mental health services: Systems of care for children's mental health* (pp. 305–329). Baltimore: Brookes.

Cavalli-Sforza, L. L., Menozzi, P., & Piazza, A. (1994). *The history of geography of human genes.* Princeton, NJ: Princeton University Press.

Chao, R. K. (1994). Beyond parental control and authoritarian parenting style: Understanding Chinese parenting through the cultural notion of training. *Child Development, 65,* 1111–1119.

Chao, R. K. (2001). Extending research on the consequences of parenting style for Chinese Americans and European Americans. *Child Development, 72(6),* 1832–1843.

Cohen, A. (1974). Introduction: The lesson of ethnicity. In A. Cohen (Ed.), *Urban ethnicity* (pp. ix–xxiv). London: Tavistock.

Cooper, C. R., Jackson, J. F., Azmitia, M., & Lopez, E. M. (1998). Multiple selves, multiple worlds: Three useful strategies for research with ethnic minority youth on identity, relationships, and opportunity structures. In V. C. McLoyd & L. Steinberg (Eds.), *Studying minority adolescents: Conceptual, methodological, and theoretical issues* (pp. 111–125). Mahwah, NJ: Erlbaum.

Cose, E. (1993). *The rage of a privileged class.* New York: HarperCollins.

Davis, F. (1991). *Who is black?: One nation's definition.* University Park: Pennsylvania State University Press.

Dilworth-Anderson, P., Burton, L., & Johnson, L. B. (1993). Reframing theories for understanding race, ethnicity, and families. In P. G. Boss, W. J. Doherty, R. LaRossa, W. R. Schumm, & S. K. Steinmetz (Eds.), *Sourcebook of family theories and methods: A conceptual approach* (pp. 627–645). New York: Plenum Press.

Dollard, J. (1937). *Cast and class in a southern town.* New Haven, CT: Yale University Press.

Drake, St. C., & Cayton, J. R. (1945). *Black metropolis: A study of Negro life in a northern city.* New York: Harcourt, Brace.

Du Bois, W. E. B. (1908). *The Negro American family: Atlanta study No. 13.* Atlanta, GA: Atlanta University Press.

Elder, G., & Johnson, M. (2002). Perspectives on human development in context. In C. von Hofsten & L. Baeckman (Eds.), *Psychology at the turn of the millennium: Vol. 2. Social, developmental and clinical perspectives* (pp. 153–172). Florence, KY: Taylor & Francis/Routledge.

Esses, V., Dovidio, J., Jackson, L., & Armstrong, T. (2001). The immigration dilemma: The role of perceived group competition, ethnic prejudice and national identity. *Journal of Social Issues, 57,* 389–412.

Foster, H. J. (1983). African patterns in the Afro-American family. *Journal of Black Studies, 14,* 201–232.

Frazier, E. F. (1940). *Negro youth at the crossways.* Washington, DC: American Council on Education.

Freeman, H. E., Armor, J., Ross, M., & Pettigrew, T. J. (1966). Color gradation and attitudes among middle income Negroes. *American Sociological Review, 31,* 365–374.

Furstenberg, F. F., Belzer, A., Davis, C., Levine, J. A., Morrow, K., & Washington, M. (1993). How families manage risk and opportunity in dangerous neighborhoods. In W.J. Wilson (Ed.), *Sociology and the public agenda* (pp. 231–258). Newbury Park, CA: Sage.

Gans, H. J. (1979). Symbolic ethnicity: The future of ethnic groups and cultures in America. In H. J. Gans (Ed.), *On the making of Americans: Essays in honor of David Riesman* (pp. 193–220). Philadelphia: University of Pennsylvania Press.

Garcia Coll, C., Maberty, G., Jenkins, R., McAdoo, H. P., Cmic, K., Wasik, B., & Garcia, H. (1996). An integrative model for the study of developmental competencies in minority children. *Child Development, 67,* 1891–1914.

Garcia Coll, C. T., Meyer, E. C., & Brillon, L. (1995). Ethnic and minority parenting. In M. H. Bornstein (Ed), *Handbook of parenting: Vol. 2. Biology and ecology of parenting* (pp. 189–209). Mahwah, NJ: Erlbaum.

Gilliam, F. D., Jr. (1986). Black America: Divided by class. *Public Opinion, 9,* 53–57.

Gjerde, P. F. (2004). Culture, power, and experience: Toward a person-centered cultural psychology. *Human Development, 47,* 138–157.

Glazer, N. (1975). Universalisation of ethnicity. *Ecounter, 2,* 16.

Guthrie, R. (1991). The psychology of African Americans: An historical perspective. In R. Jones (Ed.), *Black psychology* (pp. 33–45). Berkeley, CA: Cobb & Henry.

Hall, M. L., & Allen, W. R. (1989). Race consciousness among African American college students. In G. L Berry & J. K. Asamen (Eds)., *Black students: Psychosocial issues and academic achievement* (pp. 172–192). Newbury Park, CA: Sage.

Harris, D. (1995). Exploring the determinants of adult Black identity: Context and process. *Social Forces, 74,* 227–241.

Hill, M. E. (2000). Color differences in the socioeconomic status of African American men: Results from a longitudinal study. *Social Forces, 78,* 1437–1460.

Hill, N. E. (1997). Does parenting differ based on social class?: African-American females' perceived socialization for achievement. *American Journal of Community Psychology, 25*(5), 675–697.

Hill, N. E. (2001). Parenting and academic socialization as they relate to school readiness: The role of ethnicity and family income. *Journal of Educational Psychology, 93*(4), 686–697.

Hill, N. E., & Adams, J. D. (2005). *Socioeconomic context and parenting among African American and Euro-American families.* Manuscript under review.

Hill, N. E., & Bush, K. (2001). Relations between parenting environment and children's mental health among African American and Euro-American mothers and children. *Journal of Marriage and the Family, 63,* 954–966.

Hill, N. E., Bush, K. R., & Roosa, M. W. (2003). Relations between parenting and family socialization strategies and children's mental health: Low income, Mexican American and Euro-American mothers' and children's perspectives. *Child Development, 74,* 189–204.

Hill, N. E., Ramirez, C. L., & Dumka, L. E., (2003). Adolescents' career aspirations: A qualitative study of perceived barriers and family support among low income ethnically diverse adolescents. *Journal of Family Issues, 24,* 934–959.

Hill Collins, P. (1990). *Black feminist thought: Knowledge, consciousness and the politics of empowerment.* New York: Routledge.

Hoff-Ginsberg, E., & Tardiff, T. (1995). Socioeconomic status and parenting. In M. H. Bornstein (Ed.), *Handbook of parenting: Vol. 2. Biology and ecology of parenting* (pp. 161–188). Mahwah, NJ: Erlbaum.

Holden, G., & Edwards, L. (1989). Parental attitudes toward child rearing: Instruments, issues and implications. *Psychological Bulletin, 106,* 29–58.

Hughes, M., & Hertel, B. R. (1990). The significance of color remains: A study of life chances, mate selection, and ethnic consciousness among Black Americans. *Social Forces, 68,* 1105–1120.

Hunter, A. G., & Johnson, D. J. (in press). A certain kind of vision: Revealing structure, process, and meaning in African American families. In J. Jackson, C. Caldwell, & S. Sellers (Eds.), *Research methodology in African American communities.* Thousand Oaks, CA: Sage.

Hurlbert, J. (1989). The Southern Region: A test of the hypothesis of cultural distinctiveness. *Sociological Quarterly, 30,* 245–66.

Hutchinson, J., Rodriguez, N., & Hagan, J. (1996). Community life: African Americans in multiethnic residential areas. *Journal of Black Studies, 27*(2), 201–223.

Hutnik, N. (1991). *Ethnic minority identity: A social psychological perspective.* Oxford, UK: Clarendon Press.

Iceland, J. (2004). Beyond black and white metropolitan residential segregation in multi-ethnic America. *Social Science Research, 33,* 248–271.

Iceland, J., Weinberg, D., & Steinmetz, E. (2002). *Racial and ethnic residential segregation in the United States: 1980–2000* (U.S. Bureau of the Census, Series CENSR-3). Washington, DC: U.S. Government Printing Office.

Jaynes, G., & Williams, R. (Eds.). (1989). *A common destiny: Blacks and American society.* Washington, DC: National Academy Press.

Johnson, S. D., Jr. (1990). Toward clarifying culture, race and ethnicity in the context of multicultural counseling. *Journal of Multicultural Counseling and Development, 18,* 41–50.

Jones, R. K., & Lui, Y. (1999). The culture of poverty and African American culture: An empirical assessment. *Sociological Perspectives, 42,* 439–459.

Keith, V. M., & Herring, C. (1991). Skin tone and stratification in the Black community. *American Journal of Sociology, 97,* 760–778.

Knight, G. P., & Hill, N. E. (1998). Measurement equivalence in research involving minority adolescents. In V. C. McLoyd & L. Steinberg (Eds.), *Research on minority adolescents: Conceptual, methodological, and theoretical issues* (pp. 183–210). Mahwah, NJ: Erlbaum.

Krysan, M. (2000). Prejudice, politics, and public opinion: Understanding the sources of racial policy attitudes. *Annual Review of Sociology, 26,* 135–168.

Landrine, H., & Klonoff, E. A. (1994). The African American Acculturation Scale. *Journal of Black Psychology, 20,* 104–127.

Marable, M., & Mullings, L. (1994). The divided mind of Black America: Race, ideology, and politics in the post civil rights era. *Race and Class, 36,* 61–72.

McAdoo, H. P. (1997). *Black families.* Thousand Oaks, CA: Sage.

McLoyd, V. C. (2004). Linking race and ethnicity to culture: Steps along the road from inference to hypothesis testing. *Human Development, 47,* 185–191.

Mitchell, H. H. (1975). *Black belief: Folk beliefs in America and West Africa.* New York: Harper & Row.

Moynihan, D. (1965). *The Negro family: The case for national action.* Washington DC: Office of Policy Planning and Research, United States Department of Labor.

Murry, V. M. (2000). Extraordinary challenges and ordinary life experiences of Black American families. In P. C. McKenry & S. H. Price (Eds.), *Family stress and change* (2nd ed., pp. 333–358). Thousand Oaks, CA: Sage.

Murry, V. M., Bynum, M. S., Brody, G. H., Willert, A., & Stephens, D. (2001). African American single mothers and children in context: A review of studies on risk and resilience. *Clinical Child and Family Psychology Review, 4,* 133–155.

Murry, V. M., Smith, E. P., & Hill, N. E. (2001). Race, ethnicity, and culture in studies of families in context. *Journal of Marriage and the Family, 63,* 911–914.

Nissimov, R. (2002, August 25). Some blacks irritated by immigrant influx. *Houston Chronicle,* pp. A33, A62.

Nobles, W. (1991). African philosophy: Foundations of black psychology. In R. Jones (Ed.), *Black psychology* (pp. 47–64). Berkeley, CA: Cobb & Henry.

Ogbu, J. U., & Stern, P. (2001). Caste status and intellectual development. In R. J.

Sternberg & E. L. Grigorenko (Eds.), *Environmental effects on cognitive abilities* (pp. 3–37). Mahwah, NJ: Erlbaum.

Omi, M., & Winant, H. (1986). *Racial formation in the United States: From the 1960s to 1980s.* New York: Routledge.

Pattillo-McCoy, M. (1999). *Black picket fences: Privilege and perils among the Black middle class* (Vol. 22). Chicago: University of Chicago Press.

Pattillo-McCoy, M. (2000). The limits of out-migration for the Black middle class. *Journal of Urban Affairs, 22,* 225–241.

Phinney, J. S. (1996). When we talk about American ethnic groups, what do we mean? *American Psychologist, 51,* 918–927.

Pinderhughes, E. E., Dodge, K. A., Pettit, J. E., & Zelli, A. (2000). Discipline responses influences of parents' socioeconomic status, ethnicity, beliefs about parenting, stress, and cognitive emotional functioning. *Journal of Family Psychology, 14,* 380–400.

Robb, J. (1995). Affirmative action for immigrants: The entitlement nobody wanted. *Social Contract, 6,* 86–94.

Rohner, R. (1984). Toward a conception of culture for cross-cultural psychology. *Journal of Cross-Cultural Psychology, 15,* 111–138.

Roosa, M. W., Morgan-Lopez, A., Cree, W., & Specter, M. (2002). Ethnic culture, poverty, and context: Sources of influence on Latino families and children. In J. Contreras, A. Neal-Barnett, & K. Kerns (Eds.), *Latino children and families in the United States: Current research and future directions.* Westport, CT: Greenwood Press.

Rueter, R. E. (1918). *The mulatto in the United States: Including a study of the role of mixed-blood races throughout the world.* Boston: Richard G. Badger.

Sampson, R. J., & Groves, W. B. (1989). Community structure and crime: Testing social disorganization theory. *American Journal of Sociology, 94,* 775–802.

Schmidley, D. (2003). The foreign-born population in the United States: March 2002 (*Current Population Reports,* Series P20-539). Washington, DC: U.S. Bureau of the Census.

Selby, H. A., Murphy, A. D., & Lorenzen, S. A. (1990). *The Mexican urban household.* Austin: University of Texas Press.

Seltzer, R., & Smith, R. C. (1985). Race and ideology: A research note measuring liberalism and conservatism in Black America. *Phylon, 46,* 105–118.

Seltzer, R., & Smith, R. C. (1991). Color differences in the Afro-American community and the difference they make. *Journal of Black Studies, 21,* 279–285.

Sigelman, C. K., Sigelman, L., Walkosz, B. J., & Nitz, M. (1995). Black candidates, White voters: Understanding racial bias in political perceptions. *American Journal of Political Science, 39,* 243–265.

Smelana, J. G., Campione-Barr, N., & Daddis, C. (2004). Longitudinal development of family decision making: Defining healthy behavioral autonomy for middle class African-American adolescents. *Child Development, 75,* 1418–1434.

Sollors, W. (1996). Foreword: Theories of American ethnicity. In W. Sollors (Ed.), *Theories of ethnicity: A classical reader* (pp. 10–44). New York: New York University Press.

Stack, C. (1997). Writing ethnography: Feminist critical practice. In M. Gergen &

S. Davis (Eds.), *Toward a new psychology of gender.* Florence, KY: Taylor & Francis/Routledge.

Tajfel, H. (1978a). *Differentiation between social groups: Studies in the social psychology of intergroup relations.* Oxford, UK: Academic Press

Tajfel, H. (1978b). *The social psychology of minorities.* London: Minority Rights Group.

Tatum, B. D. (1987). *Assimilation blues: Black families in a White community.* New York: Greenwood Press.

Thomas, A., & Sillen, S. (1972). *Racism and psychiatry.* New York: Brunner/Mazel.

Thornton, M. C., Tran, T.V., & Taylor, R. J. (1997). Multiple dimensions of racial group identification among Black adults. *Journal of Black Psychology, 23,* 293–309.

Trimble, J. E. (1990). Ethnic specification, validation prospects and future of drug abuse research. *International Journal of the Addictions, 25,* 149–169.

Turner, J. C., Hogg, M. A., Oakes, P. J., Reicher, S. D., & Wetherell, M. S. (1987). *Rediscovering the social group: A self-categorization theory.* Oxford, UK: Basil Blackwell.

U.S. Bureau of the Census. (2003). *Current population reports* (Series P-20, No. 541). Washington, DC: U.S. Government Printing Office.

U.S. Bureau of the Census. (2000). Profile of the foreign-born population in the United States: 1997 (*Current Population Reports*, Series P23-195). Washington, DC: U.S. Government Printing Office.

U.S. Department of Education, National Center for Education Statistics. (2002). *The Condition of Education, 2002* (Based on U.S. Department of Commerce, Bureau of the Census, October Current Population Surveys, 1972–2000). Washington, DC: U.S. Government Printing Office.

Valsiner, J., & Litvinovic, G. (1996). Processes of generalization in parental reasoning. In C. Super & S. Harkness (Eds.), *Parents' cultural belief systems* (pp. 56–82). New York: Guilford Press.

Wainryb, C. (2004). The study of diversity in human development: Culture, urgencies, and perils. *Human Development, 47,* 131–137.

Warner, W. L., & Lunt, P. S. (1942). *The status system of a modern community.* New Haven, CT: Yale University Press.

Warren, R. (1978). *The community in America.* Lanham, MD: University Press of America.

Weber, M. (1922). Ethnic groups. In G. Roth & C. Wittich (Eds.), *Economy and society* (pp. 385–398). Berkeley: University of California Press.

Welch, S., & Foster, L. (1987). Class and conservatism in the Black community. *American Political Quarterly, 15,* 445–470.

Williams, D. R. (1996). Introduction: Racism and health, a research agenda. *Ethnicity and Disease, 6,* 1–6.

Wilson, W. J. (1996). *When work disappears.* New York: Random House.

Yee, A. H., Fairchild, H. H., Weizmann, F., & Wyatt, G. E. (1993). Addressing psychology's problem with race. *American Psychologist, 48,* 1132–1140.

CHAPTER 3

Trends in African American Child Well-Being, 1985–2001

Vicki L. Lamb, Kenneth C. Land,
Sarah O. Meadows, *and* Fasaha Traylor

As the United States has become an increasingly multiracial society, major concerns about child well-being have focused both on the circumstances of children's lives within specific racial groups and how these circumstances compare with the pattern and trend of improvement in all children's lives relative to the past. Social scientists should be engaged in monitoring and reporting on the condition of African American children, because these issues are important both in their own right and as a mirror to the nation about how far we have come.

The purpose of this chapter is to describe trends in child well-being of African American children for the years 1985–2001, building on the component social indicator time series and summary well-being indices that have been compiled by the Child Well-Being Index Project (Land, Lamb, & Mustillo, 2001; Meadows, Land, & Lamb, 2005). Our base year, 1985, represents the earliest time most racial data were collected on indicators of child well-being. National trends of child well-being for all U.S. children are also presented for the same time period to compare and contrast with African American patterns and trends of child well-being.

DATA SOURCES FOR CHILD WELL-BEING INDICATORS AND DOMAINS

Data sources available for the operationalization and measurement of trends in child well-being in the United States are limited, particularly

45

for studies based on race or ethnicity. Children are less likely to be included as respondents or subjects in national surveys. In addition, most time series data on children that identify separate racial or ethnic groups were not collected or made available until the 1980s or later. Basic demographic data on family structures and incomes for households with children under age 18 are available on an annual basis from the Annual Demographic Supplements to the March *Current Population Surveys* (U.S. Bureau of Labor Statistics and U.S. Bureau of the Census [BLS/BC], 2004). Additional annual data on selected mortality and other vital statistics also are available from the sample surveys and vital statistics compiled by the National Center for Health Statistics (Centers for Disease Control and Prevention and National Center for Health Statistics [CDC/NCHS], 2004). In addition, there are three data sources based on replications of annual sample surveys that were developed in response to the Social Indicators Movement of the 1960s and that date back to the mid-1970s: (1) the National Crime Victimization Survey, which provides data on crime victimization down to age 12 as well as data on the perceived ages of offenders (U.S. Department of Justice, 2004); (2) the High School Senior Survey, which evolved into the Monitoring the Future (MTF) study, which provides data on illicit drug use (including cigarettes, alcohol, marijuana, cocaine, and heroin) and other teen behaviors and attitudes such as religiosity (Monitoring the Future, 2004); and (3) the National Assessment of Educational Progress (NAEP), which provides reading, mathematics, and other subject test scores from samples of children at ages 9, 13, and 17 (U.S. Department of Education, 2004).

To chart trends of child well-being for African American children, we have collected 25 nationally representative time series of demographic and social indicators.[1] The indicators have been categorized into seven quality-of-life domains: material well-being, health, safety/behavioral concerns, education, place in community, social relationships, and emotional/spiritual well-being. Table 3.1 presents the list of indicators used in the project, and the ages covered by each indicator, arranged by quality-of-life domains. Time series for all of the indicators were collected for the years 1985–2001.[2]

As other chapters in this book emphasize, African Americans now occupy diverse positions in American society. However, our research on general trends indicate that African American children, on average, remain disadvantaged in a number of areas as compared with national averages for all U.S. children. For example, our data show that in 2001 the African American child poverty rate of 26.6% was 1.7 times higher than the national average of 15.8%. In 2001 the infant death rate for African American infants, 14.2 deaths per 1,000 live births, was 2.5 times that of European American infants, 5.7 deaths, and the gap is not closing.

TABLE 3.1. Component Domains of Child Well-Being Indices

I.   Material Well-Being
   1. Rate of children in poverty
   2. Median family income (in 2001 dollars)
   3. Secure parental employment rate
   4. Rate of children with health insurance coverage

II. Health
   1. Rate of children with activity limitations
   2. Low birth weight rate
   3. Infant mortality rate
   4. Child mortality rate, ages 1–14

III. Safety/Behavioral Concerns
   1. Rate of cigarette smoking, grade 12
   2. Rate of alcoholic drinking, grade 12
   3. Rate of illicit drug use, grade 12
   4. Teen birth rates, ages 10–17
   5. Rate of victimization of serious violent crimes, ages 12–17

IV. Educational Well-Being
   1. Reading test scores, ages 9, 13, and 17
   2. Math test scores, ages 9, 13, and 17

V.   Place in Community
   1. Preschool enrollment rate, ages 3–4
   2. Rate of persons receiving high school diploma, ages 18–24
   3. Rate of youth not working or in school, ages 16–19
   4. Rate of persons receiving bachelor's degree, ages 25–29
   5. Rate of voting in presidential elections, ages 18–24

VI. Social Relationships
   1. Rate of children living in a single-parent household
   2. Rate of children who have moved in the past year

VII. Emotional Well-Being
   1. Suicide rate, ages 15–19
   2. Rate of weekly religious ceremony attendance, grade 12
   3. Percent who report that religion is very important, grade 12

Note. Unless otherwise noted, the indicators refer to children ages 0–17.

Some educational gaps are closing. We have found that by the year 2001 the high school graduation rate of African Americans (86%) was equivalent to the U.S. average (87%), and the preschool enrollment rate for African American children ages 3–4 (56%) slightly exceeded the national average (54%). However, college graduation rates for persons ages 25–29 indicate that in 2001 African Americans still lagged behind the national average, 18% versus 29%.

This chapter focuses on trajectories of change in African American child well-being from 1985 to 2001. It also focuses on the disparities in African American child well-being as compared with U.S. averages for all children. African American children and their families do not live in a vacuum, but rather are part of the larger U.S. society. As the preceding discussion indicates, there continue to be gaps or disparities in well-being, and although some gaps are shrinking, other gaps are not closing. Accordingly, growing disparities in child well-being for African American populations are a matter of public concern, for which researchers should engage in monitoring and social reporting. Throughout this chapter we discuss the disparities that African American children experience, as reflected in the social indicators we examine, compared with U.S. averages and, for some indicators, European American averages. All of the figures show both African American and U.S. trends in child well-being. Hence, we can consider the changes and improvements African American children have experienced in a number of social domains, and we can also observe the gaps in child well-being that remain.

THE CHILD WELL-BEING INDEX: METHODS OF CONSTRUCTION

Since the 1960s researchers in social indicators and quality-of-life measurement have argued that well-measured and consistently collected social indicators provide a means to monitor, over time, the condition of groups in society, including children and families (Land, 2000). The information that is obtained from social indicators can be instrumental in shaping how we think about important issues in our personal lives and in the life of the nation. Indicators of child and youth well-being are used by numerous groups—including child advocacy groups, policymakers, researchers, the media, government agencies at all levels, and service providers—for a variety of purposes. Social indicators can be used to describe the condition of children, to monitor or track child outcomes, and to set goals for the future.

In the case of overall child well-being, there are multiple indicators of well-being to be compared (Pollard & Lee, 2003). Over any period of years, some indicators of child well-being likely will have risen and some will have fallen. The problem is how to combine the relative changes in many indicators pertaining to child well-being into a single number that can meaningfully be interpreted as a measure of the relative change over time in a fairly comprehensive selection of social conditions encountered by children and young people.

In its broadest sense, an index number is a measure of the magnitude of a variable at one point (such as a specific year that is termed the "current year") relative to its value at another point (called the "reference" or "base year"). Index numbers are widely used in economics, such as in the Consumer Price Index (CPI), to compare the general price levels of goods at different points in time. Although persons may not consume all of the items used to calculate the CPI, most consumers are interested in how general price levels are changing and fluctuating. Similarly, in any given year no single child encounters all of the social conditions that are part of the overall Child Well-Being Index (CWI) that we develop in this study. However, fluctuations over time in the CWI can be interpreted as signaling changes in the overall social context of social conditions encountered by children and youth. Such changes would be of interest to policymakers, government officials, adults, parents, and young persons to understand how well children and youth are doing at one point in time, say 1999, as compared with another point in time, such as 1985.

As noted, the variable, or index number, to be compared over time is the overall well-being of children in the United States—defined in terms of *averages of social conditions encountered by children and youth*. The statistical theory of index numbers deals with the development and assessment of functional forms or aggregation functions for the construction of indices (Jazairi, 1983). In this project, index formulas of the following type are applied:

Index of child well-being in year t = $(1/N) \Sigma_i \{100 + [(\Delta R_{it} / R_{ir}) \times 100]\}$

where N denotes the number of basic indicators on which the index is based, R_{it} denotes the ith child well-being indicator rate in the year $t > r$, R_{ir} denotes the i^{it} rate in the *reference or base year* r, R_{it} and R_{ir} are *rate relatives*, and the summation is taken over N indicator rates. In the equation, $\Delta R_{it} = R_{it}-R_{ir}$ denotes the numerical value of the *finite-difference* or *change* in indicator i from the base year r to year t. Each change rate ratio in the equation is multiplied by 100 in order to measure the percentage change in the rate from the base year value. In index number terminology, the formula in the equation is a *mean of percentage change rate ratios index*, is additive, and applies equal weights to all component rates.

There is little consensus among individuals (social scientists, policymakers, and citizens) regarding differential weights to be assigned to components of composite indices of well-being in general and indices of child and youth well-being in particular. Furthermore, a methodological study by Hagerty and Land (2004). found that, in the absence of a strong consensus on differential weights for indices of a single social unit, such as a nation, for multiple time periods (time-series data), an equal-weighting strategy is privileged in that it minimizes disagreement among all possible individuals' weights. Therefore, we have adopted an equal-weighting strategy for construction of the composite indices studied herein.

As Table 3.1 shows, both positive and negative indicators are used in constructing the CWI. Positive indicators are those in which higher numbers denote improved conditions, such as median family income or high school graduation rate. Negative indicators are those in which higher numbers signify worsening conditions, such as infant death rate or cigarette smoking rate. In order to track indicator trends in a consistent manner, the change rate ratio values for positive indicators will be added to the base year index of 100 and the change rate ratios for negative indicators will be subtracted from the base year index of 100. The trend of indicator performance relative to the base year value will then be in the same direction regardless of whether the particular indicator is positive or negative. Therefore, index values for years subsequent to the base year that are greater, equal, or lesser than 100, indicate "improvement," "no change," or "deterioration" in the time series relative to its base year value. For example, the African American index value for child poverty is 131 in the year 2000; this means that in 2000 there was a 31% improvement in the African American child poverty rate relative to 1985.

There are three steps in the development of the child well-being indices, and these steps have been taken with regard to African American children. First, the basic well-being indicators cited in Table 3.1 are grouped by the domain categories and the equation is applied to each indicator series within the well-being domains for African American children and for all U.S. children. For example, for the material well-being domain, the equation would be applied separately to the rates of child poverty, median family income, secure parental employment, and health insurance coverage. Then the arithmetic average of the domain-specific indicators is calculated to obtain the CWI trends for each of the seven domains.[3] Finally, the arithmetic average of the seven domain-specific child well-being indices is calculated to obtain an overall summary CWI for African American children and for all children.

As noted earlier, 100 is used as the reference point for the base year (1985) and the values of the indices for subsequent years are presented as percentages of this base year value. Thus, an index value that is greater than 100 for a subsequent year indicates improvement as compared with 1985 and a value less than 100 indicates deterioration as compared with the base year. Figures will be presented showing the domain trends in child well-being for African American and for all U.S.

children. Each trend line indicates the trend for the group as compared with that group's status in 1985.

FINDINGS

Domain-Specific Trends

Figure 3.1 presents trends in the *material well-being* domain. The material well-being domain represents resources that families are able to provide for their children. The indicators used to represent material well-being include child poverty rates, median family income, secure parental employment (having at least one parent employed full-time year-round), and health insurance coverage. Both African American children and all U.S. children follow a similar trend in that conditions are rather stable until 1989, deteriorate with the economic recession of the early 1990s until around 1993, and improve through 2001. The lower levels of material well-being during the early 1990s were due to higher rates of child poverty (39% for African American children and 22% for the national average) and lower median family incomes. Families were having a harder time providing for their children during this recessionary period.

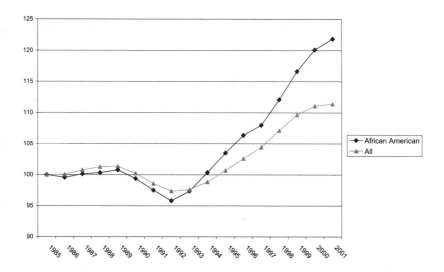

FIGURE 3.1. Trends in material well-being, 1985–2001: African American children and all children.

The consequences of poverty during childhood are far-reaching, resulting in potential deprivation of basic necessities of food, housing, and clothing (see, e.g., Duncan & Brooks-Gunn, 1997). A number of studies show that children living in poverty experience poorer health outcomes and compromised cognitive development through their formative years (Aber, Bennett, Conley, & Li, 1997; Bradley & Corwyn, 2002; Brooks-Gunn & Duncan, 1997; Dawson, 1991; Goodman, 1999; Guo, 1998; Guo & Harris, 2000; McLoyd, 1998; Montgomery, Kiely, & Pappas, 1996; Smith, Brooks-Gunn, & Klebanov, 1997), and the parents also experience emotional distress and hardship (McLoyd, 1990). In addition, research findings indicate that poor children are more likely to have school behavioral problems, get lower grades, drop out of school, become pregnant as teenagers, and do worse in the labor force as adults (Bradley & Corwyn, 2002; Brooks-Gunn & Duncan, 1997; Duncan & Brooks-Gunn, 1997; Haveman & Wolfe, 1995; Mayer, 1997; Smith et al., 1997; Zedlewski, 2002).

African American children show greater improvement in material well-being, as compared with the trend for all children, in that the African American children's level of material well-being in 2001 is 22% greater than in 1985, whereas the national trend improved 11%. The African American improvements are due to reductions in child poverty rates (from 36% in 1985 to 27% in 2001) and increases in rates of secure parental employment (from 48% to 65%) and median family income (from $25,281 in 1987 to $30,339 in 2001, calculated in 2001 dollars). The African American levels, however, continue to be well below the national and European American averages. Nationally, the child poverty rates in 1985 and 2001 were 20.1% and 15.8%, and the European American rates were 13.3% and 10.9%, respectively. The median family income, in 2001 dollars, for U.S. families with minor children was $46,151 in 1987 and $51,407 in 2001. For European American families the numbers are $51,524 and $60,861.

Between 1997 and 2000 there has been an increase in privately funded health insurance coverage for African American and all U.S. children. However, since 2000 there has been a decline in the percentage of children covered with private health insurance. In the late 1990s states were able to create State Children's Health Insurance Programs (SCHIP) to provide health insurance coverage for children in families that were ineligible to be covered by Medicaid. Research indicates that uninsured children enrolled in SCHIP benefit through improved access, continuity, and quality of health care (Szilagyi et al., 2004). Initially, many eligible children were not being covered by SCHIP because of administrative hurdles, waiting periods, and other barriers (Fairbrother et al., 2004; Kronebusch & Elbel, 2004). Public health insurance coverage, which in-

cludes Medicaid and SCHIP, as well as Medicare and CHAMPUS/
Tricare, was unchanged between 1997 and 2000, but there has been an
increase in coverage since 2001. Thus, total health insurance coverage,
either publicly or privately funded, has changed very little over the period under study and is between 84 and 88% for both African American
children and all children for most of the period under study. The exception is the period when total health insurance for African American children hovered around 80 to 81%, from 1996 to 1998.

Trends in the *health domain* are shown in Figure 3.2. Indicators in
the health domain consist of parental assessment of a child's limitations
in performing daily activities because of chronic health conditions, low
birth weight rates, infant death rates, and child death rates. African
American children experienced declines in health between 1988 and
1993, as compared with 1985 levels. The indicator that most influences
this downward trend is the increased rate of reported activity limitations
due to chronic health conditions. In 1985, 5.8% of African American
children ages 0–17 were reported to have activity limitations. In 1994,
the rate rose to 8.9%. Since that time the rate has shown a bumpy decline to just less than 7% in 2001. The national trend of children with
activity limitations also increased during the early to mid-1990s; however, the increase was not as steep as that for African American children.
Nationally, the 1985 level was 5.1%, which increased to a high of 6.7%
in 1994 and has since stabilized at approximately 6%.

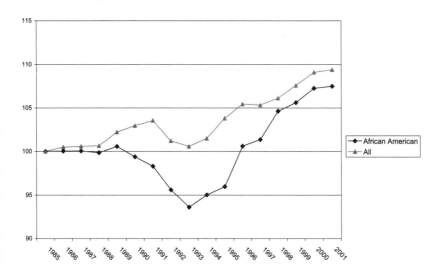

FIGURE 3.2. Trends in health domain, 1985–2001: African American children and
all children.

Both the African American and U.S. trends for activity limitations were higher in 2001 than they were in 1985, indicating a somewhat higher rate of reported health problems, particularly asthma; neurodevelopmental disorders, such as mental retardation; and learning-behavioral disorders, such as attention-deficit disorders (Msall et al., 2003; Newacheck & Halfon, 1998). Given the increasing poverty rate and declining economic status of families from 1990 to 1994, it is likely that economic factors were contributing to the increased trends in activity limitations of children in the United States. Studies have documented a significant link between childhood poverty and activity limitations, physical disablement, health problems, and chronic conditions that lead to disabilities (Alaimo, Olson, Frongillo, & Briefel, 2001; Goodman, 1999; Hogan, Msall, Rogers, & Avery, 1997; Montgomery et al., 1996; Newacheck & Halfon, 1998; Newacheck, Stein, Bauman, & Huang, 2003). There are racial disparities in children's rates of disability and poor health, although many of the disparities are associated with poverty, family structure, and use of health care services (Elster, Jarosik, VanGeest, & Fleming, 2003; Flores, Bauchner, Feinstein, & Nguyen, 1999; Montgomery et al., 1996; Newacheck et al., 2003).

Since 1993 there has been an upward trajectory in the overall trend of African American children's health well-being, primarily due to reductions in infant and child death rates. Infant death rates record the number of deaths of infants before their first birthdays. For African American infants, this rate dropped from 19.0 to 14.2 per 1,000 live births between 1985 and 2001. Child death rates reflect the annual number of deaths of children ages 1–14, and between 1985 and 2001 that rate dropped from 58.1 to 41.8 per 100,000 African American children in those age groups. At the national level, declines in infant and child death rates also contributed to improved overall child health well-being from the mid-1990s to the end of the series. By 2001, the overall health well-being of African American children had improved 7.5%, which is close to the rate of improvement in health well-being for all U.S. children, at 9.4%.

Although the health of African American children has improved since 1985, their health lags behind the national average. African American infants have much higher infant mortality rates (IMRs) than European American infants. In 2001 the African American IMR of 14.2 deaths per 1,000 live births was 2.5 times greater than the European American rate of 5.7 deaths. Recent research has indicated that most of the African American–European American gap in IMR is due to economic factors, including income and mother's education, as well as timing and frequency of prenatal health care, mother's health and behavior (e.g., smoking, drinking alcohol), and adverse birth outcomes, such as low birth weight (Hummer, 1993; Hummer et al., 1999). Another factor contributing to the racial disparities in IMRs are differences in rates of breastfeeding in the first year of life (Forste, Weiss, & Lippincott, 2001).

African Americans also have higher proportions of births of children with low birth weight (LBW), which is less than 2,500 grams (5.5 pounds). The percentage of LBW births has been increasing over the time series, and the disparity between African American and European American LBW rates has not decreased (Branum & Schoendorf, 2002; Muhuri, MacDorman, & Ezzati-Rice, 2004). Between 1985 and 2001, the rate of African American LBW births rose from 12.6% to 13.1%, which is significantly higher than the national rates of 6.8% and 7.7%, or the European American rates of 5.6% and 6.8%, for the same years. As with infant mortality rates, lower socioeconomic status is strongly associated with LBW rates (Starfield et al., 1991). However, controlling for economic disparities, prenatal care, and maternal characteristics fails to fully explain the higher African American LBW rates (Frisbie, Biegler, de Turk, Forbes, & Pullum, 1997; Kleinman & Kessel, 1987; Shiono, Klebanoff, Graubard, Berendes, & Rhodes, 1986; Starfield et al., 1991). Studies of Chicago neighborhoods have shown that important neighborhood characteristics, such as the presence of violence, poverty, perception of social support, and percent African American, help to account for LBW births to African American mothers (Buka, Brennan, Rich-Edwards, Raudenbush, & Earls, 2003; Morenoff, 2003; Roberts, 1997). Low birth weight is an important long-term health issue because research has associated LBW, particularly very low birth weights of less than 1,500 grams, with developmental problems in cognition and neuromotor functioning, disabilities, hyperactivity, and school problems (Avchen, Scott, & Mason, 2001; Behrman, Rosenzweig & Taubman, 1994; Boardman, Powers, Padilla, & Hummer, 2002; Conley & Bennet, 2000; Hack, Klein, & Taylor, 1995; Hediger, Overpeck, Ruan, & Troendle, 2002; McCormick, Gortmaker, & Sobel, 1990).

Figure 3.3 shows trends in the *safety/behavioral well-being domain*, which are based on indicators of rates of serious violent crime victimization for youth ages 12–17, teen births for girls ages 10–17, and consumption of cigarettes, illicit drugs, and alcohol by 12th graders. For African American children the safety/behavioral well-being trend deteriorated in the late 1980s, primarily due to large increases in the rate of serious violent crime victimization. In 1985 the rate of African American children ages 12–17 who were victims of aggravated assault, rape, robbery, or homicide was 35.2 per 1,000. By 1990 the rate had peaked at 77.0 per 1,000. Since 1993, the rate of serious violent crime victimization for African American youth dropped to a low of 23.4 in 2000 (the 2001 data are not available at this time). The national average for seri-

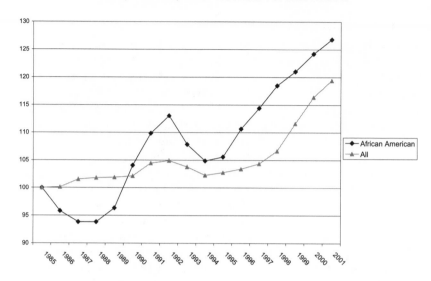

FIGURE 3.3. Trends in safety/behavioral well-being, 1985–2001: African American children and all children.

ous violent crime victimization in 1985 was 34.3 per 1,000. It rose to a high of 43.2 in 1990 and declined to 16.3 in 2000.

Beginning at about 1985 there was an "epidemic" (Cook & Laub, 1998, 2002) of youth violence in the United States, which peaked in 1993 and then declined precipitously. The youth violence epidemic has been attributed to the increased use of handguns rather than knives or fists to settle disputes, particularly among African American males under the age of 25 (Blumstein, 2002; Cook & Laub, 2002). More guns came into the hands of youth as a result of the growing crack cocaine market during the 1980s, which recruited young people who were willing to work for lower wages, were prone to take more personal risks than adults, were less vulnerable to the penalties of the adult justice system, and who could then afford to buy and use guns for protection (Blumenstein, 1995; Cork, 1999; Grogger & Willis, 2000). The reason for the steep drop in violent crimes by youth since 1993 is less clear (Blumstein & Wallman, 2000; Cook & Laub, 2002). The decline in the crack market has reduced the need for young drug sellers with guns (Johnson, Golub, & Dunlap, 2000). There has been a reduction in the proportion of teens who are carrying handguns owing to more aggressive police tactics in the pursuit of illegal weapons, more community activities to reduce gang violence and negotiate treaties between gangs, and changing community norms that discourage teens from carrying and using guns

(Blumstein, 2002; see also Freed, Webster, Longwell, Carrese, & Wilson, 2001; Molnar, Miller, Azrael, & Buka, 2004). In addition, with the economic recovery of the mid-1990s, jobs were more readily available and more young people found employment in the legitimate sector (Blumstein, 2002).

The initial deterioration in African American safety/behavioral well-being was also due to increases in teen birth rates in the late 1980s and early 1990s. In 1985, the birth rate for African American girls ages 10–17 was 36.9 births per 1,000 girls. It reached a peak of 43.6 births in 1990. These rates declined markedly at the end of the 1990s, to 23.0 births in 2001, which contributed to a much improved trend in safety/behavioral well-being for African American children. The birth rate for all U.S. girls ages 10–17 was 16.1 in 1985, reaching a high of 20.1 in 1990, and falling to 13.0 in 2001.

The decline in teen birth rates in the 1990s was accompanied by a decline in the number of teen pregnancies, which is based on rates of births, fetal losses (stillbirths and miscarriages), and abortions (Ventura, Matthews, & Hamilton, 2001); thus, fewer teenage girls were getting pregnant in the 1990s. The reduction in teen pregnancies and births during the 1990s was due to a number of factors. Between 1991 and 2001 there was a 16% increase in the percent of all teens in grades 9–12 who reported that they had never been sexually active, with a 35% increase for African American teens (Centers for Disease Control [CDC], 2002). Of those teens who were sexually active, there was a 35% increase in the reported use of condoms, and a 40% increase for African Americans (CDC, 2002). In addition, there was a 23% reduction in African American adolescents who reported that they were "currently sexually active," whereas there was little change in this rate overall.

Other factors that contributed to improved safety/behavioral well-being trends for African American children in the late 1990s were reductions in the consumption of cigarettes, illicit drugs, and alcohol by 12th graders. Overall, African American youth showed greater improvements in safety/behavioral concerns at the end of the period under study as compared with the U.S. national trends, 26.8% versus 19.4%.

The *education domain* of the CWI was created to represent educational achievement. The CWI uses indicators of children's achievements with respect to their schooling activities based on levels and trends in average test scores in the reading and mathematics tests administered as part of the continuing National Assessment of Educational Progress series for children ages 9, 13, and 17, which is conducted by the U.S. Department of Education's National Center for Education Statistics (2004). The educational well-being trend, presented in Figure 3.4, is composed of the changes in the average of the three age-group–specific scores for both reading and mathematics. For the most part, there has been little sustained improvement in these scores for U.S. students or for African American students. At the end of the time series, the U.S. average indicated only a 1.7% improvement over the 1985 test scores. African American students showed some improvements at the beginning of the time series, but their scores dropped from 1988 to 1992, primarily owing to declines in reading scores. Their scores were flat through most of the 1990s, and showed a downward trend at the end of the series because of declines in both math and reading scores, particularly for 17-year-olds.

These data point to a disturbing trend—that African American students may be falling further behind in educational achievement, particularly in comparison to European American children. The largest African American–European American difference in reading scores occurs for 9-year-olds. In 1988 the average reading score of African American 9-year-olds was 29 points lower than that of European Americans. By 1999 the gap had grown to 35 points. It is likely that this gap reflects the effect of racial differences in school readiness. Research has shown that, on average, African American children start first grade a year behind European American students in vocabulary knowledge and skills, primarily owing to the effects of poverty and limited family resources (see Farkas, 2003). The racial differences in reading test scores are not greatly reduced for

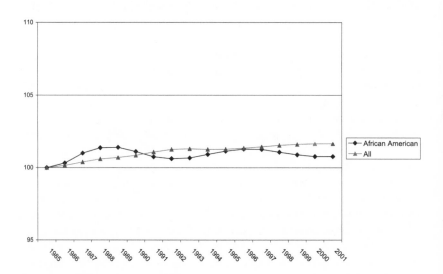

FIGURE 3.4. Trends in educational well-being, 1985–2001: African American children and all children.

older students, in that the 1999 African American–European American gap for 13- and 17-year-olds was 29 and 31 points, respectively. The largest racial gap in math test scores was for the 13-year-olds during the early to mid-1990s. However, by the end of the 1990s both 13- and 17-year-old African American students averaged 30 to 32 points behind European American math test scores. The racial gap in learning for older students has been attributed to a number of factors, including opportunities for learning, such as courses taken, teacher perceptions and actions, and school environment; curriculum/tracking and resources; and student efforts to learn (Farkas, 2003). Discrimination in the allocation of resources to minority students and minority schools has also been cited as an important factor contributing to racial differences in academic achievement for all grade levels (Farkas, 2003; Michelson, 2001, 2003).

The *place in community domain* indicator series broadly represents participation in age-appropriate activities associated with major societal institutions. The indicators refer to children's attachments to such productive activities as schooling and work and participation in the electoral process. Specifically, we use the rates of preschool enrollments for ages 3–4, receipt of high school diploma for ages 18–24, inactivity (not working or in school) for ages 16–19, receipt of bachelor's degree for ages 25–29, and voting in presidential elections for ages 18–24.

Figure 3.5 presents the trends for the place in community domain. African American children show improvement through the time series, with the exception of the early 1990s, in which they experienced a temporary drop in the series. This drop, from 1990 to 1992, was due to declines in the rates of preschool attendance for children ages 3–4 and college graduation for persons ages 25–29, and an increase in the rate of inactivity for youth ages 16–19. Since 1993, the trend in the place in community domain has risen steadily for African American children, resulting in a 25% improvement in 2001 over the 1985 levels.

The African American trend for the place in community domain rises more sharply than that for all U.S. children, which registers a 10% improvement in 2001 over 1985 levels. The major indicators contributing to the African American trend of improvement have been larger increases in preschool enrollments (up 62% in 2001 as compared with 1990) and college graduation rates (up 54% in 2001 as compared with 1985). The trend for African American high school graduation rates rose slowly from 81% in 1985 to 86% in 2001, which was comparable to the U.S. average.

Our data indicate that young children are spending more time in nonfamily childcare and preschool programs. In 2001, 59% of African

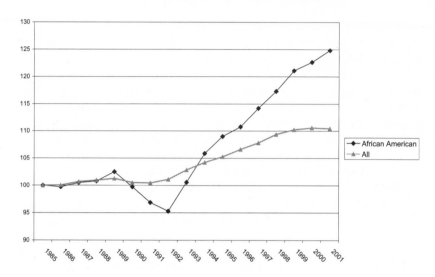

FIGURE 3.5. Trends in place in community domain, 1985–2001: African American children and all children.

American children and 55% of all U.S. children ages 3–4 were enrolled in preschool programs, though the quality of many of these programs is much below what is required to improve children's school readiness (see, e.g., Cost, Quality, and Child Outcomes Study Team, 1995). There are questions regarding the adequacy and benefits of such care. Research indicates that childcare programs can benefit child outcomes, including cognitive abilities, language development, and academic achievement in grade school, particularly for poor children; however, such benefits are strongly affected by the quality of childcare programs (Anderson et al., 2003; Currie, 2001; Loeb, Fuller, Kagan, & Carrol, 2004; Love et al., 2003; National Institute of Child Health and Human Development [NICHD] Early Child Care Research Network, 2000; NICHD Early Child Care Research Network & Duncan, 2003; Peisner-Feinberg et al., 2001).

The early 1990s saw an increase in youth ages 16–19 who were neither working nor in school. In 1991 and 1992 the rates for African American adolescents were 16.8% and 16.9%, and the national rates were 10.5% and 10.1%. Such rates of disconnected youth were lower than the 1985 rates of 18.1% and 11.1%. With the economic expansion of the 1990s, there was a steady decline in the rate of inactivity for African Americans and all youth. In 2001 the rates were 14% and 9%, respectively.

The *social relationships domain* represents a child's circle of intimate and supportive relationships with family and friends. This is a difficult domain to track because of the lack of appropriate measures reflecting social relationships available at the national level over time. Two indicators are used: single-parent-headed families and residential mobility for children under the age of 18. Both measures represent possible disruptions or reductions in an individual's circle of family members and friends and other community connections, which are all part of a person's social capital, and the two measures are found to be interrelated.

Social science research has found that children in single-parent households are less likely, on average, to have regular, open, and pleasant contact and associations with members of both sides of their biological parents' families than are children in families with both parents present (Furstenberg & Cherlin, 1991; King, 1994; Mott, 1990; Seltzer & Brandreth, 1994). Moreover, children in single-parent families are more likely to grow up in poverty, to have cognitive and behavioral problems as youth, and to have less parental supervision, especially from fathers (see McLanahan, 1997). Children in single-parent families experience higher incidences of residential mobility as compared with children in two-parent families (London, 2000; South, Crowder, & Trent, 1998). Moving residences and/or schools can disrupt regular contact with friends, classmates, and the community, and it has been associated with negative impacts on social capital, school achievement, and other child outcomes, particularly for children in single-parent households (Adam & Chase-Lansdale, 2002; Coleman, 1988; Hagan, MacMillan, & Wheaton, 1996; Mehana & Reynolds, 2004; Pettit & McLanahan, 2003; Pribesh & Downey, 1999; Tucker, Marx, & Long, 1998; Wood, Halfon, Newacheck, & Scarlatta, 1993), although part of the negative effects of moving may be due to selection effects in that the movers may be more disadvantaged than those who do not move (Pettit & McLanahan, 2003; Pribesh & Downey, 1999). A study of college students who were children of divorced parents found that if either parent moved after the divorce, the students were more likely to experience a variety of negative effects, including more hostility in interpersonal relations, poorer emotional and general health, less financial support from parents, and less favorable perceptions that their parents were sources of emotional support and role models (Braver, Ellman, & Fabricius, 2003). Residential moves during childhood have also been negatively associated with physical and mental health in midlife (Bures, 2003).

As Figure 3.6 indicates, the social relationship domain trends for African American and all U.S. children tracked below the 1985 levels for most of the period under study. Much of the pattern of greater decline for African American children is due to changes in the annual rates of residential mobility for minor children. In 1988 (the first year for which these data are available) 18.8% of all African American children moved residences. The next year the rate jumped to 23.2%. Since that time the annual residential mobility rate has fluctuated, averaging over 21%. The percentage of African American children living in single-parent households increased slightly during the middle of the period. Approximately 54% were in single-parent households in 1985. The rate increased to 58% in 1991 and hovered around 57% from 1992 through 1997. Since that time the rate has been dropping, such that in 2000 and 2001 the rate was 53%.

The national trend for the social relationship domain has not declined as greatly as that of African American children because the general U.S. rate for residential mobility for children has declined from 18.9% in 1988 to 15.2% in 2001. There have been increases in the U.S. trend for percentage of children living in single-parent families, from 23.4% in 1985 to more than 27% from 1991 to 1997. Since that time the national rate of children living in single-parent households has dropped to below 27%.

The *emotional/spiritual well-being domain* was developed to track children's emotional and psychological health, morale, and spiritual well-being. This domain is also difficult to capture with currently available time series of child well-being indicators. As shown in Table 3.1, three measures are used: rates of suicide for adolescents ages 15–19 and

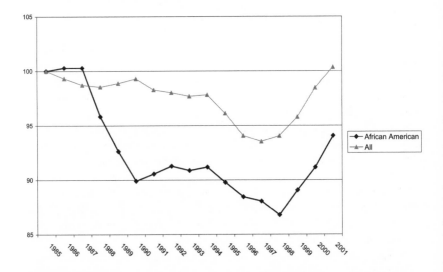

FIGURE 3.6. Trends in social relationship domain, 1985–2001: African American children and all children.

rates of weekly religious ceremony attendance and self-reported spiritual attitudes for 12th graders.

In a review of psychological autopsy studies of youth suicides and epidemiological studies of youth suicidal behaviors, Gould and Kramer (2001) found the risk factors for youth suicide to be significant psychiatric problems, including depressive disorders, substance abuse, and previous suicidal behavior. Stressful personal life events, and high rates of parental psychopathology, especially depression and substance abuse, were also found to be associated with youth suicide attempts and completions. In addition, adolescents who were drifting—not working or in school—were at higher risk of committing suicide.

Religion has been found to have a positive effect on a number of domains in the lives of adolescents, including physical and emotional health, school work and educational outcomes, volunteering and political involvement, family well-being, and avoidance of risky behaviors such as drinking, drug use, sexual activity, and delinquency (see review by Regnerus, 2003). Religious beliefs and participation in religious services have proven to be effective buffers against delinquent behavior for high-risk youth (Johnson, Li, Larson, & McCullough, 2000; Johnson et al., 2001), for high-risk youth exposed to violence (Pearce, Jones, Schwab-Stone, & Runchkin, 2003), for African American adolescents in disordered neighborhoods (Johnson, Jang, Li, & Larson, 2000), and for low-risk youth (Regnerus & Elder, 2003). Regarding emotional well-being, research indicates that higher levels of religiousness, including attendance, personal faith, and positive religious experiences, is associated with lower levels of depressive symptoms (Pearce, Little, & Perez, 2003). In addition, religious involvement has been associated with lower levels of suicide ideation and attempts (Donahue & Benson, 1995; Greening & Stoppelbein, 2002; Nonnemaker, McNeely, & Blum, 2003).

Figure 3.7 shows African American and U.S. trends in emotional and spiritual well-being. In general, the African American trend takes a "U" shape, in that the trend declines to 1993–1994 and then improves since that time. The African American downward trend is very pronounced, declining more than 27% in 1993, as compared with the 1985 base year, before tracking upward after that time. This large drop was due to a marked increase in suicide rates for teens ages 15–19. In 1985 the suicide rate for African American teens was 4.9 per 100,000 teens. In 1992, 1993, 1994, and 1995 the rates had jumped to 8.4, 8.0, 9.6, and 8.1 suicides per 100,000 teens, respectively. Since that time, African American suicide rates dropped to 5.6 in 2000, and the trend of emotional/spiritual well-being has increased accordingly. The initial decline in the U.S. trend in emotional/spiritual well-being is less pronounced because there was not the dramatic rise in suicide rates as compared with

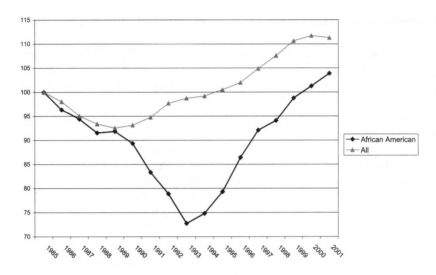

FIGURE 3.7. Trends in emotional/spiritual well-being, 1985–2001: African American children and all children.

the African American trend. In the United States in 1985, 9.9 teens per 100,000 committed suicide, which was double the African American rate of 4.9 for 1985. The U.S. teen suicide rate rose to around 11.0 between 1988 and 1994, after which time the rate dropped to 8.2 in 2000, which continues to be much higher than the African American teen suicide rate.

Suicide rates for African American youth have always been lower than those of European American youth. The spike in suicide rates for African American adolescents to the early 1990s, which narrowed the gap between African American and European American youth, was cause for concern (CDC, 1998). The heightened suicide rates during the late 1980s and early 1990s for 15–19-year-olds were due to increased rates of suicides for males of all races, as the female rates were quite stable (Gould & Kramer, 2001). The rise in the suicide rates of African American adolescent males has been linked to the general increase in lethal youth violence resulting from the growing number of teens carrying handguns or having access to firearms, as described earlier in this chapter (CDC, 1998; Fingerhut & Christoffel, 2002; Joe & Kaplan, 2001; Kaplan & Geling, 1998; Woods et al., 1997), and due to firearms being present in the home (Willis, Coombs, Drentea, & Cockerham, 2003). The CDC (1998, p. 194) reported that "firearm-related suicides accounted for 96% of the increase in suicide rate [between 1980 and

1995] for blacks aged 10–19 years." Nationally, the rate of firearm-related suicides by adolescents has declined between 1992 and 2001 (CDC, 2004). Research also has found cocaine use to be associated with suicides by African American adolescents (Marzuk et al., 1992; Willis et al., 2003; Woods et al., 1997).

Since the mid-1990s, there also have been modest increases in the percentage of African American 12th graders who attend religious services weekly as well as report religion to be very important, which has also contributed to the improved trend of their emotional/spiritual well-being. The upswing in the national trend of emotional/spiritual well-being since 1989 is due primarily to increases in the percentage of 12th graders who report that religion is very important. The national trend of 12th graders attending religious services on a weekly basis has tracked below the 1985 level of 35.3% for the entire period of study. However, there was an increase in the rate of African American 12th graders attending religious services over the period of study. In 1985, 36.3% reported attending religious services, and in 2001 the rate had risen to 44.3%.

Figures 3.8 and 3.9 show the trends for all seven domains for African American and all U.S. children, respectively. The same scale is used for both figures to illustrate that there is much more fluctuation in the African American trends as compared with those of the United States. A

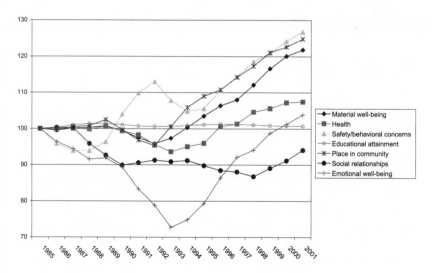

FIGURE 3.8. Domain-specific indices of child well-being for African American children, 1985–2001.

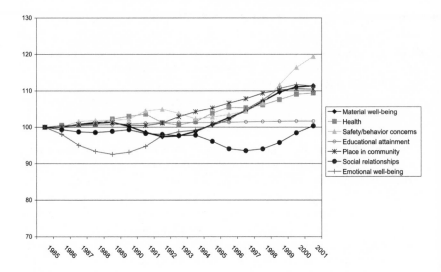

FIGURE 3.9. Domain-specific indices of child well-being for all children, 1985–2001.

number of the African American trends initially decline until 1992 or 1993, and then show great improvements after that time. The safety/ behavioral concerns, place in community, and material well-being domains each exhibit improvements of more than 20%, as compared with 1985 levels. The health and emotional well-being domains also have an upward trajectory, such that their levels are now above those in 1985. The U.S. trends show less fluctuation over the period under study, and except for safety/behavioral concerns, the 2001 improvements are rather modest as compared with 1985 levels.

Trends in Summary Indices

Figure 3.10 presents summary child well-being indices, which are the arithmetic averages of the seven domains for each group. The indices show that, as compared with 1985 levels, the overall well-being of African American children declined to a low point in 1993. This is not surprising, inasmuch as the trends for the health and emotional/spiritual domains were lowest in 1993 and the trends for material well-being, educational, and place in community domains were lowest in 1992, as can been seen in Figure 3.8. After 1993, the summary trend for African American child well-being improved at an accelerated rate such that their trend of improvement outpaces the U.S. trend. The data indicate

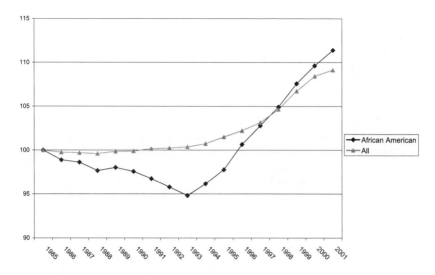

FIGURE 3.10. Summary child well-being index, 1985–2001: African American children and all children.

that by the year 2001 African American children had experienced an 11% overall improvement in child well-being, as compared with 1985. The national CWI trend shows little improvement until 1993–1994, at which time the trend begins to track upward. Nationally, child well-being improved approximately 9% in 2001, as compared with the 1985 level, which is slightly lower than the African American end point. Improvements in material well-being, health, and safety/behavioral domains contributed to the accelerated African American trend of improvement in the late 1990s.

DISCUSSION

The early 1990s mark the low point in our examination of African American child well-being. The United States was in a recession, and African American families felt the economic consequences: More than 39% of African American children were living in poverty, median family income was at its lowest point in the period under study, less than 50% of African American children had at least one parent working full time year-round, and 58% of African American children were living in single-parent families. Such depressed economic conditions resulted in a larger number of African American teens who were neither working nor in school, and slightly reduced graduation rates from high school and college. During the 1990s there was also an increase in the rate of African American children with activity limitations, which has been found to be more prevalent among children in poor households.

The economic expansion of the late 1990s had a positive effect on the well-being of African American children. Families were doing better economically and were able to provide more resources to their children, as indicated by the upward trend in material well-being. In turn, there was great progress in the place in community domain, which represents connections to mainstream social institutions and appropriate social roles. More African American young children were enrolled in preschool (although there are serious questions regarding the quality of childcare programs, as noted earlier), and graduation rates from high school and college increased as well. Education increases an individual's human capital, and it also increases social capital through maintaining a connection to educational institutions and the community. Such connections create opportunities to form social ties with others, which may be utilized in later life. Coupled with the trend of improvements in material well-being and place in community domains have been advances in safety/behavioral well-being and emotional/spiritual well-being domains. African American teen birth rates, alcohol consumption rates, and suicide rates have dropped, and there has been an increase in rates of weekly attendance at religious services and self-reported religiosity. Clearly, a more favorable economic climate benefits African American children and families in a number of different ways.

Despite the general improvement in African American child well-being over the period of study, there remain serious disparities and disadvantages for such children as compared with U.S. averages, and particularly in comparison with European American children. Much of the racial disparities can be attributed to the effects of poverty. However, as we have noted throughout this chapter, poverty alone does not fully explain the racial differences and disparities that have been found in many of our measures of child health and development, educational progress, and other indicators of child well-being. More research is needed to identify causes of racial disparities in child well-being and to find solutions to decrease such differences.

Some intervening factors that we have not been able to study more fully are the impacts of connections to family and social institutions in buffering the effects of poverty, inappropriate peers, violent neighborhoods, and other disadvantages. Studies using the National Longitudinal Study on Adolescent Health (AddHealth) of students in grades 7–12 indicate that students are less likely to engage in risky behaviors when the students are more connected to parents, family, and school (Resnick et al., 1997; Sieving, McNeely, & Blum, 2000). As noted earlier, religion exerts a positive effect on many areas of children's lives (Regnerus, 2003). Parental involvement has been found to partially counteract the negative effects of violent neighborhoods on children's behavior and psychological well-being (Ceballo, Ramirez, Hearn, & Maltese, 2003; Pearce, Jones, et al., 2003). Research on families in poverty indicate that mother's self-esteem may help shield African American children from some of the ill effects of poverty (McLeod & Nonnemaker, 2000).

Social indicators, although fundamental, do not completely determine any social reality, and this leads to several concluding thoughts. First, it is not known how much society's increasingly sophisticated methods for detecting and identifying certain conditions contribute to the rise in an indicator over time. For example, the incidence of child abuse may not actually be higher today than before 1985, but because of the existence of programs designed to identify this and other conditions, authorities may be reporting it more. Such factors affect our decisions regarding the types of indicators we use in our study. Second, further research, particularly on the spike in African American teen suicide and the role of church attendance in African American family life over time, is needed. Other areas in which African American children and youth seem to be "outperforming" the U.S. average—cigarette smoking, alcohol consumption, and teen births—also deserve closer looks. Finally, beyond the need to investigate further some of the trends presented here is the importance of developing, validating, and collecting a more complete set of measures in the emotional/spiritual and the social relationships domains. These areas of social life are too important to go unmeasured, measured partially, or measured poorly. All American children deserve a comprehensive and unflinching look at their own (average) well-being over time.

ACKNOWLEDGMENT

The Child Well-Being Index Project, on which this chapter is based, is supported by a grant from the Foundation for Child Development.

NOTES

1. Because of space limitations, details about data measurement and sources are not provided in this chapter. They have been published in Land, Lamb, and Mustillo (2001) and Meadows, Land, and Lamb (2005). Information about the Child Well-being Indicator project and data can also be found on our website: www.soc.duke.edu/~cwi

2. Four of the time series begin after 1985 and are included in the CWI calculations the

year the data are available. These indicators and the years in which their series began are Median Family Income, 1987; Health Insurance Coverage, 1987; Preschool Enrollment, 1990; and Residential Mobility, 1988. In addition, three of the indicators are not recorded annually: NAEP Reading Tests (1988, 1990, 1992, 1994, 1996, and 1999), NAEP Mathematics Tests (1986, 1990, 1992, 1994, 1996, and 1999), and Voting in Presidential Elections (1988, 1992, 1996, and 2000). Linear interpolation is used to complete the missing years.
3. There is more over-time variability in the domain-specific trends for African American children owing to more statistical variability from smaller populations. To reduce the year-to-year variability so that trends can be more easily deciphered, we applied three-year moving averages to the domain-specific indices for both the African American and U.S. children.

REFERENCES

Aber, J. L., Bennett, N. G., Conley, D. C., & Li, J. (1997). The effects of poverty on child health and development. *Annual Review of Public Health, 18,* 463–483.

Adam, E. K., & Chase-Lansdale, P. L. (2002). Home sweet home(s): Parental separations, residential moves, and adjustment problems in low-income adolescent girls. *Developmental Psychology, 38,* 792–805.

Alaimo, K., Olson, C. M., Frongillo, E. A., Jr., & Briefel, R. R. (2001). Food insufficiency, family income, and health in U. S. preschool and school-aged children. *American Journal of Public Health, 91,* 781–786.

Anderson, L. M., Shinn, C., Fullilove, M. T., Scrimshaw, S. C., Fielding, J. E., Normand, J., et al. (2003). The effectiveness of early childhood development programs: A systematic review. *American Journal of Preventive Medicine, 24*(3S), 32–46.

Avchen, R. N., Scott, K. G., & Mason, C. A. (2001). Birth weight and school-age disabilities: A population-based study. *American Journal of Epidemiology, 54,* 895–901.

Behrman, J. R., Rosenzweig, M. R., & Taubman, P. (1994). Endowments and the allocation of schooling in the family and in the marriage market: The twins experiment. *Journal of Political Economy, 102,* 1131–1174.

Blumstein, A. (1995). Youth violence, guns and the illicit-drug industry. *Journal of Criminal Law and Criminology, 86,* 10–36.

Blumstein, A. (2002). Youth, guns, and violent crime. *The Future of Children, 12,* 39–53.

Blumstein, A., & Wallman, J. (2000). *The crime drop in America.* New York: Cambridge University Press.

Boardman, J. D., Powers, D. A., Padilla, Y. C., & Hummer, R. A. (2002). Low birth weight, social factors, and developmental outcomes among children in the United States. *Demography, 39,* 353–368.

Bradley, R. H., & Corwyn, R. F. (2002). Socioeconomic status and child development. *Annual Review of Psychology, 53,* 371–399.

Branum, A. M., & Schoendorf, K. C. (2002). Changing patterns of low birthweight and preterm birth in the United States, 1981–98. *Paediatric and Perinatal Epidemiology, 16,* 8–15.

Braver, S. L., Ellman, I. M., & Fabricius, W. V. (2003). Relocation of children after divorce and children's best interests: New evidence and legal considerations. *Journal of Family Psychology, 17,* 206–219.

Brooks-Gunn, J., & Duncan, G. J. (1997). The effects of poverty on children. *The Future of Children, 7,* 55–71.

Buka, S. L., Brennan, R. T., Rich-Edwards, J. W., Raudenbush, S. W., & Earls, F. (2003). Neighborhood support and the birth weight of urban infants. *American Journal of Epidemiology, 157,* 1–8.

Bures, R. M. (2003). Childhood residential stability and health at midlife. *American Journal of Public Health, 93,* 1144–1148.

Ceballo, R., Ramirez, C., Hearn, K. D., & Maltese, K. L. (2003). Community violence and children's psychological well-being: Does parental monitoring matter? *Journal of Clinical Child and Adolescent Psychology, 21*(4), 586–592.

Centers for Disease Control and Prevention (CDC). (1998). Suicide among black youths—United States, 1980–1995. *Morbidity and Mortality Weekly Report, 47,* 193–196.

Centers for Disease Control and Prevention (CDC). (2002). Trends in sexual risk behaviors among high school students—United States, 1991–2001. *Morbidity and Mortality Weekly Report, 51,* 856–859.

Centers for Disease Control and Prevention (CDC). (2004). Methods of suicide among persons aged 10–19 years—United States, 1992–2001. *Morbidity and Mortality Weekly Report, 53,* 471–474.

Centers for Disease Control and Prevention, National Center for Health Statistics (CDS/NCHS). (2004). National Center for Health Statistics. Retrieved from www.cdc.gov/nchs/deeafault.htm

Coleman, J. (1988). Social capital in the creation of human capital. *American Journal of Sociology, 94,* S95–S120.

Conley, D., & Bennet, N. G. (2000). Is biology destiny? Birth weight and life chances. *American Sociological Review, 65,* 458–467.

Cook, P. J., & Laub, J. H. (1998). The unprecedented epidemic in youth violence. In M. Tonry & M. H. Moore (Eds.), *Youth violence* (pp. 101–138). Chicago: University of Chicago Press.

Cook, P. J., & Laub, J. H. (2002). After the epidemic: Recent trends in youth violence in the United States. *Crime and Justice: A Review of Research, 29,* 117–153.

Cork, D. (1999). Examining space–time interaction in city-level homicides data: Crack markets and the diffusion of guns among youth. *Journal of Quantitative Criminology, 15,* 379–406.

Cost, Quality, and Child Outcomes Study Team. (1995). *Cost, quality, and child outcomes in child care centers public report.* Denver: Economics Department, University of Colorado–Denver.

Currie, J. (2001). Early childhood education programs. *Journal of Economic Perspectives, 15,* 213–238.

Dawson, D. A. (1991). Family structure and children's health: United States, 1988. *Vital Health Statistics, 10*(178), 1–54.

Donahue, M. J., & Benson, P. L. (1995). Religion and the well-being of adolescents. *Journal of Social Issues, 51,* 145–160.

Duncan, G. J., & Brooks-Gunn, J. (Eds.). (1997). *Consequences of growing up poor.* New York: Russell Sage Foundation.

Duncan, G. J., Yeung, W. J., Brooks-Gunn, J., & Smith, J. R. (1998). How much does childhood poverty affect the life chances of children? *American Sociological Review, 63,* 406–423.

Elster, A., Jarosik, J., VanGeest, J., & Fleming, M. (2003). Racial and ethnic disparities in health care for adolescents: A systematic review of the literature. *Archives of Pediatrics and Adolescent Medicine, 157,* 867–872.

Fairbrother, G., Dutton, M. J., Bachrach, D., Newell, K-A., Boozang, P., & Cooper, R. (2004). Costs of enrolling children in Medicaid and SCHIP. *Health Affairs, 23*(1), 237–243.

Farkas, G. (2003). Racial disparities and discrimination in education: What do we know, how do we know it, and what do we need to know? *Teachers College Record, 105,* 1119–1146.

Fingerhut, L. A., & Christoffel, K. K. (2002). Firearm-related death and injury among children and adolescents. *The Future of Children, 12,* 25–37.

Flores, G., Bauchner, H., Feinstein, A. R., & Nguyen, U-S. D. T. (1999). The impact of ethnicity, family income, and parental education on children's health and use of health services. *American Journal of Public Health, 89,* 1066–1071.

Forste, R., Weiss, J., & Lippincott, E. (2001). The decision to breastfeed in the United States: Does race matter? *Pediatrics, 108,* 291–296.

Freed, L. H., Webster, D. W., Longwell, J. J., Carrese, J., & Wilson, M. H. (2001). Factors preventing gun acquisition and carrying among incarcerated adolescent males. *Archives of Pediatrics and Adolescent Medicine, 155,* 335–341.

Frisbie, W. P., Biegler, M., de Turk, P., Forbes, D., & Pullum, S. G. (1997). Racial and ethnic differences in determinants of interuterine growth retardation and other compromised birth outcomes. *American Journal of Public Health, 87,* 1977–1983.

Furstenberg, F. F., & Cherlin, A. (1991). *Divided families: What happens to children when parents part.* Cambridge, MA: Harvard University Press.

Goodman, E. (1999). The role of socioeconomic status gradients in explaining differences in adolescents' health. *American Journal of Public Health, 89,* 1522–1528.

Gould, M. S., & Kramer, R. A. (2001). Youth suicide prevention. *Suicide and Life-Threatening Behavior, 31*(Suppl.), 6–31.

Greening, L., & Stoppelbein, L. (2002). Religiosity, attributional style, and social support as psychosocial buffers for African American and white adolescents' perceived risk for suicide. *Suicide and Life-Threatening Behavior, 32,* 404–417.

Grogger, J., & Willis, M. (2000). The emergence of crack cocaine and the rise of urban crime rates. *Review of Economics and Statistics, 82,* 519–529.

Guo, G. (1998). The timing of the influences of cumulative poverty on children's cognitive ability and achievement. *Social Forces, 77,* 257–288.

Guo, G., & Harris, K. M. (2000). The mechanisms mediating the effects of poverty on children's intellectual development. *Demography, 37,* 431–447.

Hack, M., Klein, N. K., & Taylor, H. G. (1995). Long-term developmental outcomes of low birth weight infants. *The Future of Children, 5,* 176–196.

Hagan, J., MacMillan, R., & Wheaton, B. (1996). New kid in town: Social capital and the life course effects of family migration on children. *American Sociological Review, 61,* 368–385.

Hagerty, M. R., & Land, K. C. (2004). *Constructing summary indices of social well-being: A model for the effect of heterogeneous importance weights.* Revision of a paper presented at the annual meeting of the American Sociological Association in Chicago, 2002.

Haveman, R., & Wolfe, B. (1995). The determinants of children's attainments: A review of methods and findings. *Journal of Economic Literature, 33,* 1829–1878.

Hediger, M. L., Overpeck, M. D., Ruan, W. J., & Troendle, J. F. (2002). Birthweight and gestational age effects on motor and social development. *Paediatric and Perinatal Epidemiology, 16,* 33–46.

Hogan, D. P., Msall, M. E., Rogers, M. E., & Avery, R. C. (1997). Improved disability population estimates of functional limitation among American children aged 5–17. *Maternal and Child Health Journal, 1,* 203–216.

Hummer, R. A. (1993) Racial differentials in infant mortality in the U. S. : An examination of social and health determinants. *Social Forces, 72,* 529–554.

Hummer, R. A., Biegler, M., de Turk, P. B., Forbes, D., Frisbie, W. P., Hong, Y., & Pullum, S. G. (1999). Race/ethnicity, nativity, and infant mortality in the United States. *Social Forces, 77,* 1083–1118.

Jaziari, N. T. (1983) Index numbers. In S. Kotz, N. L. Johnson, & C. B. Read (Eds.), *Encyclopedia of statistical sciences* (Vol. 4, pp. 54–62). New York: Wiley-Interscience.

Joe, S., & Kaplan, M. S. (2001). Suicide among African American men. *Suicide and Life-Threatening Behavior, 31,* 106–121.

Johnson, B., Golub, A., & Dunlap, E. (2000). The rise and decline of hard drugs, drug violence, and violence in inner-city New York. In A. Blumstein & J. Wallman (Eds.), *The crime drop in America* (pp. 164–206). New York: Cambridge University Press.

Johnson, B. R., Jang, S. J., Larson, D. B., & Li, S. D. (2001). Does adolescent religious commitment matter? A reexamination of the effects of religiosity on delinquency. *Journal of Research in Crime and Delinquency, 38,* 22–43.

Johnson, B. R., Jang, S. J., Li, S. D., & Larson, D. (2000). The "invisible institution" and black youth crime: The church as an agency of local social control. *Journal of Youth and Adolescence, 29,* 479–498.

Johnson, B. R., Li, S. D., Larson, D. B., & McCullough, M. (2000). A systematic review of the religiosity and deviance literature. *Journal of Contemporary Criminal Justice, 16,* 32–52.

Kaplan, M. S., & Geling, O. (1998). Firearm suicides and homicides in the United

States: Regional variations and patterns of gun ownership. *Social Science and Medicine, 46,* 1227–1233.

King, V. (1994). Nonresident father involvement and child well-being: Can dads make a difference? *Journal of Family Issues, 15,* 78–96.

Kleinman, J. C., & Kessel, S. S. (1987). Race differences in low birth weight: Trends and risk factors. *New England Journal of Medicine, 317,* 749–753.

Kronebusch, K., & Elbel, B. (2004). Simplifying children's Medicaid and SCHIP. *Health Affairs, 23*(3), 233–246.

Land, K. C. (2000). Social indicators. In E. F. Borgatta & R. V. Montgomery (Eds.), *Encyclopedia of sociology* (rev. ed.; pp. 2682–2690). New York: Macmillan.

Land, K. C., Lamb, V. L., & Mustillo, S. K. (2001). Child and youth well-being in the United States, 1975–1998: Some findings from a new index. *Social Indicators Research, 56,* 241–320.

Loeb, S., Fuller, B., Kagan, S. K., & Carrol, B. (2004). Child care in poor communities: Early learning effects of type, quality, and stability. *Child Development, 75,* 47–65.

London, R. A. (2000). The dynamics of single mothers' living arrangements. *Population Research and Policy Review, 19,* 73–96.

Love, J. M., Harrison, L., Sagi-Schwartz, A., van Ijzendoorn, M. H., Ross, C., Ungerer, J. A., et al. (2003). Child care quality matters: How conclusions may vary with context. *Child Development, 74,* 1021–1033.

Marzuk, P. M., Tardiff, K., Leon, A. C., Stajie, M., Morgan, E. B., & Mann, J. J. (1992). Prevalence of cocaine use among residents of New York City who committed suicide. *American Journal of Psychiatry, 149,* 371–375.

Mayer, S. (1997). Trends in the economic well-being and life chances of America's children. In G. J. Duncan & J. Brooks-Gunn (Eds.), *Consequences of growing up poor* (pp. 49–69). New York: Russell Sage Foundation.

McCormick, M. C., Gortmaker, S. L., & Sobol, A. M. (1990). Very low birth weight children: Behavior problems and school difficulty in a national sample. *Journal of Pediatrics, 117,* 687–693.

McLanahan, S. S. (1997). Parent absence or poverty: Which matters more? In G. J. Duncan & J. Brooks-Gunn (Eds.), *Consequences of growing up poor* (pp. 35–48). New York: Russell Sage Foundation.

McLeod, J. D., & Nonnemaker, J. M. (2000). Poverty and child emotional and behavioral problems: Racial/ethnic differences in processes and effects. *Journal of Health and Social Behavior, 41,* 137–161.

McLoyd, V. C. (1990). The impact of economic hardship on black families and children: Psychological distress, parenting, and socioemotional development. *Child Development, 61,* 311–346.

McLoyd, V. C. (1998). Socioeconomic disadvantage and child development. *American Psychologist, 53,* 185–204.

Meadows, S. O., Land, K. C., & Lamb, V. L. (2005). Assessing Gilligan versus Sommers: Gender-specific trends in child and youth well-being in the United States. *Social Indicators Research, 70,* 1–52.

Mehana, M., & Reynolds, A. J. (2004). School mobility and achievement: A meta-analysis. *Children and Youth Services Review, 26,* 93–119.

Michelson, R. A. (2001). Subverting Swann: First- and second-generation segregation in the Charlotte-Mecklenburg schools. *American Educational Research Journal, 38,* 215–252.

Michelson, R. A. (2003). When are racial disparities in education the result of racial discrimination? A social science perspective. *Teachers College Record, 105,* 1052–1086.

Molnar, B. E., Miller, M. J., Azrael, D., & Buka, S. L. (2004). Neighborhood predictors of concealed firearm carrying among children and adolescents. *Archives of Pediatrics and Adolescent Medicine, 158,* 657–664.

Monitoring the Future. (2004). *Monitoring the Future study.* Retrieved from www.monitoringthe future.org/

Montgomery, L. E., Kiely, J. L., & Pappas, G. (1996). The effects of poverty, race, and family structure on U. S. children's health: Data from the NHIS, 1978 through 1980 and 1989 through 1991. *American Journal of Public Health, 86,* 1401–1405.

Morenoff, J. D. (2003). Neighborhood mechanisms and the spatial dynamics of birth weight. *American Journal of Sociology, 108,* 976–1017.

Mott, F. L. (1990). When is father really gone? Paternal–child contact in father-absent homes. *Demography, 27,* 499–517.

Msall, M. E., Avery, R. C., Tremont, M. R., Lima, J. C., Rogers, M. L., & Hogan, D. P. (2003). Functional disability and school activity limitations in 41,300 school-aged children: Relationship to medical impairments. *Pediatrics, 111,* 548–553.

Muhuri, P. K., MacDorman, M. F., & Ezzati-Rice, T. M. (2004). Racial differences in leading causes of infant death in the United States. *Paediatric and Perinatal Epidemiology, 18,* 51–60.

National Institute of Child Health and Human Development Early Child Care Research Network. (2000). The relation of child care to cognitive and language development. *Child Development, 71,* 960–980.

National Institute of Child Health and Human Development Early Child Care Research Network & Duncan, G. J. (2003). Modeling the impacts of child care quality on children's preschool cognitive development. *Child Development, 74,* 1454–1475.

Newacheck, P. W., & Halfon, N. (1998). Prevalence and impact of disabling chronic conditions in childhood. *American Journal of Public Health, 88,* 610–617.

Newacheck, P. W., Stein, R. E. K., Bauman, L., & Huang, Y-Y. (2003). Disparities in the prevalence of disability between black and white children. *Archives of Pediatrics and Adolescent Medicine, 157,* 244–248.

Nonnemaker, J. M., McNeely, C. A., & Blum, R. W. (2003). Public and private domains of religiosity and adolescent health risk behaviors: Evidence from the National Longitudinal Study of Adolescent Health. *Social Science and Medicine, 57,* 2049–2054.

Pearce, M. J., Jones, S. M., Schwab-Stone, M. E., & Runchkin, V. (2003). The protective effects of religiousness and parent involvement on the development of conduct problems among youth exposed to violence. *Child Development, 74,* 1682–1696.

Pearce, M. J., Little, T. D., & Perez, J. E. (2003). Religiousness and depressive symptoms among adolescents. *Journal of Clinical Child and Adolescent Psychology, 32,* 267–276.

Peisner-Feinberg, E. S., Burchinal, M. R., Clifford, R. M., Culkin, M. L., Howes, C., Kagan, S. L., & Yazejian, N. (2001). The relation of preschool child-care quality to children's cognitive and social developmental trajectories through second grade. *Child Development, 72,* 1534–1553.

Pettit, B., & McLanahan, S. (2003). Residential mobility and children's social capital: Evidence from an experiment. *Social Science Quarterly, 84,* 632–649.

Pollard, E. L., & Lee, P. D. (2003). Child well-being: A systematic review of the literature. *Social Indicators Research, 61,* 59–78.

Pribesh, S., & Downey, D. B. (1999). Why are residential and school moves associated with poor school performance? *Demography, 36,* 521–534.

Regnerus, M. D. (2003). Religion and positive adolescent outcomes: A review of research and theory. *Review of Religious Research, 44,* 394–413.

Regnerus, M. D., & Elder, G. H. (2003). Religion and vulnerability among low-risk adolescents. *Social Science Research, 32,* 633–658.

Resnick, J. D., Bearman, P. S., Blum, R. W., Bauman, K. E., Harris, K. M., Jones, J., et al. (1997). Protecting adolescents from harm: Findings from the National Longitudinal Study on Adolescent Health. *Journal of the American Medical Association, 278,* 823–832.

Roberts, E. M. (1997). Neighborhood social environments and the distribution of low birthweight in Chicago. *American Journal of Public Health, 87,* 597–603.

Seltzer, J. A., & Brandreth, Y. (1994). What fathers say about involvement with children after separation. *Journal of Family Issues, 15,* 49–77.

Shiono, P. H., Klebanoff, M. A., Graubard, B. I., Berendes, H. W., & Rhodes, G. G. (1986). Birth weight among women of different ethnic groups. *Journal of the American Medical Association, 255,* 48–52.

Sieving, R. E., McNeely, C. S., & Blum, R. W. (2000). Maternal expectations, mother–child connectedness, and adolescent sexual debut. *Archives of Pediatrics and Adolescent Medicine, 154,* 809–816.

Smith, J. R., Brooks-Gunn, J., & Klebanov, P. K. (1997). Consequences of living in poverty for young children's cognitive and verbal ability and early school achievement. In G. J. Duncan & J. Brooks-Gunn (Eds.), *Consequences of growing up poor* (pp. 132–189). New York: Russell Sage Foundation.

South, S. J., Crowder, K. D., & Trent, K. (1998). Children's residential mobility and neighborhood environment following parental divorce and remarriage. *Social Forces, 77,* 667–694.

Starfield, B., Shapiro, S., Weiss, J., Liang, K. Y., Ra, K., Paige, D., & Wang, X. B. (1991). Race, family income, and low birth weight. *American Journal of Epidemiology, 134,* 1167–1174.

Szilagyi, P. G., Dick, A. W., Klein, J. D., Shone, L. P., Zwanzinger, J., & McInerny,

T. (2004). Improved access and quality of care after enrollment in the New York State Children's Health Insurance Program (SCHIP). *Pediatrics, 113,* E395–E404.

Tucker, C. J., Marx, J., & Long, L. (1998). "Moving on": Residential mobility and children's school lives. *Sociology of Education, 71,* 111–129.

U.S. Bureau of Labor Statistics and U.S. Bureau of the Census. (2004). *Current Population Survey.* Retrieved from www.bls.census.gov/cps/cpsmain.htm

U.S. Department of Education, National Center for Education Statistics. (2004). *National Assessment of Educational Progress: The Nation's Report Card.* Retrieved from nces.ed.gov/nationsreportcard/

U.S. Department of Justice, Bureau of Justice Statistics. (2004). *National Crime Victimization Survey.* Retrieved from ojp.usdoj.gov/bjs/cvict.htm#Programs

Ventura, S. J., Mathews, T. J., & Hamilton, B. E. (2001). Births to teenagers in the United States, 1940–2000. *National Vital Statistics Report, 49,* 10.

Willis, L. A., Coombs, D. W., Drentea, P., & Cockerham, W. C. (2003). Uncovering the mystery: Factors of African American suicide. *Suicide and Life-Threatening Behavior, 33,* 412–429.

Wood, D., Halfon, N., Newacheck, P., & Scarlata, D. (1993). Impact of family relocation on children's growth, development, school function and behavior. *Journal of the American Medical Association, 270,* 1334–1338.

Woods, E. R., Lin, Y. G., Middleman, A., Beckford, P., Chase, L., & DuRant, R. H. (1997). The association of suicide attempts in adolescents. *Pediatrics, 99,* 791–796.

Zedlewski, S. R. (2002). Family economic resources in the post-reform era. *The Future of Children, 12,* 120–145.

CHAPTER 4

Racial Wealth Inequality and the Black Family

William Darity Jr. *and*
Melba J. Nicholson

Wealth is grossly unequally distributed in the United States, starkly more unevenly distributed than income. Edward Wolff's (2003) estimates indicate that by the mid-1980s, 56% of all wealth in the United States was owned by the upper 5% of all wealth holders. This compares quite unfavorably with estimates for other affluent countries during the same time span: The top 5% of the distribution held 38% of the wealth in Canada; the top 5% of the distribution held 43% of the wealth in France; the top 5% of the distribution held 31% of the wealth in Sweden, and the top 5% of the distribution held 25% of Japan's wealth. Moreover, in the United States the top 1% of the wealth distribution possessed a 38.5% share, whereas the lowest two quintiles—the bottom 40%—held only 0.2% of the nation's wealth (Rose, 2000).

In general, the most significant component of wealth for most Americans with positive net worth is equity in their homes. Sixty-six percent of net worth for the bottom 80% of wealth holders takes the form of home equity. In contrast, for the top 1% of wealth holders—the very richest Americans—only 6% of their net worth is generated by home ownership. The rest of their portfolios consist of a wide array of financial assets. Indeed, this small fraction of the American population owned close to 60% of all the nation's financial assets. The bottom 90% of the wealth distribution held less than 13% of the nation's financial assets (Rose, 2000).

In parallel, racial differences in wealth are far more pronounced than racial differences in income. Data extracted from the Survey of Income and Program Participation (SIPP) presented by Oliver and Shapiro (1995) indicate that the average or mean net worth of White families was $127,237 in 1988, whereas mean Black wealth was just $31,678. Hence, the Black–White wealth ratio was 0.25, substantially lower than the Black–White per capita income ratio, which was only 50% during the same year, or the Black–White household income ratio, which was 63% (Chiteji, 1999). Shapiro (2001) reports, using the same data, that this gap cannot be explained by demographic differences between Blacks and Whites:

> Taking the average black household and endowing it with the same income and age and with comparable occupational, educational, and other attributes as the average white household still leaves a $25,794 racial gap in financial assets. . . . (p. 17)

That would constitute a down payment on a home, a year's tuition at a tony university, college, or private high school, or the price of an automobile. Furthermore, Shapiro (2001) observes:

> More than two-thirds of African Americans have zero or negative net financial assets, as compared with fewer than a third of whites. This near absence of assets has extreme consequences for the economic and social well-being of the black community and for the ability of families to plan future social mobility. If an average black household were to lose an income stream, it would not be able to support itself without access to public support. Nearly eight out of ten African American families would not be able to survive for three months, even at a poverty level of consumption, on their net financial assets, and nine out of every ten black children live in such households. Comparable figures for whites— though large in their own right—are one-half those of African Americans. . . . (pp. 17–18)

By 1993 Blacks had a mere 9.7% of the median net worth of White Americans ($4,418 vs. $45,740; Shapiro, 2001, p. 17). Black net worth is less than 10% of White median net worth. In addition, more disaggregated detail on the racial wealth gap reviewed home ownership and stock holdings (Wolff, 2001, pp. 49–55). For example, the Black household homeownership rate in 1998 was 46%, in contrast with a 70% rate among Whites. About 30% of African Americans owned stock in 1998, in comparison with 54% of White Americans. Mean stock holdings for Blacks were valued at $31,767, whereas mean White stock holdings were valued at $162,789. Moreover, the Black incidence of

stock ownership and the value of holdings were lower than the White incidence and value at every income level (Wolff, 2001).

Hurst, Chingluoh, and Stafford (1998) observed that not only is
there a racial gulf in the magnitude of wealth held, but there also is a
major difference in the composition of portfolios by race; they observe
that Black wealth is more "concentrated in consumable assets—namely,
auto wealth and home equity." Although 23% of White-owned assets
took the form of stocks in 1998, only 11% of Black-owned assets was
held as stocks (Wolff, 2003).

Although Bostic and Surrette (2000) demonstrate that there was
some movement toward closure of the racial homeownership gap during
the 1990s, as noted earlier, a wide disparity persists. To compound matters, among those owning homes, the prevailing market value of homes
owned by Blacks is generally lower than the value of homes owned by
Whites.

The racial differential in portfolio composition matters because of
specific advantages associated with possession of financial assets. First,
financial assets typically offer a greater return than physical assets. Assets that function as consumables often tend to depreciate over time; for
example, most automobiles undergo substantial depreciation.

Second, Chiteji (1999) observes that financial assets necessarily afford greater liquidity in emergencies than physical assets. Furthermore,
she notes that the Black–White discrepancy in portfolio holdings with
respect to financial assets is greater than the overall racial wealth disparity. Even ownership of bank accounts is significantly lower among Black
Americans; Chiteji reports that only 45% of Black families have bank
accounts, as compared with 85% of White families.

Why is Black wealth lower? Customarily, economists consider
wealth accumulation as a consequence of a two-tier decision: first, a sav-
ing decision, and second, a portfolio decision applied to the portion of
income saved. To the extent that there are racial differences in income,
this would lead to racial differences in accumulated savings, given comparable savings rates.

Black earnings are lower as a consequence of long-term historical
factors, particularly adverse intergenerational transmission effects (see
Darity, Dietrich, & Guilkey, 2001) and current discrimination (see
Bertrand & Mullainathan, 2004). There is no evidence of significant differences in savings rates between Blacks and Whites at similar income
levels; if anything, some evidence actually suggests that the income-
adjusted Black savings rate is slightly higher than the income-adjusted
White savings rate (Gittleman & Wolff, 2004). To reinforce this point,
even if all Black families saved 100% of their income in a given year,
that would not suffice to close the racial wealth gap.

Regardless, the primary sources of personal wealth today in the United States are not careful and deliberate acts of forgone consumption; they are a combination of *in vivo* transfers of wealth (Shapiro, 2001) and inheritance (Blau & Graham, 1990). Although inheritances, when they occur, appear to be much larger, *in vivo* transfers can have great importance as a wealth-maintaining and a wealth-increasing mechanism because of the timing of such transfers during the course of the life cycle. Shapiro (2001, p. 16) lists critical events at which "intergenerational transfers" are made "throughout the life course, especially at markers of important life events such as graduation, marriage, and the birth of children; no event other than the death of a parent triggers a greater transfer of wealth than buying a first home."

Data from the 1989 Panel Study of Income Dynamics (PSID) indicate that not only do a much smaller proportion of Blacks receive inheritances than Whites (6%, as compared with 24%), but Black inheritances also tend to be much smaller than White inheritances ($41,985, as compared with $144,652; Wilhelm, 2001, p. 141). Although the differential between the racial incidence of *in vivo* transfers (18% for Blacks, compared with 20% for Whites) in a single year appears to be much narrower than the differential in the racial incidence of inheritances, the magnitudes are markedly different ($805 for Blacks, compared with $2,824 for Whites; Wilhelm, 2001, p. 141). There is no extant study that assesses the cumulative racial differential in receipt of *in vivo* transfers over the course of the life cycle.

The combination of *in vivo* transfers and inheritances—both intergenerational transfers of wealth—are central to the preservation of racialized economic stratification in the United State. Econometric research has placed the contribution of intergenerational transfers (both *in vivo* and bequests) to the wealth position of subsequent generations anywhere from 50% to 80% (Shapiro, 2001). Patently, the survey data also show that, quite reasonably, there are vastly different expectations by race of the likelihood of receiving an inheritance (Shapiro, 2001; Wilhelm, 2001).

Charles and Hurst (2002) find that Blacks are less likely to become homeowners than Whites, in large measure because Blacks are less likely to apply for mortgage loans. This reluctance, they acknowledge, may be due to a chilling effect associated with a long history of negative encounters with lending and other types of financial institutions.

In a straightforward manner, wealth begets wealth. Similarly, lack of wealth begets lack of wealth. Racialized processes of intergenerational transmission of wealth are the heart of the racial gap. After all, inherited wealth—nonmerit resources—also provides additional resources for education, insurance against emergencies, greater capacity to opt for self-

employment and business ownership, and the political influence to protect one's own position.

So why did previous generations of Black families have less wealth
to bestow upon their descendants? The obvious answer is historical.
First is the role of slavery. In slavery times Blacks typically constituted
property for others, rather than persons free to acquire property of their
own. Kirk White's (2003) research using a dynamic programming exer-
cise shows that the conditions of wealth inequality at emancipation
could dictate current disparity even in the absence of further bumps in
the road.

The conditions at emancipation were characterized by the failure to
compensate the ex-slaves for their "time on the cross"—the failure to
provide an initial property base for the propertyless. Uncompensated
emancipation meant the failure to allocate land to those formerly
enslaved—the denial of the promised 40 acres and a mule. The failure
was exemplified by the abrogation of Sherman's Special Order No. 15,
which had resulted in the settlement of 40,000 ex-slaves on 485,000
acres of land along the south Atlantic coast by June 1865. However, by
late 1865 the Black settlers had been removed, their "possessory title"
on the land vacated, and the properties restored to the former slave owners. Despite the best efforts of stalwart Radical Republicans like Thaddeus
Stevens and Charles Sumner, a comprehensive racial land reform never
took place in the post–Civil War United States (McPherson, 1964).

Second, there were several large bumps in the road. After all, with
the end of Reconstruction in 1876, Jim Crow laws and practices and a
climate of terror crystallized in the postbellum South and often, de facto,
in the North. The seizure of Black-owned land and other property became a common action by Whites. An Associated Press report published
in 2001 (Lewan & Barclay, 2001) documented 406 cases of Black landowners who lost 24,000 acres of farm- and timberland owing to theft
and illegal seizure during the first three decades of the 20th century; the
investigation was limited to cases that could be established based on
existing records, a task made extremely difficult by the fact that White
perpetrators of Black land theft "often colluded with local, state, and
even the federal government to defraud African-Americans of property. . . . [W]holesale burning of courthouses, Black churches, and homes
were common ways of destroying evidence of Black land ownership ille-
gally obtained by white terrorists" (Winbush, 2003, p. 98). Raymond
Winbush (Barclay, 2001) also hazards that the lynching trail was also a
trail of stolen Black property, speculating that lynching victims were disproportionately Black landowners.

In some cases, prosperous Black communities were subject to vir-
tual extermination. These instances include White massacres of Blacks in

Wilmington, North Carolina, in 1898; in Tulsa, Oklahoma, in 1921; and in Rosewood, Florida, in 1923. Later urban renewal and/or highway expansion would become an instrument to abolish Black-owned commercial districts. A major example is the Hayti District in Durham, North Carolina, which had all but vanished by 1980 and only now is staging a modest comeback with an entirely new array of small Black businesses. The American economy writ large can be viewed as a machine for routinized destruction of Black wealth and maintenance of a racial income gap.

Consider next the second tier of the decision process that influences wealth accumulation. Why do Blacks tend not to acquire financial assets? A simple answer may be that Blacks may be more risk averse on average than Whites for good reason, given their history of being subjected to appropriation of accumulated property and the greater fragility of their wealth position. Indeed, the history of losses of accumulated Black property may also explain the greater reluctance to use bank accounts, a problem potentially compounded by residential segregation. Black neighborhoods are comparatively starved for conventional services from both the public and private sectors, including banks and bank branches, and are disproportionately dependent on "fringe banking" institutions that charge usurious interest rates (Caskey, 1994).

Chiteji and Stafford (1999) also propose a different variant of an intergenerational transmission effect. If there is less exposure to stock ownership in a person's family, that person is less likely to purchase shares of stock him- or herself. The potential demonstration effect will be truncated.

In addition, Chiteji and Hamilton (2005; see also Hefflin & Patillo, 2002) cite "kin effects" that reduce Blacks' capacity to purchase financial assets. They theorize that Blacks who possess positive net worth may have poorer family members whom they need to assist, so they may be less able to commit to financial investments.

We conclude with the following observations:

• The racial wealth gap is so substantial and pervasive across all levels of income, it is misleading to regard Black and White families that are similarly relatively well situated on the basis of income, educational attainment, and/or occupational status as equivalently "middle class." Wealth positions differ sharply for middle-class Black and White families; they are not similar in terms of resources and options, as standard social science practice implies.

• The combination of markedly lower access to inheritances and *in vivo* transfers of income and markedly greater kin support responsibilities means that Black "middle-class" families generally have less financial flexibility and opportunity to accumulate wealth than White families.

• Income differences are more important than savings rate differences in explaining Black–White wealth differences. But most important are historical, inherited differences in initial endowments of wealth for Black families. Thus, the racial wealth gap will not be closed by focusing on changing the financial practices or savings behavior of Black Americans, who are no more profligate than most other non-Black Americans. Closing the racial wealth gap will require a racial redistribution of wealth.

• Steps to engineer a racial redistribution of wealth could focus narrowly on improving opportunities for homeownership among Blacks or targeted programs to build savings with federal matching funds for each dollar saved. But to genuinely alter the profile of racial wealth inequality in the United States would require a program of a magnitude akin to the Malaysian scheme of wealth redistribution on behalf of the native Malays. Dalton Conley (2001, p. 363) commented, "If wealth differences by race could be erased by providing equal access to housing and credit markets, this would point to a clear policy solution. However, class differences that result from the wealth of one's ancestors are not so easy to redress." Class differences overlap with racial difference with such ferocity in the United States that conditions indicate the need for a reparations program for historical and systemic wealth deprivation for Black Americans.

REFERENCES

Barclay, D. (2001, December 2). Torn from the land: The lynching trail. *The Sunday Herald-Sun* (Durham, NC), pp. A1, A3.

Bertrand, M., & Mullainathan, S. (2004). Are Emily and Greg more employable than Lakisha and Jamal? A field experiment on labor market discrimination. *American Economic Review, 94*(4), 991–1013.

Blau, F., & Graham, J. W. (1990). Black–white differences in wealth and asset composition. *Quarterly Journal of Economics, 105*(2), 321–329.

Bostic, R. W., & Surrette, B. T. (2000). *Have the doors opened wider? Trends in home ownership rates by race and income* (Finance and Economics Discussion Series Working Paper No. 2000–31). Washington, DC: Board of Governors of the Federal Reserve System.

Caskey, J. P. (1994). *Fringe banking: Check-cashing outlets, pawnshops, and the poor.* New York: Russell Sage Foundation.

Charles, K., & Hurst, E. (2002). The transition to home ownership and the black–white wealth gap. *Review of Economics and Statistics, 84*(2), 281–297.

Chiteji, N. (1999). Wealth holding and financial market participation in Black America. *African-American Research Perspectives 5*(1), 16–24.

Chiteji, N., & Hamilton, D. (2005). Family matters: Kin networks and asset accumulation. In M. Sherraden (Ed.), *Inclusion in the American Dream: Assets, poverty and public policy.* New York: Oxford University Press.

Chiteji, N., & Stafford, F. (1999). Portfolio choices of parents and their children as young adults: Asset accumulation by African American families. *American Economic Review, 89*(2), 377–382.

Conley, D. (2001). Why assets? Toward a new framework on social stratification. In T. N. Shapiro & E. Wolff (Eds.), *Assets for the poor: The benefits of spreading asset ownership* (pp. 360–363). New York: Russell Sage Foundation.

Darity, W., Jr., Dietrich, J., & Guilkey, D. (2001). Persistent advantage or disadvantage? Evidence in support of the intergenerational drag hypothesis. *American Journal of Economics and Sociology, 60*(2), 435–470.

Gittleman, M., & Wolff, E. N. (2004). Racial differences in patterns of wealth accumulation. *Journal of Human Resources, 39*(1), 193–227.

Hefflin, C. M., & Patillo, M. (2002). Kin effects on black–white account and home ownership. *Sociological Inquiry, 72*(2), 220–239.

Hurst, E., Chingluoh, M., & Stafford, F (Eds.). (1998). *Brookings papers on economic activity I.* Washington, DC: Brookings Institution Press.

Lewan, T., & Barclay, D. (2001, December 9). Inquiry: Black landowners cheated. *Sunday Herald-Sun* (Durham, NC), pp. A1, A3.

McPherson, J. M. (1964). *The struggle for equality: Abolitionists and the negro in the Civil War and Reconstruction.* Princeton, NJ: Princeton University Press.

Oliver, M., & Shapiro, T. (1995). *Black wealth/white wealth: A new perspective on racial inequality.* New York: Routledge.

Rose, S. J. (2000). *Social stratification in the United States: The new American profile poster revised and updated.* New York: New Press.

Shapiro, T. (2001). The importance of assets: The benefits of spreading asset ownership. In T. N. Shapiro & E. Wolff (Eds.), *Assets for the poor: The benefits of spreading asset ownership* (pp. 11–33). New York: Russell Sage Foundation.

White, K. (2003). *Initial conditions at emancipation: The long run effect on black–white wealth and income inequality.* Unpublished manuscript, Duke University.

Wilhelm, M. O. (2001). The role of intergenerational transfers in spreading assets. In T. N. Shapiro & E. Wolff (Eds.), *Assets for the poor: The benefits of spreading asset ownership* (pp. 132–161). New York: Russell Sage Foundation.

Winbush, R. (2003). The earth moved: Stealing black land in the United States. In R. Winbush (Ed.), *Should America pay? Slavery and the raging debate over reparations.* New York: HarperCollins.

Wolff, E. (2001). Recent trends in wealth ownership from 1983 to 1998. In T. N. Shapiro & E. Wolff (Eds.), *Assets for the poor: The benefits of spreading asset ownership* (pp. 34–73). New York: Russell Sage Foundation.

CHAPTER 5

New Families, New Functions

Postmodern African American Families in Context

M. Belinda Tucker *and* Angela D. James

One hundred years ago, W. E. B. DuBois presciently observed that the "color line" would be the problem of the 20th century (1903). As mounting concerns about the construction, maintenance, and validity of families vie with race for preeminence among modern social dilemmas, it is perhaps the intersection of complex notions of human identity and family that poses the most formidable societal challenge for the next 100 years. That is, the family has proven to be the primary engine of human organization and survival. Yet, in the United States, our conceptualizations of family and the perceived legitimacy of particular forms are fashioned in large part by the observer's and the observed's relative positions in a social structure shaped powerfully by race, ethnicity, gender, and sexual orientation. For example, the new, less overt articulations of racial discrimination (referred to by many writers as the "new racism") and contemporary discussions of family are mutually reinforcing. As race has become increasingly "coded as culture" (Gann, 2000; Silverman, 1999), family structure is used as a central marker of cultural difference and implied status differentiation. Scholarly attempts to understand African American family forms and functions have long been substantially influenced by political interests and demands.

The focus of this chapter is the evolving nature of African American families and its implications for public policy. Building on the early, classic analyses of Black families offered by DuBois (1899, 1908), Frazier

(1939), Billingsley (1968, 1993), and others, change in African American family structure is situated within the context of overarching social forces and historical experiences and events. We aim to accomplish several tasks in this chapter: (1) to examine current and emerging conceptualizations of family, (2) to cite the trends that have led to new family forms, (3) to discuss how family functions have changed in response to new demands, and (4) to offer recommendations for public policy that address a range of new needs among 21st-century African American families. Comparative analysis will be employed judiciously in this discussion without assuming as the idealized referent the dominant societal trends of the 1950s (as is often the case in family research). We have labeled our focus "the postmodern family," at the risk of contributing to rampant overuse of the term. Stacey (1991) first applied postmodernist theorizing to the analysis of domestic relationships in order to describe how family had evolved beyond common residence to refer to one's social network—as a function of its meaning to a particular individual. Our notions of family today are therefore more individualized and subjective and, as such, full of possibilities.

CONCEPTUALIZATIONS OF FAMILY

Cultural Variation in the Construction of Family

An analysis of current African American family forms must be carried out within the context of present-day variations in both the construction and meaning of family more generally. Too often family is conceptualized within a remarkably constrained view of structural options. Though the notion of family is universal, anthropologists have long observed that conceptions of family are culture-bound, with considerable variation in how relationships are determined and what obligations and responsibilities specific ties entail. There is disagreement even within the discipline about whether universal elements exist and, if so, what those might be (e.g., Ember & Ember, 1983). Some argue (and we concur) that within cultures the definition of "family" changes as the needs of the larger society evolve.

Ongoing academic debates (most notably within sociology) illustrate that even within the narrow views of family that predominate in the United States, conceptions of family are quite divergent (cf. Coontz, 1992; Popenoe, 1999). Moreover, there is a pronounced tendency in some influential circles to view a single type of family structure as functionally superior to others. Proponents of marriage in the United States cite numerous benefits of the nuclear family ideal, a permanent structure composed of biological parents and two or three children (e.g., Waite &

Galleghar, 2000). Others have argued that, whatever the benefits, the reality is that our society has essentially abandoned this model, in favor of serial monogamy or multiple relationships and more complex romantic and familial associations, and that societal aims should reflect and support this new reality (Pinsof, 2002). There is some support for this idea. Currently, less than two thirds of children in the United States, as a whole, live with their biological parents (Fields, 2003).

Having said this, we believe, nonetheless, that most readers of this chapter would have difficulty imagining just how far removed from our normative notions present-day family forms can be. Two examples have stirred recent interest among social scientists. Hua (2001) and Kong (1999) describe the Naxi people of China, whose notion of marriage precludes coresidence and who have no word for "father." In a practice referred to as "walking marriage" Naxi couples may spend the night together, but males must leave for their natal residences when morning arrives. Childrearing is the responsibility of the child's mother and her family of origin (which may include a maternal uncle). At the other end of the spectrum of father involvement, a number of lowland South American cultures[1] recognize multiple or "partible" paternity—under the belief that more than one man's sperm can contribute to fetal development (Beckerman & Valentine, 2002). Despite their fairly radical departure from modern Western notions of family constellation, these structures apparently produce functional adults.

We believe that these two examples have special relevance for the current discussion, as much of the debate around African American family forms has focused on the evolving role of men (as partners and fathers) in families. The enduring centrality of this concern is demonstrated by the fact that the issue was also a vital component of the discussions of family by early African American scholars (cf. Cox, 1940; Drake & Cayton, 1962; DuBois, 1899, 1908; Frazier, 1939). The key point here is that the role of men in families can take many forms without undermining the existence or importance of the family as the core societal institution.

Family as an Evolving and Dynamic Construct

In 1968, Andrew Billingsley wrote a now classic work that documented, in the form of typologies, the array of family formation patterns displayed among African Americans. He demonstrated that Black families varied widely on the basis of the number and type of adults present, the presence and nature of co-resident children, and the basis of the bond among family members. (Twenty-five years later, he found even more extensive variation; Billingsley, 1993.) Billingsley's (1968) book actually set the stage for later acknowledgements that American families in general no longer (and in many ways never did) conform to a single modal form (Casper & Bianchi, 2001; Coontz, 1992). There is greater awareness today that the dominant portrayals of American families—displayed most prominently by the signature shows of early television (e.g., *Father Knows Best*)—were based on family patterns typical of the 1950s and early 1960s but historically aberrant. In contrast to times both before and after, this period was distinguished by early marriage, less divorce, less singlehood, greater reliance on fathers as sole earners, and the dominance of nuclear family structures (Cherlin, 1992; Skolnick, 1991; Tucker & Mitchell-Kernan, 1995b). Today, American families display greater diversity in composition and longevity and may be characterized most by the dynamic nature of family arrangements as they adapt to separation and divorce, changing custodial arrangements for children, new and evolving relationships, and new forms of residential circumstances. More traditional constructions of family in the United States have been primarily kin-based and focused on the rearing and support of children. However, as models for romantic attachments have evolved to focus more on individual interests and are less defined by the marital model, and as sexual relationships are less bound by the institutionalized commitment of marriage, family constellations have changed as well. Family structures, on the whole, have become less kin-based, less specific to childrearing, less permanent, more permeable, and more flexible. These trends are evident in the United States at large, though the growing separation of childbearing and rearing from marriage has been displayed among African Americans for a longer period of time (Tucker & Mitchell-Kernan, 1995b).

Another concern with even scholarly conceptualizations of family in the United States are the assumptions regarding the association between family and residential patterns. The definition of family used in most empirical work, as well as in most institutional contexts, considers family as a subset of households. Extrahousehold familial relationships are generally considered outside the purview of state interest, with the notable exception of fathers who do not co-reside with the children for whom they are considered normatively responsible. In this case, lack of co-residence is treated as deviant. Although there is consideration given to the fact that there may be more than one family in a given household, the familial relationship of people across households is given scant official recognition. So although research typically considers a household composed of a woman and her children to be a "single-parent family," children who spend substantial amounts of time with two parents who live apart (or a grandparent and parent, etc.) could more accurately be described as "two-home children" (a concept that has taken hold in

New Zealand, but apparently nowhere else; see, e.g., Statistics New Zealand, 2003). This means that even the best empirical work on family is often limited to household groups and is therefore inconsistent with commonly held views and widespread spatial realities of family life. Unfortunately, the unit of measurement has become the unit of analysis. Economic, social, and psychological understandings of family in the United States therefore tend to be based largely on assessing the nature of *household* relationships.

CURRENT TRENDS IN AFRICAN AMERICAN DOMESTIC ORGANIZATION

African American Families Today

In some significant ways, African American domestic organization has become the prototypical postmodern family. By necessity, family roles have had to be renegotiated and reconstructed when functions dictated by the "modern" nuclear model were unattainable, inappropriate, or no longer desirable. For example, many African American women will never become wives in the traditional sense (i.e., legal marriage), due in large part to sociostructural factors outside their control, but increasingly also owing to personal choice. Yet their roles in their family systems are crucial. Postmodern African American family roles display a fluidity and, in some sense, a freedom that was not characteristic of Black family life earlier in the 20th century.

African American family formation underwent fairly dramatic change over the latter third of the 20th century, which we have documented in earlier publications (Taylor, Tucker, Chatters, & Jayakody, 1997; Tucker, 2000; Tucker & Mitchell-Kernan, 1995b; Tucker, Subramanian, & James, 2004). We do not repeat those fairly extensive analyses here, but briefly summarize the key trends in domestic living arrangements that are relevant to the present discussion.

• *There is much more variation in family forms.* Although the nuclear family, composed of children with their male and female biological or adoptive parents, has always been less characteristic of Black families than most other U.S. populations, this form is far less prevalent than in previous times. In 2002, under 40% of Black children in the United States lived with both biological parents (U.S. Bureau of the Census, 2003e).

• *More people have never married.* Between 1970 and 2000, the percentage of African Americans who had never married increased from 36% to 45% among men and from 28% to 42% among women (U.S.

Bureau of the Census, 2003c) and now exceeds the proportion currently married—39% and 31%, respectively.

• *Divorce increased dramatically after 1960 and has stabilized in recent years, but remains at extraordinarily high levels.* Between 1970 and 1990, the African American divorce ratio (the number of divorced persons per 1,000 married persons) increased from 104 to 358, then stabilized in the mid-1990s (Norton & Miller, 1992; Tucker & Mitchell-Kernan, 1995b).[2] Black women are more likely than women of other U.S. racial/ethnic groups to experience the disruption of their first marriages, but are less likely to complete divorce proceedings once separated (financing being a probable barrier) (Bramlett & Mosher, 2002). Raley and Bumpass (2003) estimate that 70% of Black women's first marriages will end in divorce.

• *Singlehood is more prevalent.* Because of changing marital trends (later and less marriage, more divorce, less remarriage), a greater proportion of the African American population is single. In 1970, 43% of Black men and 46% of Black women were not married (including those who were divorced, separated, or widowed); by 2000, these figures had increased to 57% and 64%, respectively (U.S. Bureau of the Census, 2003c). Individuals also spend greater proportions of their lives as singles. These changes have made being single more normative, thereby shifting the societal context for singlehood.

• *Couples are more likely to cohabitate.* The overall number of unmarried couples living together increased elevenfold between 1960 and 2000 (U.S. Bureau of the Census, 1999, 2000). As a proportion of total couples, the extent of cohabitation (defined by the Census Bureau as persons who reported that they "shared living quarters and had a close personal relationship with each other") among African Americans is 17%, which is comparable to that of Native Americans, but higher than that of all other groups (Simmons & O'Connell, 2003). In 2000, just over 11% of all African Americans reported that they were cohabitating (Fields & Casper, 2001).

• *Births to Black teenagers have declined dramatically.* Birth rates for Black females ages 15–19 declined by 32% overall between 1980 and 2002 (from 98 to 67 per 1,000) (from a compilation of census statistics by the Child Trends Data Bank, 2005; Martin, Park, & Sutton, 2002). This is a historic low and is 20 points below the Hispanic rate—a group with a similar income and educational distribution.

• *There are more diverse living arrangements for children.* The living arrangements of children overall in the United States have become more diverse. Though there has always been a fairly high level of "child fosterage" among African Americans (McDaniel, 1994), it appears that there are unique elements to the current trends. Between 1970 and 2000,

Black children became less likely to live with two parents (58% to 36%), more likely to live with their mothers only (30% to 49%), and slightly more likely to live with their fathers only (2% to 4%) (Guttman, 2002). Approximately 10% in both time periods lived with neither parent. The actual composition of both single-parent and two-parent families varies greatly. Though published data detailing the exact circumstances of childrearing are rare, a report based on the 1991 Survey of Income and Program Participation (SIPP) is revealing (Furukawa, 1994). That year, 20% of Black children were living in blended families (i.e., with at least one stepparent, stepsibling, and/or half-sibling)—including nearly a quarter of those in single-parent situations. Twenty-two percent of Black children lived in extended households (including at least one parent and someone, related or unrelated, beyond the nuclear family). Black and Latino children are nearly three times more likely to live in extended family situations than White children. These extended households often involve grand- and great-grandparents. However, in a number of situations, and in a growing trend, members of this older generation become the children's primary caretakers. In 2000, one in nine African American children lived in their grandparents' household, and in two thirds of these cases, the grand- or great-grandparent was the principal provider (Bryson & Casper, 1999).

• *Married Black women are having fewer children.* A number of the trends in childbearing and childrearing actually reflect a very distinctive phenomenon among African Americans—a steep decline in the fertility of married Black women. The birthrate (number of births per 1,000 women) for married Black women ages 15–44 fell from 130 in 1970 to 89 in 1980 and 67 in 1999 (Centers for Disease Control and Prevention, 2003). In comparison, the overall birthrates for married women in the United States over the same time period per 1,000 were 121, 97, and 87, respectively. This trend lowers the overall birthrate (the denominator in birthrate calculations) for African Americans and makes the proportion of nonmarital births greater. That is, even if nonmarital births remained constant, the decrease in marital births makes the proportion contributed by nonmarital births higher.

• *Older persons are more likely to live alone.* In 2000, 22% of Black men and 39% of Black women age 65 and older lived alone—which closely parallels the living arrangements of elderly Whites (Federal Interagency Forum on Aging-Related Statistics, 2003). Both groups are far more likely to live alone than elderly Asian Americans or Hispanics. Fitch and Ruggles (2000) found that during the 20th century Blacks were more likely than Whites to live with family members, but that this tendency declined dramatically until the 1970s when there was a slight increase in such arrangements.

• *There are more interracial families.* The proportion of African Americans who are married to persons of other races has steadily increased, but is much more likely to involve Black men than women (U.S. Bureau of the Census, 1998a, 2003a). Unmarried partners who are living together are more than twice as likely as married couples to be interracial (Simmons & O'Connell, 2003), a trend that is supported by our own data on dating patterns (Taylor, Tucker, & Mitchell-Kernan, under review). In addition, in 1990 just over 6% of families with at least one Black parent included children who differed racially from at least one parent (U.S. Bureau of the Census, 1998b).

Implications of Recent Trends in African American Family Constellation

As others have observed, key developments in late 20th-century African American family formation foreshadowed trends in the general population, including declines and delays in marriage, higher divorce rates, increases in the proportion of single-parent families, and the increased separation of childbearing from marital behavior (e.g., Staples, 1999). Whether the signifying African American patterns represented a "canary in the coal mine" (a warning, in effect), or were simply the leading edge of less valenced evolutionary development, is a question, inasmuch as their likely sources include adverse conditions as well as progressive change: economic forces of various kinds, social policy, racism, sex ratio imbalance, women's economic progress, gender role development, contraceptive advances, value shifts, individuation, and so on (Dilworth-Anderson, Burton, & Boulin-Johnson, 1993; Franklin, 1997; Hill et al., 1993; Jewell, 1988; Wilson, 1996).

Recently, some of the identified patterns of domestic organization have stabilized or have begun a slight reversal among African Americans, as well as in the United States at large (i.e., the decline in two-parent families, births to teenagers). These reversals seem to have taken place during a period of unusually robust economic activity and opportunity in the mid to late 1990s. African American jobless rates declined to new lows, and home ownership soared to new highs (Ferguson, 2002). Currently, the nation is mired in an extended economic recession that has been particularly devastating for African Americans and Latinos (Kong, 2003; Solis, 2003), so we should be alert to changing marital and childbearing behaviors in this context.

All of these trends suggest that the "typical" course of family life for African Americans, and for Americans in general, has changed substantially in the last several decades. The experience of family life is very different today than it was in 1970. Taken as a whole, the recent trends in the constellation of African American families have several implications. First, a greater proportion of the economic burden of family maintenance now rests with African American women. Because they are far more likely today to have primary responsibility for families and, relative to some sectors of African American men, are becoming better economically situated, Black women now have greater responsibility for the economic support of families. Although a greater economic role implies greater power (which may be desirable in a society that remains fundamentally sexist), other findings from our own program of research suggest that Black women are not necessarily seeking such a role and that many would prefer that men function as family providers (Taylor, Tucker, & Mitchell-Kernan, 1999). Continued movement in this direction is likely to exact a psychological and social toll on African American women. Furthermore, such a change requires renegotiation of gender roles, which is likely to further destabilize opposite-sex relationships, at least in the short run.

These trends also suggest an increasing isolationism that has more dramatic consequences at opposite ends of the age spectrum—the rearing of children and the care of older persons. It appears that parenting is becoming a more isolated and isolating activity (as single-caretaker households increase). This could result in increased stress among parents, but also a loss of the community aspect of childrearing that has characterized the maintenance of African American families for generations. Similarly, growing old is becoming a solitary activity, most particularly for African Americans. This social and psychological disconnection of a whole segment of our society who have much to offer families and communities is a disturbing trend. During a severe heat wave in 1995 in Chicago, relative to Latinos and Whites, significantly more elderly African Americans fell victim to the heat (Klinenberg, 2002). One hypothesis for the high mortality rate was the disconnection of older Blacks from support systems whose members might have checked on their welfare.

Another implication of new family patterns of African Americans is the increased emphasis on economic production, which is often in conflict with core family activities—particularly for families with one primary caretaker for children. As individuals work longer hours and often have to take on more than one means of generating income to survive (including the informal economy), they can barely manage to take care of immediate family needs. The group functions that encourage greater family cohesion (e.g., dining together, attending church together) fall by the wayside.

Perhaps the most controversial and most discussed implication of these trends is the apparent retreat of African American men from the

roles of husband and involved father. Much of the discussion has focused on the barriers that prevent African American men from fulfilling
the provider role—that is, what this society has traditionally viewed as
the primary function of men in families (Bowman, 1988; Darity &
Myers, 1995; Wilson, 1996). Because higher-income men are also less
inclined to marry, theories offered to explain this trend must go beyond
economic constraints (Tucker & Mitchell-Kernan, 1995a). Black men
are as likely as ever, however, to produce children, so the focus of a rapidly expanding body of literature has been on fathering behavior outside
of marital bonds. At the same time, societal conceptions of proper fatherhood have evolved to emphasize the socioemotional functions as
well as the economic (Coltrane, 2004). If African American men are far
less likely to be living with their biological children, what does this mean
in terms of their relationships with them and their ability to provide
guidance, instruction, and support?

The research provides a complex portrait of fathers who are not
with their children. Although all studies find men who have no contact
with their children, many nonresident fathers are quite involved in their
children's lives and are attempting to be active coparents (e.g., Carlson
& McLanahan, 2002; Hamer, 2001; Rivara, Sweeney, & Henderson,
1986). Hamer (2001) described how low-income "live-away" fathers
redefined appropriate fathering behavior in order to better reflect their
reality of limited resources and constrained hopes.

THE CHANGING FUNCTIONS
OF AFRICAN AMERICAN FAMILIES

At the same time that African American families in general have undergone fundamental changes in form, the basic functions of these families
have also been evolving. Though there are varying assumptions (some con-
flicting) about the core universal tasks of families (see, for example,
Gittens, 1998), in our view there are several critical domains of activities
for most contemporary U.S. families: socioemotional, economic, caretaking/
socialization, and role development. The socioemotional functions include activities that fulfill the affiliative and emotional needs of families.
Economic functions refer to tasks undertaken for the economic and
material support of family members. Caretaking functions encompass behaviors centered on tending to dependent others, including childrearing
and socialization, elder care, and supporting those who are ill or infirm.
Role development refers to the work required to adapt individual roles to
new or changing needs of the family as an institution. Clearly, an additional enduring function of African American families is that of coping

with and protecting members from the daily assaults incurred as a consequence of living in a society that devalues persons of African descent.

Not every function will have ongoing relevance for all families. For example, though childrearing and socialization are key tasks during the life course of most family members, for an increasing proportion of the population, they have no relevance. However, most of these functions will have to be addressed at one time or another by most family units. Within each of these central functional domains, we have identified areas that, in our view, represent significant shifts in the responsibilities and functions of postmodern African American families.

Socioemotional Functions: Maintaining Family Cohesion in the Context of Greater Geographic Dispersion

A different affiliative obligation has developed in response to new migration and residential patterns displayed by family members. Like other segments of American society, African American families are becoming more geographically dispersed. In 2002–2003, Blacks were more likely to have moved during the preceding year than Whites (18 vs. 12%), though they were not as mobile as Asian Americans and Latinos (Schachter, 2004). Also, the recent dramatic return of African Americans to southern cities from all over the nation (Frey, 2001) may reunite some family segments while increasing distances between immediate family members (e.g., as children stay where they were raised). Although the great migrations from the South to northern cities in the 1940s and 1950s also led to disruptions in family life, we view the present-day demands as decidedly distinctive. A half century ago, the expectations for contact with far-flung kin were not great. When relatives moved very far away, the occasional letter would suffice. The proportion of families that are geographically distant is constantly increasing. The demands on kin to maintain familial connections and support systems is ever more challenging in this context and may be a crucial factor in the increased isolation of the elderly. The African American investment in the tradition of family reunions is one strategy for counteracting this tendency toward greater dispersion.

Economic Functions: Managing Work and Home

The nature of the support of families and households has evolved over the last quarter century in at least two major ways: the increased reliance on women's incomes and the ever more encompassing demands of the workplace. Taken together, these trends make integration of work and family far more challenging. For most workers, men and women, time available for family or other non-job-related responsibilities has declined, even as the burdens of family life have increased (Hochschild, 1997; Schor, 1992). Inasmuch as African American women are more likely to hold full-time jobs and the jobs themselves have become more demanding, more conflicts between family and workplace are likely to arise. Of course, low-income and low-wage-earning employees have seldom had job flexibility, but the demands for overtime work and potentially undesirable schedules (e.g., being pressured to work the night shift) are becoming greater in the present economic environment (as firms seek to maximize the "bottom line" and employees seek to get as much as they can out of insecure positions) (Bluestone & Rose, 1997). Such employees may have little recourse but to accept assignments that will pose difficulties for parenting or caring for other relatives, or will limit time spent with a partner. Higher-status jobs may present the illusion of flexibility, but many arenas (including major corporations and universities) have become ever more competitive and more demanding of employee time (despite the perks of on-site childcare or time "off the clock" for childbearing). As mentioned, dual-earner couples make up the majority of African American married couples. We suspect that increases in the competing demands of work and family life may be a particular burden for African American women, in that they are typically employed for longer hours in lower-status jobs (with less flexibility).

Caretaking Functions: Supporting Young Adults

With the increased need for postsecondary schooling and the decreasing ability of young adults to secure jobs that can support independence, more young adults are dependent on their parents (or other older adults) for financial support. Although race-specific statistics are not available, the trend in the general population is noteworthy. In 2000, young adult women and men were more likely than they were in recent decades to live in their homes of origin. For women ages 18–24, the percentage living at home steadily increased over the last half-century, from 34.9% in 1960 to 47.1% in 2000; the figures for men were 52.4% and 57.1% (U.S. Bureau of the Census, 2003d). Clearly, the change in women's living arrangements is partially a result of the rise in age at first marriage. However, more recent trends cannot be influenced by the marital age, because entry into marriage was already later or not at all. This trend is also a function of the increasing costs of housing in urban centers. Even with a college education, young adults are unable to finance their independence. Notably, other nations are observing similar trends with very different responses. Some Japanese writers have termed subjects of this phenomenon "parasite singles" (Takahashi & Voss, 2000).

Role Development

The Reevaluation and Renegotiation of Gender Roles

Several changes have dictated the reconstruction of gender role expectations. First, among the most influential social changes in the last 50 years has been the increase in the proportion of women who work throughout much of their lives. This change in women's work behavior accompanied a wide array of new social and cultural perceptions about the role of women in society and, increasingly, the role of men in families. Although Black women have always been more likely than White women to be part of the labor force, the rate of employment of married Black women has grown dramatically in the last half century. In 1940, barely a quarter of married Black women were in the labor force; by 2002 nearly 70% worked outside the home and 80% of those with children under 18 held jobs (U.S. Bureau of the Census, 1961; U.S. Department of Labor and Bureau of Labor Statistics, 2004).

Second, in a related development, African American families have become more reliant on women's economic contributions. Although the median salary for African American men is still higher than women's salaries, the Black gender salary gap is much smaller than that observed for Whites and it continues to shrink. Salaries of Black women are also closer to those of White women than Black men's are to those of White men (median incomes in 2001 were $16,282 vs. $16,652 for women, respectively, as compared with $21,466 vs. $30,240 for men; U.S. Bureau of the Census, 2004). This phenomenon, coupled with the substantially increased presence of families maintained by women alone, has resulted in greater provider role responsibilities among Black women. Many African American families have been forced to reconsider traditional gender-based role differentiation.

The Reformulation and Expansion of Family Roles and Responsibilities

We also note the increased importance and prominence of expansive family ties. As people live longer and marriages continue to be somewhat fragile and less prevalent, a wider range of kinship ties have become progressively more central to everyday family life. There are a range of family members outside the coresident household who are potentially available to be called upon to perform family functions. For example, our research team has noted the presence and importance of the "beloved aunt" in many African American families. This usually single and child-free woman often has a particularly close and influential role in young peoples' lives. Similarly, male role models for many young men are their mothers' brothers, rather then their biological fathers. We expect that as the population of never-married and child-free individuals increases, so will the presence of this special relationship. Another family trend, which might be expected, is the increasingly important family roles and responsibilities of grandparents. Grandparents have already become more critical resources for many families, as evidenced by the dramatic increases in the numbers of grandparents acting as parents for their grandchildren. We believe that people are increasingly taking advantage of a wider range of family members in order to offset the uncertainties of marriage and family life. This reflects the adaptive nature of families, both conceptually and practically.

POLICY IMPLICATIONS

Marriage versus Family Policy

The changes in both form and function that have characterized African American families overall in recent times have implications for public policy that concern the welfare of families. We note, however, that in the current political environment, family policy tends to be bound up with policies designed to influence marital behavior. This has been most apparent in the so-called welfare reform movement and laws designed to reduce the dependency of poor families on governmental support. Both the House of Representatives and the Senate are considering versions of the Personal Responsibility, Work and Family Promotion Act of 2005, which contains the Bush administration's "marriage initiative"—a provision of $600 million to promote "healthy" marriages. If passed, as expected, the measure will take effect on October 1 (Library of Congress, 2005). Specific activities cited in the Act include public advertising campaigns and high school curriculum on the value of marriage, relationship skill programs (including financial management and conflict resolution) for nonmarried expectant parents, and premarital education (TheOrator.com, 2004). States, tribes, and territories may apply competitively for funds to establish their own "healthy marriage education activities" (Administration for Children and Families, 2003).

We do believe that there is a need to strengthen existing marriages, and a particular need to address the array of known assaults that serve to destabilize Black couples (which are in large part economic). However, we question the focus on marriage, rather than the institution of family more broadly, given the realities of life for most African Americans (who are not currently married). This legislation suggests that marriage is a panacea that will lift families out of economic distress and provide homes that enrich the well-being of all family members. We believe that the path to marriage and lasting relationships is extremely complex (and not even particularly well understood by social scientists who have spent their entire careers examining this very issue). The notion that the struggle is made easier with a partner (an "economies of scale" argument) may make sense as a marriage incentive for econometric models, but for poor and working-class men and women, there has to be a much greater incentive to engage in the daily struggle of emotional management and the explosive and ongoing emotional labor involved in power sharing and negotiation of identities and roles. Marriage is not like having a roommate, and today's men and women know that.

Fathering

There has been a staggering growth in initiatives and programs designed to provide support for fathering—with many focused in particular on so-called absent fathers and low-income African American men. This proliferation was stimulated in large part by the federal government's "Fathering Initiative," which was a response to President William Jefferson Clinton's call in 1995 for federal agencies to do more to support fathers' involvement in children's lives (U.S. Department of Health and Human Services, 2000). The goals of most programs focused on poor non-coresident fathers include increasing work effort and employment levels and the provision of child support, increasing father–child involvement, and enhancing child well-being. However, actual results for programs geared toward increasing "emotional" attachment have been "disappointing" (McLanahan & Carlson, 2003) and the literature is not consistent on the question of child outcomes as a function of nonresident fathering, independent of resource discrepancies (see, e.g., Martin, Emery, & Peris, 2004; Sandefur & Mosley, 1997).

We certainly endorse the continued development of programs that support fathers' involvement in children's lives. Gavanas (2002) views the fatherhood movement as two distinct wings—one being the "fragile families" groups, concerned chiefly with increasing labor market opportunities for low-income men of color, and the other the pro-marriage groups (see our earlier comments). She presents an elegant, compelling analysis of the movement and the distinct notions of race and gender that underlie each wing's sociopolitical perspectives. Although we cannot do justice to her arguments in this limited space, it is important to note that family policy in this regard is based on assumptions about gender relations, racial stereotypes, and visions of proper family life that may not be endorsed by or in the interests of the other parties in this equation (mothers, children, communities). We recall the issues we raised at the outset of this discussion about the various ways that families can be constructed and the many forms the contributions by mothers, fathers, and others can take. Public policy must be innovative in this regard and not aim to recreate nostalgic visions.

Diversity and Economics

The changes in family formation and function that we have described here suggest a focus on several issues. First, and foremost, there is no "one size fits all" policy that would apply to even most African Americans. The population of African descent in the United States is more diverse than ever on every possible measure (e.g., ethnicity, income, education, political interests, etc.). Second, economic development is fundamental to most concerns. Strong economic policy that benefits working-class men and women, as well as the poor, may well be the most effective policy for family preservation and actualization. The recent stabilization of trends in teen pregnancy, nonmarital childbearing, and divorce have all occurred in the context of a relatively robust economy. The current economic downturn, which, as noted earlier, is having a disproportionate impact on African Americans, could well be associated with the destabilization of Black families and marriages. The economic outlook for men has long been central to family formation decisions. It appears that women's economic prospects have become increasingly important to decisions to marry. Uncertainty and career immaturity, particularly among young men, dampens the willingness of young men and women to marry for a variety of reasons (Oppenheimer, 1988). African Americans' labor market position is particularly sensitive to economic change. Hence, the structure and health of local and national economies is central to decisions to form long-term unions. Beyond the issue of marriage and mating, however, is the need for more general support of families (including elderly persons, foster children, etc.). In order for individuals to create the financial base necessary to support today's families, the involvement of other institutions is required, including childcare providers and elder care.

Institutional Reform

Key institutions, such as schools, medical facilities, and government offices, must adapt to the not-so-new realities of work and family life. For example, schools generally operate on a schedule that bears no relationship to the constraints of most working families and single parents. Many families struggle to fill the gap between school hours and their work hours. The problem is particularly acute for middle school–age children, who may seem too old for traditional "childcare" and may believe that they can care for themselves. Innovative thinking by government agencies, community leaders, and employers is urgently needed to develop options that better meet the needs of families. Besides a stable economic outlook with general availability of good jobs, flexibility and responsiveness to the needs of all families are in everyone's best interest. As parents, caregivers for the elderly, and spouses, men and women must have flexibility to meet the various needs of families without sacrificing their mental health. The provision of flexible work schedules and family leave is a good place to start. However, in every facet of our society we need to rethink how to reframe schedules and expectations apart from the idea that families are equal to households, that men are breadwinners and women are primarily responsible for duties of home and family, and that family concerns are private affairs that do not affect the whole of society.

In this chapter we have chosen to focus on trends in the constellations and functions of African American families, broadly speaking, which in our view are new or represent new directions. Thus, we have not focused on many of the core problems and challenges faced by families that have continued—often unabated (such as the need for economic development in communities, crises in health care, racism, sexism, high incarceration levels, and crime). This is not meant to diminish their salience. Indeed, there are already a number of exceptionally well-argued calls for family policy reform on these grounds (e.g., Franklin, 1997; Wilson, 1996). Our intent has been to call attention to the continuing evolution of families generally and African American families most specifically. The inherent adaptability of the family as institution has been the linchpin of African American survival and advancement.

NOTES

1. Some form of "partible paternity" has been observed among the Aché of Paraguay, the Mehinaku, Kaingan, Arawete, and Curipaco of Brazil, the Matis of Peru, and the Yanamami and Bari in Venezuela (Beckerman & Valentine, 2002). Moreover, there is evidence from some of these cultures that children with "multiple fathers" display higher birth weight and are more likely to survive through adolescence than single-fathered children (Beckerman et al., 2002; Hill & Hurtado, 1996). Though this phenomenon is clearly an exception among South American populations, its adaptive function is apparent. Hrdy (2001) argues that in societies where male support is unreliable (such as those dependent on hunting and fishing) and where father mortality or defection rates are high, reliance on several fathers is beneficial to both mother and child (p. 92).

2. Owing to the suspension of detailed collection analysis of marriage and divorce data by race by the National Center for Health Statistics, as of January 1996, it is impossible to assess these trends beyond that date (U.S. Bureau of the Census, 2003b).

REFERENCES

Administration for Children and Families. (2003). *Healthy marriage matters to the Administration for Children and Families.* Retrieved June 4, 2004, from www.welfare.state.nv.us/main/ACFHealthyMarriageMatters.pdf

Beckerman, S., Lizarralde, R., Lizarralde, M., Bie, J., Ballew, C., Schroeder, S., et al. (2002). The Barí partible paternity project: Phase 1. In S. Beckerman & P. Valentine (Eds.), *Cultures of multiple fathers: The theory and practice of partible paternity in South America* (pp. 27–41). Gainesville: University of Florida Press.

Beckerman, S., & Valentine, P. (Eds.). (2002). *Cultures of multiple fathers: The theory and practice of partible paternity in South America.* Gainesville: University of Florida Press.

Billingsley, A. (1968). *Black families in white America:* Englewood Cliffs, NJ: Prentice-Hall.

Billingsley, A. (1993). *Climbing Jacob's ladder: The enduring legacy of African American families.* New York: Simon & Schuster.

Bluestone, B., & Rose, S. (1997). Overworked and underemployed: Unraveling an economic enigma. *The American Prospect, 31*(8). Retrieved from www.prospect.org/print/V8/31/bluestone-b.html

Bowman, P. J. (1988). Post-industrial displacement and family role strains: Challenges to the Black family. In P. Voydanof & L. S. Majka (Eds.), *Families and economic distress* (pp. 75–96). Newbury Park, CA: Sage.

Bramlett, M. D., & Mosher, W. D. (2002). Cohabitation, marriage, divorce, and remarriage in the United States. *Vital Health Statistics, 23*(22). (National Center for Health Statistics). Retrieved August 3, 2003, from www.cdc.gov/nchs/mardiv.htm

Bryson, K., & Casper, L. (1999). Coresident grandparents and grandchildren (*Current Populations Reports,* Series P23-198). Washington, DC: U.S. Bureau of the Census.

Carlson, M., & McLanahan, S. (2002). Fragile families, father involvement, and public policy. In C.S. Tamis-LeMonda & N. Cabrera (Eds.), *Handbook of father involvement: Multidisciplinary perspectives* (pp. 461–488). Mahwah, NJ: Erlbaum.

Casper, L. M., & Bianchi, S. M. (2001). *Continuity and change in the American family.* Thousand Oaks, CA: Sage.

Center for Disease Control and Prevention. (2003). *Table 1-19. Birth Rates for Married Women by Age of Mother, According to Race and Hispanic Origin: United States, 1950 and 1955 and Each Year 1960–99.* Retrieved October 5, 2003, from www.cdc.gov/nchs/data/statab/t991x19.pdf

Cherlin, A. (1992). *Marriage, divorce, remarriage* (2nd ed.). Cambridge, MA: Harvard University Press.

Child Trends Databank. (2005). *Table 1. Birth rates (births per 1,000) for males and females ages 10–19, Selected years 1960–2003.* Retrieved April 24, 2005, from www.childtrendsdatabank.org/tables/13_Table_1.htm

Coltrane, S. (2004). Fathering: Paradoxes, contradictions, and dilemmas. In M.

Coleman & L. H. Ganong (Eds.), *Handbook of contemporary families: Considering the past, contemplating the future* (pp. 224–243). Thousand Oaks, CA: Sage.

Coontz, S. (1992). *The way we never were: American families and the nostalgia trap.* New York: Basic Books.

Cox, O. C. (1940). Sex ratio and marital status among Negroes. *American Sociological Review, 5,* 937–947.

Darity, W. A., & Myers, S. A., Jr. (1995). Family structure and the marginalization of Black men: Policy implications. In M. B. Tucker & C. Mitchell-Kernan (Eds.), *The decline in marriage among African Americans: Causes, consequences and policy implications* (pp. 263–308). New York: Russell Sage Foundation.

Dilworth-Anderson, P., Burton, L. M., & Boulin-Johnson, L. (1993). Reframing theories for understanding race, ethnicity, and family. In P. Boss, W. Doherty, R. Larossa, W. Schumm, & S. Steinmetz (Eds.), *Sourcebook of family theories and methods: A contextual approach* (pp. 627–646). New York: Plenum Press.

Drake, St. C., & Cayton, H. R. (1962). *Black metropolis: A study of Negro life in a northern city* (Vol. 2). New York: Harper & Row.

Du Bois, W. E. B. (1899). *The Philadelphia Negro* [Online]. New York: Lippincott. Retrieved August 31, 2004, from www2.pfeiffer.edu/~lridener/DSS/DuBois/pntoc.html

Du Bois, W. E. B. (1903). *Souls of black folk* [Online]. Chicago: A.C. McClurg. (New York: Bartleby.com, 1999).

Du Bois, W. E. B. (1908). *The Negro American family* (Atlanta Study No. 13). Atlanta, GA: Atlanta University Press.

Ember, M., & Ember, C. R. (1983). *Marriage, family, and kinship.* New Haven, CT: Human Relationships Area Files (HRAF) Press.

Federal Interagency Forum on Aging-Related Statistics. (2003). *Older Americans 2000: Key indicators of well-being.* Retrieved August 3, 2003, from www.agingstats.gov/chartbook2000/

Ferguson, R. W. (2002). *Economic progress and small business: Remarks by Federal Reserve Board Vice Chairman Roger W. Ferguson, Jr. before the African American Chamber of Commerce of Western Pennsylvania, November 12.* Retrieved September 7, 2004, from www.federalreserve.gov/boarddocs/speeches/2002/200211123/default.htm

Fields, J. (2003). Children's living arrangements and characteristics: March 2002 (*Current Population Reports,* Series P20-547). Retrieved August 1, 2003, from www.census.gov/prod/2003pubs/p20–547.pdf

Fields, J., & Casper, L. (2001). America's families and living arrangements. Population characteristics (*Current Population Reports,* Series P20-537). Washington, DC: U.S. Census Bureau. Retrieved August 1, 2003, from www.census.gov/prod/2001pubs/p20-537.pdf

Fitch, C. A., & Ruggles, S. (2000). Historical trends in marriage formation: The United States, 1850–1990. In L. J. Waite, C. Bachrach, M. Hindin, El Thomson, & A. Thorton (Eds.), *The ties that bind: Perspectives on marriage and cohabitation* (pp. 59–88). New York: Aldine de Gruyter.

Franklin, D. (1997). *Ensuring inequality: The structural transformation of the African American family.* New York: Oxford University Press.

Frazier, E. F. (1939). *The Negro family in America.* Chicago: University of Chicago Press.

Frey, W. (2001). *Census shows large Black returns to the south reinforcing the region's "White–Black" demographic profile* (Population Studies Center Research Report No. 01-473). Ann Arbor: ISR, University of Michigan. Retrieved from www.psc.isr.umich.edu/pubs/papers/rr01–473.pdf

Furukawa, S. (1994). The diverse living arrangements of children: Summer 1991 (*Current Population Reports*, Series P-70, No. 38). Washington, DC: U.S. Census Bureau.

Gann, R. (2000, April). *Postmodern perspectives on race and racism: Help or hindrance?* Paper presented at the 50th Annual Conference of the Political Studies Association, London.

Gavanas, A. (2002). The Fatherhood Responsibility Movement: The centrality of marriage, work and male sexuality in reconstructions of masculinity and fatherhood. In B. Hobson (Ed.), *Making men into fathers: Men, masculinities and the social politics of fatherhood* (pp. 213–242). London: Cambridge University Press.

Gittens, D. (1998). The family in question: What is the family? Is it universal? In S. J. Ferguson (Ed.), *Shifting the center: Understanding contemporary families.* Mountain View, CA: Mayfield.

Guttman, B. (2002). *Trends in the well-being of America's children and youth.* Washington, DC: U.S. Department of Health and Human Services. Retrieved August 1, 2003, from aspe.hhs.gov/hsp/01trends/index.htm

Hamer, J. (2001). *What it means to be daddy: Fatherhood for Black men living away from their children.* New York: Columbia University Press.

Hill, K., & Hurtado, A. M. (1996). *Ache life history: The ecology and demography of a foraging people.* New York: Aldine.

Hill, R. B., Billingsley, A., Engram, E., Malson, M. R., Rubin, R. H., Stack, C. B., et al. (1993). *Research on African American families: A holistic perspective.* Boston: William Monroe Trotter Institute, University of Massachusetts.

Hochschild, A. (1997). *The time bind: When work becomes home and home becomes work.* New York: Henry Holt.

Hrdy, S. B. (2001, February). *The past, present, and future of the human family.* Paper presented at the Tanner Lectures on Human Values, University of Utah. Retrieved September 5, 2004, from www.tannerlectures.utah.edu/efgh.html

Hua, C. (2001, February). *A society without fathers or husbands: The Na of China* (A. Hustvedt, Trans.). Cambridge, MA: MIT Press.

Jewell, K. S. (1988). *Survival of the Black family: The institutional impact of U.S. social policy.* New York: Praeger.

Klinenberg. (2002). *Heat wave: A social autopsy of disaster in Chicago.* Chicago: University of Chicago Press.

Kong, D. (2003, August 2). Minorities affected the most. *Daily News of Los Angeles*, Business, p. 1.

Kong, L. K. (1999). Chinese marriages and family: Diversity and change. In S. L.

Browning & R. R. Miller (Eds.), *Till death do us part: A multicultural anthology on marriage*. Stamford, CT: JAI Press.

Library of Congress. (2005). Thomas: Legislative information on the Internet: Bill Summary & Status for the 109th Congress; Personal Responsibility, Work, and Family Promotion Act of 2005. Retrieved April 27, 2005, from thomas.loc.gov/

Martin, J. A., Park, M. M., & Sutton, P. D. (2002, June 6). Births: Preliminary data for 2001. *National Vital Statistics Reports, 50*(10).

Martin, M. T., Emery, R. E., & Peris, T. S. (2004). Single-parent families: Risks, resilience, and change. In M. Coleman & L. H. Ganong (Eds.), *Handbook of contemporary families: considering the past, contemplating the future* (pp. 282–301). Thousand Oaks, CA: Sage.

McDaniel, A. (1994). Historical racial differences in living arrangements of children. *Journal of Family History, 19*, 57–77.

McLanahan, S. S., & Carlson, M. J. (2002). Welfare reform, fertility, and father involvement. *Children and Welfare Reform, 12*. Retrieved April 24, 2005, from www.futureofchildren.org/pubs-info2825/pubs-info_show.htm?doc_id= 102547

Norton, A.J., & Miller, L. F. (1992). Marriage, divorce and remarriage in the 1990's. (*Current Population Reports*, Series P-23, No. 180). Washington, DC: U.S. Government Printing Office.

Oppenheimer, V. K. (1988). A theory of marriage timing. *American Journal of Sociology, 94*, 563–591.

Pinsof, W. (2002). The death of "till death us do part": The transformation of pair-bonding in the 20th century. *Family Process, 42*(3). Retrieved September 5, 2004, from www.findarticles.com/p/articles/mi_m0AZV/is_2_41

Popenoe, D. (1999). *Life without father: Compelling new evidence that fatherhood and marriage are indispensable for the good of children and society.* Cambridge, MA: Harvard University Press.

Raley, R. K., & Bumpass, L. (2003). The topography of the divorce plateau: Levels and trends in union stability in the United States after 1980. *Demographic Research, 8*, 245–260. Retrieved September 5, 2004, from www.demo-graphic-research.org

Rivara, F., Sweeney, P., & Henderson, B. (1986). Black teenage fathers: What happens when the child is born? *Pediatrics 78,* 151–158.

Sandefur, G. D., & Mosley, J. (1997). Family structure, stability, and the well-being of children. In R. M. Hauser, B. V. Brown, & W. R. Prosser (Eds.), *Indicators of children's well-being* (pp. 328–325). New York: Russell Sage Foundation.

Schachter, J. P. (2004). Geographical mobility: 2002–2003 (*Current Population Reports*, Series P20-549). Retrieved September 20, 2004, from www.census.gov/population/www/socdemo/migrate.html

Shor, J. B. (1992). *The overworked American: The unexpected decline of leisure.* New York: Basic Books.

Silverman, M. (1999). *Facing modernity.* London: Routledge.

Simmons, T., & O'Connell, M. (2003). *Married-couple and unmarried-partner households: 2000.* Washington, DC: U.S. Bureau of the Census.

Skolnick, A. (1991). *Embattled paradise: The American family in an age of uncertainty.* New York: Basic Books.

Solis, D. (2003, July 30). Blacks pay for weak job market. *Los Angeles Daily News,* Business, p. 1.

Stacey, J. (1991). Backward toward the postmodern family: Reflections on gender, kinship and class. In A. Wolfe (Ed.), *America at century's end in the Silicon Valley* (pp. 17–34). Berkeley: University of California Press.

Staples, R. (1999). Patterns of change in the postindustrial Black family. In R. Staples (Ed.), *The Black family: Essays and studies* (6th ed., pp. 281–290). Belmont, CA: Wadsworth.

Statistics New Zealand. (2003). *2006 census of population and dwellings: Preliminary views on content.* Retrieved September 2, 2004, from www.stats.govt. nz/domino/external/pasfull/pasfull.nsf/0/4c2567ef00247c6acc256d11007 18de0/$FILE/PVC(2006).pdf

Sylvester, K., & Reich, K. (2002). *Making fathers count: Assessing the progress of responsible fatherhood efforts.* Baltimore: Annie E. Casey Foundation. Retrieved April 24, 2005, from www.aecf.org/publications/browse.php?filter=6

Takahashi, H., & Voss, J. (2000). "Parasite singles"—A uniquely Japanese phenomenon? [Online]. *Japanese Economic Institute Report, 31.* Retrieved August 1, 2003, from www.jei.org/Archive/JEIR00/0031f.html

Taylor, P. L., Tucker, M. B., & Mitchell-Kernan, C. (1999). Ethnic variations in perceptions of men's provider role. *Psychology of Women Quarterly, 23,* 759–779.

Taylor, P. L., Tucker, M. B., & Mitchell-Kernan, C. (under review). *"I do" but to whom: Attitudes toward intermarriage in 21 U.S. cities.*

Taylor, R. J., Tucker, M. B., Chatters, L. M., & Jayakody, R. (1997). Recent demographic trends in African American family structure. In R. J. Taylor & L. Chatters (Eds.). *Family life in Black America* (pp. 14–62). Newbury Park, CA: Sage.

Tucker, M. B. (2000). Considerations in the development of family policy for African Americans. In J. S. Jackson (Ed.), *New directions: African Americans in a diversifying nation* (pp. 162–206). Washington, DC: National Policy Association.

Tucker, M. B., & Mitchell-Kernan, C. (1995a). African American marital trends in context: Towards a synthesis. In M. B. Tucker & C. Mitchell-Kernan (Eds.), *The decline in marriage among African Americans: Causes, consequences and policy implications* (pp. 345–362). New York: Russell Sage Foundation.

Tucker, M. B., & Mitchell-Kernan, C. (1995b). Trends in African American family formation: A theoretical and statistical overview. In M. B. Tucker & C. Mitchell-Kernan (Eds.), *The decline in marriage among African Americans: Causes, consequences and policy implications* (pp. 3–26). New York: Russell Sage Foundation.

Tucker, M. B., Subramanian, S., & James, A. D. (2004). Diversity in African American families: Trends and projections. In M. J. Coleman & L. H. Ganong (Eds.), *Handbook of family diversity: Considering the past, contemplating the future* (pp. 352–368). Thousand Oaks, CA: Sage.

U.S. Bureau of the Census. (1961). *U.S. Census of the Population: 1960* (Subject Reports). Employment status and work experience (Final Report PC(2)-6A). Washington, DC: U.S. Government Printing Office.

U.S. Bureau of the Census. (1998a). Interracial tables. *Table 1. Race of wife by race of husband: 1960, 1970, 1980, 1991, and 1992.* Retrieved September 5, 2004, from www.census.gov/population/www/socdemo/interrace.html

U.S. Bureau of the Census. (1998b). Interracial tables. *Table 4. Race of child by race of householder and of spouse or partner: 1990.* Retrieved September 5, 2004, from www.census.gov/population/www/socdemo/interrace.html

U.S. Bureau of the Census. (1999). *Table AD-2. Unmarried-Couple Households, by Presence of Children 1960 To Present.* Retrieved April 24, 2005, from www.census.gov/population/socdemo/ms-la/tabad-2.txt

U.S. Bureau of the Census. (2000). *Table 2. Hispanic origin and race of opposite-sex unmarried-partner households for the United States: 2000.* Retrieved April 24, 2005, from www.census.gov/population/www/cen2000/phc-t19.html

U.S. Bureau of the Census. (2003a). Hispanic origin and race of coupled households: 2000. *Table 1. Hispanic origin and race of wife and husband in married-couple household for the United States: 2000* (Census 2000 PHC-T-19). Retrieved September 5, 2004, from www.census.gov/population/www/cen2000/tablist.html

U.S. Bureau of the Census. (2003b). *Statistical Abstract of the United States, Vital Statistics, Section 2.* Retrieved September 5, 2004, from www.census.gov/prod/www/statistical-abstract-02.html

U.S. Bureau of the Census. (2003c). *Table MS-1. Marital status of the population 16 years old and over, by sex and race: 1950 to present.* Retrieved August 4, 2003, from www.census.gov/population/socdemo/hh-fam/tabMS-1.xls

U.S. Bureau of the Census. (2003d). *Table AD-1. Young adults living at home: 1960 to present.* Retrieved August 1, 2003, from www.census.gov/population/socdemo/hh-fam/tabAD-1.pdf

U.S. Bureau of the Census. (2003e). *Table C1. Household Relationship and Family Status of Children Under 18 Years, by Age, Sex, Race, Hispanic Origin, and Metropolitan Residence: March 2002.* Retrieved April 24, 2005, from www.census.gov/population/www/socdemo/hh-fam/cps2002.html

U.S. Bureau of the Census. (2004). Historical Income Tables—People, Table P-2. *Race and Hispanic origin of people by median income and sex: 1947 to 2001.* Retrieved September 7, 2004, from www.census.gov/hhes/income/histinc/p02.html

U.S. Department of Health and Human Services. (2000). HHS' fatherhood initiative. HHS Fact Sheet, June 17. Retrieved September 7, 2004, from fatherhood.hhs.gov/factsheets/fact20000617.html

U.S. Department of Labor and Bureau of Labor Statistics. (2004). *Women in the labor force: A databook* (Report 973). Retrieved September 10, 2004, from www.bls.gov/cps/wlf-databook.pdf

Waite, L. J., & Gallagher, M. (2000). *The case for marriage: Why married people are happier, healthier, and better off financially.* New York: Doubleday.

Wilson, W. J. (1996). *When work disappears: The world of the new urban poor.* New York: Knopf.

PART II

AFRICAN AMERICAN FAMILIES IN COMMUNITY CONTEXTS

CHAPTER 6

Marital Relationships of African Americans

A Contextual Approach

Chalandra M. Bryant
and K. A. S. Wickrama

Only about 47% of the African American population in the United States is married, as compared with 81% of the White population, 82% of Asian/Pacific Islanders, and 69% of Latinos (Benokraitis, 2002; Smith, 2000). Moreover, African Americans are more likely to experience marital dissolution than any other racial/ethnic group (Benokraitis, 2002; Kposowa, 1998; Saluter, 1994; White, 1991). For example, 17% of marriages among White women are likely to dissolve by the end of 15 years, whereas almost half of the marriages among African American women are likely to dissolve by that time (Kposowa, 1998). Previous research suggests that the formation and maintenance of close social relationships in general, and romantic relationships in particular, are associated with emotional and physical well-being (House, Landis, & Umberson, 1988; Simon & Marcussen, 1999; Wickrama, Lorenz, Conger, & Elder, 1997). Given (1) the high divorce rate of African Americans and (2) the link between close relationships and emotional/physical health, in addition to (3) the health disadvantages experienced by African Americans (National Center for Health Statistics, 1998; Williams, Yu, Jackson, & Anderson, 1997), there is a pressing need to explore unique social circumstances experienced by African American couples

111

that may impact their marital quality. The ecological perspective can help us gain a better understanding of the influence of these social circumstances. Ecologists focus on the relationship between organisms and the environments in which they live. In this case, the organisms of interest are families. The environment can be operationalized as the social context in which the families live. Thus, the ecological perspective views families as functioning within a set of embedded social contexts. For those of us who study relationships—particularly marriage—this suggests that both the structure of one's social context and one's experiences in a social context outside the family may affect the quality of marital relationships (Bronfenbrenner, 1986; Leventhal & Brooks-Gunn, 2000). Community is an important social context that may influence marriages. Much of the work linking community context (broadly defined) to African American family patterns focuses on the shortage of marriageable men or mate availability (Kiecolt & Fosset, 1995; Trent & South, 2003). Other community characteristics are worth considering too.

Previous community studies (Brooks-Gunn, Duncan, Klebanov, & Sealand, 1993; South & Crowder, 1999; Sucoff & Upchurch, 1998) generally suggest that community socioeconomic disadvantage negatively influences relationships, family formation, and family transitions over and above the influence of individual and family socioeconomic characteristics. Although Wilson (1987) noted, early on, that in socioeconomically disadvantaged neighborhoods marriage was weakly supported, it was not until quite recently that researchers began to empirically examine the association between marital attributes and neighborhood socioeconomic disadvantage (South, 2001). In other words, researchers finally began to ask what impact communities had on existing marriages. Although South (2001) found no significant influence of neighborhood socioeconomic status on marital dissolution, relatively little is known about the influence of neighborhood characteristics on the *quality* of marriages. There is a pressing need to build on the existing work and to extend the current literature by focusing on African American couples who choose to stay together. We are specifically interested in the community context of marital quality as captured by marital happiness—in other words, we focus on the influence of community factors (as a social context) on marital happiness. Just because couples stay together does not mean that they are happy. Likewise, just because community characteristics have little effect on marital *stability* does not mean that they have no impact on marital *happiness*. The goal of this chapter is to identify sets of community characteristics that influence marital happiness. First, we present a small set of preliminary findings, and then we discuss the policy implications of those findings. For now, we return to our discussion of communities.

The community disorganization perspective (Masey & Denton, 1993; Wilson, 1987) suggests that community poverty, ethnic segregation, and residential instability negatively influence family relationships. Although these characteristics represent parallel community processes (Wilson 1987), we contend that they are not completely confounded by each other and may, instead, each independently influence African American marriages. Very little is known about the unique direct contribution (direct effects) of these structural community adversities on the marriages of African Americans and the social processes through which these community factors exert their influences (indirect effects). We will discuss (as depicted in Figure 6.1) the manner in which the marriages of African Americans are influenced by (1) community poverty, (2) residential instability, and (3) the percentage of minorities residing in their communities.

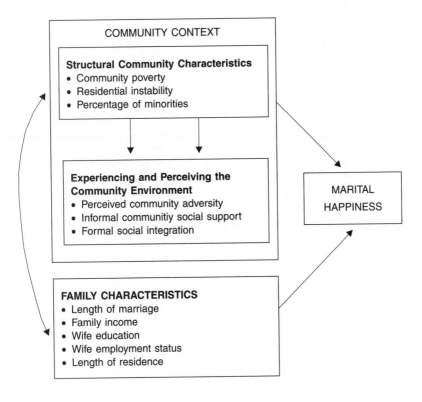

FIGURE 6.1. The theoretical model.

Many previous community studies have focused on the linear or additive influences of community characteristics on youth development, family, and marriage. Although there is a reason to expect multiplicative influences of community characteristics, only a few studies have investigated such influences. In particular, Ross, Reynolds, and Geis (2000) demonstrated that the influence of neighborhood stability is contingent on the level of community poverty. We feel that work in this area should be extended by exploring the additive and multiplicative influences of various other community characteristics on individual/family well-being. For that reason, we examine the multiplicative influence of residential instability and the percentage of minorities in the community on the marital happiness of African Americans.

INFLUENCE OF STRUCTURAL COMMUNITY CHARACTERISTICS

Community Poverty

Our discussion includes both direct and indirect influences of community poverty on marital happiness. Community poverty exerts a significant influence on the daily lives of individuals (Sampson, Squires, & Zhou, 2002; Wilson, 1987). Therefore, we expect a community's level of poverty to *directly* influence marital happiness. Lack of accessibility, affordability, and availability of resources in poor communities hinders the ability of residents to obtain services (i.e., counseling, recreation) that may facilitate the maintenance of successful, healthy marriages. These structural constraints limit the quality of day-to-day family/marital functioning of residents, thus contributing to marital distress.

In addition—consistent with the community disorganization perspective (Wilson, 1987)—we expect community poverty to indirectly influence marital happiness through social processes. Community poverty erodes formal and informal social networks. Community poverty is not only characterized by high rates of unemployment, low-skilled jobs, and female-headed households, but also by the withdrawal of government and private services, as well as by the withdrawal of businesses and organizations, thus contributing to high levels of residential instability.

Residential Instability

Residential instability is another structural community characteristic. According to community adversity models, as previously noted, residential instability and community poverty are parallel community processes. Some families move out of deteriorating communities, whereas poor minorities, in particular, move into such communities in search of less expensive housing (see Burton & Clark, Chapter 8, in this book). We believe that residential instability may influence the marital happiness of African Americans directly and indirectly through various social processes. As in the case of community poverty, we contend that the degree of residential instability prevalent in the community may directly influence marital happiness through structural constraints. Residentially unstable communities may lack adequate infrastructural facilities—such as reliable transportation, adequate housing, recreational facilities, parks, and a safe environment—all of which may influence marital/familial activities, thus contributing to marital dysfunction. Because the level of residential instability may differ in communities with similar levels of poverty, the influence of any given community's residential instability may be independent of the level of poverty in the community.

Both residential instability and community poverty may influence marital happiness indirectly through social disorganization processes. Residential instability inhibits the formation of formal and informal social ties (Ross et al., 2000). Moreover, adverse structural conditions may cause social trust to deteriorate, leading to the breakdown of formal and informal social networks in the community (Elliot et al., 1996; Ross, Mirowsky, & Pribesh, 2001; Sampson & Groves, 1989; Shaw & McKay, 1942; Wilson, 1991).

Sampson (2001) argues that there are three mechanisms through which lack of social ties can lead to detrimental outcomes. These mechanisms relate to rules, resources, and routines. Although they were originally used to explain the association between community structural adversities and delinquent behavior, we believe that they can also be used to explain the association between community adversity and marital outcomes.

Rules (Shared Actions/Expectations and Social Controls Guiding Behavior)

When residents do not know each other in a neighborhood, they are unable to operate as agents of social control for each other, and in the absence of social control or social monitoring, individuals may engage in high-risk behaviors to a greater extent than they would in a more closely knit neighborhood (Cutrona, Russell, Hessling, Brown, & Murry, 2000). High-risk behaviors may extend to marital behaviors. For example, perhaps couples who are prone to violence and do not know others in their neighborhood are more likely to continue engaging in violent behaviors with one another—because they lack ties to agents of social control. Those agents can enforce, directly or indirectly, norms regarding the manner in which relationships should function. High-risk behaviors may also lead to emotional distress (Cutrona et al., 2000), which, in turn, can influence marital happiness.

Resources (Social Capital and Institutional Resources)

Role models, peer groups, informal or formal groups, and family ties are social resources that can contribute to one's marital relationship. Disadvantaged communities may lack social resources that promote the maintenance of successful marital role models. Moreover, the presence of stable families, as conventional role models, as well as the social resources supporting them, may relay the message that "family stability is the norm, not the exception" (Anderson, 1991; Fernandez-Kelly, 1994; Wilson, 1987, p. 56). Neighborhood peer groups can also be crucial sources of influence; such groups may transmit or model certain behaviors (Ellen & Turner, 1997), such as positive marital interactions. Social ties (or lack thereof) to such peer groups can influence one's behavior and relationship outcomes. If the structural characteristics of a community hinder the formation of bonds with others, then the residents of that community may have fewer sources of social support. Lack of support can lead to distress, which, in turn, can affect marital happiness. Interestingly, this suggests that social policies aimed at strengthening community members' ties to one another may impact marital happiness.

Routines (Prevalence and Mix of Different Types of Behaviors)

Community characteristics impact residents' daily routines. Hostile, aggressive behaviors can become habitual. This means that if couples are faced with hostile, aggressive behaviors on a daily basis in their communities, that manner of behavior may spill over into their marital interactions. You may ask how we could possibly make that leap. Well, we know that communities characterized by adverse conditions (e.g., crime, litter, violence) can cause strain and distress (Cutrona et al., 2000; Latkin & Curry, 2003). We also know that distress can have a negative impact on marital happiness (Conger, Rueter, & Elder, 1999). If we put these pieces together, they suggest that there may be some type of link between community characteristics and marriage.

Residential *stability* may positively contribute to the quality of life of individuals in any given community (South & Crowder, 1997), in that residential stability promotes social ties and a sense of cohesiveness. Stability increases the likelihood that neighbors will know each other, share norms and values, and exert informal social control (Shaw & McKay, 1942). This suggests a need to examine the indirect association between residential instability and marital relationships, through social network variables. Again, we seem to come back to the importance of social ties among residents and the need for social policies that encourage the formation and strength of those ties, as well as policies that foster a sense of social cohesion. Remember, another structural community characteristic that should be addressed is racial/ethnic diversity (or minority presence).

Percentage of Minorities in the Community

Community studies suggest that racial segregation is closely associated with community poverty and residential instability (LaVeist, 2002; Massey & Denton, 1993); such studies point to the deleterious consequences of racial segregation for the youth and families in disadvantaged communities. We contend that much of the current research concerning community influences on family outcomes has mainly focused on the general population (some analyses even combine various ethnic and racial groups), with very little consideration of specific ethnic and racial groups living in those communities. Therefore, many of the disorganization models based on community socioeconomic adversity are insensitive to the differential impact of community characteristics on various racial/ethnic groups. This is particularly true with regard to the influence of the community environment on the family functioning of various racial groups (Wickrama, Noh, & Bryant, 2005). Although the impact of community socioeconomic adversity—such as community poverty, residential instability, and ethnic segregation—on youth outcomes and families has been well documented, *we expect the impact of these characteristics to differ depending on the outcomes under study and the specific group under study.* We argue that the percentage of minorities in a community has both direct and indirect beneficial effects, specifically on African American family/marital functioning, regardless of the level of community poverty and residential instability.

The degree of ethnic diversity in a community may directly affect psychological and behavioral outcomes of its residents by determining their social status in the community (i.e., minority vs. nonminority status) (Massey & Denton, 1993; Sampson et al., 2001). The social/psychological literature suggests that perceived minority status, as determined by the ethnic composition of the community, may itself be stressful and may contribute to psychological distress (Meyer, 1995), which can, in turn, contribute to adverse marital relationships. Although African Americans living in less diverse neighborhoods are, in general, economically better off, evidence still suggests that African Americans living in those neighborhoods are neither liked nor respected and are subject to hostility (Boardman, Finch, Ellison, Williams, & Jackson, 2001; Welch, Sigelman, Bledsoe, & Combs, 2001). Consider this: A recent study of White

Americans' preferences in regard to purchasing a home in certain neighborhoods indicates that "Asian and Hispanic neighborhood composi-
tions do *not* matter to whites," but "Black neighborhood composition
does matter, and matters even more for white Americans with children
under age 18" (Emerson, Yancey, & Chai, 2001, p. 922). Interestingly,
in ethnically diverse communities, African Americans live in relatively
supportive and empowered social environments despite community impoverishment (Korbin, 2001). Thus, African Americans living among
other African Americans, or among other minorities, or among more ra-
cially/ethnically diverse groups of residents may have greater positive
feelings. Those greater positive feelings may, in turn, contribute to their
marital relationships.

We believe that ethnic diversity (regardless of community poverty
and residential instability) contributes to African American marriages by
promoting informal community social resources among African Americans such as collective socialization and intergenerational closure, by
which we mean bonding across generations (Coleman, 1988). This is
what leads us to believe that ethnic diversity exerts a positive influence
on African American marriages through *informal community support.*
LaVeist (2002) argues that the concentration of minorities in communities has increased "Black political power," which, in turn, has contributed to the well-being of African Americans, independent of the effect of
poverty. Thus, independent of community socioeconomic adversity, we
argue that there is a need to examine the degree to which ethnic and racial minorities are present in the communities under study. If their presence has a positive effect, then this suggests the need to implement policies that promote the diversification of communities, particularly to the
degree to which no one group in the community feels as though it has
minority status.

So far, we have discussed the possible influence of structural community characteristics on marital happiness. Spouses' experiences in and
perceptions of their community environment may also play a role—
directly or indirectly—in marital happiness. We now turn our attention
to these experiences and perceptions.

EXPERIENCING AND PERCEIVING
COMMUNITY ADVERSITY

An important individual-level variable that may influence marital relationships is spouses' *perceptions* of the community environment or
spouses' *experiences* in the community. Such perceptions and experiences may partially mediate the influence of structural community disad-

vantages on marital relationships (Ross et al., 2000). People construct the environment in which they live through their cognitions (Demo, Small, & Savin-Williams, 1987). Thus, perceiving community adversity is not exactly the same as an objective, structural characteristic such as community poverty. *Perceptions* of the community environment can be measured by assessing (1) the residents' own beliefs about the amount of crime or the quality of schools in their area and (2) the degree to which residents feel supported by their community. Community socioeconomic adversity influences residents' beliefs and feelings through their day-to-day experiences with adverse community characteristics. In adverse communities, residents experience social disorder and physical decay; they frequently encounter various community pathologies such as vandalism, graffiti, noise, crime, drug use, and physical hazards (e.g., abandoned buildings, trash). The daily stress associated with living in a potentially harmful, uncontrollable, threatening, and noxious environment can generate distressful feelings such as fear, powerlessness, and hopelessness among residents (Ross et al., 2000). According to Brown (2003), racial disadvantage causes a number of mental health problems among minorities, including suppressed anger, anti-self issues, and nihilistic tendencies that can contribute to psychological distress. As previously noted, feelings of distress inhibit the ability to engage in close family relationships (see family stress model; Conger et al., 1990; Matthews, Wickrama, & Conger, 1996). What does this suggest? Again, it suggests the need for community-focused policies—in this case, policies aimed at fostering a sense of power and hope among residents. In terms of research, it suggests the need to investigate the possible mechanisms (i.e., perceived community adversity, informal community social support, and formal social integration) through which community structural characteristics may influence African American marriages. This is an instance in which research can inform policy, by identifying proximal mechanisms linking distal community characteristics and family/marital functioning. Of course, numerous other factors must be taken into account in explaining this link.

CONTROLS: FAMILY CHARACTERISTICS

As we examine the impact of community context on marital happiness, certain factors should be taken into account—namely, length of marriage, family-level economic hardship, employment status, length of residence, and education. Family economic (income) factors have a strong influence on the marital interactions and marital outcomes of African Americans (Brown, 1996; Taylor, Tucker, & Mitchell-Kernan, 1999).

For example, marriage rates among African Americans declined following increased levels of unemployment among African American men. Among African American couples, the increasing unemployment of men has been linked to divorce (Taylor, Jackson, & Chatters, 1997). A key component of the family stress model proposed by Conger and colleagues concerns experiences of adversity, particularly financial strain (Conger et al., 1990; Conger & Elder, 1994; Conger, Rueter, & Elder, 1999; Matthews et al., 1996). Adversity such as family strain predicts the deterioration of the quality of interactions between family members. Interaction quality, in turn, predicts perceived marital success.

Family economic hardship may have a particularly negative impact on African American couples. Traditionally, in African American households, both husbands and wives have typically had to assume responsibility for the financial well-being of the family; economic circumstances have called for the full participation of African American women in securing the financial well-being of their families (Burgess, 1994).

The other controls we recommend are education and length of marriage. Education and income are typically correlated, although they are distinct constructs; we control for both. The longer couples are married and the longer they have lived in the same community, the greater their stability; however, length of marriage may not necessarily reflect greater marital happiness. Given the information we have presented thus far, a small test of our ideas seems in order. This will determine whether we have empirical evidence for our proposed association between community characteristics and martial happiness. With such evidence we will have a better chance of convincing policymakers—particularly those interested in the institution of marriage in this country—that making improvements in how and where people live will essentially improve other aspects of their lives, namely, their marital/family relationships.

A PRELIMINARY TEST OF OUR IDEAS

To test our ideas, we use data from Wave 1 (1995) of the National Longitudinal Study of Adolescent Health (Add Health), which is a longitudinal school-based study of U.S. adolescents that focuses on their lives, particularly their health and health behaviors. Ninety-minute interviews were completed by 20,745 adolescents during the first wave of data collection in 1995. Nearly 79% of the adolescents were from two-parent families. During Wave 1, adolescents ranged in age from 13 to 19 years. The average age of parents was 40 years.

The sample included 69.2% Whites, 14.1% African Americans, and 11.8% Hispanics. About 51.1% of the adolescents were male, and

48.9% female. About 14.1% of the mothers and 11.1% of the fathers had less than a high school education; 24.4% of the households were below the poverty line. In 40% of the families, at least one parent was employed as a manual laborer (Goodman, 1999).

The present study uses the in-home data collected from the parents, as well as 1990 census data. Sample weights were used in our analyses to ensure the national representativeness of the study participants. Interview data were provided by 17,500 parents. The mother or mother figure of the targeted adolescent (15,983) was the desired respondent; however, in some cases the father or father figure (1,142) was interviewed. There were 1,718 African American married mother-respondents (or wives) in 95 school catchment areas. Thus, the average number of respondents in a level 2 unit was 18. The present within-group analyses use only African American wives' reports about marital happiness. We chose to focus only on the wives because gender of reporter may affect the results. Given that even the marriage pattern of African American men differs from that of African American women—*according to the 2000 census reports, 46% of African American males between the ages of 25 and 64 are married with a spouse present, as compared with 34% of African American females*—we felt that reports about marriage may differ. We were unable to run separate analyses for husbands due to sample size constraints. (Listwise deletion yielded a sample of 90 African American husbands.) Many of the items used in the Add Health data set were adopted from various standardized, validated instruments that have been used in national and state surveys of adolescents.

Dependent Variable

The construct marital happiness was identified using one item that asked, "How would you rate your relationship with your current spouse/partner?" It was rated on a 10-point Likert scale ranging from 1 (completely unhappy) to 10 (completely happy). The item was coded such that higher scores reflected greater marital happiness. This served as the dependent variable.

Measures of Structural Community Variables

A score representing community poverty was generated by summing four indicators corresponding to respondents' census tract information from the 1990 U.S. Census (contextual data set). Those indicators included (1) the proportion of families living in poverty, (2) the proportion of single-parent families, (3) the proportion of adults employed in service occupations, and (4) the proportion of unemployed males (Wickrama & Bryant, 2003; adopted from Sucoff & Upchurch, 1998). Communities were based on school catchment areas. We computed and used school catchment area level averages of individual scores obtained from the 1990 U.S. Census data.

Residential instability was assessed in terms of the percentage of households residing in the community less than five years, according to the 1990 census data. We computed the percentage of minorities residing in the communities. As in the case of community poverty, we computed and used school-catchment-area-level averages of individual scores obtained from the 1990 U.S. census data.

Measures Assessing Experiences in and Perceptions of Community

An index assessing an individual's experience with and perception of disorder in the community was created by standardizing and summing four items. Three items asked whether the individual (1) lived in the community because there is less crime there, (2) lived in the community because there is less drug use and other illegal activities, and (3) lived in the community because the schools are better than in other neighborhoods. The fourth item was a question asking, "In this neighborhood, how big a problem is litter or trash on the streets and sidewalks?"

Informal community social support was assessed by asking parents to respond to the question, "If a neighbor saw your child getting into trouble, would your neighbor tell you about it?" The second item asked adolescents to respond to the statement, "People in this neighborhood look out for each other." The third item asked adolescents to respond to a question asking, "How much do you feel adults care about you?" The items were coded such that higher scores reflected greater informal support. The responses were summed after standardization, and the average across census tracts was computed to create a community-level measure of collective socialization.

An individual-level measure of formal social integration was generated by summing five items and averaging across census tracts. These items asked whether the parent participating in the study was a member of formal community organizations (1 = yes, 0 = no), such as parent-teacher organizations, civic or social organizations, sports groups, labor unions, or military/veterans organizations. Items were summed and averaged to create a score representing formal social integration. Higher scores reflected greater social integration.

The number of years married was computed, and the number of years families resided in the same community was computed. A measure of family income was assessed by computing the total income of all the family members as reported by the parent in the family completing the questionnaire. Education was assessed using the years of formal education of the wives. These constructs—length of marriage, length of residence, employment status, family income, and education—were used as controls.

We tested multilevel random intercept regression models for the individual-level outcome variable (marital happiness) in the model, using family and community-level predictors. Because of the nested nature of the data (individuals within communities), individual error terms may be correlated within communities. Therefore, ordinary least square estimates, standard errors in particular, may be biased (Bryk & Raudenbush, 1992). To take into account this dependency among individuals within communities, we estimated random intercept models using the SAS PROC MIXED procedure.

We examined the between- and within-community variability of marital happiness by estimating the unconditional random intercept model (null model). Between- and within-community-level variances of marital happiness were 0.148 and 1.936. The between-community variance accounts for about 7% of the total individual differences, indicating that there is a difference in marital happiness between the various communities. Then we estimated several nested multilevel models as a means of exploring the associations between the proposed variables.

Model 1 in Table 6.1 presents the effects of structural community characteristics on the marital happiness of African American women, after controlling for individual/family characteristics. Thus, after controlling for *length of marriage, length of residence, family income, education of wives,* as well as *employment status of wives,* the structural community characteristics (community poverty, residential instability, and proportion of minorities in the community) still had an impact on marital happiness. The model indicates that community poverty has an additive negative effect on marital happiness ($\beta = -0.94$, $t = -1.95$). The bivariate (multilevel model) association between community poverty and marital happiness was significant ($\beta = -0.86$, $t = -2.50$). Residential instability has a significant negative effect on marital happiness, meaning that the more transient (or unstable) residents are in the community, the less satisfied wives are with their marriages ($\beta = -2.87$, $t = -2.56$). Residents in more stable communities enjoy higher levels of marital happiness than do residents in unstable communities. The percentage of minorities residing in the community has a beneficial effect on the marital happiness of the African Americans under study. Higher percentages of minorities in the community were associated with greater marital happiness (3.33, $t = 2.15$). Although community poverty is highly correlated with the percentage of minorities in the community ($r = .52$), those two structural characteristics have the exact *opposite* effect on African American marriages when these characteristics are examined together. Whereas community poverty has a *negative* effect on African American marriages, living in an environment where there are more minorities has a *positive* effect on the marital happiness of African Americans. More important, the interaction between residential instability and the percentage of minorities in the community was significant ($\beta = 4.50$, $t = 2.00$), suggesting that the detrimental influence of residential instability is moderated (reduced) by the high percentage of minorities in the community. These results suggest that the higher percentage of minorities in the community positively contributes to marital happiness both through its additive as well as its moderating influences. The reduction in the second-level variance from .15 in the null model to .12 in Model 1 shows that these structural community characteristics and control variables accounted for 20% of the between-community variance of marital happiness.

Model 2 adds perceived community adversity in order to determine whether perceptions of adversity in the community mediate the relationship between the structural community characteristics (community poverty, residential instability, percentage of minorities) and marital happiness. Perceived community adversity had a negative effect on marital happiness. However, results suggest that perceived community adversity operates as an independent contributor to marital happiness. Influences of structural community characteristics remained the same even after the addition of perceived community adversity.

Model 3 adds both perceived community adversity and two community social support variables. Thus, both informal and formal community social support variables are in the model. They were included in order to determine whether the social constructs—informal community social support and formal social integration—mediate the relationship between perceived community adversity and marital happiness. Of the community social support variables, only informal community support had a significant positive influence on the marital happiness of African Americans ($\beta = 0.13$, $t = 3.04$). Formal social integration had no significant effect on marital happiness ($\beta = 0.03$, $t = 0.11$). It seems that, for African Americans, informal community support partially mediates the influence of structural community characteristics on marital happiness. In particular, the additive and multiplicative influences of the percentage of minorities in the community on marital happiness were partially mediated by informal community support.

Table 6.1 also includes a fit index, Akaike's information criteria (AIC). The smaller the index's value, the better the model fit. The AIC index decreases substantially from Model 1 to Model 3. This suggests

TABLE 6.1. Predicting Marital Happiness: Random Intercept Models—Unstandardized Regression Coefficients

Independent variables	M1	M2	M3
Structural community characteristics			
Community poverty	-0.94 (-1.95)**	-0.88 (-1.80)*	-0.85 (-1.84)*
Residential instability	-2.87 (-2.56)**	-2.77 (-2.45)**	-2.27 (-2.02)**
Percentage of minorities	3.33 (2.15)**	3.29 (2.21)**	2.52 (1.67)
Residential instability × percentage of minorities	4.50 (2.00)**	4.46 (2.04)**	3.48 (1.58)
Experiences with and perceptions of community environment			
Perceived community adversity		-0.09 (-2.41)***	-0.12 (-2.84)***
Informal community social support			0.13 (3.04)***
Formal social integration			0.03 (0.11)
Family characteristics: Controls			
Length of marriage	0.01 (0.79)	0.00 (0.28)	0.01 (0.78)
Family income	0.00 (0.19)	0.00 (0.05)**	-0.00 (-0.36)
Wife education	0.00 (0.19)	0.00 (0.05)**	-0.00 (-0.36)
Wife employment status	0.20 (2.07)**	0.16 (1.60)	.12 (1.17)
Length of residence	0.00 (0.48)	0.00 (-0.08)	.00 (-0.06)
Intercept	6.06	7.44	8.00
AIC	7767	7393	7176
First-level variance	1.90	1.85	1.80
Second-level variance	0.12	0.13	0.09

*$p < .10$; **$p < .05$; ***$p < .01$; t-values in parentheses.

that more elaborate models with additional parameters fit better than the corresponding reduced model (Little, Milliken, Stroup, & Wolfinger, 1996).

TYING TOGETHER OUR IDEAS AND THE PRELIMINARY TEST OF THOSE IDEAS

This study is not without limitations. First, analyses were based largely on cross-sectional data (except for 1990 census data). Thus, issues regarding causality cannot be fully addressed. Second, our measure of informal community support may not be specific enough to capture the informal support of married couples. Similarly, our measure of perceived community adversity may not be specific enough. Third, school catchment areas were used as communities in our analyses. Fourth, the sample of African Americans may not be nationally representative. This is because the initial sampling procedure of Add Health focused on adolescents; thus, the sample included those who had a child attending grades 7 through 12. Despite these limitations, this study yielded important findings.

For example, the effects of community poverty and residential instability on marital happiness are consistent with previous research. They have a harmful effect on marriage. Although the influence of community poverty is marginal, it seems that residential instability has a strong, robust direct effect on the marital happiness of African American wives, even after controlling for length of residence, length of marriage, family income, and wives' education and employment status. That is, these deleterious structural processes in communities harm residents regardless of their individual/family factors. It seems that structural constraints in poor and unstable communities limit or hinder marital/family activities, thus contributing to marital distress.

In contrast to community poverty and residential instability, the other structural community characteristic—the higher presence of minorities in the community—has a direct beneficial effect on the marital happiness of African Americans. This is *not* consistent with the community disorganization perspective that suggests that ethnic segregation is not only closely associated with community poverty and residential instability, but that it also produces deleterious effects on residents' lives. Previous research focusing on community context fails to reveal the beneficial effect of the presence of minorities in communities. This shortcoming may be attributed to the fact that most community studies used neither race-specific samples nor interaction terms involving race when the influences of community characteristics on the well-being of residents were examined. For example, the beneficial influence of the presence of minorities is completely lost when models are run using the entire sample (Whites, African Americans, Hispanics, etc., together) in the Add Health data set. Thus, this study demonstrates the importance and value of exploring the effect of community context on specific racial/ethnic groups. It also calls into question the implementation of broad, sweeping policies meant to cover and solve the ills of all groups. Various groups may be affected differently by structural community characteristics and experiences in and perceptions of community characteristics. Social policies must be sensitive to the different effects community factors have on various racial/ethnic groups.

The interaction term (residential instability × percentage of minorities in the community) also yielded significant results suggesting that the increase in the percentage of minorities moderates (reduces) the detrimental influence of residential instability. (Alternatively, the detrimental influence of residential instability is stronger in communities with fewer minorities). It seems that ethnic and racial diversity may buffer the deleterious influence of residential instability. However, we did not find such a buffering or protective effect (an interaction) in relation to community poverty.

It appears that ethnic diversity—operationalized as greater percentages of non-Whites in the community—plays a significant role in determining the degree of happiness in African American marriages. The direct beneficial influence of the presence of greater numbers of minorities may be attributed to the enhanced social status of African Americans in the community. Perhaps in communities where more minorities are present, African Americans live in relatively supportive and empowered social environments, despite community impoverishment (Korbin, 2001). Thus, African Americans living among other African Americans or among other minorities tend to have greater positive feelings, which may, in turn, contribute to their marital relationships. In those communities with low percentages of minorities, minority status may itself be stressful and may contribute to psychological distress (Meyer, 1995), which would, in turn, contribute to adverse marital relationships.

We expected the higher percentage of minorities in the community to exert a positive influence on African American marriages through *informal community support*, because the presence of other minorities may promote informal community social resources such as collective socialization and intergenerational closure (Coleman, 1988). The results support this hypothesis. Informal community social support partially mediates both the additive and multiplicative influences of the higher percentage of minorities on the marital happiness of African American wives. This may be attributed to the fact that the beneficial influence of minority concentration on African American marriages is confounded with the beneficial influence of informal community support on those marriages. However, contrary to our expectations, community social support variables do not mediate the influence of community poverty and residential instability on African American marriages. This may be attributed to the fact that our community social support variables do not adequately capture the degree to which African American wives experience community support.

Although previous research using samples of multiple racial/ethnic groups suggests that formal social integration has a beneficial effect on the well-being of residents, our results showed that this effect may not be as important for African American wives. We attempted to capture the degree of formal social integration using membership in clubs, voluntary organizations, and unions. The absence of the influence of membership in formal social organizations may be attributed to several factors. First, African Americans may not have the opportunity to participate in formal social institutions at a level that may influence their lives, because such institutions may be rare in the communities in which they live. Second, their participation in such institutions may not be encouraged or supported. Third, they may be members of formal social institutions, but are not active/key participants. Given that formal social integration has a beneficial effect on the well-being of other racial/ethnic groups, policymakers should identify ways of increasing the participation of African Americans in *formal* community social support programs. A key question that policymakers must address relates to identifying roadblocks—perceived or real—for African Americans that hinder their participation in these more formal social institutions.

We also hypothesized that perceiving community adversity may influence the marital happiness of African Americans. Interestingly, contrary to expectations, perceived community adversity does not mediate the influence of structural community adversities; instead, it exerts a unique independent influence on the marital happiness of African Americans. That is, in addition to structural constraints imposed by community poverty and residential instability, community socioeconomic adversity generates feelings of distress through day-to-day experiences of community hazards, social disorder, and the physical decay of the surroundings (Ross et al., 2000). Feelings of distress compromise marital quality (Conger et al., 1990; Matthews et al., 1996). The unique influences of individual-level perceptions of and experiences in communities on the marital happiness of African Americans again highlight the need for further race-specific studies as well as the need for theoretical explanations that account for factors that may be uniquely associated with specific racial groups. This raises a possible controversial issue, in that it suggests that the policies promoting well-being may need to be race-specific.

The significant role played by the percentage of minorities in the community on the marital happiness of African Americans has serious implications. If, in an attempt to help economically disadvantaged couples, we relocate them—in other words, move them—into predominantly White communities, which are typically more economically advantaged, they will lose the benefit of residing in more diverse neighborhoods. Researchers and politicians tend to talk about community poverty and the percentage of minorities present as though these two constructs are similar or even interchangeable. They do correlate highly, but they have the exact opposite effects on the marital happiness of African Americans. This is not to suggest segregation. In fact, it suggests just the opposite. We use the percentage of minorities in the community as a proxy for diversity, although not an exact one. It is meant to underscore the positive influence of the presence of various racial/ethnic groups.

Much of the work focusing on community context fails to reveal the beneficial effect of the presence of minorities. It seems that some of the community influences are obscured when various racial/ethnic groups are analyzed together rather than separately. This has serious theoretical, research, and policy implications. Future research should focus on race-specific samples when examining the influence of community characteristics on the lives of different ethnic/racial groups. Variables that may be uniquely associated with a particular racial or ethnic group under study should be identified and used in analyses. For example, perhaps variables associated with immigration or racial identity should be included for some groups under study. In a similar vein, it may not be appropriate to use generalized community models to study the lives of specific ethnic/ racial groups. Likewise, as mentioned earlier, it may not be appropriate or effective to use *generalized* policies in an attempt to implement positive change in the lives of *specific* ethnic/racial groups.

This study underscores the importance of considering community context. There does, indeed, appear to be a link between community characteristics and marital happiness. One possible mechanism explaining this link is that marriages formed in communities that are economically distressed, unstable, or disorganized are relatively unhappy when they begin. It might be particularly difficult to find a well-matched or desirable spouse under such environmental conditions.

In our efforts to create the optimal organism–environment fit—or in this case, the optimal community–spouse fit—we cannot ignore race/ ethnicity. This means that we cannot assume that contextual factors such as community characteristics, perceived or real, have the same effect across racial/ethnic lines, because they *don't*. Our preliminary findings made that quite clear. By focusing on one racial/ethnic group, we were able to illustrate the impact of community context variables; the effects of some of these variables are lost when all racial/ethnic groups are analyzed together. Groups differ across racial lines. Has it become so politically incorrect to point this out that we would ignore it to the detriment of the groups most in need of attention by researchers and policymakers? Why waste money on more broad-based policies, such as those aimed at increasing the number of married couples? Such increases may be only temporary, because other factors (e.g., community context) are working against the success of those relationships. Instead of stepping *outside* the box, as we are so often challenged to do in developing solu-

COMMUNITY CONTEXTS

tions to social problems, we propose that policymakers step *inside* the box. In other words, step *inside* the communities in which these families or spouses live. Only by immersing ourselves in the social context of a particular group will we be able to adequately identify factors that have the greatest impact on their marital happiness. It is okay to be different. Let's acknowledge our differences and create policies sensitive to those differences. We know that African Americans are more likely to experience marital dissolution than any other racial/ethnic group (Benokraitis, 2002; Kposowa, 1998; Saluter, 1994; White, 1991). Let's determine why this disparity exists and create group-specific policies aimed at correcting a problem that has dire emotional and financial consequences.

ACKNOWLEDGMENTS

This research is based on data from the Adolescent Health Project, a project designed by J. Richard Udry (Principal Investigator) and Peter Bearman and funded by Grant No. P01-HD31921 from the National Institute of Child Health and Human Development to the Carolina Population Center, University of North Carolina at Chapel Hill, with cooperative funding participation by the National Cancer Institute; the National Institute of Alcohol Abuse and Alcoholism; the National Institute on Deafness and Other Communication Disorders; the National Institute on Drug Abuse; the National Institute of General Medical Sciences; the National Institute of Mental Health; the National Institute of Nursing Research; the Office of AIDS Research, National Institutes of Health (NIH); the Office of Behavior and Social Science Research, NIH; the Office of the Director, NIH; the Office of Research on Women's Health, NIH; the Office of Population Affairs, Department of Health and Human Services (DHHS); the National Center for Health Statistics, Centers for Disease Control and Prevention, DHHS; the Office of Minority Health, Centers for Disease Control and Prevention, DHHS; the Office of Minority Health, Office of Public Health and Science, DHHS; the Office of the Assistant Secretary for Planning and Evaluation, DHHS; and the National Science Foundation. Persons interested in obtaining data files from the National Longitudinal Study of Adolescent Health should contact Add Health Project, Carolina Population Center, 123 West Franklin Street, Chapel Hill, NC 27516-3997 (e-mail: addhealth@unc.edu).

REFERENCES

Anderson, F. (1991). *Streetwise, race, class and change in an urban community.* Chicago: University of Chicago Press.

Benokraitis, N. V. (2002). *Marriages and families: Changes, choices, and constraints.* Upper Saddle River, NJ: Pearson Education.

Boardman, J., Finch, B., Ellison, C., Williams, D., & Jackson, J. (2001). Neighborhood disadvantage, stress, and drug use among adults. *Journal of Health and Social Behavior, 42*, 151–165.

Bronfenbrenner, U. (1986). Ecology of the family as a context for human development: Research perspectives. *Developmental Psychology, 22*, 723–742.

Brooks-Gunn, J., Duncan, G. J., Klebanov, P. K., & Sealand, N. (1993). Do neighborhoods influence child and adolescent development? *American Journal of Sociology, 99*, 353–395.

Brown, D. R. (1996). Marital status and mental health. In H. W. Neighbors & J. S. Jackson (Eds.), *Mental health in black America* (pp. 77–94). Thousand Oaks, CA: Sage.

Brown, N. T. (2003). Critical race theory speaks to the sociology of mental health: Mental health problems produced by racial stratification. *Journal of Health and Social Behavior, 44*, 292–301.

Bryk, A., & Raudenbush, S. (1992). *Hierarchical linear models: Applications and data analysis methods.*. Newbury Park, CA: Sage.

Burgess, N. (1994). Determinants of social psychological well-being: The impact of race and employment status on married women in the United States. In R. Staples (Ed.), *The Black family*. Belmont, CA: Wadsworth.

Coleman, J. S. (1988). Social capital in the creation of human capital. *American Journal of Sociology, 94*(Suppl.), 95–120.

Conger, R. D., & Elder, G. H., Jr. (1994). *Families in troubled times: Adapting to change in rural America*. New York: Aldine de Gruyter.

Conger, R. D., Elder, G. H., Jr., Lorenz, F. O., Conger, K., Simons, R., Whitbeck, L., et al. (1990). Linking economic hardship to marital quality and instability. *Journal of Marriage and the Family, 52*, 643–656.

Conger, R. D., Rueter, M. A., & Elder, G. H., Jr. (1999). Couple resilience to economic pressure. *Journal of Personality and Social Psychology, 76*, 54–71.

Cutrona, C. E., Russell, D. W., Hessling, R. M., Brown, P. A., & Murry, V. (2000). Direct and moderating effects of community context on the psychological well-being of African American women. *Journal of Personality and Social Psychology, 79*, 1099, 1101.

Demo, D., Small, S., & Savin-Williams, R. (1987). Family relations and the self-esteem of adolescents and their parents. *Journal of Marriage and the Family, 49*, 705–715.

Ellen, I. G., & Turner, M. A. (1997). Does neighborhood matter? Assessing recent evidence. *Housing Policy Debate, 8*(4), 833–866.

Elliot, D. S., William, J. W., Huizinga, D., Sampson, R. J., Elliot, A., & Rankin, B. (1996). Effects of neighborhood disadvantage on adolescent development. *Journal of Research in Crime and Delinquency, 33*, 389–426.

Emerson, M., Yancey, G., & Chai, K. (2001). Does race matter in residential segregation? Exploring the preferences of white Americans. *American Sociological Review, 66*, 922–935.

Fernandez-Kelly, P. (1994). Towanda's triumph: Social and cultural capital in the transition to adulthood in the urban ghetto. *International Journal of Urban and Regional Research, 18*(1), 88–111.

Goodman, E. (1999). The role of socioeconomic status gradients in explaining differences in U.S. adolescents' health. *American Journal of Public Health, 89*(10), 1522–1528.

House, J., Landis, K., & Umberson, D. (1988). Social relationships and health. *Science, 241,* 540–545.

Kiecolt, K. J., & Fossett, M. (1995). Mate availability and marriage among African Americans: Aggregate and individual-level analyses. In M. B. Tucker & C. Mitchell-Kernan (Eds.), *The decline in marriage among African Americans* (pp. 121–135). New York: Russell Sage Foundation.

Korbin, J. E. (2001). Context and meaning in neighborhood studies of children and families. In A. Booth & A. C. Crouter (Eds.), *Does it take a village? Community effects on children, adolescents and families* (pp. 87–94). Mahwah, NJ: Erlbaum.

Kposowa, A. J. (1998, Fall). The impact of race on divorce in the United States. *Journal of Comparative Family Issues, 29,* 529–548.

Latkin, C. A., & Curry, A. (2003). Stressful neighborhoods and depression: A prospective study of the impact of neighborhood disorder. *Journal of Health and Social Behavior, 44,* 34–44.

LaVeist, T. A. (2002). Segregation, poverty, and empowerment: Health consequences of African Americans. In T. A. LaVeist (Ed.), *Race, ethnicity, and health: A public health reader* (pp. 76–96). San Francisco: Jossey-Bass.

Leventhal, T., & Brooks-Gunn, J. (2000). The neighborhoods they live in: The effects of neighborhood residence on child adolescent outcomes. *Psychological Bulletin, 126,* 309–337.

Little, R. C., Milliken, G. A., Stroup, W. W., & Wolfinger, R. D. (1996). *SAS System for mixed models.* Cary, NC: SAS Institute.

Massey, D. S., & Denton, N. A. (1993). *American apartheid: Segregation and the making of the underclass.* Cambridge, MA: Harvard University Press.

Matthews, L., Wickrama, K. A. S., & Conger, R. D. (1996). Predicting marital instability from spouse and observer reports of marital interactions. *Journal of Marriage and the Family, 58,* 641–655.

Meyer, I. (1995). Minority stress and mental health in gay men. *Journal of Health and Social Behavior, 36,* 38–56.

National Center for Health Statistics. (1998). *Health, United States, 1998, with socioeconomic status and health chartbook.* Hyattsville, MD: Public Health Service, U.S. Department of Health and Human Services.

Ross, C. E., Mirowsky, J., & Pribesh, S. (2001). Powerlessness and the amplification of threat: Neighborhood disadvantage, disorder, and mistrust. *American Sociological Review, 66,* 568–591.

Ross, C. E., Reynolds, J., & Geis, K. (2000). The contingent meaning of neighborhood stability for residents' psychological well-being. *American Sociological Review, 65,* 581–597.

Saluter, A. F. (1994). Marital status and living arrangements: March 1993 (*Current Population Reports,* Series P20-478). Washington, DC: U.S. Government Printing Office.

Sampson, R. J. (2001). How do communities undergird or undermine human development? Relevant contexts and social mechanisms. In A. Booth & A. C. Crouter (Eds.), *Does it take a village? Community effects on children, adolescents, and families* (pp. 2–30). Mahwah, NJ: Erlbaum.

Sampson, R. J., & Groves, W. B. (1989). Community structure and crime: Testing social disorganization theory. *American Journal of Sociology, 94,* 776–802.

Sampson, R. J., Squires, G. D., & Zhou, M. (2002). *How neighborhoods matter: The value of investing at the local level.* Washington, DC: American Sociological Association.

Shaw, C. R., & McKay, H. D. (1942). *Juvenile delinquency and urban areas.* Chicago: University of Chicago Press.

Simon, R., & Marcussen, K. (1999). Marital transitions, marital beliefs, and mental health. *Journal of Health and Social Behavior, 40,* 111–125.

Smith, T. W. (2000). *Taking America's Pulse II: A survey of intergroup relations.* Chicago: University of Chicago, The National Conference for Community and Justice, National Opinion Research Center.

South, S. J. (2001). The geographic context of divorce: Do neighborhoods matter? *Journal of Marriage and Family, 63,* 755–766.

South, S. J., & Crowder, K. (1997). Escaping distressed neighborhoods: Individual, community, and metropolitan influences. *American Journal of Sociology, 102,* 1040–1084.

South, S. J., & Crowder, K. D. (1999). Neighborhood effects on family formation: Concentrated poverty. *American Sociological Review, 64,* 113–132.

Sucoff, C. A., & Upchurch, D. M. (1998). Neighborhood context and the risk of childbearing among metropolitan-area Black adolescents. *American Sociological Review, 63,* 571–585.

Taylor, P., Tucker, M. B., & Mitchell-Kernan, C. (1999). Ethnic variations in perceptions of men's provider role. *Psychology of Women Quarterly, 23,* 741–761.

Taylor, R. J., Jackson, J.S., & Chatters, L. M. (Eds.). (1997). *Family life in black America.* Thousand Oaks, CA: Sage.

Trent, K., & South, S. J. (2003). Spousal alternatives and marital relations. *Journal of Family Issues, 24,* 787–810.

Welch, S., Sigelman, L., Bledsoe, T., & Combs, M. (2001). *Race and place: Race relations in an American city.* New York: Cambridge University Press.

White, L. K. (1991). Determinants of divorce. In A. Booth (Ed.), *Comparative families: Looking forward, looking back* (pp. 150–161). Minneapolis, MN: National Council on Family Relations.

Wickrama, K. A. S., & Bryant, C. M. (2003). Community context of social resources and adolescent mental health. *Journal of Marriage and Family, 65,* 850–866.

Wickrama, K. A. S., Lorenz, F. O., Conger, R. D., & Elder, G. H., Jr. (1997). Marital quality and physical illness: A latent growth curve analysis. *Journal of Marriage and the Family. 59,* 143–155.

Wickrama, K. A. S., Noh, S., & Bryant, C. (2005). Racial differences in adolescent distress: Differential effects of the family and community for blacks and whites. *Journal of Community Psychology, 33,* 261–282.

Williams, D., Yu, Y., Jackson, J., & Anderson, N. (1997). Racial differences in physical and mental health: Socioeconomic status, stress, and discrimination. *Journal of Health Psychology, 2*, 335–351.

Wilson, W. J. (1987). *The truly disadvantaged*. Chicago: University of Chicago Press.

Wilson, W. J. (1991). Studying inner-city social dislocations: The challenge of public agenda research. *American Sociological Review, 56*, 1–14.

CHAPTER 7

Work and African American Family Life

Vonnie C. McLoyd
and Noemí Enchautegui-de-Jesús

Questions about linkages between work and African American family life have commanded little scholarly attention since the late 1970s and early 1980s, a period that witnessed a burgeoning of research on this topic (McLoyd, 1993). This trend is perplexing, given the recent growth in research studies on the family lives of African Americans generally (Burton & Jarrett, 2000; McLoyd, Cauce, Takeuchi, & Wilson, 2000; Taylor, Jackson, & Chatters, 1997), the continued prominence of paid employment in the lives of African American women, and the large share of time that work consumes relative to other activities. Enriching our understanding of how employment-related issues influence core aspects of African American family functioning requires a reinvigoration of this area of study. Along with theory-guided, basic research on this topic, there is a pressing need for careful explication of the implications of research findings for practice and policy, and for systematic research assessing how social policies influence the work–family nexus. Efforts to promote the well-being of African American families deserve the benefit of knowledge generated by social science. This is an especially opportune time to undertake such research because of the unprecedented wealth of data sets from nationally representative samples available for secondary data analyses—many of which are longitudinal and include an oversampling of African Americans—and because of recent advances in statistical procedures for analyzing family-level and longitudinal data.

It is in the spirit of reinvigoration that this chapter sets forth research questions and policy issues pertinent to the interface between work and African American family life. As backdrop to this discussion, we assemble a statistical portrait of the employment status and work life of African Americans relative to their European American counterparts. Drawing on research literatures in sociology and psychology, we explore the implications of these factors for within- and between-race differences in family and marital functioning, parenting, and children's development and identify important gaps in our knowledge base. Finally, we discuss policy issues in light of knowledge about the employment status and work life of African Americans, identifying policies that can be expected to enhance indirectly the stability, cohesion, and well-being of African American families by improving employment conditions and circumstances.

The chapter is organized around four themes that capture the essential ways in which the employment status and work lives of African Americans differ from those of their European American counterparts: (1) higher labor force participation among African American women and mothers; (2) increased difficulty in finding and maintaining employment among African Americans; (3) less favorable employment conditions, circumstances, and experiences (i.e., longer work hours, increased likelihood of working nonstandard hours, decreased likelihood of having a flexible work schedule and other family-friendly employee benefits, lower wages) among African Americans; and (4) prejudice and discrimination against African Americans. As we discuss in more detail later, many of these differences are stubborn legacies of institutionalized racism in education, employment, and housing. America's racial caste system, legalized until the mid-1960s, has weakened under the weight of social protest, legal remedies, and changing attitudes, but its economic and social vestiges are evident still (Jargowsky, 1994; Jaynes & Williams, 1989; Oliver & Shapiro, 1995).

HIGHER LABOR FORCE PARTICIPATION AMONG AFRICAN AMERICAN WOMEN AND MOTHERS

In concert with the increasing prevalence of maternal employment in contemporary mainstream America over the past three decades or so, questions about the effects of maternal employment as compared with nonemployment have gradually given way to questions about the impact of employment *conditions* and *circumstances*. The latter issues are the primary foci of this chapter, but we begin with a discussion of racial disparities in rates of women's and mothers' employment to provide context for our examination of employment conditions and policy issues.

In his classic book, *The Strengths of Black Families*, sociologist Robert Hill (1971) identified a strong work orientation as one of the key factors responsible for the survival, stability, and advancement of African American families. There is no shortage of evidence that this orientation continues, coexisting as it always has alongside structural disadvantages in the labor market for both African American women and men. African American women have long had the highest rates of labor force participation among women in the United States and have been considerably more likely than European American women to work steadily most of their adult lives (Flippen & Tienda, 1999).

However, the pattern of racial disparity varies by maternal status. In 2004, rates of employment among women ages 16 and over *with no minor children* were higher among European Americans than African Americans (51.3% versus 48.3%, respectively), regardless of marital status (Bureau of Labor Statistics, 2005). The reverse pattern is seen among women with children. The largest racial differential continues to be among married women with preschool children. In 2004, the employment rate for African American wives with children under 3 years old was 66.9%, as compared with 51.9% for their European American counterparts. However, among wives with children 6 to 17 years old (none younger), the rates for the two groups were far less discrepant (76.8% vs. 72.8%, respectively) (Bureau of Labor Statistics, 2005). These patterns reflect the tendency of African American married mothers to work continuously, regardless of the presence of preschool children, in contrast to the tendency of a substantial proportion of European American mothers to withdraw from the labor force when they have preschool children and return to the labor force when the youngest child enters school or when the children are older.

Research conducted during the 1970s and 1980s identified several factors that account for the comparatively high rate of labor force participation among African American mothers, among them, greater economic need, increased exposure to a working mother during childhood, direct socialization during childhood that emphasizes the value of being an economic provider, and normative approval of maternal employment (McLoyd, 1993). These factors instantiate the strong work orientation that Hill (1971) observed.

Because rates of employment are higher overall among African American mothers than among mothers from other racial/ethnic groups, African American children are more likely than other children to live with parents who are employed. In 2001, 75% of African American children had resident parents who were employed, as compared with 68% of European American and 59% of Latina/o children. The late 1990s witnessed a marked increase in the percentage of African American children under age 6 with employed parents (between 1996 and 2001 the percentage increased from 58% to 72%, as compared with increases from 58% to 61% and from 43% to 53% for European American and Hispanic children, respectively). Virtually all of this increase occurred among children living in single-mother families (Office of the Assistant Secretary for Planning and Evaluation, 2002).

Increases in employment among single mothers during the late 1990s have been linked to (1) the booming economy of the late 1990s, which allowed low-income single mothers to enter jobs that had been added to the economy, mostly in retail trade and services; (2) welfare reform policies (the cornerstone of which is Temporary Assistance for Needy Families, TANF) that mandated an increase in paid work effort from welfare recipients; and (3) expansions in the Earned Income Tax Credit, a provision intended to offset the burden of Social Security payroll taxes, supplement low-wage earnings, and promote work as a viable alternative to welfare (Chapman & Bernstein, 2003; Winkler, 2002). As the U.S. economy took a downturn in 2001, a sharp decrease occurred in the number of jobs in the sectors that had previously employed low-income single mothers, precipitating higher unemployment rates in this group. In 2002, the average unemployment rate of low-income single mothers was 12.3%, an increase from 9.8% in 2000 (Chapman & Bernstein, 2003).

Given African American mothers' relatively high rates of employment, policies that affect employees' labor conditions have the potential to affect African American families with children disproportionately (e.g., policies affecting availability and affordability of quality daycare, government subsidies and tax credits, and other supports to balance paid work and family responsibilities; Winkler, 2002). Likewise, as recent changes in maternal employment rates precipitated by welfare reform illustrate, employment-related policies directed at single-mother families will affect African American families disproportionately owing to the larger representation of single mothers among African Americans. In 2000, 63% of all African American families were headed by single parents (90% of whom were mothers) and more than half (58%) of all African American children lived with one parent (Cantave & Harrison, 2001).

INCREASED DIFFICULTY FINDING AND MAINTAINING EMPLOYMENT

Over the last two decades, employment rates increased among African American women ages 16 and over (from 53.1% to 62.9%), but decreased among African American men (from 70.3% to 68.5%) (U.S.

Bureau of the Census, 2002). Throughout the lifespan, African American men have the lowest labor force participation rates of men from different racial/ethnic groups in the United States (Flippen & Tienda, 1999). African American women have been a majority of the African American labor force since 1990, with even larger differences evident since 1996. By 1998, they were 53.4% of the Black labor force, whereas European American women made up 46.5% of the White labor force (Cantave & Harrison, 1999).

Underemployment is a disadvantage distinctive to African American men, but African American men and women alike contend with comparatively high rates of unemployment. In 2003, African American men and women 20 years and over had unemployment rates of 10.3% and 9.2%, respectively, as compared with 5% and 4.4% among their European American counterparts, respectively. Racial disparities also exist in the duration of unemployment. In 2003, the average duration of unemployment among African American men and women 16 years and over was 24.2 and 21.2 weeks, respectively, as compared with 18.5 and 17.3 weeks among European American men and women, respectively (Bureau of Labor Statistics, 2004).

A partial explanation for racial disparities in employment concerns the residential location of African Americans in relation to the location of jobs—an explanation labeled "the spatial mismatch hypothesis" (Kain, 1992). The proportion of African Americans living in cities far surpasses that of European Americans. In 2002 the proportion of African Americans living inside the central city in metropolitan areas was twice that of European Americans (51.5% vs. 21.1%). Most European Americans (56.8%) lived in suburbs (outside the central city of metropolitan areas), whereas only a minority of African Americans did (36%) (McKinnon, 2003). Suburban residents enjoy higher rates of employment than city residents regardless of their educational attainment, with the most pronounced disparities by location appearing among African Americans (Bureau of Labor Statistics, 1998). In 1997 the labor force participation rate of African Americans living in cities versus suburbs was 60.2% versus 73.3%, respectively, contrasting with a much smaller gap among European Americans (66.2% vs. 69.8%, respectively) (Bureau of Labor Statistics, 1998). It is noteworthy that these figures indicate that the overall employment rate in suburbs is higher for African Americans than European Americans. The problems of residential segregation and industry suburbanization are compounded by unavailability of public and private transportation resources to access job opportunities in suburban locations (McLafferty & Preston, 1996; Raphael & Stoll, 2000). Even African Americans living in suburbs are disadvantaged by their mode of transportation to work. For instance, African American women in the suburbs of the New York metropolitan region have longer commutes than European American suburban women because they rely more on mass transit (McLafferty & Preston, 1996).

The sparse research published since the 1980s on the interface between work and African American family life focuses primarily on the processes by which financial strain affects marital relations and parenting (Brody, Stoneman, & Flor, 1995; Clark-Nicolas & Gray-Little, 1991; Conger et al., 2002; Elder, Eccles, Ardelt, & Lord, 1995; Gomel, Tinsley, Parke, & Clark, 1998; Gutman & Eccles, 1999; Jackson, Brooks-Gunn, Huang, & Glassman, 2000; Lawson & Thompson, 1995; McLoyd, Jayaratne, Ceballo, & Borquez, 1994). In general, these studies have found that financial strain predicts increased psychological distress in parents (e.g., depression, hostility) that, in turn, fosters marital or partner discord and less nurturant and involved parenting. The findings are consonant with other work indicating that the economic marginalization of African American men is a major source of conflict in heterosexual relations (Dixon, 1998). In keeping with Elder's (1974) research with European American families of the Great Depression, the studies report few direct effects of economic hardship on children's functioning. Rather, economic hardship increases internalizing and externalizing symptoms in children indirectly through its negative effects on parents' psychological functioning, marital relations, and parenting behavior. The family processes that link economic hardship to child functioning appear to operate similarly for African American and European American families (Conger et al., 2002; Gutman & Eccles, 1999; Jackson et al., 2000; Taylor, Rodriguez, Seaton, & Dominguez, 2004). What is now needed is a better understanding of factors that attenuate these mediational processes and encourage more positive marital functioning, parenting, and child functioning in the face of economic stress (Chadiha, 1992).

LESS FAVORABLE EMPLOYMENT CONDITIONS, CIRCUMSTANCES, AND EXPERIENCES

The range of employment factors that have important implications for family life extends well beyond low wages, job loss, underemployment, unemployment, and other precipitants of economic stress. Indeed, the venerable body of research on the interplay between employment and family relations has shifted its primary attention from employment status to employment conditions and experiences. However, virtually none of this work has focused on African American families qua African

American families. In studies based on racially diverse samples, researchers have typically cast race as a control variable—a practice that may be
dictated partly by small sample sizes. Redress of this neglect is essential
if the circumstances, needs, and pressures experienced by African American families are to be reflected in discussions of employment and workplace policies.

Future research might proceed along two tracks—one track documenting the extent to which work conditions account for variation
within African American families and the other track clarifying a range
of issues concerned with race differences (e.g., whether African Americans and European Americans respond to work conditions similarly,
whether mediating and moderating processes are similar, the extent to
which differences in work conditions account for race differences in
marital, parental, and child functioning). In the sections that follow, we
consider the status of African Americans with respect to selected employment conditions and work experiences, briefly discuss key findings
from studies (based primarily on European American samples) linking
these conditions/experiences to marital relations, parenting behavior,
and child functioning, and consider their implications for African American family life and social policy.

Number of Hours

African American mothers of children under 18 years of age are more
likely to be employed full time and less likely to be employed part time
than mothers from other racial/ethnic groups. In 2001, 63% of African
American mothers were employed full time, as compared with 50% of
European American mothers and 47% of Latina mothers (Office of the
Assistant Secretary for Planning and Evaluation, 2002). Full-time maternal employment, as compared with part-time maternal employment, has
been associated with less positive outcomes for children. Studies based
on economically and ethnically diverse families (where race is typically a
control variable) indicate that net of maternal background factors and
other work characteristics (e.g., hourly wage), children whose mothers
work part time (20–34 hours/week) have greater verbal facility than
children whose mothers work full time, who in turn, have better verbal
skills than children whose mothers routinely work overtime (Parcel &
Menaghan, 1990, 1994). Mothers' work hours appear to have no main
effect on children's behavior problems, but the combination of overtime
hours and having a job high in routinization and low in autonomy has
been found to exacerbate children's behavior problems (Parcel & Menaghan, 1990, 1994). Parental work that routinely exceeds 40 hours/
week may hinder children's cognitive, social, and physical well-being by

diminishing the quality of parenting and constraining parents' social capital and involvement with their children.

We do not know, on the basis of the available research, whether full-time maternal employment, as compared with part-time employment, is linked to less positive outcomes in African American children (studies of the effects of maternal employment in African American families typically ignore variation in number of hours employed as a predictor), but there are cultural factors that may mitigate against such an effect. Research conducted during the 1980s suggested that African Americans, as compared with their European American counterparts, were more likely to view maternal employment favorably and as compatible with maternal and marital roles. In addition, African American women reported higher levels of confidence in their ability to fulfill these roles simultaneously and successfully and were less likely to anticipate feeling guilty about working (see McLoyd, 1993, for a discussion of these studies). Consequently, African American mothers who work full time may demand higher levels of maturity and responsibility of their children and experience more success in their efforts to secure instrumental and parenting supports to balance employment demands. If these factors distinguish African Americans from European Americans in the contemporary context, they may lessen the probability that full-time employment or even overtime hours will be associated with less positive outcomes for African American children.

However, this hypothesized effect may be conditional on household structure, with the risks of deleterious effects of full-time employment and overtime hours being greater for children in female-headed households because parental and domestic responsibilities fall to one, rather than two adults. The question of whether the effects of maternal work hours on the functioning of African American children depend on household structure is highly pertinent and deserves study, given the high proportion of African American children who live in female-headed households (in 2002, 48% of African American children were living with a single mother) (Fields, 2003).

Work Schedule

People who work nonstandard hours tend to have less education than those who work 9:00 to 5:00, Monday through Friday. African Americans are more likely than European Americans to work night, evening, and variable shifts—a disparity that has existed for decades. In 2001, for example, 12% of African Americans worked evening and night shifts, as compared with 7% of European Americans. A total of 20% of full-time wage and salary African American workers were on shift schedules (evening, night, rotating, split, irregular), as compared with 13.6% of European American workers (U.S. Bureau of the Census, 2002).

These disparities are associated with race differences in education as well as family structure. Never married mothers, more prevalent among African Americans than among European Americans, are more likely than married or divorced mothers to work nonstandard hours because they have lower levels of education, lack alternative employment opportunities, and are disproportionately represented in jobs that demand these work hours. Remarkably, their employment schedules, unlike those of married mothers, are unrelated to caregiving demands (e.g., having a child under the age of 5, number of children under age 14) (Beers, 2000; Presser & Cox, 1997).

Nonstandard work schedules have been linked to poor-quality and insufficient sleep, problems with appetite, digestion, and elimination, increased risk of cardiovascular disease, and risky health behaviors (e.g., smoking, high levels of alcohol consumption, use of hypnotics) (Barak et al., 1995, 1996; Boggild & Knutsson, 1999; Simon, 1990). Because workers on afternoon and rotating shifts have less regular eating times, they may substitute snacks for main meals, a practice that over time can result in weight gain, weight loss, and/or nutritional deficiency (Duchon & Keran, 1990). These health problems and health-related behaviors are thought to result because nonstandard shifts upset diurnal and circadian rhythms that control sleep and wakefulness, body temperature, the cardiopulmonary system, cortisol and growth hormone secretion, metabolic activity, and digestive and eliminative processes (Simon, 1990).

Shift workers are also more susceptible to mental health problems. This is thought to be the result of greater social isolation, less access to community services, and more difficulty in participating regularly in recreational and social groups in their neighborhoods and communities, as compared with those who work standard hours (Bohle, 1997; Muhammad & Vishwanath, 1997; Schmieder & Smith, 1996). Sleep disturbances appear to be a key source of physical and mental health problems in shift workers. Shift workers who experience sleep disturbances have higher blood pressure, are more likely to use antihypertensive medications, report more anxiety, marital difficulties, and dissatisfaction with work, and perceive fewer opportunities to spend time with friends (Simon, 1990).

Given their links to physical and mental health problems, it is not surprising that nonstandard work schedules are associated with more family problems (e.g., divorce, marital conflict) (Aldous, 1969; Mott, Mann, McLoughlin, & Warwick,1965; Presser, 2000; White & Keith, 1990). A recent study by Presser (2000) using a subsample of 3,500 married couples drawn from two waves of the National Survey of Families and Households (NSFH) found that among fathers who were married less than five years at Wave 1, working fixed nights made separation or divorce six times more likely relative to working days. Among mothers married more than five years at Wave 1, working fixed nights increased the odds of separation or divorce by three times. When mothers (but not fathers) worked rotating shifts, separation or divorce was 1.5 times more likely than when they worked fixed days. Presser found no evidence that spouses who take jobs with night or rotating shifts are in less stable marriages to begin with—an important finding suggesting that the relations found in the study are not simply due to self-selection. Minorities were oversampled in the NSFH from which the subsample was drawn, but Presser did not examine effects within race/ethnicity. The study did not identify processes that mediate these effects, but evening and rotating shifts probably increase marital disruption by interfering with stabilizing, cohesion-enhancing routines like a couple's having dinner together, socializing with friends and family as a couple, and participating jointly in activities with children.

African Americans historically have had higher divorce rates than others in the general population. Data from the 1995 National Study of Family Growth indicated that after 10 years, first marriages had dissolved among 47% of African Americans, as compared with 32% among European Americans (Bramlett & Mosher, 2002). African American couples also report less marital happiness and satisfaction than European American couples, even when economic resources, education, premarital cohabitation, family constellation, and patterns of marital interaction are taken into account (Adelmann, Chadwick, & Baerger, 1996; Broman, 1991; Oggins, Veroff, & Leber, 1993). A substantial body of knowledge has accumulated about factors and processes that undermine marital quality and encourage marital dissolution within African Americans and mediate racial disparities (Goodwin, 2003; McLoyd et al., 2000), but several issues remain unresolved. A popular explanation of racial disparity in marital happiness is African Americans' greater exposure to racial discrimination and negative conditions in the workplace (Oggins et al., 1993), but remarkably few empirical tests of this hypothesis have been undertaken (Johnson, 1989). (We return to this issue later.) Consideration of the causal role of nonstandard work schedules seems warranted in light of Presser's (2000) findings and the increased tendency of African Americans to hold jobs with nonstandard work schedules.

In addition to posing threats to marital stability, nonstandard work schedules may jeopardize children's well-being. Parents' nonstandard work schedules are associated with lower school achievement and less positive psychological functioning among children (Barton, Aldridge, &

Smith, 1998; Heymann, 2000; Landy, Rosenberg, & Sutton-Smith, 1969; Mott et al., 1965). Early research found that daughters had poorer quantitative skills in high school if their fathers worked night shifts when the daughters were in early and middle childhood (Landy et al., 1969). More recent evidence from the National Longitudinal Study of Youth indicates that the more hours a parent worked evenings or nights, the lower his or her child's math and reading achievement scores and the more likely the child was to have repeated a grade and to have been suspended from school, even after taking account of family income, parental education, marital status, the child's gender, and the total number of hours the parent worked (Heymann, 2000). Daughters (but not sons) whose fathers work non-day shifts report more dysphoria, lower self-esteem, and less perceived academic competence, as compared with daughters whose fathers work day shifts (Barton et al., 1998). A standard daytime work schedule affords more parent–child contact than a nonstandard work schedule because it is generally more synchronous with children's daily school schedules. Consequently, parents who work these hours may find it easier to monitor a child's behavior, to set and enforce limits/rules, and to engage in shared activities with the child (Heymann, 2000). They may also be more available to enforce a consistent and appropriate bedtime (i.e., one that allows sufficient sleep) for children than parents who work nonstandard hours. Given these differences, it seems likely that nonstandard work schedules undermine children's well-being partly by reducing parent–child interaction, parental involvement in the children's schooling, and parental supervision of children's time use and activities. Documentation of these potential pathways is needed.

A recent study by Toyokawa and McLoyd (2004) testing a hypothesized model linking maternal work demands to adjustment in African American children ages 10–12 suggests the importance of family routines as a potential pathway by which parental work characteristics may influence children's psychological well-being. Family routines were defined as family-level activities, and child behaviors and activities supervised or arranged by parents that occur with predictable regularity, often daily or weekly (e.g., eating meals together, going to bed at a regular time each night, doing homework at a regular time, participation in regular after-school activities). The key work-related variable in this study was work demands, a composite variable based on four variables reflecting objective, structural conditions or circumstances of employment: (1) whether the mother had a nonstandard work schedule, (2) number of hours the mother worked per week, (3) commuting distance from home to the workplace, and (4) frequency of the home–workplace commute. A nonstandard work schedule, more hours of employment per week, greater commuting distance, and greater frequency of commuting were all assumed to reflect greater work demands. We assessed the cumulative effect of these factors, rather than the unique contribution of each.

Consistent with our hypothesized model, in single-mother African American families greater work demands increased externalizing symptoms (e.g., aggression) and internalizing symptoms (e.g., depression) in children by decreasing family routines and increasing work–family conflict. Work–family conflict predicted increased depressive symptoms in single mothers, which in turn predicted less family routinization. We found substantially more support for our model in single-mother than in two-parent families. It would be useful to extend this work by simultaneously examining the work demands of mothers and fathers in two-parent families and assessing the unique contribution of each of the work demands to work–family conflict, parents' psychological functioning, family routines, and child outcomes.

Wage Level

Both African American women and men have long been and continue to be overrepresented in less lucrative occupations. As compared with their European American counterparts, African American women are less likely to be employed in managerial and professional occupations (in 2002, 37% vs. 26%, respectively), less likely to be employed in technical, sales, and administrative support occupations (40% vs. 36%), and more likely to be employed in service occupations (15% vs. 27%). A similar racial disparity exists among men (McKinnon, 2003).

Workers in service occupations are at a major disadvantage in terms of wages. In 2001, service occupations were the lowest paid of all occupational groups; half or more of the workers in these occupations (e.g., food preparation and serving, building and grounds cleaning and maintenance, personal care and service) earned less than $8.50 per hour, on average (Bureau of Labor Statistics, 2002). Occupational segregation based on race/ethnicity is widespread in the United States (Kmec, 2003), and the racial and gender distributions in occupations affect wage levels. For example, hourly wages in occupations with a higher proportion of African American men and women tend to decline over time—an effect observed for decades in relation to the share of African American men, but observed only more recently in relation to the share of African American women (Catanzarite, 2003). Data also indicate that working in female-dominated occupations has greater penalties in earnings for African American women than for Latinas and European American women (Cotter, Hermsen, & Vanneman, 2003).

What are the implications of differential wage levels for family life? Research indicates that even within low-income families, variation in parents' wage levels and, in turn, family income influences children's home environment and well-being. Income effects on children's cognitive functioning and completed years of education are nonlinear, with positive impacts being much larger among children in families with incomes below or near the poverty line than among children in middle-class families (Duncan & Brooks-Gunn, 1997; Duncan, Brooks-Gunn, Yeung, & Smith, 1998). Within low-income families with some history of welfare receipt, girls whose mothers work have fewer behavioral problems and higher math achievement scores, but only if mothers earn relatively high wages. Outcomes for girls whose mothers earn very low wages are similar to those for girls with nonworking mothers (Moore & Driscoll, 1997).

These effects are mediated through a variety of pathways. Especially low wages may impose severe restrictions on parents' ability to procure material goods that help provide children a stimulating home environment (Duncan, Brooks-Gunn, & Klebanov, 1994). Low wages also may diminish the quality of parenting and parent–child relations by increasing psychological distress in parents (Dubow & Ippolito, 1994; Garrett, Ng'andu, & Ferron, 1994). Research indicates that the quality of children's home environment worsens when single mothers enter low-wage jobs with low complexity (i.e., routine, repetitive, heavily supervised activities with little opportunity for initiative), but not when they enter jobs with higher wages and complexity (Menaghan & Parcel, 1995; Parcel & Menaghan, 1997). Low-complexity jobs tend to present minimal cognitive demands for those who hold them. This job characteristic is thought to indirectly and negatively affect the learning, academic, and language stimulation children receive in their home environment (e.g., books, toys that teach academic and language skills, quality of verbal explanation to child, etc.) by constricting parents' cognitive functioning and, in turn, lessening their value for cognitive achievement in their children.

Employer-Sponsored Benefits

Although African Americans have higher rates of union affiliation than European Americans, they are less likely than their European American counterparts to have health insurance coverage, the most coveted of employer-sponsored benefits. In 2002, 20.2% of African Americans were without health insurance coverage for the entire year, as compared with 14.2% of European Americans; in 2001, 14.3% of African American children under 19 years of age were not covered by private or government health insurance, as compared with 7.6% of non-Hispanic Whites (Bhandari & Gifford, 2003; Mills & Bhandari, 2003).

Just as health insurance is important for protecting the physical and emotional well-being of family members, so too is flexibility in parents' work schedule, whether achieved by paid sick leave, paid vacation leave, or flexible hours. Meeting children's health and developmental needs occasionally requires time off from work to take children to well-child or illness-related medical appointments, to care for sick children, to manage chronic disease exacerbations (e.g., asthma), and to have children evaluated for cognitive and behavior problems. Flexibility in work schedule influences parents' ability to meet these needs while maintaining employment. Parents use their sick leave not only to care for themselves but also to care for their children. Paid vacation is sometimes used to meet children's routine health and developmental needs, but is less frequently used to meet children's sick care needs because of the advance notice typically required for such leave (Heymann & Earle, 1999).

African Americans are less likely than European Americans to have flexible work schedules and other family-friendly benefits. In 2001, 21% of African Americans 16 years old and over had flexible work schedules, as compared with 30% of European Americans (U.S. Bureau of the Census, 2002). A recent study by Caputo (2000) used national longitudinal data to examine predictors of women's access to family-friendly employee benefits over the course of 17 years (women were age 41–51 at the time of the last interview). Family-friendly employee benefits included family leave (paid and unpaid leave—usually occasioned by medical emergency, childbirth, adoption, need for dependent care), flexible work hours, and time off for child care. Women who spent more years in full-time employment in the private sector as union members, had higher levels of education, spent less time on public assistance, and were European American rather than African American, worked more years for employers providing family-friendly benefits. That African American women were less likely than European American women to work for employers providing family-friendly benefits, after taking account of other factors, is striking because they were employed full time for more years than European American women (10.26 years vs. 8.49 years).

PREJUDICE AND DISCRIMINATION

Although European Americans' endorsement of the principles of racial equality and integration has increased markedly over the past few decades, substantial proportions of European Americans still hold negative stereotypes about African Americans. In the 1990 national General

Social Survey, European Americans rated African Americans as less intelligent than European Americans (54%), lazier (62%), more prone to violence (56%), and having a greater preference for living on welfare (78%) (Bobo, 2000). More than half of the respondents in Plous and Williams's (1995) survey of Whites in "liberal" Connecticut endorsed at least one negative stereotype about the "innate" abilities of people of color or differences in physical anatomy.

In view of these data, it is hardly surprising that African Americans are more likely than European Americans to report discriminatory events (both lifetime and in the past year), many of which occur in the workplace or employment sector (Gary, 1995; Klonoff & Landrine, 1999). Nor is it surprising that the vast majority of African American adults in national surveys believe that European Americans are racially prejudiced, that their economic and educational opportunities are not equal to those available to European Americans, and that their treatment in the workplace, schools, courts, housing, and credit markets is less favorable than the treatment accorded European Americans (Duke, 1994; Holmes, 1994).

There is no shortage of evidence corroborating African Americans' perceptions of unequal treatment. Note the results of a recent experiment in which Bertrand and Mullainathan (2004) submitted multiple resumes from phantom job seekers to 1,300 help-wanted ads in Boston and Chicago newspapers. The resumes were patterned after those of people who were actually seeking similar jobs; job openings involved administrative, sales, clerical, and managerial positions. The researchers randomly assigned the first names on the resumes, choosing from one set names particularly common among African Americans (e.g., Lakisha, Jamal) and from another set names common among European Americans (e.g., Emily, Greg). Apart from their names, the phantom applicants had the same experience, education, and skills. Those with Black-sounding names were 50% less likely to be called for interviews than were those with White-sounding names. Moreover, the likelihood of being called for an interview rose sharply with an applicant's credentials (e.g., experience, honors) for those with White-sounding names, but much less for those with Black-sounding names. As the authors point out, this practice may dampen incentives for African Americans to acquire job skills, producing a self-fulfilling prophecy that perpetuates prejudice and misallocates resources.

Perceived discrimination is highly salient in African Americans' evaluation of their work experience. Institutional discrimination and interpersonal prejudice in the workplace have been found to be more potent predictors of perceived job quality among African American women than other occupational stressors such as low task variety, low decision authority, heavy workloads, and poor supervision (Hughes & Dodge, 1997). The notion that discrimination in the workplace adversely affects marital functioning is quite plausible, given its psychological salience. It is consistent with a burgeoning empirical literature linking perceived discrimination to greater psychological distress, lower subjective well-being, psychiatric symptoms, poorer self-reported health, higher blood pressure, and a greater number of bed-days among African Americans (Clark, Anderson, Clark, & Williams, 1999; Williams, Spencer, & Jackson, 1999; Williams, Yu, Jackson, & Anderson, 1997).

However, if discrimination in the workplace can disrupt marital relations, it might also serve as a unifying force, drawing the couple closer in mutual support. Research conducted during the 1970s and 1980s on the effects of job and income loss on marital relations makes an especially strong case for differential response to stressors. Whether economic loss had positive, negative, or no effects on conjugal relations was found to depend to a considerable degree on the status of preexisting conjugal relations. The essential effect of economic loss was one of accentuation or exaggeration of preexisting marital states. Though economic loss tended to increase the frequency of marital quarrels overall, quarrels were most frequent and acrimonious in previously weak, unsatisfying marriages. These marriages tended to disintegrate under the pressures created by economic loss, whereas previously happy, stable marriages gained renewed commitment and resilience under the same circumstances (see Ray & McLoyd, 1986, for a fuller discussion of these studies). The assumption that racial discrimination does not have uniformly negative effects on marital relations—an assumption that seems tenable in light of the research on economic loss—calls for systematic study of the conditions that influence how marital relations are affected by racial discrimination in the workplace.

We are aware of only one empirical study that examines linkages between perceived discrimination in the workplace and marital processes among African Americans. Johnson's (1989) investigation of African American police officers found that the perception of being barred from assignments because of race predicted increased marital discord and the tendency for couples to consider divorce, by increasing feelings of fatigue and emotional depletion and increasing officers' desire to quit their jobs. The perception of being judged by the actions of other African American officers had an especially potent and negative impact on marital interaction, mediated through an increased tendency to behave callously and impersonally toward the spouse. Analyses of data from a comparable sample of European American police officers indicated that desire to quit the job was more predictive of marital discord among African Americans than among European Americans, apparently because it constitutes a more serious economic threat as a result of the reduced job opportunities available to African Americans. This study raises a cornucopia of issues that deserve systematic study. Studies are needed to establish the replicability and generalizability of the findings and to identify psychological and contextual factors that buffer the negative effects of workplace discrimination on marital relations.

Perceived racial discrimination in the workplace also appears to have implications for the socialization messages that parents transmit to their children. Hughes and Chen's (1997) study of dual-earner, two-parent African American families with children ages 4–14 found that parents who perceived prejudicial attitudes or racial stereotypes in their daily interpersonal transactions at work (interpersonal prejudice) reported engaging in more racial socialization of their children. In particular, they were more likely to make efforts to prepare their children for experiences of racial prejudice (e.g., talking about the fight for equality among African Americans, explaining television programs showing poor treatment of African Americans). Those who perceived racial inequities in the distribution of valued resources such as salaries, benefits, job assignments, and opportunities for promotion (institutional discrimination) were more likely to socialize their children to mistrust European Americans.

It is highly plausible that perceived job discrimination and the messages that parents transmit to their children about race, rather than being causally related, are merely two indicators of an underlying construct of perceived discrimination or racial attitudes. Clarification of this issue would stand as a major contribution, as would methodologically sophisticated studies (e.g., multimethod designs, use of multiple informants) that document the influence of different types of racial socialization messages on children's racial identity, educational and occupational aspirations and expectations, achievement behavior, and their capacity to interpret and cope with experiences of racial prejudice (McLoyd et al., 2000). Hughes and Chen's (1997) research raises the broader issue of the extent to which the workplace shapes parents' childrearing values, beliefs, and behavior through the nature of the work adults perform, the competencies they must possess to perform their jobs satisfactorily, and other pathways. A rich and intriguing literature on this topic has developed over the past two decades (e.g., Greenberger, O'Neil, & Nagel, 1994; Kohn, 1969; Kohn & Schooler, 1983; Parcel & Menaghan, 1994; Whitbeck et al., 1997), but virtually no examination of this issue has been directed at African American families.

POLICY ISSUES

Scholars have linked higher rates of underemployment and unemployment and less favorable employment conditions among African Americans to a range of historical factors and social conditions. These include (1) inferior schools and restricted educational resources; (2) overt and de facto racial discrimination in employment practices (e.g., limiting job advertisements to ethnic, neighborhood, or suburban newspapers that cater to Whites, rather than advertising in metropolitan newspapers; recruiting exclusively in predominantly White schools; refusal to recruit from state employment service programs; reliance on referrals of employees instead of screening applicants who respond to newspaper ads); (3) the decline and suburbanization of industries that employ low- or semiskilled workers; and (4) spatial mismatch, some of which is due to segregationist practices that restrict low-income housing and racial diversity in suburban areas and effectively keep African Americans out of suburban neighborhoods where job opportunities tend to be more plentiful (Brueckner & Zenou, 2003; Burgess, 1995; Charles, 2003; Heinicke, 2000; Quillian, 2003; Wilson, 1996).

Schooling

A number of policy analysts give high priority to improving the quality of schooling and increasing the academic performance and educational attainment of African American students as long-term solutions to the problem of unemployment, underemployment, and unfavorable employment conditions among African Americans. Numerous proposals have been offered to achieve these ends, including school vouchers, charter schools, performance contracts, merit pay, culturally responsive curricula, supplementary educational programs (e.g., after-school and weekend programs), school-to-career programs, and a system of national performance standards that young people must meet before they can graduate from high school, akin to the system in industrial democracies like Japan and Germany (Ogbu, 2003; Wilson, 1996). A detailed discussion and evaluation of each of these educational strategies is beyond the scope of this chapter. Rather, we focus on two (i.e., after-school programs, school-to-career programs) that show considerable promise as preventive strategies.

After-school programs deserve comment because of their special relevance to working parents and because they have been the focus of empirical research more often than the aforementioned educational strategies. This research provides a reasonably strong case for state and federal appropriations to create and support educationally oriented after-school programs on a widespread basis, especially for children of low-income parents. The gap between parents' work hours and children's school hours may be 20–25 hours per week or more. It is during this time, when they are most likely to be unsupervised, that children are most vulnerable to accidents, delinquency, and poor choices in time use (Chung, 2000; Snyder & Sickmund, 1999).

Growing evidence indicates that formal after-school care lessens these risks and affords numerous advantages as well. Children who participate in formal after-school programs are at less risk of poor cognitive development and academic failure, have better study habits, are less truant, are less likely to drop out, and have fewer externalizing behavior problems and better interpersonal skills (Chung, 2000; Posner & Vandell, 1994). These benefits appear to accrue because these programs provide structure and supervision, cognitive and academic enrichment, help with homework, and opportunities for positive social interactions and leadership roles (Chung, 2000). Participation in these programs may also lower the risk of academic failure by reducing the amount of time children watch television. Elementary school–age children in self-care spend more time watching television and less time in enriching after-school activities (Posner & Vandell, 1994). The negative effects of self-care appear to be especially strong for low-income children (Marshall, Coll, & Marx, 1997; Pettit, Laird, Bates, & Dodge, 1997).

Research also points to school-to-career programs in high schools as a credible antidote to the problem of unemployment, underemployment, and low-wage employment. These programs are well suited to address needs and problems that are especially acute among economically disadvantaged youth. The virtually nonexistent link between high schools and careers is particularly problematic for youth whose parents and friends are unemployed or in unskilled jobs, because such a family and social context makes it difficult to learn about or gain connections to skill-based careers through informal channels. Scripts are largely unavailable to non-college-bound youth about how to get skilled jobs in careers that do not initially require academic degrees (e.g., carpenter, electrician, plumber) (Lerman, 1999; Wilson, 1996). Congress passed the School-to-Work Opportunities Act in 1994, in part, to promote integration of academic and occupational learning through a variety of activities and approaches including youth apprenticeships, career academies, tech-prep programs, internships, and cooperative education. This Act offers time-limited investments to state and local governments willing to adopt, modify, and/or extend these approaches to prepare young people for the job market. Nonetheless, America is a long way from instituting such programs on a scale sufficient to reach the number of youth who desperately need them (Lerman, 1999).

Advocates point out several benefits of well-structured school-to-career programs: (1) the use of learning in context motivates students to do better in school, reengages disconnected youth in the learning process, and increases the rate of entry into postsecondary education programs by helping students to see the relevance of what they are studying and gain self-confidence by accomplishing work-related tasks; (2) young people gain recognized work experience, and the mismatch between what schools do and what employers demand is reduced; (3) the negative influence of peers is lessened by increasing young people's exposure to constructive adult peer groups and informal mentors at work sites; and (4) the disadvantages of poor youth with respect to informal channels to jobs (e.g., the "word of mouth" channel) are reduced by improving the formal system of placement in training and jobs. These programs also help inner-city high school students learn more about job and career opportunities in suburbs and other parts of a city. Research documenting positive effects of such programs is growing (Lerman, 1999).

Spatial Mismatch

Learning about job and career opportunities in suburbs is of limited usefulness if transportation problems thwart inner-city residents' ability to pursue these opportunities. Because of the marked disparity in job opportunities in inner-cities versus suburbs, a comprehensive plan to deal with the employment problems of inner-city residents should encompass efforts to establish cheap, efficient public transit systems that make suburbanized employment sites more accessible to inner-city residents (Wilson, 1996). The benefits of such transit systems will fall disproportionately to African Americans because they reside in cities in disproportionate numbers as compared with European Americans.

Another policy option to address spatial mismatch is to help low-income inner-city residents move to better neighborhoods that are closer geographically to employment opportunities and offer other advantages (e.g., greater safety, better schools). Moving to Opportunity (MTO) is especially interesting in this regard. MTO is a demonstration program conducted by the U.S. Department of Housing and Urban Development that helps poor urban families (about two-thirds are African American; more then 90% are single-parent families) move out of poor, inner-city high-risk neighborhoods and settle in low-poverty neighborhoods (where less than 10% of the population is poor) (Orr et al., 2003). Presumably, the latter neighborhoods are closer spatially to employment opportunities. The program's experimental design (i.e., random assignment) provides a strong test of the causal link between neighborhood characteristics and outcome variables. The experimental group received Section 8 housing vouchers (i.e., housing subsidies) usable only in low-poverty areas, along with counseling and assistance in finding a private rental unit; the control group was not offered vouchers but continued to live in public housing or receive other project-based housing assistance. To retain their vouchers, experimental families were required to stay in low-poverty areas for one year, after which they could move without locational constraints.

A recent interim evaluation of families four to seven years after random assignment found no significant effects on adult or youth employment or earnings, or on receipt of public assistance, but longitudinal administrative data over the entire follow-up period indicated a trend of increasingly favorable effects over time for these outcomes. This may be an indication that it will take more years for the full effects of the program on economic well-being to manifest. Positive effects were found for adult mental health (e.g., lower depressive symptomatology) and adolescent girls' functioning (e.g., reductions in psychological distress and risky behaviors such as smoking and marijuana use; higher perceived chances of going to college and getting a well-paying, stable job), but MTO did not improve functioning among adolescent boys. MTO had a small but positive effect on the characteristics of the schools the sample children attended (e.g., marginally higher school-level performance on state exams). It is plausible that the latter effect, along with the higher expectancies for education and employment produced by MTO, may ultimately result in better adult employment outcomes among children in the MTO experimental group.

Employer-Sponsored Benefits

Because employer-sponsored benefits facilitate family functioning in myriad ways, we need to understand why they are race-linked as a first step toward elimination of racial disparities. Policy discussions would also benefit from systematic documentation of the strategies used by parents without family-friendly benefits to meet their children's health and developmental needs. These naturally occurring strategies may provide insight into how best to structure community-based services to support these families. We also need to better understand the *costs* of lack of family-friendly benefits for work productivity, families' long-term economic well-being, parenting quality, and children's development in relation to whatever *benefits* employers accrue from nonprovision of family-friendly benefits. We know, for instance, that having young children is a stronger predictor of transition to joblessness among African American women than among European American and Latina women, and that marriage is a stronger predictor of returns to the labor force among African American women than among European American and Latina women (Reid, 2002; Taniguchi & Rosenfeld, 2002), but whether these patterns are linked to differences in employee benefits is unclear.

Gerstel and McGonagle (1999) found that African American workers are more likely than European American workers to report needing to take leaves from their jobs for reasons covered in the Family and Medical Leave Act, yet they are less likely to take such leaves. The most common reason given for not taking leaves was that they were unpaid. Because current policy does not provide wage replacement, this pattern probably points to underlying inequalities in income and health care resources that render African Americans less able to take job leaves. An amended policy is needed that eases the financial pressures of workers and their families by providing paid leave for circumscribed time periods.

The share of the American population without health insurance rose in 2002, the second consecutive annual increase (Mills & Bhandari, 2003). A confluence of labor market conditions forecasts a continuation of this pattern as well as an increase in the number of workers contending with less desirable employment conditions. Job growth is concentrated in the service sector, especially in entry-level or secondary-sector jobs (e.g., cashier, waitress, sales clerk) that typically pay near minimum wage and generally do not offer benefits such as health insurance, paid sick leave, or vacations. Growth is also occurring in part-time, contingency, subcontracted, and temporary jobs, all of which tend to have irregular work schedules, high layoff and turnover rates, and disadvantages with respect to pay, benefits, and job security. Union coverage and the protections it offers also are decreasing (Glass & Fujimoto, 1995; Seccombe, 2000). African Americans are likely to be disproportionately affected by these trends, given their overrepresentation in service occupations. Although job growth is concentrated in the service sector, this advantage is counteracted by the fact that service jobs are often unstable and offer little economic security. An analysis of 2002 unemployment data showed that 17.9% of workers in service occupations were long-term unemployed (Stettner & Wenger, 2003). The erosion of employee benefits can be counteracted to some extent by passage of universal health care and expansion of the Earned Income Tax Credit. These proposals would especially benefit African Americans, because they are more likely than European Americans to lack health insurance coverage and to work in low-wage jobs (Bureau of Labor Statistics, 2002; McKinnon, 2003; Mills & Bhandari, 2003).

Child Care and Maternal Work Itensity

Many of the jobs projected to have the highest growth during the next decade have disproportionately high rates of nonstandard schedules, are in female-dominated occupations, and include jobs most commonly held by women with low levels of education (e.g., cashier, janitor, maid, waiter; nursing aide, orderly) (Silvestri, 1995). Increasing numbers of working poor mothers will hold these jobs to satisfy the work effort mandated by welfare reform. These trends forecast increased need for government initiatives to help low-income working parents pay for *quality* child care. Poor women's ability to maintain employment will be enhanced as well by policies that encourage growth in high-quality childcare facilities in urban areas and expansion of available childcare during nonstandard hours and/or days.

The Bush administration's proposal for reauthorization of welfare reform calls for single-parent welfare recipients to be involved in work and work-related activities 40 hours per week instead of the current 30 hours per week (Thompson, 2003). This is yet another reason to determine whether maternal part-time versus full-time versus overtime hours have differential effects on African American children living in female-headed versus two-parent households. A recent study, although not addressing this specific question, suggests that this proposed policy may not portend negative effects for children. This longitudinal study of low-income children and mothers (46% were African American) found that transitions into and out of welfare and employment—whether for one or more hours or for 40 hours per week—were not associated with negative outcomes (e.g., lower levels of cognitive achievement, more problem behaviors) for preschoolers or young adolescents (Chase-Lansdale et al., 2003). More work is needed to determine if these findings hold over the long term (the study's findings concerned children's development over a 16-month period) irrespective of race/ethnicity and the broader economic environment (the study was conducted during the recent economic boom that lowered unemployment and raised wages among low-skilled workers).

Prejudice and Discrimination

Racial/ethnic discrimination should be routinely monitored by audit studies similar to those conducted by Bertrand and Mullainathan (2004). Ultimately, fairness and justice mandate the elimination of racial/ethnic discrimination. The repercussions of discrimination for workers' economic and psychological well-being, attitudes toward the job, and the quality and content of interactions with spouses and children underscore the importance of implementing policies to combat racial/ethnic discrimination and harassment in the workplace. Two types of policy actions are needed—one that establishes accountability for discriminatory and harassing behaviors, and one that fosters a climate of respect and understanding. The first type of policy establishes clear and expedient procedures for presenting complaints inside and outside the organization and, more important, makes individuals and the organization accountable and subject to disciplinary action. The second type of policy establishes programs that enhance cultural competence among individuals at all levels of the organization, increases representation of diverse racial/ethnic groups in work groups and positions, creates opportunities for interaction, and rewards success in achieving these goals.

REFERENCES

Adelmann, P. K., Chadwick, K., & Baerger, D. R. (1996). Marital quality of Black and White adults over the life course. *Journal of Social and Personal Relationships, 13,* 361-384.

Aldous, J. (1969). Wives' employment status and lower-class men as husbands-fathers: Support for the Moynihan thesis. *Journal of Marriage and the Family, 31,* 469–476.

Barak, Y., Achieron, A., Kimh, R., Lampi, Y., Ring, A., Elizur, A., & Sarovo-Pinhas, I. (1996 Nov–Dec). Health risks among shift workers: A survey of female nurses. *Health Care for Women International, 17,* 527–533.

Barak, Y., Achiron, A., Lample, Y., Gilad, R., Ring, A., Elizur, A., & Sarovo-Pinhas, I. (1995). Sleep disturbances among female nurses: Comparing shift to day work. *Chronobiology International, 12,* 345–350.

Barton, J., Aldridge, J., & Smith, P. (1998). The emotional impact of shift work on the children of shift workers. *Scandinavian Journal of Work, Environment and Health, 24,* 146–150.

Beers, T. (2000). Flexible schedules and shift work: Replacing the "9-to-5" workday? *Monthly Labor Review, 123,* 33–40.

Bertrand, M., & Mullainathan, S. (2004). Are Emily and Greg more employable than Lakisha and Jamal? A field experiment on labor market discrimination. *American Economic Review, 94*(4), 991–1013.

Bhandari, S., & Gifford, E. (2003). Children with health insurance: 2001. *Current Population Reports.* Washington, DC: U.S. Bureau of the Census.

Bobo, L. D. (2000). Racial attitudes and relations at the close of the twentieth century. In N. Smelser, W. J. Wilson, & F. Mitchell (Eds.), *America becoming: Racial trends and their consequences.* Washington, DC: National Academy Press.

Boggild, H., & Knutsson, A. (1999). Shift work, risk factors and cardiovascular disease. *Scandinavian Journal of Work, Environment and Health, 25,* 85–99.

Bohle, P. (1997). Does "hardiness" predict adaptation to shiftwork? *Work and Stress, 11,* 369–376.

Bramlett, M. D., & Mosher, W. D. (2002, July). Cohabitation, marriage, divorce, and remarriage in the United States. In *Vital Health Statistics* (Series 23, No. 22). Washington, DC: National Center for Health Statistics. Retrieved from www.cdc.gov/nchs/data/series/sr_23/ sr23_022.pdf

Brody, G., Stoneman, Z., & Flor, D. (1995). Linking family processes and academic competence among rural African American youths. *Journal of Marriage and the Family, 57,* 567–579.

Broman, C. L. (1991). Gender, work–family roles, and psychological well-being of blacks. *Journal of Marriage and the Family, 53,* 509–520.

Brueckner, J. K., & Zenou, Y. (2003). Space and unemployment: The labor-market effects of spatial mismatch. *Journal of Labor Economics, 21,* 242–266.

Bureau of Labor Statistics. (1998, December). Labor-market outcomes for city dwellers and suburbanites. *Issues in Labor Statistics* (Summary 98-12). Washington, DC: U.S. Department of Labor. Retrieved from www.bls.gov/ opub/ils/pdf/opbils27.pdf

Bureau of Labor Statistics. (2002, November 6). *Occupational employment and wages, 2001.* Washington, DC: U.S. Department of Labor, Division of Occupational Employment Statistics. Retrieved from www.bls.gov/news.release/ ocwage.nr0.htm

Bureau of Labor Statistics. (2004). *Labor force statistics from the current population survey.* Retrieved from www.bls.gov/cps/home.htm#data

Bureau of Labor Statistics. (2005, May). *Women in the labor force: A databook* (Report 985). Table 6. Employment status of women by presence and age of youngest child, marital status, race, and Hispanic or Latino ethnicity, 2004. (pp. 16–17). Retrieved from www.bls.gov/cps/wlf-tables3.pdf

Burgess, N. (1995). Looking back, looking forward: African American families in sociohistorical perspective. In B.B. Ingoldsby & S. Smith (Eds.), *Families in multicultural perspective* (pp. 321–334). New York: Guilford Press.

Burton, L., & Jarrett, R. (2000). In the mix, yet on the margins: The place of families in urban neighborhood and child development research. *Journal of Marriage and the Family, 62,* 1114–1135.

Cantave, C., & Harrison, R. (1999, June). *Employment and unemployment: Fact sheet.* Washington, DC: Joint Center for Political and Economic Studies. Retrieved from jointcenter.org/DB/factsheet/employ.htm

Cantave, C., & Harrison, R. (2001, August). *Single parent families: Fact sheet.* Washington, DC: Joint Center for Political and Economic Studies. Retrieved from www.jointcenter.org/DB/factsheet/sigpatn.htm

Caputo, R. K. (2000). The availability of traditional and family-friendly employee benefits among a cohort of young women, 1968–1995. *Families in Society, 81,* 422–436.

Catanzarite, L. (2003). Race–gender composition and occupational pay degradation. *Social Problems, 50,* 14–37.

Chadiha, L. A. (1992). Black husbands' economic problems and resiliency during the transition to marriage. *Families in Society: The Journal of Contemporary Human Services, 73,* 542–552.

Chapman, J., & Bernstein, J. (2003, April 11). *Falling through the safety net: Low-income single mothers in the jobless recovery* (Issue Brief #191). Washington, DC: Economic Policy Institute. Retrieved from www.epinet.org/Issuebriefs/ib191/ib191.pdf

Charles, C. Z. (2003). The dynamics of racial segregation. *Annual Review of Sociology, 29,* 167–207.

Chase-Lansdale, P., Moffitt, R., Lohman, B., Cherlin, A., Coley, R., & Pittman, L. D. (2003). Mothers' transitions from welfare to work and the well-being of preschoolers and adolescents. *Science, 299,* 1548–1552.

Chung, A. (2000). *Working for children and families: Safe and smart after-school programs.* Washington, DC: U.S. Department of Education and U.S. Department of Justice.

Clark, R., Anderson, N.B., Clark, V.R., & Williams, D.R. (1999). Racism as a stressor for African Americans: A biopsychosocial model. *American Psychologist, 54,* 805–816.

Clark-Nicolas, P., & Gray-Little, B. (1991). Effects of economic resources on marital quality in Black married couples. *Journal of Marriage and the Family, 53,* 645–655.

Conger, R. Wallace, L., Sun, Y., Simons, R., McLoyd, V. C., & Brody, G. (2002). Economic pressure in African American families: A replication and extension of the family stress model. *Developmental Psychology, 38,* 179–193.

Cotter, D. A., Hermsen, J. M., & Vanneman, R. (2003). The effects of occupational gender segregation across race. *Sociological Quarterly, 44,* 17–36.

Dixon, P. (1998). Employment factors in conflict in African American heterosexual relationships: Some perceptions of women. *Journal of Black Studies, 28,* 491–505.

Dubow, E., & Ippolito, M. F. (1994). Effects of poverty and quality of the home environment on changes in the academic and behavioral adjustment of elementary school-age children. *Journal of Clinical Child Psychology, 23,* 401–412.

Duchon, J. C., & Keran, C. M. (1990). Relationships among shiftworker eating habits, eating satisfaction, and self-reported health in a population of U.S. miners. *Work and Stress, 4,* 111–120.

Duke, L. (1994, March 3). Blacks, Asians, Latinos cite prejudice by whites for limited opportunity. *Washington Post,* p. A9.

Duncan, G. J., & Brooks-Gunn, J. (Eds.). (1997). *Consequences of growing up poor.* New York: Russell Sage Foundation.

Duncan, G. J., Brooks-Gunn, J., & Klebanov, P. (1994). Economic deprivation and early childhood development. *Child Development, 65,* 296–318.

Duncan, G. J., Brooks-Gunn, J., Yeung, W. J., & Smith, J. R. (1998). How much does childhood poverty affect the life chances of children? *American Sociological Review, 63,* 406–423.

Elder, G. H. (1974). *Children of the Great Depression.* Chicago: University of Chicago Press.

Elder, G. H., Eccles, J. S., Ardelt, M., & Lord, S. (1995). Inner-city parents under economic pressure: Perspectives on the strategies of parenting. *Journal of Marriage and the Family, 57,* 771–784.

Fields, J. (2003). Children's living arrangements and characteristics: March 2002. *Current Population Reports* (P20–547). Washington, DC: U.S. Bureau of the Census.

Flippen, C., & Tienda, M. (1999). *Pathways to retirement: Patterns of labor force participation and labor market exit among the pre-retirement population by race, Hispanic origin, and sex* (Princeton University Office of Population Research Working Paper No. 1). Princeton, NJ: Princeton University. Retrieved from opr.princeton.edu/papers/opr9901.pdf

Garrett, P., Ng'andu, N., & Ferron, J. (1994). Poverty experiences of young children and the quality of their home environments. *Child Development, 65,* 331–345.

Gary, L. (1995). African American men's perceptions of racial discrimination: A sociocultural analysis. *Social Work Research, 19,* 207–217.

Gerstel, N., & McGonagle, K. (1999). Job leaves and the limits of the Family and Medical Leave Act: The effects of gender, race, and family. *Work and Occupations, 26,* 510–534.

Glass, J., & Fujimoto, T. (1995). Employer characteristics and the provision of family responsive policies. *Work and Occupations, 22* (4), 380–411.

Gomel, J. N., Tinsley, B. J., Parke, R., & Clark, K. M. (1998). The effects of economic hardship on family relationships among African American, Latino, and Euro-American families. *Journal of Family Issues, 19,* 436–467.

Goodwin, P. (2003). African American and European American women's marital well-being. *Journal of Marriage and the Family, 65,* 550–560.

Greenberger, E., O'Neil, R., & Nagel, S. K. (1994). Linking workplace and homeplace: Relations between the nature of adults' work and their parenting behaviors. *Developmental Psychology, 30*(6), 990–1002.

Gutman, L. M., & Eccles, J. S. (1999). Financial strain, parenting behaviors, and adolescents' achievement: Testing model equivalence between African American and European American single- and two-parent families. *Child Development, 70,* 1464–1476.

Heinicke, C. W. (2000). One step forward: African-American married women in the South, 1950–1960. *Journal of Interdisciplinary History, 31,* 43–62.

Heymann, J. S. (2000). *The widening gap: Why America's working families are in jeopardy and what can be done about it.* New York: Basic Books.

Heymann, J. S., & Earle, A. (1999). The impact of welfare reform on parents' ability to care for their children's health. *American Journal of Public Health, 89*(4), 502–505.

Hill, R. (1971). *The strengths of black families.* New York: Emerson Hall.

Holmes, S. (1994, March 3). Survey finds minorities resent one another almost as much as they do whites. *New York Times,* p. B8.

Hughes, D., & Chen, L. (1997). When and what parents tell children about race: An examination of race-related socialization among African American families. *Applied Developmental Science, 1,* 200–214.

Hughes, D., & Dodge, M. (1997). African American women in the workplace: Relationships between job conditions, racial bias at work, and perceived job quality. *American Journal of Community Psychology, 25,* 581–599.

Jackson, A. P., Brooks-Gunn, J., Huang, C., & Glassman, M. (2000). Single mothers in low-wage jobs: Financial strain, parenting, and preschoolers' outcomes. *Child Development, 71,* 1409–1423.

Jargowsky, P. (1994). Ghetto poverty among Blacks in the 1980s. *Journal of Policy Analysis and Management, 13,* 288–310.

Jaynes, G., & Williams, R. (1989). (Eds.). *A common destiny: Blacks and American society.* Washington, DC: National Academy Press.

Johnson, L. B. (1989). The employed black: The dynamics of work–family tension. *Review of Black Political Economy, 17,* 69–85.

Kain, J. F. (1992). The spatial mismatch hypothesis: Three decades later. *Housing Policy Debate, 3,* 371–460.

Klonoff, E. A., & Landrine, H. (1999). Cross-validation of the schedule of racist events. *Journal of Black Psychology, 25,* 231–254.

Kmec, J. A. (2003). Minority job concentration and wages. *Social Problems, 50,* 38–59.

Kohn, M. (1969). *Class and conformity: A study of values.* Homewood, IL: Dorsey.

Kohn, M., & Schooler, C. (1983). *Work and personality: An inquiry into the impact of social stratification.* Norwood, NJ: Ablex.

Landy, F., Rosenberg, B. G., & Sutton-Smith, B. (1969). The effect of limited father absence on cognitive development. *Child Development, 40,* 941–944.

Lawson, E. J., & Thompson, A. (1995). Black men make sense of marital distress and divorce: An exploratory study. *Family Relations, 44,* 211–218.

Lerman, R. I. (1999). Improving links between high schools and careers. In D. Besharov (Ed.), *America's disconnected youth: Toward a preventive strategy* (pp. 185–212). Washington, DC: Child Welfare League of America Press.

Marshall, N. L., Coll, C. G., & Marx, F. (1997). After-school time and children's behavioral adjustment. *Merrill-Palmer Quarterly, 43,* 497–514.

Menaghan, E. G., & Parcel, T. L. (1995). Social sources of change in children's home environments: The effects of parental occupational experiences and family condition. *Journal of Marriage and the Family, 57,* 69–84.

McKinnon, J. (2003, April). The Black population in the United States: March 2002 (*Current Population Reports,* Series P20-541). Washington, DC: U.S. Bureau of the Census. Retrieved from www.census.gov/prod/2003pubs/p20-541.pdf

McLafferty, S., & Preston, V. (1996). Spatial mismatch and employment in a decade of restructuring. *Professional Geographer, 48,* 420–431.

McLoyd, V. C. (1993). Employment among African American mothers in dual-earner families: Antecedents and consequences for family life and child development. In J. Frankel (Ed.), *The employed mother and the family context* (pp. 180–226). New York: Springer-Verlag.

McLoyd, V. C., Cauce, A. M., Takeuchi, D., & Wilson, L. (2000). Marital processes and parental socialization in families of color: A decade review of research. *Journal of Marriage and the Family, 62,* 1070–1093.

McLoyd, V. C., Jayaratne, T., Ceballo, R., & Borquez, J. (1994). Unemployment and work interruption among African American single mothers: Effects on parenting and adolescent socioemotional functioning. *Child Development,* 65, 562–589.

Mills, R., & Bhandari, S. (2003). Health insurance coverage in the United States: 2002 (*Current Population Reports*). Washington, DC: U.S. Bureau of the Census.

Moore, K. A., & Driscoll, A. K. (1997). Low-wage maternal employment and outcomes for children: A study. *The Future of Children,* 7, 122–127.

Mott, P. E., Mann, F. C., McLoughlin, Q., & Warwick, D. P. (1965). *Shift work: The social, psychological, and physical consequences.* Ann Arbor: University of Michigan Press.

Muhammad, J., & Vishwanath, V. (1997). Shiftwork, burnout, and well-being: A study of Canadian nurses. *International Journal of Stress Management,* 4, 197–204.

Office of the Assistant Secretary for Planning and Evaluation. (2002). *Trends in the well-being of America's children and youth 2002.* Washington, DC: U.S. Department of Health and Human Services. Retrieved from aspe.hhs.gov/hsp/02trends/index.htm

Ogbu, J. U. (2003). *Black American students in an affluent suburb: A study of academic engagement.* Mahwah, NJ: Erlbaum.

Oggins, J., Veroff, J., & Leber, D. (1993). Perceptions of marital interaction among Black and White newlyweds. *Journal of Personality and Social Psychology,* 65, 494–511.

Oliver, M., & Shapiro, T. (1995). *Black wealth/white wealth: A new perspective on racial inequality.* New York: Routledge.

Orr, L., Feins, J., Jacob, R., Beecroft, E., Sanbonmatsu, L., Katz, L. F., et al. (2003). *Moving to Opportunity for Fair Housing Demonstration Program: Interim impacts evaluation.* Washington, DC: U. S. Department of Housing and Urban Development.

Parcel, T. L., & Menaghan, E. G. (1990). Maternal working conditions and children's verbal facility: Studying the intergenerational transmission of inequality from mothers to young children. *Social Psychology Quarterly,* 53, 132–147.

Parcel, T. L., & Menaghan, E. G. (1994). Early parental work, family social capital, and early childhood outcomes. *American Journal of Sociology,* 99, 972–1009.

Parcel, T. L., & Menaghan, E. G. (1997). Effects of low-wage employment on family well-being. *The Future of Children,* 7, 116–121.

Pettit, G. S., Laird, R. D., Bates, J. E., & Dodge, K. A. (1997). Patterns of after-school care in middle childhood: Risk factors and developmental outcomes. *Merrill-Palmer Quarterly,* 43, 515–538.

Plous, S., & Williams, T. (1995). Racial stereotypes from the days of American slavery: A continuing legacy. *Journal of Applied Social Psychology,* 25, 795–817.

Posner, J. K., & Vandell, D. L. (1994). Low-income children's after-school care: Are there beneficial effects of after-school programs? *Child Development,* 65, 440–456.

Presser, H. (2000). Nonstandard work schedules and marital instability. *Journal of Marriage and the Family, 62,* 93–110.

Presser, H., & Cox, A. G. (1997, April). The work schedules of low-educated American women and welfare reform. *Monthly Labor Review, 120,* 25–34.

Quillian, L. (2003). The decline of male employment in low-income black neighborhoods, 1950–1990. *Social Science Research, 32,* 220–250.

Raphael, S., & Stoll, M. A. (2000). *Can boosting minority car-ownership rates narrow inter-racial employment gaps?* (Northwestern University/University of Chicago Joint Center for Poverty Research Working Paper No. 200). Retrieved from www.jcpr.org/wpfiles/raphael_stollSG2000.pdf

Ray, S. A., & McLoyd, V. C. (1986). Fathers in hard times: The impact of unemployment and poverty on paternal and marital relations. In M. Lamb (Ed.), *The father's role: Applied perspectives* (pp. 339–383). New York: Wiley.

Reid, L. L. (2002). Occupational segregation, human capital, and motherhood: Black women's higher exit rates from full-time employment. *Gender and Society, 16,* 728–747.

Schmieder, R. A., & Smith, C. S. (1996). Moderating effects of social support in shiftworking and non-shiftworking nurses. *Work and Stress, 10,* 128–140.

Seccombe, K. (2000). Families in poverty in the 1990s: Trends, causes, consequences, and lessons learned. *Journal of Marriage and the Family, 62,* 1094–1113.

Silvestri, G. (1995). Occupational employment to 2005. *Monthly Labor Review, 118,* 60–87.

Simon, B. L. (1990). Impact of shift work on individuals and families. *Families in Society* [Special issue], *71,* 342–348.

Snyder, H. W., & Sickmund, M. (1999). *Children as victims* (1999 National Report Series. Juvenile Justice Bulletin). Rockville, MD: Juvenile Justice Clearinghouse.

Stettner, A., & Wenger, J. (2003, May 15). *The broad reach of long-term unemployment* (Issue Brief #194). Washington, DC: Economic Policy Institute. Retrieved from www.epinet.org/Issuebriefs/ib194/ib194.pdf

Taniguchi, H., & Rosenfeld, R. A. (2002). Women's employment exit and reentry: Differences among whites, blacks, and Hispanics. *Social Science Research, 31,* 432–471.

Taylor, R. D., Rodriguez, A. U., Seaton, E., & Dominguez, A. (2004). Association of financial resources with parenting and adolescent adjustment in African American families. *Journal of Adolescent Research, 19*(3), 367–283.

Taylor, R. J., Jackson, J., & Chatters, L. (Eds.) (1997). *Family life in black America.* Thousand Oaks, CA: Sage.

Thompson, T. G. (2003). *Welfare reform: Building on success* (Testimony before the United States Senate Committee on Finance). Retrieved from www.os.hhs.gov/asl/testify/t030312.html

Toyokawa, T., & McLoyd, V. C. (2005). *Maternal work demands and child adjustment in African American families: The mediating role of family routines.* Manuscript submitted for publication.

U.S. Bureau of the Census. (2002). *Statistical abstract of the United States: 2002.* Washington, DC: Author.

Whitbeck, L. B., Simons, R. L., Conger, R. D., Wickrama, K. A. S., Ackley, K. A., & Elder, G. H., Jr. (1997). The effects of parents' working conditions and family economic hardship on parenting behaviors and children's self-efficacy. *Social Psychology Quarterly, 60,* 291–303.

White, L., & Keith, B. (1990). The effect of shift work on the quality and stability of marital relations. *Journal of Marriage and the Family, 52,* 453–462.

Williams, D. R., Spencer, M. S., & Jackson, J. S. (1999). Race, stress, and physical health: The role of group identity. In R. J. Contrada & R. D. Ashmore (Eds.), *Self, social identity, and physical health* (pp. 71–100). New York: Oxford University Press.

Williams, D. R., Yu, Y., Jackson, J. S., & Anderson, N. B. (1997). Racial differences in physical and mental health: Socioeconomic status, stress and discrimination. *Journal of Health Psychology, 23,* 335–351.

Wilson, W. J. (1996). *When work disappears: The world of the new urban poor.* New York: Knopf.

Winkler, A. E. (2002, June). *A new chapter in women's labor force participation: Rising rates among never-married mothers* (University of Missouri, St. Louis, Public Policy Research Center Policy Brief 9). St. Louis: University of Missouri. Retrieved from www.umsl.edu/services/pprc/data/pbrief_009_new chapter.pdf

Homeplace and Housing in the Lives of Low-Income Urban African American Families

Linda M. Burton *and* Sherri Lawson Clark

The purpose of this chapter is twofold. First, we discuss the importance of "homeplace" in the day-to-day lives of low-income urban African American families. Drawing principally on theoretical discussions of place provided by Gieryn (2000), Stack (1996), and hooks (1990), we define the homeplace as a multilayered, nuanced family process anchored in a bounded geographic space that elicits feelings of empowerment, commitment, rootedness, ownership, safety, and renewal among family members (Burton, Winn, Stevenson, & Lawson Clark, 2004). Critical features of the homeplace include social relationships characterized by distinct cultural symbols, meanings, and rituals (Allan & Crow, 1999; Fischer, 1982; Lahiri, 1999). In the context of a defined physical place, these relationships shape individuals' and families' sense of social and cultural identity (Burton, Hurt, Eline, & Matthews, 2001; Franklin, 1997; hooks, 1990).

Second, we describe the issues low-income urban African American families face and the strategies they employ to secure permanent housing to create a homeplace. Securing permanent housing is critical for low-income African American families because, frequently, it is intertwined with their access to social service programs and their ability to garner and sustain economic security (Gilbert, 1998). When families do not have permanent housing, social service agencies (e.g., job training programs, welfare, food stamp, and Medicaid offices) often cannot communicate important, life-affecting information to them via mail, telephone, or home visits. For many poor families, having unstable housing and living arrangements can preclude parents' success in securing and sustaining employment, children's timely progression in school, and the acquisition of consistent and quality medical care for family members. Moreover, unstable living conditions not only provide daily challenges for families that are at odds with successful access to social services and building economic security: they usurp families' ability to create and sustain a homeplace.

In this chapter we discuss the importance of homeplace and securing housing, using representative case studies from the ethnographic component of Welfare, Children and Families: A Three-City Study (Burton, Lein, & Kolak, 2005; Burton, Skinner, Matthews, & Gensimore, 2004; Winston et al., 1999). We begin with a brief overview of the Three-City Study Ethnography, followed by an integrative discussion of the importance of homeplace in the lives of low-income African Americans. Next we describe the strategies to secure housing used by many of the families that participated in our study. We conclude with specific recommendations for future research and policy on housing and the homeplace relative to the lives of low-income urban African American families specifically, and America's poor, in general.

THE THREE-CITY STUDY ETHNOGRAPHY

The data on homeplace and housing featured in this chapter derive from the ethnographic component of a larger research project, Welfare, Children and Families: A Three-City Study (Burton et al., 2004; Burton et al., 2005; Winston et al., 1999). The study was carried out over a period of 4 years in Boston, Chicago, and San Antonio. The purpose of the project was to monitor the consequences of welfare reform for the well-being of children and families. The study comprises three interrelated components: (1) a longitudinal in-person survey of approximately 2,400 families with children ages 0–4 and 10–14 in low-income neighborhoods, about 40% of whom were receiving cash welfare payments when they were first interviewed in 1999; (2) an embedded developmental study of a subsample of about 630 children ages 2–4 in 1999 and their caregivers; and (3) an ethnographic study of 256 families residing in the same neighborhoods as the survey families, recruited according to the same family income criteria, and that were followed intensively until the project ended in August 2003. In all three components and in all three cities, African American, Hispanic, and non-Hispanic White families are represented. A detailed description of the Welfare, Children, and Families: Three-City Study and a series of reports are available at www.jhu.edu/~welfare.

Families were recruited into the ethnography between June 1999 and December 2000 at formal childcare settings such as Head Start; Women, Infants and Children (WIC); neighborhood community centers; local welfare offices; churches; and other public assistance agencies. Of the 256 families participating in the ethnography, 44 were recruited specifically because they had a child, ages birth–8 years, with a moderate or severe disability. We include this purposive subsample of families in the analysis reported here because, much to our surprise, they are not distinguishable on homeplace and housing issues from the larger ethnographic sample. All families that participated in the ethnography had household incomes at or below 200% of the federal poverty line.

For the purposes of this chapter, we use only the data on the African American subsample of the Three-City Study Ethnography. Thirty-eight percent ($N = 98$ families) of the total ethnography sample ($N = 256$) were African American. More than two thirds (68%) of the mothers were age 29 or younger, and a majority of the respondents (80%) had a high school diploma, a GED, or had attended trade school or college. Sixty percent of the families were receiving welfare (Temporary Assistance for Needy Families, or TANF) when they entered the study; half of these, in compliance with welfare regulations, were also working. Forty percent of the sample was not receiving TANF benefits, and the primary earner in the household was either working a low-wage labor job or unemployed. Twenty-five percent of the mothers were responsible for one child, and 28%, 25%, and 23% for two, three, and four or more children, respectively. At the time they enrolled in the study, 63% of mothers were not married and did not have a partner (e.g., boyfriend) living with them; another 19% were not married but were cohabiting with a partner; 9% were married and living with their spouses; and 9% were married or separated and their spouses were not living in the home.

To gather ethnographic data on families, we employed a method of "structured discovery" in which in-depth interviews and observations focus on specific topics, but allow flexibility to capture unexpected findings and relationships (Burton et al., 2004). Topics addressed in the interviews included homeplace and housing; neighborhood environments; health and health access experiences with TANF and other public assistance programs; education and work experiences and future plans; family economics; child development, parenting, and intimate relationships; support networks; and family routines. In addition to these interviews, ethnographers engaged in participant observation with the families. This often involved accompanying a mother and her children to the housing office, welfare office, doctor, hospital, clinic, or workplace and taking note of the interactions and contexts of those places.

Ethnographers met with each family once or twice each month, on average, for 12–18 months. In the follow-up stage, families were interviewed every 6 months to identify any changes in their lives, including housing, family composition, welfare, work, and health. Each interview was audiotape-recorded and a written record for each interview was produced. These records took at least one (and sometimes more) of the following three formats: fieldnote, complete transcription, and targeted transcription (in which all information was recovered and narrative accounts of significant events were transcribed word-for-word). The documents were then coded for entry into a Qualitative Data Management (QDM) software application and summarized into a case profile for each family. The QDM program and case profiles enabled counts across the entire sample of ethnographic families as well as detailed analysis of individual cases.

In the case of each family, a team of Qualitative Data Analysts (QDAs), using profiles developed for each family and the QDM software, assessed each family's homeplace and housing experiences. Data on each family were cross-checked through an iterative process, in which information drawn from family profiles was compared with information available from the data collection team and the data processing team (the QDAs), and with information that had been coded into our QDM software. This process ensured the most complete and reliable analysis of the data.

Our discussion of the homeplace and housing experiences of the study participants focuses on the family as the principal unit of analysis, although we primarily use mothers' voices to describe their families' circumstances. Family is defined as the mother (biological or surrogate), her partner, the children they are responsible for, and the intergenerational kinship network they are embedded within. It is important to note that in discussing the lives of the families we use pseudonyms rather than actual names to protect the families' identities.

THE IMPORTANCE OF HOMEPLACE IN THE LIVES OF LOW-INCOME URBAN AFRICAN AMERICAN FAMILIES

Two of the most profound challenges faced by many of the African American families in our study were that most did not possess a homeplace or they were struggling to maintain one. Our experiences in interviewing these families and reviewing their lives led us to conclude that a viable homeplace could potentially be a critical protective re-source for them. It could be a refuge from the daily barrage of life in poverty and a sanctuary from and opposed to the discriminatory prac-tices they experienced in larger social contexts (Clark, 1993; hooks, 1990).

Moreover, the homeplace was consistently discussed by the families as a force they reckoned with throughout the life course. In the best of circumstances, the homeplace was described by families as a source of strength and social defiance in their life victories (e.g., children attending an upper-middle-class predominately White school). However, for fami-lies who did not have one, the homeplace was manifested as unrealized dreams or a source of conflict, loss, and grief. Seventeen-year-old Benjamin's description of his ideal homeplace epitomizes comments we typically heard from individuals struggling to find one:

> "Oh, if I only had a house and home like the Cosbys! I would never be scared again. Nothing from the streets could get me. I could come home and close the door and my four sisters Rudy, Vanessa, Denise, and Sondra and my parents Claire and Cliff would be there and we would laugh and talk and everything would be good. All the prob-lems would be on the other side of the front door. Being Black would be just fine, just fine. No pain, no pain."

Although insights on the homeplace emerged in the ethnographic data, we also looked to the conceptual and empirical work of Gieryn (2000), Stack (1996), hooks (1990), and others (Clark, 1993; Gilbert, 1998; Lahiri, 1999; Perkins, Thorns, Winstanley, & Newton, 2002; Sanders, 1993; Vivero & Jenkins, 1999) to help us interpret the meaning of homeplace in the families' lives. Gieryn (2000) provides theoretical principles useful for studying the homeplace, noting that it has three es-sential features: geographic location, material form, and investment with meaning and value. He contends that home, nested in a definable space, is the crucible from which a person's social identity emerges, transforms, and is internalized and sustained over time.

In the classic ethnography, *Call to Home*, Stack (1996) recounts the return migration of adult African Americans to the poor rural South, and, in doing so, reveals the homeplace as a critical and dynamic devel-opmental process in their lives. African American families involved in her study experienced the homeplace as an omnipotent entity. It would send certain family members away in early adulthood and call them back in midlife. The homeplace would hasten some to reclaim their childhood attachment to the land and the rootedness that soil, a family house, or a community cemetery provide. It would beckon men, women, and children to assume family caregiving responsibilities anchored in the very place life began for them. It was also a safe haven from the uncompromising demands of living in high-risk urban neighborhoods. And, as a site of resistance, it shaped families' political consciousness and destiny.

The writings of bell hooks (1990) are particularly persuasive on matters of the homeplace and African Americans. In her critically acclaimed collection of essays, *Yearning: Race, Gender, and Cultural Politics*, hooks underscores the importance of the homeplace relative to the survival and coping strategies of African Americans. Recounting memories of childhood visits to her grandparents' home, hooks characterizes the homeplace as a communal experience anchored in a domestic household where "all that truly mattered in life took place, the warmth and comfort of shelter, the feeding of our bodies, the nurturing of our souls. There we learned dignity, integrity of being . . . there we learned to have faith" (pp. 41–42).

hooks's essays on the homeplace highlight the historical, political, cultural, race, and social consciousness necessary for understanding the lived experiences of many African Americans. In fact, her perspective is reified in numerous venues (Allan & Crow, 1999; Altman & Werner, 1985; Clark, 1993; Gilbert, 1998; Perkins et al., 2002; Sanders, 1993; Stack & Burton, 1993; Vivero & Jenkins, 1999). For example, Waniek (1990) and Dilworth-Williams (2003) artfully depict the cultural ethos of the homeplace in their respective collections of poetry, *The Homeplace* and *Panola: My Kinfolks's Land*. These authors' verses poignantly describe the family labor involved in men, women, and children creating a homeplace, the routines and rituals that embody it, the physical space that gives the homeplace form, and what happens in the lives of African Americans who don't have one.

African Americans experience a deep sense of yearning when they don't have a homeplace, can't create one, are embattled about keeping it, or are working to reclaim it. According to hooks (1990), this yearning is an individual's or family's psychological and emotional longing for connectedness to place, for a sense of rootedness and purpose, and for a crucible of affirmation of one's sense of social and cultural identity.

hooks (1990, p. 42) also describes the homeplace as a "site of resistance forged principally through the intergenerational labor of African American women. As a site of resistance, the homeplace is where African Americans could freely confront humanization issues, develop a political consciousness, and resist racist stereotypes and oppression." hooks (p. 42) states that African American women designed the homeplace to be a physical and social environment where "black people could strive to be subjects, not objects, where we could be affirmed in our minds and

hearts despite poverty, hardship, and deprivation, where we could re-
store to ourselves the dignity denied us on the outside in the public
world."

Figure 8.1 illustrates our conceptualization of the homeplace as a
site of resistance where, as hooks (1990, p. 47) argues, "post-slavery African Americans were able to evade the tyranny of racism." We learned
that many of the African American families in our study needed a
homeplace as a site of resistance, as a place to construct their social identities, to empower themselves by negotiating privacy, and to regulate
family routines and build legacies. The site of resistance is embedded
with meanings, symbols, and actions that allow individuals to form a
place identity that, in turn, enhances a person's well-being, forges
intergenerational networks, and builds stability (Clark, 1993; Howard,
2000; Low, 1992). Implicit in these descriptions of homeplace is the notion of process—that is, each individual must cultivate a homeplace just
as farmers tend to their crops year after year. It takes time to build a
homeplace. One does not just happen upon a homeplace. Nor can one
be arbitrarily situated into a homeplace.

Notice the semipermeable nature of the homeplace (see Figure 8.1),
as forces on the outside are continually seeking entry and forces on the
inside are being made and remade to resist dominance. hooks (1990,
p. 47) contends, "It is no accident that this homeplace [where Black
women and men went to renew their spirits and recover themselves] . . .
is always subject to violation and destruction" because "when a people
no longer have the space to construct a homeplace, we cannot build a
meaningful community of resistance." Thus, the homeplace is much
more than a physical structure located in space; it is a political and personal necessity.

Our data suggest that the homeplace serves several critical functions
in the lives of the families we studied, including the construction of social and cultural identity, the procurement of privacy and power and
control, and the development and maintenance of family routines and
legacies. We discuss these functions in greater detail in the following sections.

Constructing Social and Cultural Identity

Social and cultural identity and the homeplace are co-constructed
(Gieryn, 2000; hooks, 1990; Stack, 1996). Through the co-construction
process, individuals and families begin to identify themselves in terms of
group memberships and are able to distinguish attributes that make
them similar to and unique from others (Howard, 2000). For many of
the African American mothers in our study who lived in or near the

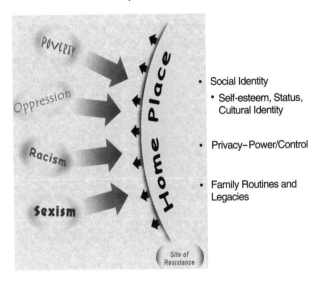

FIGURE 8.1. The homeplace as a site of resistance.

same neighborhood in which they were raised and close to extended family members, their attachment to place was essential in constructing their identities. Living in a place in which other family members are present may "provide status and enhance . . . self-esteem" (Howard, 2000, p. 369). These place attachments, which "provide people and groups with a sense of unique cultural identity" (Low, 1992, p. 11), may also provide some explanation as to why some of the African American mothers in our study who moved to the suburbs through Section 8 or other housing programs spoke highly of the experience, but eventually returned to their old neighborhoods (Rosenbaum & Harris, 2000, 2002). Meisha's homeplace dilemma illustrates this point.

Meisha, a 26-year-old mother of five, spent her entire life living in Chicago Housing Authority (CHA) developments. The housing authority gave Meisha three choices when her project housing was scheduled for demolition—scattered site housing, Section 8 voucher, or a unit in another CHA development. She chose scattered site housing in the suburbs of DuPage. She describes her experience while living there as:

"Wonderful, I mean wonderful. Forty dollars a month is what I have to pay. I had a house full of furniture, I had everything I wanted—cable, just everything, and it was just wonderful. I just miss it, I really do. It was better than CHA . . . DuPage is like global, you know . . . they got more technology than I ever seen and things that they doin' over here in Chicago, they been did over there in DuPage. It's just different, it's like goin' to another different state. DuPage is the richest county in Chicago, so it's marvelous and I like it out there. I been all out there and it's just the way you would wanta live, I mean, you go home, you don't have to worry about nothin'. It's like you stress free when you out there, you don't have to worry about all that stuff, that gang bangin', hangin' out on the front . . . "

Unfortunately, Meisha's mother, with whom she had a very close relationship, died suddenly and Meisha decided to move back to the city and her original homeplace. Meisha's mother had played a major role in sustaining Meisha's day-to-day connectedness to her Chicago homeplace. When her mother died, Meisha's most salient connection to the homeplace was lost. Subsequently, Meisha decided to return home to personally tend to her relationships with kin and to ensure that the family homeplace, as a site of refuge, was maintained. Although Meisha reminisces about moving back to DuPage in the future, she has decided to remain in her former neighborhood for the time being. For now, it is where she feels comforted and grounded.

Garnering Privacy, Power, and Control

The second reason a homeplace is important is that it allows one to garner privacy, power, and control in one's immediate environment. In addressing this issue, however, it is incumbent upon us to make the point that although privacy, power, and control are integral aspects of the homeplace, their presence is not always suggestive of positive experiences in the home. In fact, individuals are abused and neglected in the privacy of the home and some family members use their power and control over others in personally and relationally destructive ways.

Nonetheless, garnering privacy, power, and control was a challenge for many of the mothers in our study because most had lived in some form of subsidized housing all of their lives. The public nature of their lives in the form of adherence to welfare and housing authority regulations and sanctions is closely reminiscent of Bentham's (cited in Foucault, 1995, pp. 204–206) panopticon which "functions as a kind of laboratory of power . . . " applicable "to all establishments whatsoever, in which, within a space, a number of persons are meant to be kept under inspection." The privacy of a homeplace offers some relief from the inspections, studies, and other intrusions that those who receive welfare have to encounter. Young (1997, pp. 162–163) states, "Whatever her social activities, a person should have control over access to her living space, her meaningful things, and information about herself."

In the spirit of Bentham's and Young's perspectives, one of the mothers involved in our study complained that the Boston Housing Authority removed the fences that divided tenants' backyards. Although the officials may have thought nothing of the changes, this mother considered the removal of the fences not only an invasion of her privacy but also a denial of her ability to allow her children to play outside alone. As researchers, we question the motives of the housing authority in making homes more accessible to the public and less private for tenants.

For many of the mothers in our study, perceptions of a homeplace embodied power and control, and the lack thereof created a sense of subordination. The ability to establish power, control, and social boundaries around the home and to decide who is allowed to enter and under what circumstances is fixed in social relations (Allan & Crow, 1999). When mothers and their children have to live as boarders in other family members' or friends' homes, they lose the sense of power, control, and belonging, or, as Allan and Crow (1999, p. 144) describe, "They happen to live there, but it does not have the identity of home."

Consider the case of Carol, a single mother of two young daughters. Carol lived in the same Chicago neighborhood for 25 years. Although she lived in the same community for a quarter of a century, since childhood she had resided in 15 places, migrating from the household of one family member to another. She had no job and her welfare benefits had been cut; therefore, she was also at the mercy of others. She described a time when she lived with her mother who, depending on her mood, refused to buy food, and Carol and her children would go hungry. When Carol had money, she always bought food for the entire household, including her mother and siblings. Carol described this period of transience as a state of homelessness, "not out on the street homeless but nonetheless homeless. . . . I was out of my mind . . . and frequently considered suicide."

After several years of transience, Carol was able to move into her own apartment. Since moving into her own place, she describes her life as "peaceful . . . the best characteristic about the apartment is it's mine. . . . In others' homes, I had to keep my children quiet . . . felt uncomfortable using the kitchen . . . had to stay in the bathroom with my girls because I didn't want them in there alone." She credits her new home with aiding in the development of her daughters, who were able to be more independent after moving into their own place.

Creating and Maintaining Family Routines and Rituals

Some of Carol's problems during the times she spent living with her relatives were due to an inability to regulate family routines and build a legacy for her daughters. Carol's dilemma presents a third reason underscoring the importance of homeplace in the lives of low-income African American families. The case of Sonia's family further illustrates the point.

In reviewing the case of Sonia, a 25-year-old mother of two who was placed with an aunt as a young child after her mother abandoned her and her siblings, we observed the connections between the homeplace and stable family routines. Sonia described to us how difficult it was living in her aunt's house because of the "extra kids in the house" and "lots of jealousy." When she was 18, Sonia recalled her aunt coming home one day tired "of grown niggas' living in her house and she kicked everybody out." Sonia realized that it was time for her to go, especially because she had to raise a child of her own. For a short period of time, she moved in with her grandmother, who lived across the street from her aunt. Although Sonia found her grandmother's house as constricting as her aunt's house, she praised her grandmother's networking skills in getting her and her children a unit in the newly renovated Center Place Housing Development. It was only after acquiring her new home that Sonia was able to regulate and normalize her children's daily lives.

Although many of the African American mothers in our study relied on family ties in times of need, some realized the need to sever ties in an effort to keep themselves and their children afloat. Janice, a single mother of six boys, was a recovering drug addict and a victim of domestic abuse. She recalled her several moves from housing complexes rampant with gang activity to other "houses" where she had to place towels beneath her door to prevent the smell of crack cocaine from entering her home. After months of researching and filling out forms with the Boston Housing Authority, she and her children moved into a three-story townhouse.

Upon securing a stable environment for herself and her sons, Janice tried "helping out" her siblings even though they were constant reminders of the life she used to live. One brother was in a veteran's hospital; two other brothers were in jail, one of whom had AIDS; and her two sisters were addicted to drugs. Each of her five siblings lived with her and her sons at one time or another. She became emotionally drained after one of their visits and finally decided to cut off ties with them. She also instructed her boys not to open the door to them anymore. In doing so, she demonstrated the essence of the homeplace as a site of resistance, whether one is retaliating against oppressive institutions, a beleaguered economy, or impaired family members.

The stories of Janice, Sonia, Carol, and Meisha are a few examples of the complexities involved in constructing a homeplace. These mothers have overcome the major hurdle of acquiring the physical form of a homeplace and are in good positions to continue building the psychological, social, and emotional dimensions of the homeplace. However, for many other mothers involved in our study, securing the physical space and structure for a homeplace is a distant dream (Massey & Denton, 1993).

STRATEGIES FOR SECURING STABLE HOUSING AND A HOMEPLACE

Americans have long identified permanent housing as one of the most significant indicators of economic attainment (Conley, 1999; Goering & Feins, 2003; Kidder, 1999; Lawson Clark & Burton, 2003). Housing is seen as a central element in social and economic mobility and communicates a sense of stability, prestige, and status (Oliver & Shapiro, 1995). A permanent residence not only provides a psychological sense of satisfaction and well-being but also serves as an important junction for communicating with and being contacted by others (Altman & Werner, 1985). A fixed abode means that the occupants can apply for jobs, access social services, form lasting relationship with neighbors, and create a homeplace.

Recognizing the important role of housing in promoting family economic self-sufficiency for low-income families, national housing policy has paid considerable attention to the shortage of affordable and decent housing (Lawson Clark, 2002a). To alleviate the pressure on poor families in locating low-cost housing, the federal government funds public and private sector housing units, which are made available to families who meet some basic requirements for eligibility. Public housing, especially in large metropolitan areas, is characteristically composed of high-density, high-rise apartment complexes that house large numbers of poor families. The most common form of federally assisted housing is provided by the private sector. These units are normally made available to families who qualify for a Section 8 voucher or who reside in units that were built with below-market-rate loans or low-income housing tax credits. Despite the existence of these programs, there remains a dire shortage of low-rent units that poor families can afford. In areas with high residential segregation, low-income African American families are further disadvantaged in obtaining adequate housing (Bullard, Lee, Charles, Grigsby, & Feagin, 1994; Lawson Clark, 2002b; Massey & Denton, 1993).

In most urban areas the waiting lists for available public or Section 8 units are closed to new enrollees, and those who are lucky enough to get their names on a list often have to wait years before suitable units become available. Even for those low-income families fortunate enough to have subsidized housing, the financial and psychological costs of maintaining a permanent address can be daunting. A number of studies have indicated that a majority of the working poor (families earning the full-time equivalent of minimum wage, $10,712, and 120% of the median area income) experience excessive housing costs (Lawson Clark, 2002b). Many also live in dilapidated structures that posed health and safety risks for their children and themselves.

The remainder of this chapter describes some of the major issues families in our study faced and the strategies they employed to secure housing. Foremost among these issues are precarious romantic relationships, overcrowding, weak credit, housing affordability and quality, and the ability to substantiate one's "worthiness" for getting a house and complying with the housing rules.

For an illustration of the impact of these issues on acquiring and sustaining housing, consider Jasmine's experiences with precarious romantic relationships and residential crowding. Jasmine moved 11 times since she was 18 years old. Her first move occurred when she left her parents' home to live with her husband when she was 18. She lasted two years in that relationship and left because of her husband's drug addiction and physical abuse. She moved twice in a brief period after that. She first obtained a one-bedroom and then a two-bedroom unit in public housing in San Antonio. She then met another man, with whom she had a daughter, and moved out of public housing and into an apartment with him. This relationship became abusive, and Jasmine left and moved in with her biological father for a brief period. Her exposure to abusive men continued there, and she complained that during that time her father "was still being the same abusive person the way he was [when she was growing up] . . . verbally, physically."

In brief succession Jasmine tried various living arrangements with family members, but none of them worked out. Along the way, Jasmine gave birth to two more children. After the birth of her third child, she moved her family in with her mother for a while, but the conditions were too crowded so she moved on to another arrangement. At one point, she ended up in a shelter where she stayed for 5 months while she tried to work out a permanent solution to her living arrangements. Commenting about that period, Jasmine relates, "It's something I don't talk about. It's something the girls don't remember, and I don't plan on letting them remember, because it was the lowest point in my life."

Jasmine was finally approved for a Section 8 apartment; however, she and her children had only a brief stint in this apartment as well. A neighbor reported that Jasmine's boyfriend also lived in the apartment and that she was evicted for violating the terms of her lease. Jasmine subsequently moved back into her mother's apartment, which was also shared by other family members. In all, there were ten people living in Jasmine's mother's three-bedroom house—Jasmine, her three children, Jasmine's mother, her grandmother, and her sisters. The ethnographer noted that Jasmine and her daughters were "literally camping in the living room." They slept on couch cushions on the floor, and their clothes and shoes were stacked in a box in the middle of the living room. Jasmine hopes to have a place of her own in about five years. Her criteria for an apartment is as simple as "four walls and a roof . . . cheap but not dangerous, nice but not elegant, because I can't afford elegant right now."

Charnisse's situation sheds light on the problems that weak credit histories create for low-income African American mothers who attempt to secure housing. Charnisse is a 23-year-old mother of two living in Boston. She was on TANF for the entire period she was enrolled in the study. Her benefits fluctuated from month to month, and she was unsure what the reasons for this were.

Charnisse got pregnant when she was in the ninth grade at age 16. She moved into a project-based Section 8 apartment with her boyfriend shortly after her child was born and had intermittent work and welfare patterns for about 2 years. When her boyfriend left her and her child, she "made some bad choices" and readily admits that her behavior caused some problems for her and her child at the time. She got behind in her rent and had some arguments with her neighbors; she was eventually asked to leave the building and lost her Section 8. Her situation continued to deteriorate from that point.

Charnisse eventually moved in with her mother and sister, who were residing in a Section 8 apartment where both adults' names were on the lease. However, they were having housing problems of their own. The sister complained of overcrowding and was in the process of leaving the apartment. The sister had not kept up with her rent payments, and because the lease was in both of their names, the mother was also in arrears and was constantly harassed by the building manager. By now Charnisse had three children and their presence in the apartment caused additional concerns for the mother in that she could be evicted for allowing her daughter and grandchildren to stay with her as they were not legitimate tenants. Even though Charnisse could not afford to pay for an apartment of her own at the moment, her bad credit history and her inability to obtain referrals from previous landlords prevented her from finding a place of her own when she tried. Charnisse and her three children stayed in one of the bedrooms in her mother's two-bedroom apartment, but the situation was tense. Charnisse stated that everyone bickered constantly and that it was "very stressful."

Individuals' voices and personal stories of how these impediments constrain their ability to establish places of their own have received short shrift in the empirical literature on housing and the homeplace

(Burton, Quane, & Graefe, 2002; Clark, 1993). Our ethnographic accounts of mothers' rationalizations of their living situations underscore the complex array of issues they must consider when choosing where to reside. Overcrowding is sometimes endured because a young mother must remain at home to care for ailing parents or siblings. Affordability is sometimes equated with risk, as mothers must weigh the tradeoffs of a low-cost rental unit in a high-crime neighborhood. And the quality of a house can have various meanings, depending on where a person is coming from or going to. For one mother, quality housing can mean not having to protect her child from rodents or other pests likely to harm or infect the child. For another, quality can mean having two separate bathrooms instead of one. Nonetheless, low-income mothers' circumstances dictate the need to make some very difficult choices and perhaps employ questionable strategies to secure housing.

Results from our analysis of the Three-City Study ethnographic data indicated that mothers used several strategies to garner housing, including (1) purposely making only just enough income to qualify for a housing voucher; (2) using split-family living arrangements; (3) doubling up; and (4) using last-resort strategies to procure housing by filing for bankruptcy, "holding three months rent," or moving one's name up on the Section 8 list by rendering one's family homeless or declaring oneself to be drug dependent or a victim of domestic violence. Case studies illustrating these strategies follow.

Making Just Enough to Qualify

Carrie, an African American single mother of three, runs her San Antonio household on tight time and financial budgets and works a nontraditional shift of three days on, four days off, as a flight attendant. She uses the four days off to work on an associate's degree at a local college and to complete the household domestic work required for family functioning. She says she chose this employment routine because it allows her to earn enough money to make ends meet, but not enough to disqualify her eligibility for public housing assistance. According to Carrie, this is a strategy for providing the best possible home environment for her children within the double constraints of her ability to produce a family income combined with public assistance income thresholds.

> "I am what you call the 'working poor.' The only difference between me and [someone else] is that I was smart enough to go to [public housing] and not to the regular rent. Because regular rent, you just cannot do it. If you lose your apartment—I did it before!—you lose your apartment; that's it! You're evicted! Whereas here, they'll work with you, you know."

Carrie has been working 55–65 hours each month to improve her family's financial position. She says she would need to work 85 hours each month, but the trade-off would be tragically expensive. As she says:

> "I could fly and never see these kids . . . have a brand new house, you know, brand new car, but I'd never see them, see. And I would be paying [a] mortgage and be in a higher tax bracket. But now with four kids, it's not worth it. I would be just working to pay for them and my place and the material things. I could do it, but of course, I'd never see them, and it would be like that. We could have it all, but I prefer to fly just enough to where I am below the income level, where I can afford something halfway decent."

Carrie never lived in public housing until now, but her family does know what it is like to be without a place to call home. After dropping out of college in her early 20s, Carrie became an airline stewardess for a major airline, where she worked steadily until she was 30 and became pregnant with her first child. Separated from the child's father during that pregnancy, she drew sick leave from the airline as well as collecting unemployment benefits. Upon discovering her second pregnancy seven years later, Carrie again filed for unemployment benefits only to find that her earlier benefit receipt had been fraudulent, and she was ineligible to receive further unemployment benefits. This financial crisis resulted in Carrie's inability to afford the apartment in which they were living, forcing her to move, with, at the time, an 8-year-old and twin infants, into a Salvation Army shelter—an experience sufficiently stressful to change Carrie's sense of adult responsibility for independence from her own parents. Carrie had felt that grown children should take care of themselves and their own families, and not move in with relatives. Next time, she says, she will turn to her father to spare herself and her children. Carrie remarked, "Proudness, pride, tail between my legs, I will go back home to my dad, deal with my father, instead of putting my children through what we went through as far as shelter and transitional housing. Never again in life." This conviction adds to her strategic resolve to keep her children in their public housing apartment, even if it means forgoing an improvement in their financial state.

Split-Family Living Arrangements

Sandra, a 22-year-old mother of two children, was 8 months pregnant with her third child when she was served an eviction notice from her Chicago landlord, a personal friend of her deceased parents. The landlord demanded that she move out of her apartment on December 24th, Christmas Eve, also the day her third child was to due to be born. Three months earlier, the landlord had learned that he could rent Sandra's apartment for four times the amount he was getting from her. Because Sandra was 3 months behind in her rent, he decided that he would move her out, and a higher-rent-paying tenant in.

Sandra searched vigorously for an apartment, but to no avail. The morning of December 24, the landlord had Sandra's belongings moved out of the apartment onto the street. Sandra went into labor that night. Before going to the hospital, she took her children to stay with their respective grandparents where they continued to stay for 9 months thereafter. She gave birth to a baby girl on Christmas Day.

Two days later, Sandra was released from the hospital with nowhere to go. Her baby's father's mother agreed to let her new grandchild live with her and her father until Sandra could find a place to live. However, a sticking point was that the baby's grandmother would not allow Sandra to stay in her home with the baby. One of Sandra's friends, who lived 25 miles away from the area in which Sandra's children were residing, agreed to let only Sandra stay with her until she could find housing.

Although in Sandra's case, moving to a homeless shelter was an alternative to a split-family living arrangement, Sandra refused to consider this as a viable option. She believed that the split-family living arrangement was her family's best chance for having a temporary stable living environment. The family lived across four separate households—Sandra at her friend's house, her oldest son with his grandparents, her second oldest son with his grandparents, and her baby daughter with her father and grandmother—for 9 months until Sandra found an apartment she could afford. Her greatest regret is that because she lived separately from her baby girl, she was not there to hear her daughter's first words or to see her crawl for the first time.

Doubling Up

Doubling up, or "stacking," is a strategy to secure housing used by a number of the mothers in the study (Burton, Quane, & Graefe, 2002). Doubling up involves two or more families sharing a single residence and can often create significant tensions in a household. For example, Angela, age 19, experienced this conflict firsthand before going into public housing. "[My mother] was tripping because she did not want to help me with him [her son] and everything. . . . She say me and my sister are grown and she wanted to go on her own and get on with her life." Now Angela and her older, childless, sister share a place. This arrangement helps both of them. Her sister recently lost her job and had no place to live. Angela provides her with a place, and her sister provides childcare for Angela's son. However, this interferes with her sister's job search efforts, tying her down at a time when she wants to find a new job so she can get a place of her own.

Last-Resort Strategies

The experiences of the Jones family are particularly illustrative of a strategy used by several of the families to move up the list for a Section 8 voucher. The plan involves the family's moving to the "projects" so that it is viewed as having a high-priority housing need. This strategy, however, is not without costs. Unfortunately, the costs for Evette Jones were very high.

Evette and her children once lived in the suburbs and believed they were finally setting a new family path out of poverty. Evette held on tightly to her dream until one day, greatly affected by the sequential and unexpected deaths of her parents and brother, and overwhelmed by financial difficulties, she made a decision to "just stop working." Evette and her children then left the suburbs and moved back into the same housing project in which she grew up, even though she feared for her children's safety. Evette was hedging her bets, because she knew that moving back into the projects greatly increased her chances for getting a Section 8 housing voucher. Nonetheless, Evette's fears were realized when she and her family were victimized and the windows in her apartment were continually smashed by people attempting to break in. Her young daughter, Candice, was in the room during one such incident. Evette recounted:

> "When they busted the windows, my baby was in the kitchen and it was something that just knocked me off my feet. I was over overwhelmed cause I was like, my precious baby, she's just a doll, she would hurt no one. Why would you want to hurt a baby, you know? And just think that if you know the baby's in there, to hurt them and they helpless, they just babies, they don't deserve this. How you gonna just end their life or hurt them and they just, you know, babies. They gotta grow like you did to grow to bust that window. That's why I was just real overprotective and now that I am living in fear because I feel like now, you gonna bust my windows, you throw a cocktail in here, you gonna burn me up."

Evette continued to live in her apartment because she hoped she would eventually be relocated to one of the new townhomes being built for residents of her complex. To protect herself and her family, Evette had her windows boarded up, leaving only one small area exposed. In the meantime, afraid for her children's safety, she was hesitant to let them play outside. This was particularly difficult for one of her six sons who has hypertension. He, along with three of her other children, also has asthma. Evette exclaims, "[My son] feels like he is caved in, he never goes outside and he don't go outside playing and running around. [My] number one priority in life is having safety. And I don't have that right now."

Issues of housing, financial insecurity, and safety appear to have played a major role in Evette's fate. After living in the housing project a little less than a year, Evette was arrested for allegedly participating in illegal activities. She was sent to jail and relatives assumed responsibility for her children's care. Although the boarded-up windows may have helped prevent people from breaking into Evette's apartment, they appeared to be a major factor in endangering the lives of her children. While in the care of family members, a fire broke out in Evette's apartment and Candice was killed. Because she was incarcerated, Evette was not able to attend her daughter's funeral.

SUMMARY AND CONCLUSION

The purpose of this chapter was to discuss the importance of homeplace in the day-to-day lives of low-income urban African American families and to describe the issues families face and the strategies they employ to secure permanent housing to establish a homeplace. Our intent in this chapter was not to romanticize the homeplace or demonize the housing circumstances of the poor, nor was it to imply that the insights presented here are useful or relevant only for low-income urban African American families. Rather, our goal was to draw attention to the salience of the homeplace and housing issues for African Americans and to catalyze a discourse on the utility of exploring these ideas in future research. We do acknowledge that although homeplace and housing issues have distinct features and cultural meanings, depending on the ethnic/racial group being considered, there are aspects of these issues that undeniably have universal relevance or potential relevance for families of all backgrounds (Gilbert, 1998; Lahiri, 1999; Perkins et al., 2002).

Building on the homeplace perspectives of Gieryn (2000), Stack (1996), and hooks (1990), and the ethnographic data on low-income African American families derived from Welfare, Children, and Families: A Three-City Study (Burton et al., 2004), we argue that the ability to construct a homeplace as a site of resistance may greatly improve the lives of African American families in poverty. Our data illustrate that mothers who have created a homeplace have higher self-esteem and self-identity, are more empowered to draw social boundaries around their homes excluding individuals who are negative influences on the family, and are better able to manage the daily routines of their families while establishing solid foundations from which their offspring can develop.

The availability of and access to safe, high-quality, and affordable housing in high-poverty neighborhoods is another important part of the homeplace equation. As our data suggest, issues of overcrowding, bad credit, and the required ability to substantiate one's "worthiness" for getting a house and comply with the housing rules are major impediments to families' securing adequate housing. Many families' circumstances dictate the need to make some very difficult choices and perhaps employ questionable strategies to secure housing. Such circumstances underscore the dire need for public policy and the reevaluation of, and commitment to, sustainable measures to directly address the housing needs of America's poor. These measures may include (1) recalibrating income eligibility guidelines so that working single mothers can sustain levels of employment that meet their families' financial needs, but do not compromise mothers' abilities to provide care for their children; (2) instituting a well-funded national policy to provide emergency housing support for homeless pregnant mothers and their children; (3) providing alternative housing options that support some families' needs to "double up"; (4) investigating how local "urban housing myths" (e.g., in order to move up the Section 8 housing list, you should move into the projects regardless of the quality and safety of the units) influence the sometimes catastrophic decisions families make about housing; and (5) implementing a sensitively to homeplace issues in housing policies.

Clearly, much work needs to be done in evaluating the relationship between the homeplace and housing in the lives of low-income families regardless of race. We hope this chapter has raised issues that will stimulate further empirical investigation and discussion of this concern.

ACKNOWLEDGMENTS

We gratefully acknowledge the funders of the ethnographic component of Welfare, Children, and Families: A Three-City Study, including the National Institute of Child Health and Human Development; the Assistant Secretary for Planning and Evaluation, U.S. Department of Health and Human Services; the Social Security Administration; the Henry J. Kaiser Family Foundation; the Robert Wood Johnson Foundation; the W.K. Kellogg Foundation; and the John D. and Catherine T. MacArthur Foundation. We extend special thanks to our 210-member ethnographic team (see project website www.jhu.edu/~welfare) and, particularly, the Penn State team that provided the infrastructure, organization, and data management for the multisite ethnography. Most important, we thank the families that have graciously participated in the project and have given us access to their lives.

REFERENCES

Allan, G., & Crow, G. (Eds.). (1999). *Home and family: Creating the domestic sphere*. London: Macmillan.

Altman, I., & Werner, C. (Eds.). (1985). *Human behavior and environment: Advances in theory and research: Vol. 8. Home environments*. New York: Plenum Press.

Bullard, R., Lee, W., Charles, J., Grigsby, E., & Feagin, J. (Eds.). (1994). *Residential apartheid: The American legacy* (CAAS Urban Policy Series, Vol. 2). Los Angeles: CAAS.

Burton, L. M., Hurt, T. R., Eline, C., & Matthews, S. (2001, October). *"The yellow brick road": Neighborhoods, the homeplace, and life course development in economically disadvantaged families*. Keynote address presented at the second biennial meeting of the Society for the Study of Human Development, Ann Arbor, MI.

Burton, L. M., Lein, L., & Kolak, A. (2005). Health, and mothers' employment in low income families. In S. Bianchi, L. Casper, & R. King (Eds.), *Work, family health, and well-being* (pp. 493–509). Mahwah, NJ: Erlbaum.

Burton, L. M., Quane, J., & Graefe, D. R. (2002, November). *Inside which walls?: Low-income families' strategies for procuring stable housing in an era of welfare reform*. Paper presented at the annual meeting of the Association for Public Policy Analysis and Management, Dallas, TX.

Burton, L. M., Skinner, D., Matthews, S., & Gensimore, D. (2004). *Structuring discovery: A model and method for multi-site team ethnography*. Working paper, Center for Human Development and Family Research in Diverse Contexts, Pennsylvania State University.

Burton, L. M., Winn, D. M., Stevenson, H., & Lawson Clark, S. (2004). Working with African American clients: Considering the homeplace in counseling and therapy practices. *Journal of Marriage and Family Therapy, 30*(4), 397–410.

Clark, H. (1993). Sites of resistance: Place, "race," and gender as sources of empowerment. In P. E. Jackson & J. Penrose (Eds.), *Constructions of race, place, and nation* (pp. 121–142). London: UCL Press.

Conley, D. (1999). *Being black, living in the red*. Berkely: University of California Press.

Dilworth-Williams, E. (2003). *Panola: My kinfolks's land*. Bloomington, IN: 1stBooks.

Fischer, C. S. (1982). *To dwell among friends*. Chicago: University of Chicago Press.

Foucault, M. (1995). *Discipline and punish: The birth of the prison*. New York: Vintage Books.

Franklin, D. L. (1997). *Ensuring inequality: The structural transformation of the African-American family*. New York: Oxford University Press.

Gieryn, T. (2000). A space for place in sociology. *Annual Review of Sociology, 2*, 463–96.

Gilbert, M. R. (1998). Race, space, and power: The survival strategies of working poor women. *Annals of the Association of American Geographers, 88,* 595–621.

Goering, J., & Feins, J. D. (Eds.). (2003). *Choosing a better life? Evaluating the Moving to Opportunity social experiment.* Washington, DC: Urban Institute.

hooks, b. (1990). *Yearning: Race, gender, and cultural politics.* Boston: South End Press.

Howard, J. (2000). Social psychology of identities. *Annual Review of Sociology, 26,* 367–393.

Kidder, T. (1999). *House.* New York: Houghton Mifflin.

Lahiri, J. (1999). *Interpreter of maladies.* New York: Houghton Mifflin.

Lawson Clark, S. (2002a). *Policy, perceptions, and place: An ethnography of the complexities of implementing a federal housing program.* Unpublished doctoral dissertation, American University, Washington, DC.

Lawson Clark, S. (2002b). Where the poor live: How federal housing policy shapes residential communities. *Urban Anthropology and Studies of Cultural Systems and World Economic Development, 31*(1), 69–92.

Lawson Clark, S., & Burton, L. M. (2003, November). *The American dream: Homeownership and aging among American's urban poor.* Paper presented at the annual meeting of the Gerontological Society of America, San Diego, CA.

Low, S. (1992). Symbolic ties that bind: Place attachment in the plaza. In I. Altman & S. Low (Eds.), *Human behavior and environment: Advances in theory and research* (Vol. 12, pp. 165–185). New York: Plenum Press.

Massey, D., & Denton, N. (1993). *American apartheid: Segregation and the making of the underclass.* Cambridge, MA: Harvard University Press.

Oliver, M., & Shapiro, T. (1995). *Black wealth/white wealth: A new perspective on racial inequality.* New York: Routledge.

Perkins, H., Thorns, D., Winstanley, A., & Newton, B. (2002). *The study of "home" from a social scientific perspective: An annotated bibliography* (2nd ed.). Christchurch, New Zealand: University of Canterbury.

Rosenbaum, E., & Harris, L. (2000). Residential mobility and opportunities: Early impacts of the Moving to Opportunity demonstration program in Chicago. *Housing Policy Debate, 12,* 321–346.

Rosenbaum, E., & Harris, L. (2002). Low-income families in their new neighborhoods: The short-term effects of moving from Chicago's public housing. *Journal of Family Issues, 22*(2), 183–210.

Sanders, R. S. (1993). *Staying put: Making a home in a restless world.* Boston: Beacon Press.

Stack, C. (1996). *Call to home.* New York: Basic Books.

Stack, C., & Burton, L. M. (1993). Kinscripts. *Journal of Comparative Family Studies, 24*(2), 157–170.

Vivero, V. N., & Jenkins, S. R. (1999). Existential hazards of the multicultural individual: Defining and understanding "cultural homelessness." *Cultural Diversity and Ethnic Minority Psychology, 5,* 6–26.

Waniek, M. N. (1990). *The homeplace*. Baton Rouge: Louisiana State University Press.

Winston, P., Angel, R. J., Burton, L. M., Chase-Lansdale, P. L., Cherlin, A .J., Moffitt, R. A., & Wilson, W. J. (1999). *Welfare, children, and families: Overview and design*. Baltimore: Johns Hopkins University Press.

Young, I. (1997). *Intersecting voices: Dilemmas of gender, political philosophy, and policy*. Princeton, NJ: Princeton University Press.

CHAPTER 9

Religion in African American Life

Jacqueline S. Mattis

Religion and family are cultural systems that are fundamental parts of the bedrock of most societies. The word "family" denotes enduring connections and patterns of obligation borne through blood, mutual decision, or societal script. Religion, according to anthropologist Clifford Geertz, refers to "a system of symbols which acts to establish powerful, pervasive, and long-lasting moods and motivations in men by formulating conceptions of a general order of existence and clothing these conceptions with such an aura of factuality that the moods and motivations seem uniquely realistic" (1973, p. 90). Recent work in the sociology and psychology of religion suggests the need to distinguish between "religiosity" and "spirituality." Although these two terms traditionally have been used interchangeably in scholarly literature, findings from qualitative research suggest that religiosity refers to people's adherence to the core beliefs and rituals associated with worship of a divine figure or figures (Mattis, 2000). In contrast, spirituality refers to a belief in the transcendent nature of life (i.e., to the notion that existence is not limited to the physical or observable world); to a belief in the sacredness of life; and to a consequent quest to live a life of goodness and caring. For those who self-define as both religious and spiritual, spirituality also refers to the relationship that one builds with divine or noncorporeal forces (e.g., God, ancestors, spirits) (Mattis, 2000). It is important to note that whatever conceptual distinctions may exist between religiosity and spirituality, evidence drawn from lived experience suggests that for most people religiosity and spirituality are deeply intertwined. As such, throughout this manuscript I use both terms as a way of recognizing their nuanced differences as well as their interconnectedness.

When we arrive at the nexus of religion, spirituality, and family, we enter a highly particular discursive plane. Religion and spirituality insert into family life a weighty set of ideological threads that complicate, cohere, enliven, empower, lend meaning to, and sustain family relationships. These constructs introduce into family life the notion of things divine, sacred, and inviolable. When we link religion and spirituality with family, we are forced to grapple with such concepts as love, forgiveness, hope, honor, humility, respect, submission, and sacrifice. It is also important that we grapple with these existential concepts in the context of relationships (e.g., spousal and parent–child relationships) that are, by definition, permanent, religiously sanctioned, legally recognized, and historically situated.

Although religion and religious institutions are organizing forces for most African Americans, there is relatively little empirical data that help us to elucidate the specific ways in which religion and spirituality shape African American family life. Further, the concepts that are associated with religiosity and spirituality (e.g., love, forgiveness, honor) are not well studied in the social sciences. Thus, this effort to articulate the role of religion and spirituality in African American life will be interdisciplinary and will be a pastiche of empirical, archival, and anecdotal work on religion's role in community life as well as in the lives of adults and youth. In the end, I hope to paint a textured picture of the ways in which religion enhances, complicates, and otherwise influences the integrative unit that we define as family.

In the effort to delineate the link between religiosity, spirituality, and family life, it is necessary to address four organizing questions. First, what do we know about general patterns of religious involvement among African American families? Second, what do we know about the processes by which religiosity and spirituality are reproduced intra- as well as intergenerationally? Third, what do we know about the functional significance of religiosity and spirituality in the lives of African American families? Finally, what are some of the emerging core concerns related to religiosity and spirituality in African American family life? To address these questions, I begin with an overview of national data on patterns of religious affiliation (e.g., service attendance, institutional membership) among African Americans. Next I explore the family as a context for religious socialization. I turn then to the role that religious ideology and religious institutions play in influencing the quality and structure of family life, as well as their influence on the psychological well-being of families. I conclude with an enumeration of emerging research and policy concerns.

PATTERNS OF AFRICAN AMERICAN
RELIGIOUS PARTICIPATION:
A NATIONAL PERSPECTIVE

Data from the National Survey of Black Americans (NSBA) have long demonstrated that religion plays a central role in the lives of the overwhelming majority of African Americans (Levin, Taylor, & Chatters, 1995; Taylor, 1988; Taylor & Chatters, 1991a, 1991b; Taylor, Chatters, & Levin, 2004). In addition to within-group data on patterns of religious involvement among African Americans, cross-racial analyses demonstrate that African Americans outscore European Americans on various indices of organizational, nonorganizational, and subjective religious involvement (Regnerus, Smith, & Fritsch, 2003; Smith, Faris, Denton, & Regnerus, 2003; Taylor, Mattis, & Chatters, 1999). National statistics indicate that 89% of African American adults self-identify as religious. Seventy-eight percent report that they attend religious services. Further, 90% of African Americans pray, meditate, or consume religious materials (Taylor et al., 1999). Recent data on religious involvement of youth indicate that among African Americans, 51% of 8th graders, 55% of 10th graders, and 55% of 12th graders reported that religion plays a "very important" role in their lives (*Statistical Abstracts of the United States*, 2002). In comparison, among European Americans, 39% of 8th graders, 27% of 10th graders, and 29% of 12th graders identified religion as very important. Data also demonstrate that 46% of African American 10th graders and 40% of African American 12th graders report that they attend religious services weekly. Comparatively, among European Americans, 45% of 8th graders, 37% of 10th graders, and 33% of 12th graders attend services weekly (*Statistical Abstracts of the United States*, 2002). Data from the Monitoring the Future Study and the National Longitudinal Survey of Adolescent Health, indicate that relative to European, Hispanic, and Asian American youth, African American adolescents are disproportionately likely to pray and to report that faith is very important to them. Taken together, these data point both to the centrality of religion for African Americans across the developmental span, and to the reality that religion and spirituality may have greater significance for African Americans than for members of other ethnic groups.

Research has established a link between patterns of religious involvement and family configuration. Barnes (2001) found that although the overwhelming majority of African American families are religiously involved, single parents were somewhat less likely than parents from nuclear or augmented families to pray, attend religious services, read the Bible, and make financial contributions to religious institutions. These findings are consistent with findings from the NSBA indicating that relative to their single counterparts, married African Americans tend to be more involved in organizational religious life (e.g., they attend religious services more frequently), they pray more frequently, they assign a greater level of importance to religion, and they are more subjectively religious (Taylor & Chatters, 1991a, 1991b).

Our knowledge of patterns of religious involvement (e.g., service attendance) among African Americans provides us with only a partial picture of African American religious life. Also important are data on patterns of religious affiliation (e.g., religious identification) among members of this community. However, efforts to measure African American religious affiliation among African American families are complicated by at least four factors. First, scholars interested in religious affiliation have tended to focus on individuals rather than families. Indeed, any effort to assess "family religiosity" naturally raises important questions about who should be included under the rubric of family (i.e., are residential as well as nonresidential parents, grandparents, aunts, uncles, and non-blood-related kin to be included?). A second factor that complicates social scientists' efforts to operationalize "familial religious affiliation" stems from the reality that the adults within a given family and or household may belong to different faith communities (e.g., one parent may be Methodist while the other is a Muslim). Third, there may be disjoints between people's nominal affiliations and the denominations in which they worship. For example, an individual who self-identifies as Baptist may worship in an African Methodist Episcopal (AME) church for reasons of convenience, or because of a particular appreciation for the liturgical style of a given minister. Finally, categorical systems designed to capture patterns of religious affiliation among mainstream Americans often fail to include denominations in which African Americans are the majority (e.g., African Methodist Episcopal, Nation of Islam), religious communities that reflect the unique religious traditions of Blacks in particular regions of the United States (e.g., Holiness churches, Moorish Science) (see Nance, 2002), and traditions that are common among the substantial portion of Black/African Americans who are first- and second-generation immigrants from the Caribbean, Latin America, and/or Continental Africa. These limitations serve as a backdrop against which to read existing data on patterns of religious affiliation among African Americans.

Data on African American religious affiliation drawn from the American Religious Identity Survey (2001) indicate that approximately 48% of African Americans self-identify as Baptist, 8% identify as generically Christian, 8% identify as Methodist, and another 8% identify as Catholic. Less than 1% of African Americans identify as Pentecostal.

Approximately 2% of African Americans worship in other denomina-
tional groups—Church of God, Churches of Christ, Seventh-Day Adventist,
Jehovah's Witness, Episcopalian/Anglican, Presbyterian, and Assemblies
of God. Less than 1% of African Americans self-identify as Buddhist,
Jewish, or Muslim. It is notable that approximately 11% of African
Americans report that they have no religious affiliation (i.e., agnostics or
atheists). These data are consistent with findings from the NSBA (Taylor
& Chatters, 1991b, 2004).

Empirical studies have pointed to a link between religious affiliation, religious involvement, geography, education, gender, income, marital status, age, and parental status (Taylor & Chatters, 1991b). Women
score higher on indices of religious involvement, and people of higher income, those who are married, those who have children, and those who
are older tend to report greater levels of religious involvement (Taylor &
Chatters, 1991b). However, it is important to note that, in the African
American community, religious institutions historically have been "classed"
spaces. That is, denominations and individual churches are often distinguished by the average level of educational attainment, income, occupations, and social positions of their members. Thus, although family
tradition plays a powerful role in the selection of religious affiliation and
of specific sites of worship, African American families may also select
denominational affiliations and places of worship on the basis of their
real or perceived social class status or their class aspirations.

Religious involvement represents an important valence of religious
life; however, data on membership and affiliative patterns tell us little
about the functions of religion and spirituality. The significance of religiosity and spirituality in African American family life is more powerfully
captured when we attend to the ways in which religious ideologies and
religious institutions operate in everyday experience. The following sections of this chapter explore the ways that religion and spirituality inform the structure, as well as the quality, of African American family
life.

The Role of Religious Institutions in Family Life

Empirical research on African Americans generally has ignored the link
between religion and family life. However, discourses linking these two
dimensions of African American life have deep roots in America's moral
imagination. In antebellum as well as post-emancipation America, White
abolitionists and America's nascent Black leadership struggled to understand, justify, and alter an African American family structure that had
been changed irreparably by generations of slavery and postslavery oppression. Many abolitionists and Black leaders assumed that in order for

Blacks to alter their social condition, they had only to adopt the mainstream Victorian values and nuclear family structures that were presumed to be characteristic of the White middle and upper classes. Ultimately, many of these pundits concluded that the problems facing Black individuals, families, and communities could be accounted for by failings in the moral makeup of Black people—their sexual excesses, poor work ethic, inadequacy as parents, and their inability to serve as moral exemplars for their children. Black moral degeneracy was imagined as the cause of a host of problems, including poverty, violence, out-of-wedlock pregnancies, criminal behavior, abject materialism, fragile family structures, and chaotic family functioning. Religion, with its focus on piety, moral rectitude, and moderation, emerged as central in discourses about how to solve African American people's social and economic problems. Certainly, theories that link poverty, social, sociological, and psychological problems to Black moral degeneracy have never disappeared from the social sciences. These theories, and the studies that they engender, often position religion as the magical mediator between individual and community-level problems and positive Black family outcomes. Rarely, however, do these studies explore the particular processes, religious ideologies, and/or institutional factors that might inform specific aspects of family functioning.

FAMILY AS A CONTEXT
FOR CULTIVATING RELIGIOSITY

Religious Socialization of African American Youth

An important starting point for any discussion of the link between religion and family life is the process of religious socialization. Brown and Gary (1991) define religious socialization as "the process by which an individual learns and internalizes attitudes, values, and behaviors within the context of a religious system of beliefs and practices" (p. 412). These authors note that religious institutions use sermons, music, protest activities, education, economic support, and organized as well as informal systems of support, to socialize members of faith communities. Families also play a central role in the religious socialization of children and adults. Families provide the context in which people learn the practices, symbols, beliefs, and values that define religious life. Further, the existential challenges that emerge in family life (e.g., marriage, birth, death) provide the most immediate and intimate landscapes for witnessing the ways in which faith operates. In sum, family experiences, whether mundane or outrageous, adverse or beneficial, provide opportunities for youth as well as adults to learn about

God, divine love, grace, salvation, forgiveness, temptation, evil, and the transformative power of faith.

Although empirical work on religious socialization among African Americans is quite scarce, the existing work in this area demonstrates that members of families who perceive themselves as close were more likely to report that religion was important in their youth and that religious values learned in their early years still played a role in their lives (Brown & Gary, 1991). Brown and Gary (1991) also found a link between denominational affiliation and religious socialization. Pentecostals scored highest on indices of socialization—particularly the early and ongoing importance of religion and the continued use of religious values—followed by Methodists and then Baptists.

There is ample evidence that the process of religious socialization is also shaped by gender. African American girls and women report greater levels of participation in religious life and assign greater importance to religion than their male counterparts (Mattis, 1997; Taylor & Chatters, 1991b; Taylor et al., 1999). Not surprisingly, mothers play particularly crucial roles in the process of religious socialization. The importance of women in the socialization process is evident from the finding that among African Americans, maternal religious affiliation is a robust predictor of adult religious affiliation (Taylor & Chatters, 1991b). As culture bearers, women are largely responsible for educating youth about every aspect of religious life. Women (mothers, grandmothers, aunts, and other female relatives) ensure that youth participate in key rituals (e.g., baptisms, christenings) that mark or denote their identities as members of a faith community. Women involve youth in religious activities that sustain their beliefs and their religious identities (e.g., choir, Sunday or Saturday school). Women also generally serve as bridges between family members, religious institutions, and the secular world. Indeed, Tinney (1981) asserts that men, particularly those who do not attend religious services, may rely on women who do attend to pray for them and to garner, on their behalf, the material resources and social and emotional support that they need to endure life's various challenges.

The attention paid to the role of women (particularly mothers) in religious socialization has obscured attention to the broader array of people and forces that may inform the religious development of African American youth and adults. In particular, we know virtually nothing about the impact that African American men (e.g., fathers, grandfathers, uncles) have on the religious lives of children and adults. Recent work has begun to fill the gap in our knowledge about the role that fathers play in the religious socialization of their sons. African American men who attend religious services tend to report that their fathers attended services, and men who do not attend services report that their fathers did not attend (Mattis, Eubanks, et al., 2004). These findings suggest that men play important roles in shaping the religious lives of their sons—at least in regard to religious service attendance. In addition to family, however, religious leaders, teachers, and church-involved adults appear to play critical roles in shaping the early and ongoing religious and spiritual development of African Americans (Mattis, 1997). Archival sources also support the notion that religious (i.e., parochial) schools may also play significant roles in the religious socialization of some African American youth. Although we have some empirical data on the social agents involved in the religious socialization of African Americans, we have virtually no information about the ways in which patterns of religious socialization inform family dynamics. We do not know, for example, how religion and spirituality are used to shape men's and women's roles within the family, or men's and women's ability to read and respond to the emotional and social cues of the members of their families.

The importance that African American families give to religious socialization and the success of families' socialization efforts are evident in data on the religious involvement and behaviors of African American youth. African American adolescents (8th through 12th graders) are significantly more likely than adolescents of other ethnic groups to attend religious services (Smith, Denton, Faris, & Regnerus, 2002). Smith et al. (2002) also found that African American youth are significantly more likely than their European American, Latino, or Asian American counterparts to belong to a religious youth group throughout their adolescence. These data raise important questions about the functional links between formal religious involvement and adolescents' outcomes. In this regard, Stevenson (1997) found that African American youth who scored higher on a measure of spirituality were more likely to engage in emotional self-regulation and were less likely to aggress against others. Jagers (1997) found that African American youth who perceived their families to be spiritual, communal, and affective were more empathic, more likely to take the perspective of others, and less likely to engage in acts of aggression. Commenting on Jagers's (1997) findings, Mattis and Jagers (2001) asserted:

> It is possible that parents who are religiously and/or spiritually oriented may focus particular attention on teaching their children the qualities associated with good character. These parents may also focus on teaching their children how to effectively read and respond to internal and external affective and social cues. . . . Further, parents who are religious, or who are involved in church-related activities, and those who involve their children in such activities, may avail themselves of social support networks composed of people who share and perhaps reinforce crucial

values, beliefs and commitments. These relationships may provide the contexts, the tools, and the opportunities needed to actualize and reinforce religiously and spiritually consistent values and behaviors.

In sum, religious socialization shapes how adults and youth make meaning of and interpret the world, as well as how they negotiate social and emotional situations.

Religion, Religious Institutions, and the Structure and Functioning of Families

Archival and anecdotal data indicate that religion and religious institutions play powerful roles in the various stages of family life, including partner selection, family composition and family size, and childrearing practices. Religious institutions can serve as sites for meeting romantic partners (Scanzoni, 1971). These institutions actively shape mate selection by influencing peoples' perspectives on the qualities that define an appropriate partner (Scanzoni, 1971) and by explicitly prohibiting their members from socializing or partnering with people who are not affiliated with the particular faith community.

Religion and religious institutions may shape family size through mandates regarding the importance of bearing children (e.g., the importance of "being fruitful and multiplying"), sexual abstinence, and the appropriate timing of sexual intimacy (within or outside marriage), and by shaping the use of and attitudes toward contraceptives and abortion (see Brewster, Cooksey, Guilkey, & Rindfuss, 1998). Research demonstrates that African American women who score higher on religiosity (measured in terms of frequency of church attendance) and those who self-define as Protestant are more likely to hold pro-choice attitudes (Lynxwiler & Gay, 1996). However, Lynxwiler and Gay (1996) also found that, in general, religious service attendance was negatively associated with support for abortion. These findings suggest that the various domains of religious and spiritual life (e.g., religious affiliation, subjective religiosity, and religious service attendance) may operate in complex and seemingly contradictory ways to shape patterns of sexual intimacy and the entire spectrum of women's reproductive practices. Missing from the existing research are data that link religion, spirituality, attitudes toward sexual intimacy, abortion and contraceptive use, and patterns of fertility among African American men as well as women.

Religion and religious institutions may shape family composition in a number of ways. First, they may encourage adults to serve as foster parents and/or to adopt children, including their own biological relatives. A number of African American churches have, in the past decade, launched adoption initiatives. Furthermore, Gibson (2002) has found that faith in God contributes to African American grandmothers' decisions to take custody of their grandchildren. African American grandmothers indicated that religion (i.e., their faith in and relationship with God) contributed to their willingness to acknowledge that their grandchildren were being neglected or abused. These women sought God's guidance in making decisions about whether to take custody of their grandchildren. Faith also influenced these grandmothers' efforts to cope with the strain of parenting young children, their efforts to intervene with the parents of these children, and their attempts to engage in effective decision making regarding the upbringing of their grandchildren. Second, religion and spirituality appear to shape family composition by radically expanding our ideas about who makes up our families. Among religious and spiritual African Americans, family support networks may include God, spirits, and ancestors, including deceased friends and relatives (Nelson, 1997).

In addition to their impact on the structure of families, religion and spirituality also play a number of roles in informing the quality of family life. First, through couple and marriage ministries, many religious institutions may play important roles in informing the quality and longevity of marital relationships. Through these ministries institutions may help couples to understand and live their marriages (and the crises that can often accompany marriage/partnership) as extensions of their faith experience. Religious institutions may also embed couples in a network of support. Second, religions articulate for believers a pattern of expected and appropriate behaviors for siblings and for children and parents in relation to each other. More specifically, religious texts (e.g., the Bible and the Qur'an) emphasize that children should honor and remain obedient to their parents. These texts also emphasize love, strict discipline, and religious instruction as important elements of the parenting experience.

Religious texts also aptly portray the dramas and dilemmas of family life; thus, people often turn to these texts for guidance about the constructive resolution of family concerns. Many religious texts provide potent examples of family loyalty, of the nature and consequences of sibling rivalry, of parental conflicts with prodigal children, and of family grief and loss. Furthermore, these texts offer guidance regarding rules of inheritance, the roles and responsibilities that come with birth order, and appropriate responses to spousal infidelity, and they instruct people on the conditions under which annulments and divorces are permitted. The family dilemmas experienced by figures in religious texts help to underscore for believers the reality that the struggles that they face are timeless and are not unique. Even more, religious narratives provide believers with a clear understanding that faith can transform even the most painful and challenging family trials.

Empirical findings support the assertion that religiosity informs family functioning. Indeed, Brody, Stoneman, Flor, and McCrary (1994) found that religiosity positively shapes the relationship between spouses and that the positive consequences of religion filter down to the relationship between parents and their children. More specifically, these researchers found that paternal religiosity is associated with the quality of the interactions between men and their spouses, as well as the level of support and conflict that men experience as co-caregivers. Maternal religiosity was directly associated with the consistency and quality of maternal parenting.

It is important to note, in addition to religion's role in shaping the structure and function of families, that African American religious institutions and religious leaders historically have shaped family life by operating as symbolic as well as literal extensions of the family unit. Indeed, a number of scholars have suggested that African Americans replicated the institution of family in their religious institutions as a way of creatively negotiating the destructive and turbulent impact of slavery and the terrible existential losses wrought by the trade and sale of parents, children, siblings, and other kin (see Townsend-Gilkes, 2001, for example). The organic nature of the link between family and church in the African American community is immediately apparent in the vocabulary African American people use in their narratives about church and secular life (Mattis & Jagers, 2001). Terms such as "church family," "church home," "church mother," "church brother/sister," "godparents" and "godbrother/sister" are common in African American discourses about church and family. However, these relationships have been all but ignored in social science research on African American religiosity.

The "church family" and "church home" have served as stable, symbolic, as well as literal, homeplaces for individuals and families and as buffers against the forces that have proved inimical to the survival of blood-related kinship networks. For many African American families the "church home" is defined as that place where their blood relatives have worshiped for generations. These families often have a legacy of involvement in shaping the direction of the church home. Further, because these families' evolution is inextricably intertwined with the evolution of the church, the members of these families come to be crucial and stable repositories of church as well as community history. Further, church history becomes an important way of (re)telling the history of these families. Individuals and families that migrate from one geographic location to another often maintain psychological and financial allegiance to their church family and their church home. The historically transmitted memories, beliefs, and practices, the powerful sense of allegiance, and the dynamic sense of commitment that define blood-related families as coherent and meaningful social units, also bond "church families" together as coherent and socially meaningful units. As is the case with blood-related kin, one's church family and one's church home can be counted on to provide crucial material, financial, social, intellectual, and emotional supports in times of need (Moore, 1991; Porter, Ganong, & Armer, 2000).

The link between family life and the African American church is also powerfully evidenced in the unique role of the "church mothers." Church mothers are senior members of a church who, after years of dedicated service to the church and community, emerge into this position of prestige and influence. In her seminal study of church mothers, Cheryl Townsend-Gilkes (2001) asserted:

> The roles of church and community mothers represent impositions of familistic and pseudo-familistic ties upon social organizations and the process of social influence. . . . Not only are they role models, power brokers, and venerable elders, but the actuarial realities of Black life are such that elderly Black women provide the continuity necessary to promote unity in the face of ever-changing historical conditions. . . . In some religious settings . . . these women provided continuity through the crises wrought by the deaths of charismatic local and national leaders. (p. 63)

In sum, church mothers are maternal figures whose influence extends beyond the narrow confines of blood-related relationships to bind families and communities together. Church mothers are afforded great reverence in the church and, owing to their wisdom and legacy of care, they have unique authority to intervene in the affairs of the church as well as into the home lives and personal affairs of church members.

Religious Institutions as Sources of Family Support

Religious institutions play significant roles in the ability of African American families to cope with life's various demands. Among the key factors that shape institutions' impact on families are the expectations of African American people regarding the role of religious institutions in creating supports for the African American community. Most African Americans hold religious institutions accountable for resolving and addressing the substantive material, social, emotional, and political needs of the African American community (Taylor, Thornton, & Chatters, 1987). Furthermore, most African Americans look favorably on the impact that religious institutions have had in community life. Although many African Americans are critical of religious institutions, data from the NSBA demonstrate that more than 80% of African Americans believe that, historically, the church has played a positive and helpful role in the lives of Blacks (Taylor et al., 1987). According to NSBA data the benefits provided by churches include shaping and supporting people's religious beliefs, helping people manage the stresses associated with everyday life, providing for material needs and social and emotional support in times of crisis, and providing a moral base for members of the community (Taylor et al., 1987). Recent work suggests that religion and religious institutions may also be associated with a heightened sense of optimism and a decreased sense of pessimism among African Americans (Mattis, Fontenot, & Hatcher-Kay, 2003; Mattis, Fontenot, Hatcher-Kay, Grayman, & Beale, 2004).

Consistent with the tradition of guilds and self-help initiatives that defined the earliest Black churches (Lincoln & Mamiya, 1990), and consistent with the community's expectations, Black religious institutions continue to play profound roles in shaping the lives and fates of African American families. In a national survey of African American churches, Billingsley and Caldwell (1991, 1994; Billingsley, 1999) found that more than half of the churches that were surveyed sponsored family outreach programs, and 31% offered services to children and youth (see also Billingsley, 1992; Caldwell, Chatters, Billingsley, & Taylor, 1995). Billingsley (1999) identified three broad categories of support provided to families and communities by churches: expressive supports, instrumental supports, and joint expressive and instrumental supports. Expressive supports include programs that attend to the emotional, intellectual and spiritual needs of individuals and families. Such programs include individual and family counseling, couple ministries, aid to incarcerated youth and adults and their families, domestic violence supports, child welfare services, parenting workshops, and workshops on sexuality. Instrumental supports comprise tangible material and informational needs of families and individuals, including childcare, housing, medical screenings, health care, clothing, food, emergency financial support, financial aid programs for adults and youth attending college, and referrals to appropriate services. The joint expressive and instrumental supports available to families through religious institutions include health education programs (e.g., HIV/AIDS education), academic tutoring, Bible classes, cultural awareness programs, mentoring, and life skills training. In addition to these programmatic supports, religious institutions often have outreach programs that provide prayer and visitation for sick and shut-in people. Furthermore, a growing number of churches are engaging in entrepreneurial and community revitalization activities, which include opening and operating fast-food franchises that provide employment to youth and adults in low-income communities, affordable housing for families and seniors, and community centers for youth and family development enterprises (see also Lincoln & Mamiya, 1990). Collectively, these initiatives represent constructive and supportive extensions of the church into Black family life. More specifically, through these initiatives religious institutions provide critical aid to families who otherwise would have limited or no access to crucial services and opportunities (e.g., medical care, psychological counseling).

Religious institutions are important in the landscape of support. However, in assessing the impact of the church on family life, researchers must consider the reality that families often receive both formal institutional supports and supports from individual church members. During times of stress families may receive an array of informal supports (e.g., encouragement, compassion, advice, information, prayer, money, shelter) from the family members, friends, and acquaintances who are a part of their worship community (Dressler, 1985; Taylor & Chatters, 1986). The succor provided to families by individual church members may be especially important in creating and reinforcing the experience of the church as an extension of the family.

Religion and Psychological Well-Being

Much of the empirical research on the link between religion and family life has been conducted under the rubric of coping (Handal, Black-Lopez, & Moergen, 1989; Taylor, Chatters, Tucker, & Lewis, 1990). African American couples point to religion as both a source of meaning and a means of coping with the challenges of marriage (Chadia, Veroff, & Leber, 1998). Although the studies are not clear about the specific pathways via which religion influences meaning making and coping among African American couples, findings from studies conducted by Bowman (1990) and Hunter and Davis (1992) offer promising lines for investigation. Bowman (1990) found that African American families that score higher on indices of religiosity tend to extend greater levels of emotional and social support to husbands and fathers who are unemployed or underemployed, and that this heightened support was crucial to men's efforts to cope with the challenges of fulfilling their roles as providers. This finding, when considered against the backdrop of Hunter and Davis's (1992) finding that religion and spirituality shape African American men's definitions of masculinity, suggests two important possibilities. First, religion may influence coping by encouraging families to create matrices of care and support that allow them to insulate themselves from external assaults. Furthermore, religion and spirituality may shape crucial aspects of identity, including gender identity and gender role orientation, in ways that also inform families' ability to weather life's storms.

Although marital status is associated with reported religious coping, the data clearly demonstrate that religion and spirituality play powerful roles in the lives of single individuals (Barnes, 2001; Brodsky, 2000; Mattis, 2002; Neighbors, Jackson, Bowman, & Gurin, 1983; Neighbors, Musick, & Williams, 1998; Nelson, 1997). McAdoo (1995) demonstrates, for example, that African American single mothers rely principally on religious coping strategies—particularly prayer—to help them to endure adversity. The single mothers in McAdoo's (1995) study reported that religion provided emotional and moral support, cultivated family unity, and provided answers to prayers. Consistent with McAdoo's (1995) findings, Brodsky (2000) found that religion facilitated coping by shaping the meanings that women ascribed to diversity, linking women to crucial sources of emotional and instrumental support, providing a system of morality for children, providing a sense of hope, and helping women to grow emotionally. Similarly, Rogers-Dulan (1998) demonstrated that religion often helps African American families with special needs children (e.g., children with disabilities) to cope with their caregiving demands and challenges. The effectiveness of religion in coping is evident in the finding that individuals who report higher levels of religious involvement tend to report fewer family problems (Ellison, Boardman, Williams, & Jackson, 2001). It is important to note, however, that Rogers-Dulan's (1998) findings demonstrate that religiosity can also be associated with negative adjustment outcomes—that is, that caregivers who believed that their children's disabilities represented punishments from God tended to experience heightened levels of shame and guilt.

In addition to its impact on adult well-being, religiosity informs family functions by influencing the well-being of children and youth (Cook, 2000; Donahue & Benson, 1995; Haight, 1998). Religion appears to play a substantial role in mitigating risk-taking behaviors among youth (Maton & Wells, 1995). Religiosity and spirituality assist youth in emotional and behavioral self-regulation (see also Stevenson, 1997). Urban-residing African American and African Caribbean adolescents who are religiously involved are significantly less likely to engage in antisocial activity, are more likely to be employed, and report fewer psychological problems than their less involved counterparts (Cook, 2000). The data suggest that these young people rely on religious institutions and religious leaders (e.g., youth ministers) for mentorship, emotional support, advice, and moral guidance (Cook, 2000). Religious institutions also facilitate adolescent well-being by providing youth with concrete activities (e.g., religious study, sports teams, academic assistance, cheerleading, volunteer opportunities) in which to get involved (Billingsley, 1999; Lincoln & Mamiya, 1990). Many religious institutions also support well-being by publicly celebrating the academic, athletic, and personal achievements of its young members. These celebrations, and the attendant support that young people receive from adults as well as their peers within the religious community, can have powerful reinforcing functions.

In sum, some of the prophylactic effects of religious institutions are due to the willingness of leaders in these institutions to operate as extensions of the family. Certainly, religion offers ideological lenses through which young people can examine the meaning of their lives and of adverse events. However, involvement with religious institutions also situates young people in vital and supportive social networks (e.g., communities) that provide and reinforce positive values and positive activities. Activities sponsored by religious institutions provide venues for talking with their peers and with non-blood-related adults about important matters. Further, religious leaders and institutions set behavioral expectations for young people, and they provide contexts in which youth can achieve and can be positively reinforced for their achievements.

EMERGING POLICY CONCERNS

Religion has achieved and maintained a place of ascendancy in African American life because it has proved superior to any other belief system in addressing the unique existential questions, conditions, and dilemmas faced by African American families. Inarguably, African American families have been remarkably creative and agentic in the ways that they have used religion and religious institutions to respond to the seemingly insurmountable challenges they have faced. Black families and religious institutions will, without doubt, continue to respond creatively to social, economic, and political challenges. However, public policies that foster novel interfaces between families, religious institutions, and secular service providers are needed desperately. One obvious point of entry into dialogues regarding possible interfaces is the faith-based initiative movement.

Many African American churches have funded outreach ministries through local, state, and federal grant support. However, Black religious institutions traditionally have funded their outreach initiatives through the financial support of their members (e.g., through offerings, tithes) or through creative fund-raising. Recent governmental efforts to expand the availability of federal support for faith-based initiatives have spawned heated debates among scholars, religious leaders, and laypeople within the African American community. On the pro side of these debates are individuals who assert that it is untenable to believe that Black religious institutions can continue to meet the needs of increasingly desperate communities by collecting offerings from, and counting on the volunteer hours of, members of those communities. Individuals in this camp insist that the availability of federal aid will allow religious institutions, particularly smaller and less well-resourced religious institutions, to launch initiatives that they would not be able to afford otherwise. On the other side of the debate about federally funded faith-based initiatives are opponents whose critiques highlight a range of policy concerns.

Four general policy-relevant concerns have emerged from dialogues about faith-based initiatives. First, some opponents are concerned that federal funding for faith-based initiatives poses serious challenges to constitutional mandates regarding the separation of church and state. Second, some critics worry that seeking and accepting funds from government sources will undermine the tradition of self-sufficiency that has been a hallmark of Black religious institutions and will stifle the critical independent voices of Black religious leaders. Third, some critics insist that we have yet to demonstrate empirically the efficacy of faith-based programs, or to provide compelling evidence that faith-based initiatives are more effective or appealing than secular service options. An important step in evaluating faith-based programs is to distinguish between programs that are "faith based" (i.e., those that are grounded in theology and that use theology to shape beliefs and behaviors) and those that are "church based" (i.e., those that are located in religious institutions and that rely on the human resources provided by church members, but are not grounded in theology). Another important step in evaluating faith-based programs focuses on establishing the means by which we can judge the efficacy of these programs. Religions tend to highlight values and outcomes (e.g., compassion, salvation, faith) that may have little cachet for secular programs of intervention. In short, faith-based interventions may be as concerned with ameliorating symptoms of depression as they are with the capacity of individuals to engage in forgiveness or to grow by deepening their faith. These points raise important questions about the range of outcomes (secular as well as religious) that we should include in our assessments of the efficacy of faith-based interventions.

A fourth set of concerns that emerge regarding faith-based initiatives centers on issues of oversight. Here, concerns emerge about the line between religious proselytizing and providing "value-free" service. Faith-based organizations vary in their emphasis on socially conservative and liberal values. Certainly, the values held by particular religious institutions have implications for who will receive and who will be denied services, and for the kind of services that they will receive. An area of concern that has received less attention is the reality that religious leaders and paraprofessionals vary in the degree to which they are qualified (i.e., trained) to provide mental health or other outreach services. Related to this issue of training is the fact that secular professionals are often bound by principles of practice including ethical codes that provide a structure for their work. Although secularly trained professionals (e.g., psychologists, social workers, psychiatrists) who work in faith-based settings will obviously be bound to the principles of practice advocated by their professional organizations, it is unclear how and by whom nontrained service providers will be monitored.

A final area for consideration is the link between public policy and research. There is a need for funding to support studies that conceptualize African American families as integrated systems that are embedded in a larger historical, social, economic, and political landscape. Studies that explore the ways in which religious ideologies and religious institutions affect families' abilities to negotiate a range of ecological systems and demands are desperately needed. We have yet to explore the ways in which religious beliefs, values, and practices inform feelings of intimacy, mutuality, altruism/self-sacrifice, interdependence, trust, caring, and commitment within and across generations of a given family. We have yet to investigate empirically the extent to which religiosity and spirituality inform the development of a "psychological sense of family" among African Americans, or to explore the ways in which this sense of family may inform both a sense of community and willingness to engage in such prosocial behaviors as charitable giving and civic involvement.

Scholars and activists often point to the church as a site from which to receive referrals and as a site to which to refer people who are in need. However, the data demonstrate that there are barriers to establishing links between religious institutions and secular professional services (Blank, Mahmood, Fox, & Guterbock, 2002). We need policies that will create seamless links between the services offered by faith-based and secular organizations. The implicit notion that families receive services either in faith-based or in secular settings creates an unnecessary and nonconstructive divide. Policies that foster collaborative relationships between religious and secular institutions will, no doubt, prove valuable to African American families.

Finally, it is essential that policymakers recognize that faith-based institutions and the families they serve can play crucial roles in shaping policies related to a host of concerns, including child and family welfare and women's reproductive rights. Among the concerns raised by contemporary families and family activists is the point that child welfare organizations often intervene in African American family life in ways that are destructive and culturally insensitive. For example, children are often removed from the custody of their parents because of parental insistence on using religiously and culturally sanctioned practices such as corporal punishment. In other instances, poor women may be punished (via limitations on the availability of food stamps or other entitlements) for having children whom they cannot support or for refusing to divorce spouses or partners who have been identified as abusive. Events such as these highlight the ways in which public policy may directly conflict with religious (and cultural) perspectives on appropriate disciplinary practices, appropriate parent–child relationships, and the sanctity of marriage. Families who are adversely affected by existing social policies, and the religious leaders to whom these families turn in times of crisis, are quite articulate about the limitations of these policies. By developing co-creative relationships with religious institutions, policymakers may have renewed opportunities to develop policies that are culturally competent and humanistic and have heightened potential for being effective.

REFERENCES

American Religious Identity Survey. (2001). Retrieved from www.gc.cuny.edu/studies/images/image037.gif

Barnes, S. (2001). Stressors and strengths: A theoretical and practical examination of nuclear, single-parent, and augmented African American families. *Families in Society, 82,* 449–460.

Billingsley, A. (1992). *Climbing Jacob's ladder: The enduring legacy of African American families.* New York: Simon & Schuster.

Billingsley, A. (1999). *Mighty like a river: The Black church and social reform.* Oxford, UK: Oxford University Press.

Billingsley, A., & Caldwell, C. (1991). The church, the family and the school in the African American community. *Journal of Negro Education, 60,* 427–440.

Billingsley, A., & Caldwell, C. (1994). The social relevance of the contemporary Black church. *National Journal of Sociology, 8,* 1–24.

Blank, M., Mahmood, M., Fox, J., & Guterbock, T. (2002). Alternative mental health services: The role of the Black church in the South. *American Journal of Public Health, 92,* 1668–1672.

Bowman, P. (1990). Coping with provider role strain: Adaptive cultural resources among Black husband-fathers. *Journal of Black Psychology, 16,* 1–21.

Brewster, K., Cooksey, E., Guilkey, D., & Rindfuss, R. (1998). The changing impact of religion on the sexual and contraceptive behavior of adolescent women in the United States. *Journal of Marriage and the Family, 60,* 493–504.

Brodsky, A. (2000). The role of religion in the lives of resilient, urban, African American single mothers. *Journal of Community Psychology, 28,* 199–219.

Brody, G., Stoneman, Z., Flor, D., & McCrary, C. (1994). Religion's role in organizing family relationships: Family process in rural, two-parent African American families. *Journal of Marriage and the Family, 56,* 878–888.

Brown, D., & Gary, L. (1991). Religious socialization and educational attainment among African Americans: An empirical assessment. *Journal of Negro Education, 60,* 411–426.

Caldwell, C., Chatters, L., Billingsley, A., & Taylor, R. (1995). Church-based support programs for elderly Black adults: Congregational and clergy characteristics. In M. Kimble, S. McFadden, J. Ellor, & J. Seeber (Eds.), *Aging, spirituality and religion* (pp. 306–324). Minneapolis, MN: Fortress Press.

Carter, H. (1976). *The prayer tradition of Black people.* Valley Forge, PA: Judson Press.

Chadia, L., Veroff, J., & Leber, D. (1998). Newlyweds' narrative themes: Meaning in the first year of marriage for African American and White couples. *Journal of Comparative Family Studies, 29*(1), 115–130.

Cone, J. (1997). *God of the oppressed.* New York: Orbis Press.

Cook, K. (2000). "You have to have somebody watching your back, and if that's God, then that's mighty big": The church's role in the resilience of inner-city youth. *Adolescence, 35,* 717–730.

Donahue, M., & Benson, P. (1995). Religion and the well-being of adolescents. *Journal of Social Issues, 51,* 145–160.

Dressler, W. (1985). Extended family relationships, social support, and mental health in a Southern Black community. *Journal of Health and Social Behavior, 26,* 39–48.

Ellison, C., Boardman, J., Williams, D., & Jackson, J. (2001). Religious involvement, stress, and mental health: Findings from the 1995 Detroit Area Study. *Social Forces, 80,* 215–249.

Geertz, C. (1973). *The interpretation of cultures.* New York: Basic Books.

Gibson, P. (2002). African American grandmothers as caregivers: Answering the call to help their grandchildren. *Families in Society, 83,* 35–43.

Haight, W. (1998). "Gathering the spirit" at First Baptist Church: Spirituality as a protective factor in the lives of African American children. *Social Work, 43,* 213–221.

Handal, P., Black-Lopez, W., & Moergen, S. (1989). Preliminary investigation of the relationship between religion and psychological distress in Black women. *Psychological Reports, 65,* 971–975.

Hunter, A. G., & Davis, J. E. (1992). Constructing gender: An exploration of African American men's conceptualization of manhood. *Gender and Society, 6,*464–479.

Jagers, R. (1997). Afrocultural integrity and the social development of African American children: Some conceptual, empirical and practical considerations. *Journal of Prevention and Intervention in the Community, 16,* 1–2, 7–31.

Levin, J., Taylor, R., & Chatters, L. (1995). A multidimensional measure of religious involvement for African Americans. *Sociological Quarterly, 36,* 157–173.

Lincoln, C., & Mamiya, L. (1990). *The Black church in the African-American experience.* Durham, NC: Duke University Press.

Lynxwiler, J., & Gay, D. (1996). The abortion attitudes of Black women: 1972–1991. *Journal of Black Studies, 27,* 260–277.

Maton, K., & Wells, E. (1995). Religion as a community resource for well-being: Prevention, healing, and empowerment pathways. *Journal of Social Issues, 51,* 177–193.

Mattis, J. (1997). The spiritual well-being of African Americans: A preliminary analysis. *Journal of Prevention and Intervention in the Community, 16*(1–2), 103–120.

Mattis, J. (2000). African American women's definitions of spirituality: A qualitative analysis. *Journal of Black Psychology, 26,* 101–122.

Mattis, J. (2002). The role of religion and spirituality in the coping experience of African American women: A qualitative analysis. *Psychology of Women Quarterly, 26,* 308–320.

Mattis, J., Eubanks, S., Zapata, A., Grayman, N., Belkin, M., Mitchell, N., & Cooper, S. (2004). Factors influencing religious non-involvement among African American men: A multi-method analysis. *Review of Religious Research, 45,* 386–403.

Mattis, J., Fontenot, D., & Hatcher-Kay, C. (2003). Religiosity and optimism among African Americans. *Personality and Individual Differences, 34,* 1025–1038.

Mattis, J., Fontenot, D., Hatcher-Kay, C., Grayman, N., & Beale, R. (2004). Religiosity, optimism and pessimism among African Americans. *Journal of Black Psychology, 30,* 187–207.

Mattis, J., & Jagers, R. (2001). Toward a relational framework for the study of religiosity and spirituality in the lives of African Americans. *Journal of Community Psychology* [Special issue on spirituality, Vol. 2], *29,* 519–539.

McAdoo, H. (1995). Stress levels, family help patterns, and religiosity in middle- and working class African American single mothers. *Journal of Black Psychology, 21,* 424–449.

Moore, T. (1991). The African American church: A source of empowerment, mutual help, and social change. *Prevention in Human Services, 10,* 147–167.

Nance, S. (2002). Mystery of the Moorish Science Temple: Southern Blacks and American alternative spirituality in 1920s Chicago. *Religion and American Culture: A Journal of Interpretation, 12,* 123–166.

Neighbors, H., Jackson, J., Bowman, P., & Gurin, G. (1983). *Stress, coping, and Black mental health: Preliminary findings from a national study.* Newbury Park, CA.: Sage.

Neighbors, H., Musick, M., & Williams, D. (1998). The African American minister as a source of help for serious personal crises: Bridge or barrier to mental health care. *Health Education and Behavior, 25,* 759–777.

Nelson, T. (1997). He made a way out of no way: Religious experience in an African American congregation. *Review of Religious Research, 39,* 5–26.

Porter, E., Ganong, L., & Armer, J. (2000). The church family and kin: An older rural Black woman's support network and preferences for care providers. *Qualitative Health Research, 10*(4),452–470.

Regnerus, M., Smith, C., & Fritsch, M. (2003). *Religion in the lives of American adolescents: A review of the literature.* A research report of the National Study of Youth and Religion (No. 3). Chapel Hill: University of North Carolina.

Rogers-Dulan, J. (1998). Religious connectedness among urban African American families who have a child with disabilities. *Mental Retardation, 36,* 91–103.

Scanzoni, J. (1971). *The Black family in modern society.* New York: Allyn & Bacon.

Smith, C., Denton, M., Faris, R., & Regnerus, M. (2002). Mapping American adolescent religious participation. *Journal for the Scientific Study of Religion, 41,* 597–612.

Smith, C., Faris, R., Denton, M., & Regnerus, M. (2003). Mapping American adolescent subjective religiosity and attitudes of alienation toward religion. *Sociology of Religion, 64,* 111–133.

Statistical Abstracts of the United States. (2002). Washington, DC: U.S. Bureau of the Census.

Stevenson, H. (1997). Managing anger: Protective, proactive, or adaptive racial socialization identity profiles and African American manhood development. *Journal of Prevention and Intervention in the Community, 16,* 35–61.

Taylor, R. (1988). Correlates of religious non-involvement among Black Americans. *Review of Religious Research, 30,* 126–139.

Taylor, R., & Chatters, L. (1986). Patterns of informal support to elderly black adults: Family, friends, and church members. *Social Work, 31,*432–438.

Taylor, R., & Chatters, L. (1991a). Extended family networks of older Black adults. *Journal of Gerontology, 46,* S210–S217.

Taylor, R., & Chatters, L. (1991b). Religious life. In J. S. Jackson (Ed.), *Life in Black America* (pp. 105–123). Newbury Park, CA: Sage.

Taylor, R., Chatters, L., & Levin, J. (2004). *Religion in the lives of African Americans: Social, psychological, and health perspectives.* Thousand Oaks, CA: Sage.

Taylor, R., Chatters, L., Tucker, B., & Lewis, E. (1990). Developments in research on Black families. *Journal of Marriage and the Family, 52,* 993–1014.

Taylor, R., Mattis, J., & Chatters, L. (1999). Subjective religiosity among African Americans: A synthesis of findings from five national samples. *Journal of Black Psychology, 25,* 524–543.

Taylor, R., Thornton, M., & Chatters, L. (1987). Black Americans' perceptions of the sociohistorical role of the church. *Journal of Black Studies, 18*(2), 123–138.

Tinney, J. (1981). The religious experience of Black men. In L. Gary (Ed.), *Black men* (pp. 269–276). Beverly Hills, CA: Sage.

Townsend Gilkes, C. (2001). *If it wasn't for the women: Black women's experience and Womanist culture in church and community.* Maryknoll, NY: Orbis Books.

CHAPTER 10

A Model of Extended Family Support

Care of the Elderly in African American Families

Peggye Dilworth-Anderson *and* Paula Y. Goodwin

Sociohistorical evidence (Berlin, 1998; Franklin, 1997; Gutman, 1976) shows that strong cultural values in African American families, which include filial piety, family reciprocity, a sense of duty, and group survival, provide the background for intergenerational family support in African American families. Traditionally, family functioning among African Americans has been primarily based on an extended family model with distinct characteristics: existence of fluid and flexible boundaries, inclusion of blood and non-blood kin, and the norm of reciprocity (giving back) (Franklin, 1997). Thus, grandparents care for young grandchildren in their homes (Burton, 1992), older grandchildren care for and share their homes with grandparents, and middle-aged children care for the numerous generations within their households (Dilworth-Anderson, Williams, & Cooper, 1999a). Elderly parents are cared for and supported in part because family members feel obligated to give back to the older generation that cared for them.

Previous research has documented the presence of a large informal support system in African American families (Barer & Johnson, 1990; Wood & Parham, 1990), which increases the availability of a caring network to the elderly population. Aschenbrenner (1975) and Taylor and Chatters (1991) proposed that extended caregiving networks in African American families consist of a large and diverse pool of support providers who mutually assist each other. Some recent findings show, however, that the strength and size of the network in African American families may be changing. Such findings show that the size and strength of the kin network is being challenged by the needs of multiple generations in the family coupled with declining resources in the network to address the needs of family members (Jarrett & Burton, 1999; McDonald & Armstrong, 2001; Roschelle, 1997).

Because of the fluidity and flexibility of kin relations among African American families, numerous caregivers, including kin and non-kin, are incorporated into the caregiving network (Franklin, 1997). In fact, research findings show that kin caregivers to dependent older African Americans consist of an array of family members, such as adult children, spouses, nieces, nephews, in-laws, and grandchildren (Haley et al., 1995; Young & Kahana, 1995). Non-kin caregivers consist of friends and neighbors who provide care to the dependent elderly (Gibson, 1982). Lawton, Rajagopal, Brody, and Kleban (1992) reported that the quality of care to older people in African American families did not vary by relationship to the caregiver.

Although researchers assert that it is more realistic to conceptualize that families give care to their elderly members through different members of the family (Dilworth-Anderson, Williams & Cooper, 1999a; Keith, 1995; Piercy, 1998), only a few studies have addressed the issue of multiple caregivers as well as the larger helping network in providing care to elderly people (Bourgeois, Beach, Schulz, & Burgio, 1996; Taylor & Chatters, 1991; Tennstedt, McKinlay, & Sullivan, 1989). The findings from these studies show that the caregiving duties of secondary and tertiary caregivers both complement and supplement those of the primary caregivers. Dilworth-Anderson and colleagues (1999a), using both levels of responsibility and caregiving tasks, identified three types of caregivers in their research: primary, secondary, and tertiary caregivers. As found in similar studies, they reported that the primary caregiver had the highest level of responsibility regarding care and performed the largest number of caregiving tasks. They also found that secondary caregivers also provided high levels of care without the overall caregiving responsibility of primary caregivers. However, unlike other investigators, Dilworth-Anderson and colleagues examined a third type of caregiver, the tertiary caregiver who had little or no responsibility for making decisions about the care recipient and mostly performed specialized tasks.

As suggested in the literature, not only do African American families have multiple caregivers, these different caregivers create distinct arrangements or structures in which they provide care. These structures can consist of both kin and non-kin who perform different and overlapping tasks. A primary caregiver most often heads such structures. Dilworth-Anderson and colleagues (1999a) have identified four different caregiving structures in their study: (1) PST structure (primary, secondary, and tertiary), (2) PS structure (primary and secondary), (3) PT structure (primary and tertiary), and (4) PO structure (primary only). Montgomery and Williams (2001) reported that the quality of the relationship between the caregiver and care recipient largely determines whether an individual will assume the role of caregiver, particularly of the primary caregiver.

CONCEPTUAL AND THEORETICAL VIEWS IN FRAMING EXTENDED FAMILY SUPPORT

The theoretical ideas for this research were framed by the concept of wholeness from systems theory and from Keith's (1995) and Piercy's (1998) conceptual discussion on family systems of care to the elderly. Systems theory broadly defines a system as connected parts or elements that function together to manage the environment (von Bertalanffy, 1968; Whitchurch & Constanine, 1993). A central assumption of this theory is that single elements or parts of a system provide very little understanding of how a system works because each part, though distinct, is connected to other parts in the system. Thus, the concept of wholeness in systems theory provides an understanding of how extended African American family members come together to create a system of care for the dependent elderly.

In addition, Keith (1995) and Piercy (1998) provide a conceptual discussion on understanding how extended family relationships can facilitate assessing family systems of care to dependent elders. These authors suggest that when elements of the caregiving whole, such as the composition of the caregiving system, multiple caregivers, and caregiving structures or arrangements, are examined, researchers are more likely to focus on the multidimensionality of caregiving rather than on a single caregiver (e.g., the primary caregiver). Specifically, Keith suggests that by examining multiple caregivers, we gain knowledge about the cooperative arrangement families develop to support primary caregivers and care recipients. Piercy states that by examining multiple caregivers within the family, researchers can gain knowledge about the levels of responsibility different caregivers have in the caregiving system.

The Structure and Outcomes of Caregiving to Elderly Blacks Study (Williams & Dilworth-Anderson, 2002) provided evidence of an extended family support system in the care of elderly African Americans. The study participants were 330 African American caregivers who were providing care to 202 noninstitutionalized dependent older persons age 65 or older living in five contiguous counties in the Piedmont area of North Carolina (Cornoni-Huntley, Blazer, Service, & Farmer, 1990). All caregivers provided care to older care recipients who were either functionally impaired (an inability to perform two or more basic activities of daily living [ADL]; Branch, Katz, Kniepmann, & Papsidero, 1984) or cognitively impaired (a score of 3 or more on the Short Portable Mental Status Questionnaire [SPMSQ; Pfeiffer, 1975]) or both.

As shown in Table 10.1, the majority of the 330 caregivers were middle-aged women (mean age = 54.2 years) who spent an average of 8.74 years in the caregiving role. More than half (55%) of these caregivers were unmarried (divorced, widowed, or never married), and the majority of them had at least a high school education. Furthermore, about 57% of the caregivers indicated that they worked at least 30 hours per week, and more than half of the caregivers had an annual personal income of $15,000 or less.

As with caregivers, the majority of care recipients were women (80%). The care recipients' average age was 74, and more than three fourths of them were unmarried (mostly widowed). On average, care re-

TABLE 10.1. Demographic Characteristics of the 330 Caregivers

Age (years)	
M	54.2
SD	14.5
Gender (%)	
Female	79.1
Male	20.9
Time in role (years)	
M	8.74
SD	9.88
Marital status (%)	
Married/living as married	44.5
Not married	55.5
Educational status (%)	
Less than high school	36.7
High school or equivalent	63.3
Employment status (%)	
Working	57.2
Not working	42.8
Income level (%)	
0–$15,000	72.5
$15,001–$30,000	20.0
Over $30,000	7.5

Note. M, mean; SD, standard deviation.

cipients had mild physical impairments and moderate cognitive impairments. The average ADL score for care recipients was 2.4 out of 12, and they had an average cognitive score of 4.3 out of 10 on the SPMSQ. The majority (58%) of the care recipients shared households with their primary caregivers. Only 2% of care recipients lived more than 30 minutes away from their primary caregivers.

Composition of Caregivers

Consistent with the extended family model of care, the majority of caregivers in this study were family members. Approximately 89% of the 330 caregivers identified were assigned kin (i.e., related by blood or marriage to the care recipient), 7.9% were classified as created kin, which included fictive kin, foster children, friends, and godchildren.

TABLE 10.2. Caregivers' Relationship to Care Recipients

Relationship	N	%
Assigned kin	293	88.8
Blood relatives	258	
Daughter	137	
Son	42	
Granddaughter	29	
Niece	23	
Sister	10	
Nephew	9	
Grandson	5	
Cousin	3	
Wives	17	
Stepfamily/in-laws	18	
Daughter-in-law	9	
Cousin-in-law	2	
Niece-in-law	2	
Sibling-in-law	2	
Son-in-law	1	
Stepson	1	
Stepgrandson	1	
Created kin	26	7.9
Friend	20	
Fictive family	3	
Foster family	2	
Godchild	1	
Paid help	11	3.3

Note. N = 330.

Only 3.3% were paid caregivers. Table 10.2 provides a breakdown of the composition of the caregivers providing care to elderly Blacks by their relationship to the care recipient. Overall, female relatives provided the most of the care to African American elders. Among family members providing care, the majority were adult daughters, followed by sons, granddaughters, and nieces. All spousal caregivers in this study were wives of the care recipients. Daughters-in-law composed the largest group providing care among step-relatives and in-laws, and friends composed the largest group among created kin. Among the 330 caregivers identified in the study, only 3.3% were paid to provide care.

Network of Caregivers

Analyses from the larger Structure and Outcomes of Caregiving to Elderly Blacks Study showed that there was a network of care that included a range of kin from different generations that provided personal care, financial services, instrumental support, and emotional support to African American elders (Dilworth-Anderson, Goodwin, Williams, & Gibson, 2004). More than half of the primary caregivers (57%) reported they had two or more other helpers available to provide care for the older person, and almost all primary caregivers (91%) indicated that they had someone available to take their place when they were unable to care for the care recipient.

As shown in Table 10.3, multivariate regression analyses examining primary caregiver (assigned and created kin) and care recipient factors that predict the size of the network revealed that time in the caregiving role, and the number of children living within one hour of the care recipient, were significant in predicting the size of the network providing care to the care recipient (Dilworth-Anderson et al., 2004). Specifically, the longer the primary caregiver was in the role and the more of the care recipient's children were living within one hour's drive of the care recipient, the larger the size of the caregiving network. Primary caregivers' family cohesion (the closeness family members felt toward one another) approached significance in predicting the size of the network. Those primary caregivers with greater family cohesion also had larger caregiving networks.

Types of Caregivers and Caregiving Structures

From the caregiving study, three different types of caregivers were identified by their level of responsibility and by their caregiving task: primary, secondary, and tertiary (Dilworth-Anderson et al., 1999a). Primary caregivers had the highest level of responsibility regarding care and per-

TABLE 10.3. Summary of Regression Analyses for Variables Predicting Size of the Caregiving Network

	β	SE β	β
Main variables			
Cultural values	.03	.04	.06
Relationship quality	.23	.35	.06
Family cohesion	.15	.08	.15†
Caregiver characteristics			
Age	−.01	.01	−.05
Gender: female	−.32	.34	−.07
Marital status: married	−.28	.27	−.08
Time in role	−.00	.00	−.18*
Residence: lives with care recipient	−.55	.28	−.15*
Employment status: employed	.41	.31	.12
Physical functioning	.00	.01	.02
General health	−.01	.01	−.16
Care recipient characteristics			
Age	.03	.02	.12
Gender: female	.11	.36	.02
Number of children living within one hour	.21	.06	.28***
Cognitive status	−.06	.07	−.07
ADL	.08	.05	.16
Medical status	.01	.00	.13
R^2		.22	

Note. N = 181.
†$p \leq .10$; *$p \leq .05$; **$p \leq .01$; ***$p \leq .001$.

formed the largest number of caregiving tasks. Secondary caregivers were those who performed tasks at a level similar to primary caregivers but had less responsibility than primary caregivers regarding care recipients' care. Secondary caregivers provided care only in conjunction with primary caregivers. The third type of caregivers identified were tertiary caregivers, and they had little or no responsibility for making decisions regarding the care recipient. They performed specialized tasks such as grocery shopping, yard work, or paying bills. Tertiary caregivers often provided care with primary caregivers, but some provided care in the absence of other caregivers, typically to high-functioning older people.

Caregivers created five structures of care that differed according to the type and combination of caregivers: (1) primary, secondary, and tertiary; (2) primary and secondary; (3) primary and tertiary; (4) primary only; and (5) tertiary only. These structures provided varying degrees of care and support to African American elders. Analyses revealed that care recipients with greater dependency (more ADL assistance), those who used more formal support, and those having more children living within an hour's drive were more likely to be cared for in the largest structure (i.e., primary, secondary, and tertiary) than they were to be cared for in the smaller structures (Dilworth-Anderson et al., 1999a). However, care recipients in poor financial condition were least likely to be cared for in the largest structure.

CONTEXT AND CONSEQUENCES OF CAREGIVING

Church Support and Formal Support in the Care of African American Dependent Elders

Similar to African Americans in the general population, the African American caregivers in this study reported high levels of spirituality. However, only 20% of primary caregivers in this study reported receiving help from the church to provide care to elderly care recipients (Williams & Dilworth-Anderson, 2002). Prayers (92%), encouragements (88%), and visits (77%) were the types of support most often received by the 20% of caregivers receiving church support. Forty-four percent of the caregivers who received church support reported that the church provided help to them when they were ill, and only 22% indicated that church members assisted them with the care recipient so as to provide them with respite.

African American caregivers also received limited support from other formal systems, which typically provide services such as home health care, adult daycare, and transportation services. Only 26% of primary caregivers in the Structure and Outcomes of Caregiving to Black Elderly Study reported that they utilized formal support services (Williams & Dilworth-Anderson, 2002). The most often used source of formal support was that of referral services (13%). Approximately 3% of those utilizing formal support services used counseling and legal services, financial advice and planning, congregate meals, and home health care. Fewer caregivers reported the use of support groups, respite, and patient education classes.

Consequences of Caregiving

In the caregiving literature, African American caregivers are often portrayed as resilient and possessing unique strengths that buffer them from the vicissitudes of caring for elderly family members (Wood & Parham, 1990). In reality, the chronic and progressive nature of caregiving can have negative consequences even for African American caregivers who have positive appraisals of providing care to the elderly. In particular, African American caregivers may be at greater risk for negative effects of caregiving because they are often in poorer health than their European American counterparts (Smedley, Stith, & Nelson, 2003), underutilize formal support services (Sudha & Mutran, 1999), and provide care to older persons who have greater limitations (Wallace, Levy-Storms, Kington, & Andersen, 1998).

One of the negative consequences associated with caregiving is role strain, which is defined as difficulty in meeting role demands (Williams, Dilworth-Anderson, & Goodwin, 2003). Middle-aged women, the typical persons who provide care to the elderly, often fulfill the roles of spouse, parent, and employee simultaneously. The addition of the caregiver role to these other roles can make it difficult to meet role demands or can increase role strain. Williams and colleagues (2003) found that African American caregivers experienced a wide range of caregiver role strains or difficulties in meeting role demands. Caregivers who were most likely to experience high levels of role strain were those who shared a household with the care recipient, those who provided care to care recipients with greater physical limitations, those who were more educated, and those who had higher levels of depressive symptoms.

In addition to role strain, African American caregivers are also susceptible to emotional distress while caring for dependent elderly family members. It was discovered that 20% of the primary caregivers in the Structures and Outcomes of Caregiving to Elderly Blacks Study were emotionally distressed, as determined by the Brief Symptom Inventory (Dilworth-Anderson et al., 1999b). Distressed caregivers in this study were less satisfied with the social support received, had poorer physical health, experienced more caregiving role strain, and perceived less mastery in their caregiving role than those who were not emotionally distressed.

Another negative consequence of caregiving experienced by African American caregivers involves physical health. Over time the demands of caregiving can have a negative effect on the physical health of caregivers, especially those who have preexisting health problems. Longitudinal analyses of data from the larger Structure and Outcomes of Caregiving to Elderly Blacks Study revealed that culture played a significant role in helping to explain the physical health effects of caregiving over time for African American caregivers (Dilworth-Anderson, Goodwin, & Williams, 2004). Specifically, having very weak or very strong cultural reasons for caregiving (i.e., reciprocity, socialization, filial obligation) were predictive of poor self-rated health. It is believed that African American caregivers who provide care because of a very strong identification with cultural values and beliefs are doing so from a sense of duty and may be experiencing role engulfment (Skaff & Pearlin, 1992) or role captivity (Aneshensel, Pearlin, & Schuler, 1993). Howeve, caregivers with low levels of cultural beliefs and values may be providing care out of necessity because there may not be anyone else available to provide care.

CONCLUSIONS AND POLICY IMPLICATIONS

A number of findings from the larger Structure and Outcomes of Caregiving to Elderly Blacks Study are presented in this chapter. First, this study found that extended family support is prevalent in the care of older African Americans. Most of the care provided to African American elderly persons is given by adult children, particularly adult daughters. Second, it was discovered that there are strong family networks to support giving care. With the exception of high-functioning care recipients, most African American elders were provided support by multiple caregivers, who often performed a variety of services and tasks. Contrary to expectations, the majority of the caregivers in this study reported that they did not receive much church support to aid in caring for their elderly dependent family members. Limited support in the form of prayers, encouragements, and visits were given to caregivers who received church support. In addition to the lack of church support, African American caregivers also utilized few formal support services such as home health care, respite, and congregate meals.

The findings in this study can, in several ways, inform policies and programs that are designed to address the care needs of older people and their family caregivers, especially among African Americans. First, it was demonstrated that, ultimately, the care of African American elderly persons is the business of intergenerational networks of family caregivers. Although most of the caregivers positively appraised their caregiving role and perceived it as an expression of their cultural values and beliefs, the caregiving role was not without negative consequences. African American caregivers who provided care to dependent elderly family members were at risk of role strain, emotional distress, and poor physical health. Thus, interventions are needed to help strengthen systems that support African American caregivers who provide care to the elderly.

Second, although few caregivers in this study received support from the church or utilized formal support services, findings show that linking church and formal support services can be beneficial for caregivers. Specifically, it was found that the Black church served as a link between caregivers and formal support services (Williams & Dilworth-Anderson,

2002). Therefore, efforts should be made to assist churches in their efforts to support caregivers by linking them to formal services in their communities.

Finally, this study provided evidence of the negative consequences of caregiving for African Americans. Specific caregiver and care recipient characteristics were identified that make caregivers more prone to role strain and to poor emotional and physical health outcomes. Findings such as these can help to identify those caregivers who are at risk of the negative effects of caregiving and who, consequently, may not be able to provide adequate care and support to older dependent family members.

REFERENCES

Aneshensel, C. S., Pearlin, L. I., & Schuler, R. (1993). Stress, role captivity, and the cessation of caregiving. *Journal of Health and Social Behavior, 34,* 54–70.

Aschenbrenner, J. (1975). *Lifelines: Black families in Chicago.* New York: Holt, Rinehart & Winston.

Barer, B., & Johnson, C. (1990). A critique of the caregiving literature. *Gerontologist, 30,* 26–29.

Berlin, I. (1998). *Many thousands gone: The first two centuries of slavery in North America.* Cambridge, MA: Belknap Press/Harvard University Press.

Bourgeois, M., Beach, S., Schulz, R., & Burgio, L. (1996). When primary and secondary caregivers disagree: Predictors and psychological consequences. *Psychology and Aging, 11,* 327–237.

Branch, L. G., Katz, S., Kniepmann, K., & Papsidero, J. (1984). A prospective study of functional status among community elders. *American Journal of Public Health, 74,* 266–268.

Burton, L. M. (1992). Black grandparents rearing children of drug-addicted parents: Stressors, outcomes, and social service needs. *Gerontologist, 32,* 744–751.

Cornoni-Huntley, J., Blazer, D. G., Service, C., & Farmer, M. E. (1990). Introduction. In J. Cornoni-Huntley, D. G. Blazer, M. E. Lafferty, D. F. Everett, D. B. Brock, & M. E. Farmer (Eds.), *Established populations for epidemiologic studies of the elderly: Vol. 2. Resource data book* (pp. 1–7). Washington, DC: National Institute of Health (NIH Publication No. 90-495).

Dilworth-Anderson, P., Williams, S. W., & Cooper, T. (1999a). The contexts of experiencing emotional distress among family caregivers to elderly African Americans. *Family Relations, 48,* 391–396.

Dilworth-Anderson, P., Williams, S. W., & Cooper, T. (1999b). Family caregiving to elderly African Americans: Caregiver types and structures. *Journal of Gerontology: Social Sciences, 54B,* S237–241.

Dilworth-Anderson, P., Goodwin, P. Y., & Williams, S. W. (2004). Can culture help explain the physical health effects of caregiving over time among African American caregivers? *Journal of Gerontology: Social Sciences, 59,* 17–24.

Dilworth-Anderson, P., Goodwin, P. Y., Williams, S. W., & Gibson, B. (2004). *Extended relationships in African American families that support the care of dependent elders.* Manuscript in preparation.

Franklin, D. (1997). *Ensuring inequality: The structural transformation of the AfricanAmerican.* New York: Oxford University Press.

Gibson, R. C. (1982). Blacks at middle and late life: Resources and coping. *Annals of the American Academy of Political and Social Science, 464,* 79–80.

Gutman, M. G. (1976). *The Black family in slavery and freedom, 1750–1925.* New York: Pantheon.

Haley, W. E., West, C. A., Wadley, V. G., Ford, G. R., White, F. A., Barrett, J. J., et al. (1995). Psychological, social, and health impact of caregiving: A comparison of Black and White dementia family caregivers and noncaregivers. *Psychology and Aging, 10,* 540–552.

Jarrett, R. L., & Burton, L. M. (1999). Dynamic dimensions of family structure in low-income African American families: Emergent themes in qualitative research. *Journal of Comparative Family Studies, 30,* 177–187.

Keith, C. (1995). Family caregiving systems: Models, resources and values. *Journal of Marriage and the Family, 57,* 179–190.

Lawton, M. P., Rajagopal, D., Brody, E., & Kleban, M. H. (1992). The dynamics of caregiving for a demented elder among Black and White families. *Journal of Gerontology, 47,* S156–S164.

McDonald, K., & Armstrong, E. (2001). De-romanticizing Black intergenerational support: The questionable expectation of welfare reform. *Journal of Marriage and the Family, 63,* 213–223.

Montgomery, R. J. V., & Williams, K. N. (2001). Implications of differential impacts of caregiving for future research on Alzheimer care. *Aging and Mental Health, 5*(Suppl. 1), S23–S34.

Pfeiffer, E. (1975). A short portable mental status questionnaire for the assessment of organic brain deficit in elderly patients. *Journal of the American Geriatrics Society, 10,* 433–441.

Piercy, K. W. (1998). Theorizing about family caregiving: The role of responsibility. *Journal of Marriage and the Family, 60,* 109–118.

Roschelle, A. R. (1997). *No more kin: Exploring race, class, and gender in family networks.* Thousand Oaks, CA: Sage.

Skaff, M. M., & Pearlin, L. I. (1992). Caregiving: Role engulfment and the loss of self. *Gerontologist, 32,* 656–664.

Smedley, B. D., Stith, A. Y., & Nelson, A. R. (Eds.). (2003). *Unequal treatment: Confronting racial and ethnic disparities in health care.* Washington, DC: National Academies Press.

Sudha, S., & Mutran, E. J. (1999). Ethnicity and eldercare: Comparison of attitudes toward adult care homes and care by families. *Research on Aging, 21,* 570–595.

Taylor, R. J., & Chatters, L. M. (1991). Extended family networks of older Black adults. *Journal of Gerontology, 46,* S210–S217.

Tennstedt, S. L., McKinlay, J. B., & Sullivan, L. M. (1989). Informal care for frail elders: The role of secondary caregivers. *Gerontologist, 29,* 677–683.

von Bertalanffy, L. (1968). *General systems theory.* New York: Braziller.

Wallace, S., Levy-Storms, L., Kington, R. S., & Andersen, R. M. (1998). The persistence of race and ethnicity in the use of long-term care. *Journal of Gerontology: Social Sciences, 53B*, S104–S113.

Whitchurch, G. G., & Constantine, L. L. (1993). Systems theory. In P.G. Boss, W.J. Doherty, R. LaRossa, W.R. Schum, & S. K. Steinmetz (Eds.), *Sourcebook of family theory and methods: A contextual approach* (pp. 325–352). New York: Plenum Press.

Williams, S. W., & Dilworth-Anderson, P. (2002). Systems of social support in families who care for dependent African American elders. *Gerontologist, 42,* 224–236.

Williams, S. W., Dilworth-Anderson, P., & Goodwin, P.Y. (2003). Caregiver role strain: The contribution of multiple roles and available resources in African American women. *Aging and Mental Health, 7,* 103–112.

Wood, J. B., & Parham, I. A. (1990). Coping with perceived burden: Ethnic and cultural issues in Alzheimer's family caregiving. *Journal of Applied Gerontology, 9,* 325–339.

Young, R. F., & Kahana, E. (1995). The context of caregiving and well-being outcomes among African and Caucasian Americans. *Gerontologist, 35,* 225–232.

PART III

SOCIALIZATION PROCESSES IN AFRICAN AMERICAN FAMILIES

CHAPTER 11

Family Practices and School Performance of African American Children

Oscar A. Barbarin, Terry McCandies,
Cheri Coleman, *and* Nancy E. Hill

> Knowledge is the power that gives us wings to soar.
> —FREDERICK DOUGLASS

This simple but poetic declaration underscores the faith African Americans have long placed in education as a means of overcoming social inequities and economic disadvantage. This statement is more than a reminder of that faith; it is a call to action. It extols not only valuing knowledge but also pursuing excellence in education as a means of shaping the destinies of African American children. In many ways African Americans have heeded this call, nurtured high expectations of academic achievement, and retained education as a central value. Over the past 50 years, rates of high school and college graduation have steadily increased. Standardized academic test scores for African Americans rose steadily from the mid-1970s through the 1990s (Grissmer, Kirby, Berends, & Williamson, 1994). This rise is due in part to the increased levels of education attained by African American mothers. Grissmer and colleagues (1994) note, for example, that in 1970 only 7% of African American mothers of 15- to 18-year-olds had a college degree and 38% lacked a high school diploma. In 1990, 16% were college graduates and only 17% lacked a high school diploma. In 2000 the percentage of African Americans ages 25 and older who were high school graduates reached a record high, at 79% (Newburger & Curry, 2000). African Americans have gone on to higher education in increasing numbers, and once completing an undergraduate degree, have had the highest rate of applications of all ethnic groups to professional and graduate schools, at 50.1% (Adelman, 2004).

Academic achievement has been linked to a number of endogenous and extrinsic factors at multiple levels—temperament and abilities, the quality of neighborhoods and schools, socioeconomic resources, peers, and family life (Shonkoff & Phillips, 2000). Success in academic tasks is strongly linked to qualities of the social and family environments in which children are raised (Bradley, Corwyn, McAdoo, & Garcia Coll, 2001). Although neighborhood and school contexts have indisputable links to achievement, families and parents play a critical and unique role, in part because families buffer and interpret the effects of more distal contexts. Parents' day-to-day interactions, their explicit socialization practices, and their efforts to structure the child's environment are all critical to acquisition of self-regulation, social competence, and academic motivation and skills. For example, the quality of parent–child relationships indirectly influences motivational processes that, in turn, influence children's achievement (Turner & Johnson, 2003). This chapter summarizes what is known about the relationship of family life and functioning to academic outcomes among African Americans.

PARENTAL PRACTICES AND THE HOME LEARNING ENVIRONMENT

We begin by examining parenting practices—the steps families take to help children develop into competent learners and lifelong achievers. The positive effects that families have on children result from multiple factors. Of these, parenting behaviors and the home learning environments are the most fully explored. The term "parenting behaviors" refers broadly to the strategies parents use to socialize children, instill academic motivation, and nurture the development of academic and socioemotional competence; the home learning environment can facilitate or impede children's academic progress. Both are, however, intended to inculcate values, attitudes, knowledge, and skills that the family believes are essential for the child's survival and growth. For example, parenting practices related to discipline and warmth arise from specific family values, which may vary considerably across cultures (Garcia Coll, Meyer, & Brillon, 1995; Taylor, Chatters, Tucker, & Lewis, 1990), communities (Klebanov, Brooks-Gunn, & Duncan, 1994), and economic contexts (Hoff, Laursen, & Tardiff, 2002). Among the cultural values that African American families tend to pass on to their children are the notions of interdependence, perseverance, and group efforts for common interests, in addition to self-sufficiency and independence (Harrison, Wilson, Pine, Chan, & Buriel, 1990). Flowing from these African American values are parenting styles that are depicted as firm, "no-nonsense," or authoritarian, which have been associated with higher achievement levels for African Americans (Brody & Flor, 1998; Brody, Flor, & Gibson, 1999). Specifically, among African Americans, parents who create a calm and controlled environment, who reinforce clear interpersonal boundaries between themselves and their children, and who impose fair rules foster academic competencies in their children (Jenkins, 1989). Above all, the quality of parent–child relationships and communication, along with the nature of the home environment, seem to be among the most important determinants of favorable outcomes for children.

Of the many different family factors that influence academic competence in children, none has a more lasting impact than the availability of a rich language environment that promotes early language development (Dickinson & Snow, 1987). Language skills serve as a foundation of reading and strongly predict achievement later in life (Purcell-Gates, 1988). Activities as commonplace and unremarkable as parent and child talking while riding together in a car and engaging in extended conversations at mealtimes contribute greatly to children's literacy development (Reese, 1995). Dickinson and Tabors (2001) found that early reading skill in children from households of low socioeconomic status was related to the richness of the language environment in the home, particularly exposure to extended discourse, frequent joint reading, and modeling of sophisticated language structure and vocabulary. Although the quality of language exposure is as important for children from low-SES households as for other children, they received less language stimulation and entered school with more limited vocabularies and fewer skills in Standard English than high-SES children (Hart & Risley, 1995). These findings have drawn attention to the nature of early language experiences of African American children and have rekindled the debate over the influence of African American English (AAE) or Ebonics in children's literacy development. Is it different or is it deficient? Some argue that exposure to nonstandard dialect impedes the acquisition of reading skills, performance in reading, and subsequent performance in other subjects (Hart & Risley, 1995), whereas others argue that AAE is different but rich in its own right (Vernon-Feagans, Hammer, Miccio, & Manlove, 2001) and the conclusion depends on the criterion used to judge its adequacy. Until recently the major characteristics of AAE in preschool children have not been well known. Washington and Craig (1994, 1998, 2002) have provided detailed descriptions of its use by young children and their mothers. The use of AAE appears to be moderated by gender, socioeconomic status (Washington, Craig, & Kushmaul, 1998), and conversational context (Washington & Craig, 1998). However, the impact of this dialect system on acquisition of early literacy skills is undetermined. If AAE has an impact on the acquisition of reading skills, this effect would most likely occur in respect to phonological awareness skills and in the word decoding processes (see Washington & Craig, 2002, for review of early issues). As a whole, these studies draw attention to the importance of examining the influence of AAE on the development of children's reading development and school performance. However, it should be pointed out, again, that socioeconomic status moderates the use of AAE, and researchers should keep this in mind in the design of their ongoing assessments of African American children's school readiness and reading development.

Aside from the impact of families' providing a rich language environment for their children, reading to children has long been held as one of the most effective strategies for increasing children's literacy and preparing them for independent reading (Adams, 1990). Joint reading is effective not when the parent reads and the child just listens, but when parent and child interact together around and expand on the text. Accordingly, the benefits of joint reading seem to arise from the conversations, comments, questions, extended descriptions, explanations, and definitions that surround the reading material rather than reading per se. Reading is also enriching when it becomes a vehicle for recalling personal experiences, predicting or anticipating future events, and drawing inferences about things that are implied but not stated explicitly in the text. It also involves an evolving relationship by providing opportunities for repeated conversations about the shared text. The extent to which principles of expanded and dialogic reading strategies (i.e., asking what happened in the story, why it happened, and asking the child to make an evaluative judgment about the story) are incorporated into the practices of African American parents across groups of varying socioeconomic status is not well understood and is an emerging research issue.

With respect to older children, Halle, Kurtz-Costes, and Mahoney (1997) examined the family influences on school achievement in low-income third- and fourth-grade African American children and found that the provision of books was positively related to children's reading achievement; however, the use of practices such as asking questions about what is being read did not seem to significantly relate to the reading achievement of these low-income African American children. In sum, it is clear that there are cultural differences in the learning strategies that parents use; what remains unclear is whether African American parents engage in other practices that may make a difference in children's reading skills. This is an important focus of new research. An additional line of research might involve the testing of interventions, based on these expanded principles of joint reading, that rely on materials that reflect or are relevant to African American life to determine in a more rigorous way what interactive book reading styles, used with what types of reading materials, seem to most benefit African American children's reading achievement.

THE SOCIAL AND EMOTIONAL CLIMATE OF FAMILY LIFE

Although early shared reading is critically important to language growth and reading achievement, the social and emotional climate of family life is also extremely important in cultivating academic success. Research has repeatedly demonstrated that stressful living conditions have negative effects on children's learning (e.g., Brody et al., 1994; Mantzicopoulos, 1997). Although poverty has the most pervasive effect, it is not alone. Other sources of life stress, such as serious chronic illness or injury, marital disruption, death of a family member, and living under conditions of danger and violence, may also impair family functioning and have adverse consequences for children's early learning and development. The costs of such events seem to weigh heavily on African American mothers, many of whom live below the poverty line and experience much higher levels of distress than observed in mothers from other ethnic groups (McLoyd, 1990). This stress exacts a high cost for children as well. High levels of parental distress, especially that caused by economic strain, vitiate parental warmth and supplant interpersonal closeness with emotional distance and punitiveness. These factors, in turn, contribute to lower academic performance (Luster & McAdoo, 1996).

Although family life is often constrained by the weight of economic disadvantage and cultural forces, individual family strengths—such as close, supportive relationships, high expectations, and fair, consistent discipline—can sometimes mitigate the adverse effects of stressful living conditions on children's achievement. For example, low socioeconomic status often correlates with academic deficiencies; yet when poor families provide a supportive environment for learning, their children do in fact develop the social and cognitive skills necessary for academic success (Luster & McAdoo, 1996). High levels of parental distress seem to impair educational performance by children (Luster & McAdoo, 1996); conversely, the existence of warm, emotionally supportive relationships, along with a cohesive family structure, optimizes parental functioning and in turn contributes to favorable academic outcomes for children

(Jenkins, 1989). In addition, a family atmosphere that is characterized by parental acceptance, nurturance, encouragement, and responsiveness to the child's needs and level of development is positively associated with academic achievement (Hess & Holloway, 1984).

The family's social climate and the degree of strain the family unit experiences most likely affect the child by means of the effects on maternal functioning. Parents who are functioning well engage in practices that facilitate children's coping, learning, and acquisition of academic skills. However, distressed parents tend to be more punitive and less involved with their children (Miller, Cowan, Cowan, Hetherington, & Clingempeel, 1993) and provide less positive encouragement (Bigatti, Cronan, & Anaya, 2001), suggesting a poorer quality of supervision, teaching, and facilitation of the child's educational achievement. The benefit to the child of optimal maternal functioning is especially strong with respect to the quality of verbal interactions and the provision of stimulating learning materials. These occur at higher rates when parents are not distressed (Bigatti et al., 2001). It is axiomatic, then, that concern about children's academic performance must begin with some concern about the well-being of those who are principally responsible for their care and socialization.

FAMILY STRUCTURE

Structural features of African American families have received a great deal of attention with respect to their effects on children's achievement. Because a majority of African American children are being raised in households headed by single mothers and, increasingly, grandmothers, much of this work has been directed to understanding the effects of single parenthood and documenting the critical role of the extended family structure as a source of support (Wilson, 1987).

Initially, this empirical work concluded that single parenthood placed children and adolescents at risk for a variety of adverse developmental outcomes, including diminished intellectual functioning, school dropout, and lower achievement (e.g., Krein & Beller, 1988; Pong & Ju, 2000). However, a different conclusion about the relationship of single parenthood to academic achievement is drawn from studies that control for the effects of economic deprivation and disruption of the family (e.g., Huston, McLoyd, & Garcia Coll, 1994). More recent analyses suggest that single parenthood itself is not the critical issue in determining children's school achievement. Instead, it is likely to be myriad factors associated with economic disadvantage that impinge on how fully a parent is able to support the children's educational progress (e.g., lack of social support, work-related stress, and school policies and procedures that as-sume all children live in dual-parent households). Specifically, when so-cioeconomic status or poverty status is controlled, in most cases the rela-tionship between single parenthood and educational outcomes weakens considerably or disappears entirely (Grissmer, Williamson, Kirby, & Berends, 1998; Patterson, Kupersmidt, & Vaden, 1990; Ricciuti, 1999).

THE EMOTIONAL CONNECTION OF PARENT TO CHILD

As noted earlier, one of the ways parental distress is translated into an impact on children is through its effect on the quality of the affective and interpersonal connection between parent and child. A parent–child rela-tionship characterized by parental acceptance, nurturance, encourage-ment, and responsiveness to the child's needs and level of development is positively associated with academic achievement (Hess & Holloway, 1984). Research in early child development demonstrates the impor-tance of parental warmth and accessibility to the growing competence of children (see Demo & Cox, 1990, for a review). In particular, this work highlights the importance of parental sensitivity to the child's emotional state and responsiveness to the child. High levels of parental sensitivity and responsiveness are related to better cognitive and socioemotional de-velopment of children. The relationship between the child and the adult caregiver, then, may be important to both academic and socioemotional outcomes. Parents of African American children who excel academically tend to stress the importance of education and encourage the develop-ment of self-esteem and belief in personal efficacy (i.e., ability to get things done). At the same time, they acknowledge that their children may encounter racial prejudice and discrimination and try to prepare them to cope with such barriers (Sellers, Smith, Shelton, Rowley, & Chavous, 1998).

ETHNIC AND RELIGIOUS SOCIALIZATION

In addition to fostering close parent–child relationships, nurturing a strong ethnic and religious identity may provide children and adoles-cents with resources that are helpful to them in meeting the demands and overcoming the challenges associated with high levels of academic performance. Developing a positive ethnic identity may serve as a pro-tection against negative or nonencouraging responses of powerful others who may respond punitively or display low expectations for them. Religious ideologies and practices may also help youths sustain motivation and forego immediate gratification for the sake of achieving a delayed but highly valued end, such as academic skills (Steward, 1998). In comparison to European Americans, more African American youths are involved in religious services, activities, and practices (Markstrom, 1999), although all youth involvement in religion decreases with age. Nonetheless, across a number of areas of concern (e.g., underachievement, low levels of self-worth, feelings of rejection, and other maladaptive coping responses), several studies have shown that ethnic and religious socialization can shield African American adolescents against negative social stereotypes and environments that may be antagonistic (Bowman & Howard, 1985; Jeynes, 2002; Peters, 1985; Stevenson, 1994). Church attendance also appears to act as a protective influence against dropping out of school for some African American youth (Steward, 1998).

Although several years of research have shown that a healthy ethnic identity and strong sense of religiosity and spirituality influence African American adolescents' attitudes and behaviors in ways that positively impact student learning and achievement, to date, research examining the influence of ethnic identity and religion on preadolescents is very uncommon. In the rare studies that do include preadolescent children, both spirituality and racial identity have modest associations with child academic outcomes (Christian & Barbarin, 2001). To fully examine the extent to which ethnic identity and religiosity in childhood and adolescent promotes academic success, studies that follow individuals across time are needed. In light of the interest generated by faith-based initiatives, the pathways that account for the connection between religiosity and academic success is an emerging issue that needs to be fully explored.

PARENTAL ACADEMIC EXPECTANCIES AND BELIEFS

Parents' expectations about children's school performance and behavior is strongly related to child outcomes (Bempechat & Well, 1989; Grolnick, Benjet, Kurowski, & Apostoleris, 1997; Jimerson, Egeland, & Teo, 1999; Scott-Jones, 1988). Among low-income African American families, parental expectations was one of the only consistent predictors of academic achievement, once other demographic variables were controlled (Reynolds & Gill, 1994). Expectations about grades, how many years of schooling children should complete, and expectations about future career prospects were related to school performance at kindergarten for African Americans and European Americans (Hill, 2001). Longitudinally, early parental expectations are predictive of later school success and experiences. Parental expectations for children's schooling at kindergarten were related to children's school performance at third grade (Hill & Bouffard, 2003) and children's attitudes about school at fourth grade (Butterly & Hill, 2003). Parental expectations seem to affect children's school performance by increasing children's own expectations and perceptions about their own competence (Eccles, Wigfield, Harold, & Blumenfeld, 1993). Parenting practices and expectations do not operate in isolation, but sometimes combine to impact achievement. For example, Hill and Bouffard (2003) found that high expectations in combination with harsh parenting resulted in lower school performance for children from families of higher socioeconomic status. Although most research examines parenting expectations and parent–school involvement separately, an understanding of their effects in combination and a more complete understanding of the complex family dynamics associated with achievement are needed.

THE HOME–SCHOOL RELATIONSHIP

Parent involvement in children's schooling is widely regarded as a way to help students in school. Traditionally, parent involvement has included home-based activities (e.g., helping with homework, encouraging children to read, and promoting school attendance) and school-based activities (such as attending PTA meetings, parent–teacher conferences, concerts, and other school events; helping to raise money for various school-improvement projects, and volunteering at school during the day). The educational benefits of parent involvement in schools along these lines are well documented. For example, Stevenson and Baker (1987) found that parents' attendance at school events was related significantly to teacher reports of academic performance of elementary, middle, junior high, and high school students. Other researchers have found that reading at home (Morrow, 1989) and the frequency with which parents volunteered and attended school workshops relate significantly to parent and teacher ratings of school readiness, academic motivation, and social competence (Dauber & Epstein, 1993; Parker, Piotrowski, & Peay, 1987).

Although many African American parents readily volunteer their time for school-based activities and actively engage themselves in their children's learning at home, others are reluctant or unable to participate. It is often believed that family structures, values, work commitments, and time constraints are the reasons African American parents are not actively engaged in their children's school-based activities. Research directed at examining the reasons parents do not engage themselves in their children's schools has produced some interesting findings. Finders and Lewis (1994), for example, interviewed parents who were considered "hard to reach" to understand how their lives affected home–school relationships. Parents reported that their own school experiences, economic and time constraints, and differences in linguistic and cultural practices presented significant impediments to their participation in school-based activities. Relatedly, Hurley (1996) found that African American parents reported feeling less welcomed at their children's school than European American parents reported. The degree to which parents believe that they are important and efficacious in their children's learning and that their presence in schools is valued and welcomed can greatly impact the manner in which parents and families involve themselves in their children's school experiences.

In addition to work commitments and time constraints, parents' decisions to get involved in school-based activities embrace a wide set of behaviors and beliefs. The tendency for African American parents to spend more time involved in home-based school activities may be due to the beliefs they hold about their children's academic abilities and the roles they and the school play in fostering achievement. Some parents may see that the school's role is to handle academic topics and that families are responsible for handling moral, cultural, and religious education, as noted by Hill and Taylor (2004). These authors also reported that parents who had received more education were more likely to question the policies and practices of their children's schools and more actively manage their children's education. When there are differences between the beliefs and values of parents and those of the schools, this can be a hindrance to effective home–school collaboration and communication. To truly understand the complexities of African American parental school involvement, more research is needed that examines the relative importance each type of involvement has at different grade levels and its relation to different aspects of achievement.

In regard to parental school involvement across various grade levels, a recent study found that family involvement generally declines during secondary and postsecondary school (Eccles & Harold, 1996) and may thus be less salient in directly affecting older children's academic achievement. Decreased parental school involvement in middle and high school may be due to the adolescents' desire for autonomy and independence (Anderson & Keith, 1997; Jodl, Michael, Malanchuk, Eccles, & Sameroff, 2001). Alternatively, it may be due to the parents' belief about their competence in assisting with more challenging subjects (Eccles & Harold, 1993). In a national survey, 72% of students ages 10–13 and 48% of students ages 14–17 said they would like to talk to their parents about schoolwork and 40% of parents believed they were not devoting enough time to their children's education (U.S. Department of Education, 1994). In another survey conducted by Conners and Epstein (1994), 82% of inner-city high school students agreed that parent involvement was needed at the high school level, but only 50% of the students indicated that they wanted their parents involved.

Hill and Taylor (2004) recently conducted a longitudinal analysis of the influence of parent–school involvement and school behavior problems during middle school on achievement and aspirations at the end of high school. Parent–school involvement in 7th grade was negatively related to 8th grade school behavior problems and positively related to 11th grade aspirations, and school behavior problems were negatively related to 9th grade achievement. Although pathways were mostly similar across ethnicity, the relations between parental involvement and achievement, between family socioeconomic status and achievement, and between schools' behavioral problems and achievement were stronger for African Americans than for European Americans. Clearly, the benefits of involving parents are not confined to the early school years. However, the amount of involvement necessary to effect a positive impact on academic achievement, behavior, and goals needs to be identified. Prospective, longitudinal studies examining the long-term effects of parent–school involvement can help determine the optimal amount and type of parent involvement necessary to have an effect at different grade levels.

Integral to building healthy collaborative home–school relationships are mutual support, open and honest communication, and trust. Research findings on trust indicate that parents and educators consider trust to be very important for an effective parent–teacher partnership to promote children's learning (Dunst, Johanson, Rounds, Trivette, & Hamby, 1992). In a study that explored trust between homes and schools, Adams and Christenson (1998) surveyed 123 parents of regular and special education students and 152 teachers in three urban middle schools that were ethnically balanced. They found that parents' trust of teachers was significantly higher than teachers' trust of parents. Furthermore, parents who were characterized as "high trust" reported significantly more behavioral indicators of parental involvement than parents characterized as either moderate or low in trust. Contrary to predictions, however, there were no significant differences between groups that differed on the variables of income, ethnicity, or type of educational service (special education vs. regular education). Similar results were found in a subsequent study in which 1,234 parents and 209 teachers from one school district were surveyed. Adams and Christenson (2000) found that parents' trust was higher than teachers' trust at elementary, middle, and high school grade levels. They also found that parents' trust of teachers was significantly higher at the elementary than at the middle or high school levels, and teachers' trust of parents was significantly higher for elementary than for high school teachers. Regardless of school level, parents and teachers identified communication and parental dedication to education as important means to increasing mutual trust between families and schools, and satisfaction with the parent–teacher relationship was a predictor of trust for both parents and teachers. Finally, parents' trust of teachers was significantly correlated with GPA and attendance for students in grades 9–12. Most recently, Goddard, Tschannen-Moran, and Hoy (2001) found that teachers' trust in students and parents was a significant positive predictor of differences between 47 elementary urban schools in student achievement. The foregoing review confirms that, regardless of the economic, racial, or cultural background of the family, when homes and schools work together as advocates for children's education, the results are improved student achievement, better school attendance, reduced behavioral problems, and increased career aspirations.

CONCLUDING REMARKS

The research shows clearly that families make important contributions to the development and learning of children from prekindergarten to high school. In all, parents exert a powerful influence on children's academic achievement through multilevel efforts that involve activities direct and indirect, witting and unwitting. These activities guide and socialize children toward the learning goals parents have set for them. They do so through parental practices, through the socioemotional climate within the family, through the quality of the parent–child relationship, and through the relationship with schools. Parental practices take many different forms. Some are directly didactic, such as teaching a child that letters make sounds or how books work. Others indirectly reinforce language and literacy, as when parents model reading and writing (Taylor, 1983). Parents are also an important source of academic motivation. In undertaking many of the practices described in this chapter, adult caregivers unmistakably convey to children their importance to their parents and the value that parents attach to education, much more powerfully than the words parents speak. Among these actions are the creation of a climate at home that is supportive of learning. Others involve explicit efforts to draw upon resources outside the home to further educational goals. Parents may provide supplemental experiences and information, strive to get children into good schools, monitor schoolwork and homework, involve themselves with the school, and more. The use of these strategies adds another building block to the foundation of academic competence. The evidence suggests that African American parents as a rule engage in these practices, but that many face considerable impediments to exploiting them fully to their children's advantage. We know little about the compromises parents must make and how they adapt and use these strategies to support their children's learning. Additional research is needed on this subject and on the effects of these practices across socioeconomic lines.

REFERENCES

Adams, K., & Christenson, S. L. (2000). Trust and the family–school relationship: Examination of parent–teacher differences in elementary and secondary grades. *Journal of School Psychology, 38*(5), 477–497.

Adams, K. S., & Christenson, S. L. (1998). Differences in parent and teacher trust levels: Implications for creating collaborative family–school relationships. *Special Services in the Schools, 14*(1), 1–22.

Adams, M. J. (1990). *Beginning to read: Thinking and learning about print.* Champaign, IL: Center for the Study of Reading.

Adelman, C. (2004). *Answers in the tool box: Academic intensity, attendance patterns, and bachelor's degree attainment.* Washington, DC: Department of Education. Retrieved August 29, 2004, from www.ed.gov/offices/OERI/PLLI/quick_facts.html

Anderson, E. S., & Keith, T. Z. (1997). A longitudinal test of a model of academic success for at-risk high school students. *Journal of Educational Research, 90,* 259–268.

Bempechat, J., & Well, A. (1989). *Promoting the achievement of at-risk students* (Urban Diversity Series No. 99). New York: ERIC Clearinghouse on Urban and Minority Education, Columbia University, Teacher's College.

Bigatti, S. M., Cronan, T. A., & Anaya, A. (2001). The effects of maternal depression on the efficacy of a literacy intervention program. *Child Psychiatry and Human Development, 32*(2), 147–162.

Bowman, P. I., & Howard, C. (1985). Race-related socialization, motivation, and academic achievement: A study of black youths in three-generation families. *Journal of the American Academy of Child Psychiatry, 24*(2), 134–141.

Bradley, R. H., Corwyn, R. F., McAdoo, H. P., & Garica Coll, C. (2001). The home environments of children in the United States, Part 1. Variations by age, ethnicity, and poverty status. *Child Development, 72*(6), 1844–1867.

Brody, G., & Flor, D. (1998). Maternal resources, parenting practices, and child competence in rural, single-parent African American families. *Child Development, 69,* 803–816.

Brody, G. H., Flor, D. L., & Gibson, N. M. (1999). Linking maternal efficacy beliefs, developmental goals, parenting practices, and child competence in rural African American families. *Child Development, 70*(5), 1197–1208.

Brody, G. H., Stoneman, Z., Flor, D., McCrary, C., Hastings, L., & Conyers, O. (1994). Financial resources, parent psychological functioning, parent co-caregiving, and early adolescent competence in rural two-parent African American families. *Child Development, 65,* 590–605.

Butterly, B., & Hill, N. E. (2003, November). *The impact of school dislike and social competence on academic achievement.* Poster session presented at the biennial meeting of the Society for Research on Adolescence, Baltimore.

Christian, M., & Barbarin, O. (2001). Cultural resources and psychological adjustment of African-American children: Effects of spirituality and racial attribution. *Journal of Black Psychology, 27,* 43–63.

Conners, L. J., & Epstein, J. L. (1994). *Taking stock: Views of teachers, parents, and students on school, family, and community partnerships in high school* (Report No. 25). Baltimore: Johns Hopkins University, Center on Families, Communities, Schools, and Children's Learning.

Dauber, S. L., & Epstein, J. L. (1993). Parents' attitudes and practices of involvement in inner-city elementary and middle schools. In N. Chavkin (Ed.), *Families and schools in a pluralistic society* (pp. 53–72). Albany: State University of New York Press.

Demo, H. D., & Cox, M. J. (1990). Families with young children: A review of research in 1990s. *Journal of Marriage and the Family, 62,* 876–895.

Dickinson, D. K., & Snow, C. E. (1987). Interrelationships among prereading and oral language skills in kindergarteners from two social classes. *Early Childhood Research Quarterly, 2*(1), 1–25.

Dickinson, D. K., & Tabors, P. O. (2001). *Beginning literacy with language: Young children learning at home and school.* Baltimore: Brookes.

Dunst, C. J., Johanson, C., Rounds, T., Trivette, C. M., & Hamby, D. (1992). Characteristics of parent–professional partnerships. In S. L. Christenson & J. C. Conoley (Eds.), *Home–school collaboration: Enhancing children's academic and social competence* (pp. 157–174). Silver Springs, MD: National Association of School Psychologists.

Eccles, J. S., & Harold, R. D. (1993). Family involvement in children's and adolescents' schooling. In A. Booth & J. F. Dunn (Eds.), *Family–school links: How do they affect educational outcomes?* (pp. 3–34). Mahwah, NJ: Erlbaum.

Eccles, J. S., Wigfield, A., Harold, R., & Blumenfeld, P. (1993). Age and gender differences in children's self- and task perceptions during elementary school. *Child Development, 64,* 830–847.

Finders, M., & Lewis, C. (1994). Why some parents don't come to school. *Educational Leadership, 51,* 50–54.

Garcia Coll, C. T., Meyer, E. C., & Brillon, L. (1995). Ethnic and minority parenting. In M. H. Bornstein (Ed.), *Handbook of parenting: Vol. 2. Biology and ecology of parenting* (pp. 189–209). Hillsdale, NJ: Erlbaum.

Goddard, R. D., Tschannen-Moran, M., & Hoy, W. K. (2001). A multilevel examination of the distribution and effects of teacher trust in students and parents in urban elementary schools. *Elementary School Journal, 102*(1), 23–37.

Grissmer, D. W., Kirby, S. N., Berends, M., & Williamson, S. (1994). *Student achievement and the changing American family*. Santa Monica, CA: Rand Corporation (MR 488–LE). Retrieved from www.rand.org/publications/randreview/issues/RRR.winter94.5.education/The_Family.html

Grissmer, D. W., Williamson, S., Kirby, S. N., & Berends, M. (1998). Exploring the rapid rise in Black achievement scores in the United States (1970–1990). In U. Neisser (Ed.), *The rising curve*. Washington, DC: American Psychological Association.

Grolnick, W. S., Benjet, C., Kurowski, C. O., & Apostoleris, N. H. (1997). Predictors of parent involvement in children's schooling. *Journal of Educational Psychology, 89*(3), 538–548.

Halle, T. G., Kurtz-Costes, B., & Mahoney, J. L. (1997). Family influences on school achievement in low-income African American children. *Journal of Educational Psychology, 89*(3), 527–537.

Harrison, A. O., Wilson, M. N., Pine, C. J., Chan, S. Q., & Buriel, R. (1990). Family ecologies of ethnic minority children. *Child Development, 61*, 347–362.

Hart, B., & Risley, T. R. (1995). *Meaningful differences in the everyday experience of young American children*. Baltimore: Brookes.

Hess, R. D., & Holloway, S. D. (1984). Family and schools as educational institutions. In R. D. Parke, R. M. Emde, H. P. McAdoo, & G. P. Sackett (Eds.), *Review of child development research: Vol. 7. The family* (pp. 179–222). Chicago: University of Chicago Press.

Hill, N. E. (2001). Parenting and academic socialization as they relate to school readiness: The role of ethnicity and family income. *Journal of Educational Psychology, 93*(4), 686–697.

Hill, N. E., & Bouffard, S. (2003). *Socialization messages of parental school involvement in elementary school among African American and Euro-American families*. Manuscript in preparation.

Hill, N. E., & Taylor, L. C. (2004). Parent–school involvement and children's academic achievement: Pragmatics and issues. *Current Directions in Psychological Science, 13*, 161–164.

Hoff, E., Laursen, B., & Tardiff, T. (2002). Socioeconomic status and parenting. In M. H. Bornstein (Ed.), *Handbook of parenting: Vol. 2. Biology and ecology of parenting* (2nd ed., pp. 231–252). Mahwah, NJ: Erlbaum.

Hurley, C. M. (1996). *The effects of parental welcome status on desired family involvement activities*. Unpublished master's thesis, University of Minnesota, Minneapolis.

Huston, A. C., McLoyd, V. C., & Garcia Coll, C. (1994). Children and poverty: Issues in contemporary research. *Child Development, 65*, 275–282.

Jenkins, L. E. (1989). The Black family and academic achievement. In G. L. Berry & J. K. Asaneb (Eds.), *Black students: Psychosocial issues and academic achievement* (pp. 138–152). Thousand Oaks, CA: Sage.

Jeynes, W. H. (2002). A meta-analysis of the effects of attending religious schools and religiosity on Black and Hispanic academic achievement. *Education and Urban Society, 35*, 27–50.

Jimmerson, S., Egeland, B., & Teo, A. (1999). A longitudinal study of achievement trajectories: Factors associated with change. *Journal of Educational Psychology, 91,* 116–126.

Jodl, K. M., Michael, A., Malanchuk, O., Eccles, J. S., & Sameroff, A. (2001). Parents' roles in shaping early adolescents' occupational aspirations. *Child Development, 72,* 1247–1265.

Klebanov, P. K., Brooks-Gunn, J., & Duncan, G. J. (1994). Does neighborhood and family poverty affect mothers' parenting, mental health and social support. *Journal of Marriage and the Family, 56,* 441–455.

Krein, S. F., & Beller, S. H. (1988). Educational attainment of children from single-parent families. Differences by exposure, gender, and race. *Demography, 25,* 221–234.

Luster, T., & McAdoo, H. (1996). Family and child influences on educational attainment: A secondary analysis of the High/Scope Perry Preschool data. *Developmental Psychology, 32(1),* 26–39.

Mantzicopoulos, P. Y. (1997). The relationship of family variables to Head Start children's preacademic competence. *Early Education and Development, 8,* 357–375.

Markstrom, C. A. (1999). Religious involvement and adolescent psychosocial development. *Journal of Adolescence, 22(2),* 205–221.

McLoyd, V. C. (1990). The impact of economic hardship on Black families and children: Psychological distress, parenting, and socioemotional development. *Child Development, 61(2),* 311–346.

Miller, N. B., Cowan, P. A., Cowan, C. P., Hetherington, E. M., & Clingempeel, W. G. (1993). Externalizing in preschoolers and early adolescents: A cross-study replication of a family model. *Developmental Psychology, 29(1),* 3–18.

Morrow, L. M. (1989). *Literacy development in the early years: Helping children read and write.* Boston: Allyn & Bacon.

Newburger, E., & Curry, A. (2000). *Current population reports: Educational attainment in the U.S.: Population characteristics—Update.* Washington, DC: U.S. Bureau of the Census (P20-536). Retrieved from www.census.gov/prod/2000pubs/p20-536.pdf

Parker, F. L., Piotrowski, C. S., & Peay, L. (1987) Head Start as social support for mothers: The psychological benefits of involvement. *American Journal of Orthopsychiatry, 57,* 220–233.

Patterson, C. J., Kupersmidt, J. B., & Vaden, N. A. (1990). Income level, gender, ethnicity, and household composition as predictors of children's school-based competence. *Child Development, 61,* 485–494.

Peters, M. F. (1985). Racial socialization of young Black children. In H. P. McAdoo & J. L. McAdoo (Eds.), *Black children: Social, educational, and parental environments* (pp. 159–173). Newbury Park, CA: Sage.

Pong, S. L., & Ju, D. B. (2000). The effects of change in family structure and income on dropping out of middle and high school. *Journal of Family Issues, 21,* 147–169.

Purcell-Gates, V. (1988). Lexical and syntactic knowledge of written narrative held by well-read-to kindergartners and second graders. *Research in the Teaching of English, 22,* 128–160.

Reese, F. (1995). Predicting children's literacy from mother–child conversations. *Cognitive Development, 10,* 381–405.

Reynolds, A. J., & Gill, S. (1994). The role of parental perspectives in school adjustment of inner-city black children. *Journal of Youth and Adolescence, 23,* 671–694.

Ricciuti, H. N. (1999). Single parenthood and school readiness in White, Black, and Hispanic 6- and 7-year-olds. *Journal of Family Psychology, 13*(3), 450–465.

Scott-Jones, D. (1988). Families as educators. *Educational Horizon, 6,* 66–69.

Sellers, R. M., Smith, M. A., Shelton, J. N., Rowley, S. J., & Chavous, T. M. (1998). Multidimensional model of racial identity: A reconceptualization of African American racial identity. *Personality and Social Psychology Review, 2*(1), 18–39.

Shonkoff, J., & Phillips, D. (2000). *From neurons to neighborhoods: The science of early childhood development.* Washington, DC: National Academy Press.

Stevenson, D., & Baker, D. (1987). The family–school relations and the child's school performance. *Child Development, 58,* 1348–1357.

Stevenson, H. C. (1994). Racial socialization in African-American families: The art of balancing intolerance and survival. *Family Journal: Counseling and Therapy for Couples and Families, 2*(3), 190–198.

Steward, R. J. (1998). *Does spirituality influence academic achievement and psychological adjustment of African American urban adolescents?* (Report No. UD-032-189). East Lansing, MI: National Center for Research on Teacher Learning. (ERIC Document Reproduction Service No. ED417248)

Taylor, D. (1983). *Family literacy: Young children learning to read and write.* Exeter, NH: Heineman.

Taylor, R. J., Chatters, L. M., Tucker, M. B., & Lewis, E. (1990). Developments in research on black families: A decade review. *Journal of Marriage and the Family, 52,* 993–1014.

Turner, L. A., & Johnson, B. (2003). A model of mastery motivation for at-risk preschoolers. *Journal of Educational Psychology, 95*(3), 495–505.

U.S. Department of Education. (1994). *Strong families, strong schools: Building community partnerships for learning.* Washington, DC: U.S. Government Printing Office.

Vernon-Feagans, L., Hammer, C. S., Miccio, A., & Manlove, E. (2001). Early language literacy skills in low-income African American and Hispanic children. In S. B. Neuman & D. K. Dickinson (Eds.), *Handbook of early literacy research* (pp. 192–210). New York: Guilford Press.

Washington, J. A., & Craig, H. K. (1994). Dialectal forms during discourse of urban, African American preschoolers living in poverty. *Journal of Speech and Hearing Research, 31,* 816–823.

Washington, J. A., & Craig, H. K. (1998). Socioeconomic status and gender influences on children's dialectal variation. In J. Harris, A. Kamhi, & K. Pollock

(Eds.), *Literacy in African American communities* (pp. 147–168). Mahwah, NJ: Erlbaum.

Washington, J. A., & Craig, H. K. (2002). Morphosyntactic forms of African American English used by young children and their caregivers. *Applied Psycholinguistics, 23,* 209–231.

Washington, J. A., Craig, H. K., & Kushmaul, A. (1998). Variable use of African American English across two language sampling contexts. *Journal of Speech and Hearing Research, 41*(5), 1115–1124.

Wilson, W. (1987). *The truly disadvantaged: The inner city, the underclass and public policy.* Chicago: University of Chicago Press.

CHAPTER 12

The Cultural Context
of Physically Disciplining Children

Kenneth A. Dodge, Vonnie C. McLoyd,
and Jennifer E. Lansford

One of the major tasks of parenting is shaping child behavior, both for immediate compliance to expectations and norms and for long-term socialization of behavioral habits. Much of this socialization occurs around the discipline event, in which the parent responds to the child's misbehavior or noncompliance. The most important finding from analyses of discipline patterns among African American families is great heterogeneity across families. This chapter focuses on one of several disciplinary strategies used by African American parents in contemporary society, namely, physical punishment. African American parents, in general, rely on a context of warmth and acceptance of their children and employ mild physical punishment (e.g., spanking) in response to child misbehavior. Even though spanking is experienced by more than 90% of all American children (Giles-Sims, Straus, & Sugarman, 1995), one of the more striking and well-replicated findings in the child development literature is that European American parents employ spanking *less* frequently than do African American parents. The reasons for this difference, the effect on child outcomes, the mechanisms through which parenting practices exert an impact on child outcomes, and the public policy implications of this difference are all addressed in this chapter.

DISCIPLINE PATTERNS IN
AFRICAN AMERICAN FAMILIES

It is well documented in the qualitative (e.g., Young, 1970) and quantitative (e.g., Deater-Deckard & Dodge, 1997) literatures that most African American families (as well as families from other ethnic groups) provide unqualified love, acceptance, and warmth for their children. Discipline strategies employed by African American families are quite diverse. Punishment most commonly takes the form of spanking on the buttocks at a level that is well below the threshold that would be called physical abuse (Korbin, Coulton, Lindstrom-Ufuti, & Spilsbury, 2000). This parenting style is clearly intentional, in that interview studies attest that African American parents endorse these strategies as appropriate and acceptable (Flynn, 1998).

Several recent studies describe both the general pattern of spanking by African American parents and the relative differences in this style between African American and European American parents. The first study is an ongoing longitudinal examination of child development in community samples of 100 African American and 485 European American families in three communities, called the Child Development Project (Dodge, Bates, & Pettit, 1990). Begun in 1987 when the children were in preschool, this study has followed children through the end of high school with less than 1% attrition each year. At the time of the preschool assessment, socioeconomic status as measured by the Hollingshead (1979) index ranged from 11 to 66 ($M = 42.18$) for European American families and from 8 to 66 for African American families ($M = 27.04$); although families' mean socioeconomic status differed by ethnicity ($F(1, 558) = 111.50$, $p < .001$), examination of the distribution of scores reveals that both African American and European American families represented the full range of socioeconomic backgrounds. Also at the time of the preschool assessment, African American children were more likely than European American children to be living with a single parent ($\chi^2(1) = 50.58$, $p < .001$; 67% of African American children vs. 29% of European American children). When the children were age 4 or 5 years, parental discipline patterns were assessed in both mothers and fathers and found to reveal a consistent ethnic group difference favoring more mild physical punishment as reported by African American mothers and fathers about themselves and their partners. Because same-ethnic interviewers were employed and three different methods were used to collect data, it is doubtful that this finding is an artifact of measurement bias. The first method was the Conflict Tactics Scale (Straus, 1979), a standard multi-item instrument in which the parent reports frequencies of various discipline behaviors in response to child conflicts. The second method involved the presentation of five hypothetical vignettes in which the parent was to imagine that his or her child had misbehaved in a particular way (e.g., striking a younger sister, not coming when called) and was asked to report in open-ended fashion how he or she would respond and then also report how severely he or she would punish the child on a 5-point scale. The third method involved an open-ended interview in which the interviewer first asked about the child's behavioral development since birth and then asked the parent to describe how he or she typically responded and to identify the most extreme response. The interviewer then privately scored the use of physical punishment (with high interrater reliability, $r = .80$). All three methods revealed a robust main effect difference between the two cultural groups, with African American parents reporting more use of mild physical punishment than European American parents (Deater-Deckard, Dodge, Bates, & Pettit, 1996). This difference held even when socioeconomic status was controlled (Pinderhughes, Dodge, Bates, Pettit, & Zelli, 2000).

When the same children were in grades 6 and 8, two follow-up interviews were completed with mothers, in which they were asked to report their use of physical punishment on multi-item scales. Because stability across these years was moderately high ($r = .55$), scores were averaged across years. Again, African American mothers reported more use of mild physical punishment than European American mothers, and even though physical discipline occurred more frequently in single-parent than married-parent families and in families of lower than middle socioeconomic status, the ethnic group difference continued even when these factors were controlled (Lansford, Deater-Deckard, Dodge, Bates, & Pettit, 2004).

Data from the National Longitudinal Survey of Youth (NLSY) corroborate these findings (McLoyd & Smith, 2002). In a national representative sample of 550 African American and 1,039 European American children, each mother was asked whether and how frequently she spanked her 4-year-old child in the past week. In addition, interviewers noted whether or not the mother hit the child during the course of the home observation. These data were used to create a four-level ordinal scale of spanking. Whereas 64% of African American mothers spanked the child (combining mothers who reported spanking the child once in the past week, but did not hit during the interview; mothers who reported spanking more than once, but did not hit during the interview; and mothers who reported spanking more than once and hit the child during the interview), only 51% of European American mothers did so, and this difference held even when the family's income-to-needs ratio was statistically controlled. Mothers were interviewed again when the children were 10–11 years old, and a similar difference was found, although the magnitude of difference had dissipated. The diminishing difference in the rate of spanking between African American and European American families may indicate an emerging secular trend or may simply represent an age effect of the child (i.e., the largest magnitude difference in the use of spanking holds for the youngest children).

These findings join a long list of studies reporting similar effects using a wide variety of sampling methods, informants, and measures. Day, Peterson, and McCracken (1998) used data from the National Survey of Families and Households, and Giles-Sims and colleagues (1995) used the Conflict Tactics Scale with a large representative sample of parents to reveal the same pattern.

Several studies have determined that these ethnic differences in behavior extend to attitudes and endorsement of mild physical punishment. Flynn (1996a, 1996b, 1998) found that among college students, African Americans were more likely than European Americans to endorse parents' use of physical punishment. Korbin and colleagues (2000) asked parents to define child maltreatment and found that African American parents were less likely than European American parents to include physical discipline in their definitions. Deater-Deckard and Dodge (1996, 1997) found that both African American children and their mothers held more accepting attitudes toward physical punishment than did European Americans. In the Child Development Project, Deater-Deckard, Lansford, Dodge, Pettit, and Bates (2003) implemented a new five-item scale, for which scores ranged from disapproval (1) to unsure (3) to approval (5), to find that African American children mildly endorse the use of spanking ($M = 3.28$) whereas European American children mildly disapprove of this discipline strategy ($M = 2.43$), with the difference being a full standard deviation even when socioeconomic status is controlled.

UNDERSTANDING THE CONTEXT
OF PHYSICAL DISCIPLINE

Numerous explanations have been offered for these differences. Ogbu (1981) has suggested that the context of slavery within which African Americans entered this country set the stage for physical means of control of other persons as a historical legacy. In addition, researchers have found that conservative Protestants (e.g., Adventist, Baptist, Pentecostal—religious affiliations common among African Americans) are more likely than parents with other religious affiliations to use physical discipline and more likely to believe that its use will prevent children's future misbehaviors (Gershoff, Miller, & Holden, 1999).

The ethnographic literature offers insights into the meaning of physical discipline in African American families. Ward (1971) concluded that physical punishment and the use of verbal reasoning are independent practices with their own rule structures and applications. Thus, failing to use physical punishment does not imply that the parent uses verbal reasoning to respond to child misbehavior; in fact, failing to use physical punishment may mean that the parent is failing to respond at all. Young (1970) concluded that the control of child aggression, even if by coercive means, signals love for the child. A study by Mosby, Rawls, Meehan, Mays, and Pettinari (1999) offers an important caveat, however. They studied narratives of parents' reports about discipline and concluded that parents recognize that physical punishment is not effective if accompanied by anger. These studies suggest that physical punishment is a part of the culture of African American families, with a rational function and rule structure.

Stress and Challenge

Other explanations focus on the current social context of stress and economic challenge that faces many African American families, making parenting a difficult task (McLoyd, 1990). Such explanations suggest that statistical control of these confounding factors would eliminate ethnic differences in parenting behavior. Some of the apparent ethnic differences in parenting styles may indeed be accounted for by factors that correlate with ethnicity, such as rearing children in a single-parent versus two-parent household (Fox, Platz, & Bentley, 1995), in an unsafe neighborhood versus one that affords parents support and opportunities to make parenting easier (Abell, Clawson, Washington, Bost, & Vaughn, 1996), in a context of family stress versus comfort (McLoyd, Jayaratne, Ceballo, & Borquez, 1994), and in a family context of low versus middle socioeconomic status (Day et al., 1998). However, even simultaneous control of all of these factors does not completely eliminate the ethnic difference in parenting styles (Pinderhughes et al., 2000), which holds within each socioeconomic status group and which seems to have a partial basis either in culture or the unique position of African American families in contemporary society.

A possible explanation for the frequent use of physical punishment in African American families concerns the context of inevitable racial discrimination and disadvantage that African American children face in contemporary American society. This challenge presents parents with a dilemma about how to prepare their children to succeed in a world that will scrutinize their every action and will be unforgiving. To examine these factors more directly, Pinderhughes and colleagues (2000) interviewed 978 mothers and fathers of 4- and 5-year-old boys and girls, including 125 African American parents. They presented parents with five hypothetical vignettes, each depicting a misbehaving child (e.g., pushing another child to the ground, teasing a peer), and asked the parents to imagine that the child was their own. The interviewer asked several questions about how the parent would feel and think about this situation and then how the parent would respond. Consistent with past studies, African American mothers and fathers reported greater likelihood of responding with physical punishment than did European American parents. African American parents were also more likely than European American parents to attribute hostile intent to their child for his or her misbehavior, to rate their child's behavior as problematic, and to feel "worried" that their child would grow up to become a bad person. These cognitive-emotional processes were significantly correlated with the use of physical punishment, and structural equation models revealed that they accounted for 50% of the total effect of ethnicity on discipline responses. These findings suggest that the use of physical punishment by some African American parents may be a rational response to worries that their children may grow up to encounter difficulties in contemporary society.

Anger and Discipline

Although a Eurocentric explanation of ethnic differences focuses on why and how African Americans differ from a European American standard, given the ubiquity of spanking one might more reasonably ask why European American families use physical discipline sparingly. It seems that African American families follow the norm, but a minority of European American families deviate from that norm, and the number of families that are refraining from spanking is growing. One posited explanation for this trend is that White middle-class parents from Minnesota report that they experience moderate to high levels of anger when they physically discipline their children (Graziano & Hamblen, 1996), and more than half of these mothers report remorse after they use physical punishment and judge in retrospect that it was the wrong strategy. The context of anger apparently compromises the effectiveness of physical discipline and is leading some European American parents to abandon this strategy altogether.

It is plausible that African American parents do not couple anger and physical discipline in this manner, and thus physical discipline is not viewed as negatively. Gunnoe and Mariner (1997, p. 768) suggest that whereas European American families may interpret spanking as an "act of interpersonal aggression," African American families may regard it as a "legitimate expression of parental authority." Indeed, qualitative analyses of the narratives of African American parents and elders indicate the belief that physical discipline is a more effective strategy than reasoning alone, but that teaching, and not anger, must accompany the physical discipline (Mosby et al., 1999).

EFFECTS OF PHYSICAL DISCIPLINE ON CHILD OUTCOMES

Much of the furor over and interest in spanking stems from the presumed effects of various parenting practices on child behavior outcomes. Compliance with a parent's directives and cessation of misbehavior are the immediate effects that parents seek. Indeed, Gershoff's (2002) review concluded that spanking is effective in meeting these short-term goals. The long-term effects, however, are more controversial. Proponents of mild physical punishment claim that contingent application of mild negative consequences for misbehavior teaches a child an important lesson that leads to growth of character and positive habits. Opponents (e.g., American Academy of Pediatrics, 1998) claim that the practice is imitated by the child and generalized to other situations, so that the "lesson" that is learned is that physical coercion is an acceptable and effective social behavior. Furthermore, opponents argue that mild physical punishment is rarely applied in a calm and systematic way; instead, it is applied with anger by a parent who is losing self-control. The effects, they claim, are that the parent and child fail to develop a trusting, intimate relationship that is necessary for the child's development of internalized standards for behavior and that the child learns a style of losing control in conflict situations.

A broad body of research has documented the positive correlations between parents' use of physical punishment and subsequent child antisocial outcomes, including aggressive behavior (Eron, Huesmann, & Zelli, 1991), delinquency (Farrington & Hawkins, 1991), and criminality (McCord, 1991). Despite the correlational nature of these studies, Gershoff (2002) concluded that the literature supports a directional effect of spanking to increase antisocial outcomes in children. However, most of these studies were conducted with White middle-class families, ignoring the role of culture, and most ignored the affective context in which discipline is applied (Deater-Deckard & Dodge, 1997; Jackson, 1997). More than 30 years ago, Baumrind (1972) suggested that socialization effects might differ for children from different ethnic contexts.

To examine culture and context more directly, Deater-Deckard and colleagues (1996) used the ethnically diverse Child Development Project sample to find that a child's experience of mild physical discipline in the first five years of life is correlated with higher levels of externalizing behavior problems as rated by parents in early elementary school, for both African American and European American children. Because parents usually employ physical discipline in response to child misbehavior and the child's initial behavior level was not controlled statistically, this correlation can be interpreted as a child effect on parenting. However, when teacher and peer ratings of classroom behavior were examined and child behavior levels were controlled, the positive correlation held only for European American children and the correlation for African American children was in the negative direction but not significant. Because of concerns that this pattern may be an artifact of the method of measurement of parenting, these analyses were repeated for each of three independent measures (parent responses to the Conflict Tactics Scale, parent responses to hypothetical vignettes depicting child misbehavior, and an interviewer's private rating following an open discussion about parenting practices). The same interaction pattern held for each measure and for both mothers and fathers.

Still skeptical, these researchers (Lansford et al., 2004) followed up the children into grade 11 to determine whether these patterns held over the long term. Indeed, controlling for early child difficult temperament and socioeconomic status, mild physical punishment during the first five years of life predicted more adolescent externalizing problems on the Youth Self Report, school suspensions/expulsions, and criminal arrest for European American but not African American youth. To determine whether the timing of discipline in a child's life might alter these patterns, measures of mothers' use of mild physical punishment in grades 6 and 8 were correlated with adolescent outcomes as well. Not only did the same interaction pattern hold (that is, controlling for early difficult temperament and socioeconomic status, greater use of mild physical discipline at grades 6 and 8 predicted higher externalizing problems, school suspensions, and criminal arrest at grade 11 for European American but not African American youth), but the effect among African American youth was statistically significant and *negative*. That is, the use of mild physical punishment among African American children was correlated with protection against later externalizing problem outcomes.

This interaction pattern has been replicated in diverse samples using diverse methods to measure parenting and child outcomes. Gunnoe and Mariner (1997) found that parents' use of spanking was correlated with *more* fights at elementary school for European American children but *fewer* fights for African American children. Deater-Deckard, Dodge, and Sorbring (in press) sampled 102 African American and European American children in grades 1–4 to find the same interaction effect on mother-rated externalizing problem scores. Similar interaction effects have been reported with diverse samples in middle childhood by Stormshak, Bierman, McMahon, Lengua, and the Conduct Problems Prevention Research Group (2000), McLeod, Kruttschnitt, and Dornfield (1994), and Spieker, Larson, Lewis, Keller, and Gilchrist (1999). The interpretation of this robust interaction effect is still unclear, although Whaley (2000) has suggested that it represents a true socialization difference that is consistent with African American parents' report when European American clinicians have tried to change the parenting practices of African Americans—that spanking has different effects on children of different ethnic backgrounds.

The Importance of Emotional Support

McLoyd and Smith (2002) proposed a different perspective, that the effects of spanking are universal but depend on the context of emotional support in which it occurs. They cited Larzelere (1996), who had concluded that mild physical discipline by parents will not have adverse long-term effects on a child if the broader parenting context is characterized by positive parental involvement and the physical discipline is consistently applied in instrumental ways without insults or anger. McLoyd and Smith (2002) thus hypothesized that spanking will catalyze antisocial development only in a context of low emotional support and warmth. McLoyd and Smith used data from the NLSY (described earlier) to test their hypothesis. Their measure of family emotional support came from five items from the Home Observation for Measurement of the Environment (HOME; Caldwell & Bradley, 1980), which asked a home visitor to rate the mother's warmth, encouragement, and emotional support of the child. Consistent with their hypothesis, they found that emotional support moderated the impact of spanking, for both African American and European American families. They concluded, "When spanking occurs in a context of strong overall emotional support for the child, it does not appear to contribute to a significant increase in behavior problems. However, without this support in place, behavior problems tend to increase in response to increases in spanking" (McLoyd & Smith, 2002, p. 50).

Although this finding goes a long way toward resolving the apparently inconsistent findings regarding ethnic group differences in the effects of spanking, it does not completely resolve them. Two other findings from this study linger for future analysis. First, the interaction effect between ethnicity and spanking on growth in child behavior problems (which has been reported in the numerous studies noted earlier) was not reported as significant in this sample. In fact, with adjustments for income-needs ratio and emotional support, the effect of spanking was significant for both African American and European American children, although larger for the latter group (.90) than the former group (.72). It is the significant effect for the African American children that is discrepant with some previous findings, although the measure of behavior problems in this study was derived from mothers' reports, which have revealed fewer ethnic differences in effects of spanking on children's adjustment than have measures derived from teachers' or peers' reports (Deater-Deckard et al., 1996; Gunnoe & Mariner, 1997). Among other potential explanations (awaiting further analysis) are the inclusion of economic control variables (McLoyd and Smith's [2002] assessments of the effects of spanking on growth in behavior problems and the moderating influence of emotional support take account of the income–needs ratio over time) and the impact of the main effect of emotional support on child behavior, which is more highly significant for African American than European American children.

Second, African American families were rated as *lower* in emotional support than European American families. The McLoyd and Smith (2002) findings are that spanking has no effect on child antisocial behavior *among families with high emotional support.* One might explain the lack of effect of spanking on child behavior among African American families reported in previous studies as being due to the presumed ubiquity of high emotional support in those families; however, this explanation also presumed high overall levels of emotional support in African American families. The McLoyd and Smith findings indicate that overall levels are lower among African American than European American families.

The Case of Child Physical Abuse

A crucial exception to the lack of relation between physical punishment and child aggression among African American families is the case of physical maltreatment of the child. When the level of physical punishment exceeds thresholds that interviewers and society at large deem to constitute abuse, the effect on child outcomes is decisively negative. Findings by Dodge and colleagues (1990) indicate that physical maltreatment in the first 5 years of life is related to antisocial outcomes for children of both African American and European American backgrounds. Lansford and colleagues (2002) found that these effects endure for at least 12 years into adolescence and extend to outcomes that include school adjustment, for both cultural groups.

In sum, although it is quite clear that the long-term effects of physical abuse are uniformly negative, the effects of mild physical punishment remain controversial, despite Gershoff's (2002) conclusion that spanking harms children's development. The studies reviewed here suggest that spanking children might not have proven long-term negative effects *if* (1) spanking is administered in a cultural context of normative use of spanking; (2) spanking occurs in a family context of emotional support for the child; (3) spanking is applied in a systematic, nonangry manner with instrumental goals for the child; and (4) the harshness of spanking never exceeds thresholds that could constitute physical abuse. Finally, this summary applies only to established empirical findings; the ultimate concern is that it remains plausible that adverse effects of spanking could eventually be found in other domains (e.g., internalizing problems, self-esteem, identity).

The implications for African American families in contemporary society are complicated by the rapidly changing normativeness of spanking. If spanking is a well-accepted parenting practice, then its effects may not be negative. Indeed, this cultural context seems to have characterized African American families of the 1960s. Today, however, it appears that spanking may be diminishing as a practice of first resort and has become more controversial among African American families, especially among parents who have moved into the middle class. Ironically, if African American families in contemporary society are beginning to question the use of spanking, then its effects on their children may actually become more negative, *if they begin to apply spanking in a context of doubt.*

CAUSAL MECHANISMS IN THE EFFECTS OF PHYSICAL PUNISHMENT ON CHILDREN'S BEHAVIOR

The precise circumstances in which physical punishment will or will not have adverse effects may become most clear if we begin to understand the psychological mechanisms through which parenting behaviors exert an impact on the child. McLoyd and Smith (2002) suggested that emotional support is an important moderator of spanking effects because it alters the meaning of spanking for the child. They concluded, "The child may be less likely to view spanking as harsh, unjust, and indicative of parental rejection when relations with the parent are generally warm and supportive" (p. 51). Studies by Rohner and his colleagues (e.g., Rohner, Bourque, & Elordi, 1996; Rohner, Kean, & Cournoyer, 1991) support the hypothesis that the child's perception of whether or not he or she is being rejected by the parent is a crucial mediator of the effects of physical punishment. Likewise, studies of children's aggressive behavior indicate that the child's attribution that another person is acting with hostile (rather than benign) intent is an important catalyst of aggressive behavior (Dodge et al., 1990).

Children's Interpretations of Parenting Behaviors

The most plausible explanation for interaction effects between discipline practices and ethnicity in producing child outcomes is that the cultural context of a particular discipline practice alters the meaning that it conveys to the child, which is the mediator of any long-term effects on the child's adjustment outcomes. Following from the conjectures made earlier, we propose that the extent to which a discipline practice communicates contempt and rejection of the child determines the long-term adverse effects on the child's social development.

An important question concerns how the child derives meaning from a parent's discipline practice. Some of the rules that guide the meaning that is inferred by the child may follow concepts from attribution theory in social psychology (e.g., Jones & Davis, 1965). For example, when a child is the object of a practice that is highly normative and usual in a culture, the child may be less likely to infer any "special" or unique status as the recipient of that practice. In contrast, if a child is the object of a negative, nonnormative practice, that child may be more likely to attribute the source of the unique practice to him- or herself ("I must be really bad if they did this to me"), or the parent ("My parent must be a bad parent"), or the relationship ("My parent must really hate me"). All of these attributions may exacerbate the likelihood of deviant child development.

The Development of Attitudes about Spanking

Perhaps the most direct effect of physical discipline experiences on children that may be expected concerns their development of attitudes about spanking and their likelihood of using this discipline strategy in parenting their own offspring. Deater-Deckard and colleagues (2003) used data from the Child Development Project to understand the intergenerational transmission of discipline strategies. Mothers completed interviews about their discipline strategies when their children were in kindergarten, sixth grade, and eighth grade. Adolescents answered questions regarding their attitudes about physical discipline when they were in eighth grade. For both African American and European American youth, experiencing physical discipline was related to more endorsement of its use, regardless of the timing (i.e., kindergarten, sixth grade, eighth grade), chronicity, or frequency of the discipline. An important finding, however, was that there was no association between the experience of physical discipline and endorsing its use for those children who were suspected of having been physically abused.

In this study there was no overlap built into the construction of the physical abuse and physical discipline variables. First, it was determined whether the child met criteria for physical abuse (i.e., whether the child had been severely harmed, using a criterion of intentional strikes to the child by an adult that left visible marks for more than 24 hours or that required medical attention). Second, separate measures asked about the mother's use of physical punishment (e.g., how often she spanked the child). Note that abuse may have been perpetrated by someone other than the parent providing information about her own discipline strategies with that same child. Statistically, there was overlap between the physical discipline and abuse variables (i.e., they were correlated, because many but not all of the abused children also experienced their mothers' physical discipline), but it was possible to identify mutually exclusive and exhaustive categories for each of the two variables. Ratings of physical abuse were not nested within or contingent upon the parent's responses that addressed physical discipline experiences. Thus, with the exception of cases in which physical abuse is involved, these findings suggest that spanking children promotes the development of attitudes concerning the efficacy and benign nature of corporal punishment that are consistent with this experience. Because African American children are more likely to be physically disciplined than are European American children, it makes sense that African American children would develop attitudes more accepting of the use of physical discipline.

PRACTICE IMPLICATIONS

The research described here has important implications for clinical practices directed toward a change in parenting. Foremost is the obvious implication that forcible attempts to get parents to stop the use of physical discipline may well be received with resistance from parents whose cultural experiences provide them a reality check that is not consistent with that of the clinician. The outcome may be that parents do not enter these treatments or that they withdraw from them prematurely (Kumpfer, Alvarado, Smith, & Bellamy, 2002).

Instead, it is incumbent upon practitioners to become culturally sensitive and competent and to adapt their interventions to the cultural perspective of their clients. This cultural sensitivity may take several forms, such as acknowledging the legitimacy of the use of physical discipline but also proposing alternative disciplinary strategies, not expressing

opinions about whether nonphysical disciplinary strategies are prefera-
ble to the use of physical discipline (unless the practitioner has a concern
that the physical discipline is negatively affecting the particular child in
question), or giving parents suggestions about how best to administer
physical discipline if they are committed to its use. Five research studies
that contrasted a culturally adapted version of an evidence-based parent-
training program (the Strengthening Families Program) with African
American families (as well as Hispanic, Asian/Pacific Islander, and
American Indian families) indicate that cultural adaptations can increase
retention of families in treatment by up to 40% (Coard, Wallace,
Stevenson, & Miller Brotman, 2004). A remaining theoretical and empirical challenge is to define the parameters of cultural adaptation of an
evidence-based intervention that can and should be implemented without adverse effects on the efficacy of the intervention itself.

POLICY IMPLICATIONS

The policy implications of this research are far-reaching. Research on
discipline practices in Sweden is informative, because physical punishment was banned there in 1979. Although sentiment in favor of the ban
was growing at that time, it was a controversial policy. This policy was
implemented in an effort to "(1) alter public attitudes toward this practice; (2) increase early identification of children at risk for abuse; and (3)
promote earlier and more supportive intervention to families" (Durrant,
1999, p. 435). In the years since the passage of the ban, attitudes toward
spanking have become less favorable in Sweden (Durrant, 1999). However, it appears that up to a third of Swedish parents privately report that
they still employ physical discipline strategies with their children. Several
European countries (e.g., Finland, Denmark, Norway) have followed
Sweden's lead in banning corporal punishment of children, and in 1992
a bill was introduced in the United States in an effort to prohibit American parents from using corporal punishment. The bill did not make it
out of its initial committee, and since that time there has not been a
groundswell of support for its passage.

What would be the implications of policies banning parental use of
corporal punishment in the United States? Although such a policy may
seem like a reasonable approach to decreasing favorable attitudes toward and use of spanking in this country, such policies would likely encounter a number of difficulties in being passed and then implemented.
In countries that have banned the use of corporal punishment, favorable
attitudes toward its use had decreased over time prior to the ban, not

only as a result of the ban (Durrant, 1999). The fact that these laws were put forward and written into legislation is due in part to shifts in attitudes that occurred prior to implementation. Our findings, and the prior research described earlier, document the wide range of attitudes present in the United States that vary across ecological contexts (e.g., ethnicity, socioeconomic status), with prevailing attitudes supporting parents' use of this method of discipline. This diversity in attitudes is likely to prevent the establishment of policies banning corporal punishment.

If such policies were passed in the United States, enforcing them would present a number of challenges. In Sweden, 30% of children experienced physical discipline after the 1979 ban, which is only a small decrease from the 32–34% of children who had been physically disciplined before the ban (Statistics Sweden, 1996, as cited in Larzelere, 2000). Attempts to enforce such a ban in the United States would overburden an already overwhelmed Child Protective Services system. In addition, given the remarkable cultural diversity of families in the United States, and the documented cultural differences in attitudes and discipline practices, enforcement would require a great deal of sensitivity to potential abuses of the legal system that might lead to discriminatory or biased enforcement for vulnerable subgroups of parents (e.g., working poor, immigrants).

Finally, yet another potential counterintuitive implication of a policy banning corporal punishment must be considered. If such a policy were implemented, the public sanction against the use of physical discipline would become more overt and obvious to parents and children alike. A norm against its use would be established. If a parent continued to employ physical discipline in the face of this policy, the meaning of that parenting strategy might change in the eyes of the child. The research cited here suggests that the child might experience his or her discipline as an indication of a wayward parent, a deviant child who merits such horrible treatment, or a problematic parent–child relationship. In all of these cases, the effect on the child may well be negative, that is, to exacerbate the child's conduct problems. Thus, an ironic effect of a new policy may well be to transform a current practice that has benign effects in certain cultural contexts into one that has adverse effects.

We are not advocating the continued practice of physical discipline nor a continued policy of endorsement of this practice. Rather, the research suggests that in order for a new policy banning corporal punishment to have positive effects, it must have a solid basis of support from a sizeable portion of the culture and must be readily endorsed by that culture. Thus, prior to making a formal policy change, it appears that a cultural change in attitudes and practice would be a necessary first step.

REFERENCES

Abell, E., Clawson, M., Washington, W. N., Bost, K. K., & Vaughn, B. E. (1996). Parenting values, attitudes, behaviors, and goals of African American mothers from a low-income population in relation to social and societal contexts. *Journal of Family Issues, 17,* 593–613.

American Academy of Pediatrics Committee on Psychosocial Aspects of Child and Family Health. (1998). Guidance for effective discipline. *Pediatrics, 101,* 723–728.

Baumrind, D. (1972). An exploratory study of socialization effects on Black children: Some Black–White comparisons. *Child Development, 43,* 261–267.

Caldwell, B., & Bradley, R. (1980). *Home Observation for Measurement of the Environment.* Unpublished manuscript, University of Arkansas at Little Rock.

Coard, S., Wallace, S., Stevenson, H., & Miller Brotman, L. (2004). Towards culturally competent preventive interventions: The consideration of racial socialization in parent training with African American families. *Journal of Child and Family Studies, 13*(3), 277–293.

Day, R. D., Peterson, G. W., & McCracken, C. (1998). Predicting spanking of younger and older children by mothers and fathers. *Journal of Marriage and the Family, 60,* 79–94.

Deater-Deckard, K., & Dodge, K. A. (1996, September). *Parents' and children's understanding of harsh parental discipline: Individual and cultural group differences.* Poster session presented at the Developmental Section of the British Psychological Society, Oxford, UK.

Deater-Deckard, K., & Dodge, K. A. (1997). Externalizing behavior problems and discipline revisited: Nonlinear effects and variation by culture, context, and gender. *Psychological Inquiry, 8,* 161–175.

Deater-Deckard, K., Dodge, K. A., Bates, J. E., & Pettit, G. S. (1996). Physical discipline among African American and European American mothers: Links to children's externalizing behaviors. *Developmental Psychology, 32,* 1065–1072.

Deater-Deckard, K., Dodge, K. A., & Sorbring, E. (in press). Parenting, antisocial behavior, and culture. In M. Tienda & M. Rutter (Eds.), *Ethnic variations in intergenerational continuities and discontinuities in psychosocial features and disorders.* New York: Cambridge University Press.

Deater-Deckard, K., Lansford, J. E., Dodge, K. A., Pettit, G. S., & Bates, J. E. (2003). The development of attitudes about physical punishment: An 8-year longitudinal study. *Journal of Family Psychology, 17,* 351–360.

Dodge, K. A., Bates, J. E., & Pettit, G. S. (1990). Mechanisms in the cycle of violence. *Science, 250,* 1678–1683.

Durrant, J. E. (1999). Evaluating the success of Sweden's corporal punishment ban. *Child Abuse and Neglect, 23,* 435–448.

Eron, L. D., Huesmann, L. R., & Zelli, A. (1991). The role of parental variables in the learning of aggression. In D. Pepler & K. Rubin (Eds.), *The development and treatment of childhood aggression* (pp. 169–188). Hillsdale, NJ: Erlbaum.

Farrington, D. P., & Hawkins, J. D. (1991). Predicting participation, early onset and later persistence in officially recorded offending. *Criminal Behavior and Mental Health, 1,* 1–33.

Flynn, C. P. (1996a). Normative support for corporal punishment: Attitudes, correlates, and implications. *Aggression and Violent Behavior, 1,* 47–55.

Flynn, C. P. (1996b). Regional differences in spanking experiences and attitudes: A comparison of northeastern and southern college students. *Journal of Family Violence, 11,* 59–80.

Flynn, C. P. (1998). To spank or not to spank: The effect of situation and age of child on support for corporal punishment. *Journal of Family Violence, 13,* 21–37.

Fox, R. A., Platz, D. L., & Bentley, K. S. (1995). Maternal factors related to parenting practices, developmental expectations, and perceptions of child behavior problems. *Journal of Genetic Psychology, 156,* 431–441.

Gershoff, E. T. (2002). Corporal punishment by parents and associated child behaviors and experiences: A meta-analytic and theoretical review. *Psychological Bulletin, 128,* 539–579.

Gershoff, E. T., Miller, P. C., & Holden, G. W. (1999). Parenting influences from the pulpit: Religious affiliation as a determinant of parental corporal punishment. *Journal of Family Psychology, 13,* 307–320.

Giles-Sims, J., Straus, M., & Sugarman, D. (1995). Child, maternal, and family characteristics associated with spanking. *Family Relations, 44,* 170–176.

Graziano, A. M., & Hamblen, J. L. (1996). Subabusive violence in child rearing in middle-class American families. *Pediatrics, 98,* 845–849.

Gunnoe, M. L., & Mariner, C. L. (1997). Toward a developmental-contextual model of the effects of parental spanking on children's aggression. *Archives of Pediatrics and Adolescent Medicine, 151,* 768–775.

Hollingshead, A. B. (1979). *Four-Factor Index of Social Status.* Unpublished manuscript, Yale University, New Haven, CT.

Jackson, J. F. (1997). Issues in need of initial visitation: Race and nation specificity in the study of externalizing behavior problems and discipline. *Psychological Inquiry, 8,* 204–211.

Jones, E. E., & Davis, K. E. (1965). From acts to dispositions: The attribution process in person perception. *Advanced Experimental Social Psychology, 2,* 219–276.

Korbin, J. E., Coulton, C. J., Lindstrom-Ufuti, H., & Spilsbury, J. (2000). Neighborhood views on the definition and etiology of child maltreatment. *Child Abuse and Neglect, 24,* 1509–1527.

Kumpfer, K. L., Alvarado, R., Smith, P., & Bellamy, N. (2002). Cultural sensitivity and adaptation in family-based prevention interventions. *Prevention Science, 3,* 241–246.

Lansford, J. E., Deater-Deckard, K., Dodge, K. A., Bates, J. E., & Pettit, G. S. (2004). Ethnic differences in the link between physical discipline and later adolescent externalizing. *Journal of Child Psychology and Psychiatry, 45,* 801–812.

Lansford, J. E., Dodge, K. A., Pettit, G. S., Bates, J. E., Crozier, J., & Kaplow, J. (2002). A 12–year prospective study of the long-term effects of early child physical maltreatment on psychological, behavioral, and academic problems in adolescence. *Archives of Pediatrics and Adolescent Medicine, 156,* 824–830.

Larzelere, R. E. (1996). A review of the outcomes of parental use of nonabusive or customary physical punishment. *Pediatrics, 98,* 824–831.

Larzelere, R. E. (2000). Child outcomes of nonabusive and customary physical punishment by parents: An updated literature review. *Clinical Child and Family Psychology Review, 3,* 199–221.

McCord, J. (1991). Questioning the value of punishment. *Social Problems, 38,* 167–179.

McLeod, J., Kruttschnitt, C., & Dornfield, M. (1994). Does parenting explain the effects of structural conditions on children's antisocial behavior? A comparison of Blacks and Whites. *Social Forces, 73,* 575–604.

McLoyd, V. C. (1990). The impact of economic hardship on Black families and children: Psychological distress, parenting, and socioemotional development. *Child Development, 61,* 311–346.

McLoyd, V. C., Jayaratne, T. E., Ceballo, R., & Borquez, J. (1994). Unemployment and work interruption among African American single mothers: Effects on parenting and adolescent socioemotional function. *Child Development, 65,* 562–589.

McLoyd, V. C., & Smith, J. (2002). Physical discipline and behavior problems in African American, European American, and Hispanic children: Emotional support as a moderator. *Journal of Marriage and the Family, 64,* 40–53.

Mosby, L., Rawls, A. W., Meehan, A. J., Mays, E., & Pettinari, C. J. (1999). Troubles in interracial talk about discipline: An examination of African American child rearing narratives. *Journal of Comparative Family Studies, 30,* 489–521.

Ogbu, J. U. (1981). Origins of human competence: A cultural-ecological perspective. *Child Development, 52,* 413–429.

Pinderhughes, E. E., Dodge, K. A., Bates, J. E., Pettit, G. S., & Zelli, A. (2000). Discipline responses: Influences of parents' socioeconomic status, ethnicity, beliefs about parenting, stress, and cognitive-emotional processes. *Journal of Family Psychology, 14,* 380–400.

Rohner, R. P., Bourque, S. L., & Elordi, C. A. (1996). Children's perceptions of corporal punishment, caretaker acceptance, and psychological adjustment in a poor, biracial, Southern community. *Journal of Marriage and the Family, 58,* 842–852.

Rohner, R. P., Kean, K. J., & Cournoyer, D. E. (1991). Effects of corporal punishment, perceived caretaker warmth, and cultural beliefs on the psychological adjustment of children in St. Kitts, West Indies. *Journal of Marriage and the Family, 53,* 681–693.

Spieker, S. J., Larson, N. C., Lewis, S. M., Keller, T. E., & Gilchrist, L. (1999). Developmental trajectories of disruptive behavior problems in preschool children of adolescent mothers. *Child Development, 70,* 443–458.

Stormshak, E. A., Bierman, K. L., McMahon, R. J., Lengua, L. J., & the Conduct Problems Prevention Research Group. (2000). Parenting practices and child disruptive behavior problems in early elementary school. *Journal of Clinical Child Psychology, 29,* 17–29.

Straus, M. A. (1979). Measuring intrafamily conflict and violence: The Conflict Tactics Scale. *Journal of Marriage and the Family, 41,* 75–85.

Ward, M. (1971). *Them children: A study in language learning.* New York: Holt, Rinehart & Winston.

Whaley, A. L. (2000). Sociocultural differences in the developmental consequences of the use of physical punishment during childhood for African Americans. *Cultural Diversity and Ethnic Minority Psychology, 6,* 5–12.

Young, V. H. (1970). Family and childhood in a Southern Negro community. *American Anthropologist, 72,* 269–288.

CHAPTER 13

African American Families as a Context for Racial Socialization

Stephanie I. Coard *and* Robert M. Sellers

The socialization of children is the primary responsibility of families, with a general goal being to make children familiar with social roles and prescribed behavior. It is also through the process of socialization that children learn the rules, skills, and attitudes of, and gain specific knowledge about, their family and ethnic culture. For families of color, part of this process is preparing children to recognize their position within the larger social structure. Over the past several years there has been increased interest in how African American[1] parents shape children's understanding of their position in an environment that traditionally has been incompatible with realizing positive group identity (i.e., significance of racism and discrimination). How do parents shape their children's learning about their own race and ethnicity? How do they do so within the context of racism and discrimination? Evidence has emerged regarding how African American families attempt to prepare, buffer, and insulate their children and foster a positive and functional group identity. A review of this evidence and its limitations, suggestions for the future study of racial socialization, and policy implications are the foci of this chapter.

Although all families struggle with the challenges of raising children, doing so is particularly challenging for families of color—and especially African American families, in which family serves an additional critical function, given the context of race. That is, African American

families help their children to navigate and negotiate the terrain of racism in America (Abell, Clawson, Washington, Bost, & Vaughn, 1996;
Franklin, Boyd-Franklin, & Draper, 2002; Marshall, 1995, McGroder,
2000; Peters, 1988; Stevenson, Davis, & Abdul- Kabir, 2001; Ward,
2000; Wilson, 1990; Wright, 1998). African American children disproportionately face difficult obstacles such as poverty, unemployment, incarceration, and crowded urban environments (Peters, 1985; Safyer,
1994). African American families serve to insulate and lessen the negative and often deleterious consequences that accompany racial group status.
Although there is great diversity within the African American community, one commonality is that African Americans must make psychological sense of the dominant culture's openly disparaging view of them and
negotiate racial barriers in an environment that marginalizes them. That
is, as a group, African Americans, regardless of class, are forced to grapple with the significance of race in defining themselves as well as decid-
ing what it means to be Black within their own life experiences. More recently, researchers have set out to describe the many unique behavioral
practices that African American parents employ to help their children
navigate their environments (Abell et al., 1996, Barnett & Kidwell,
1997; Coard, Wallace, Stevenson, & Miller Brotman, 2004; Deater-
Deckard, Dodge, Bates, & Pettit, 1996; Denby & Alford, 1996; Hughes
& Chen, 1997; Kelly, Power, & Wimbush, 1992; McGroder, 2000;
Stevenson et al., 2001). The process by which African American parents
impart these teachings to their children has come to be referred to as racial socialization.

RACIAL SOCIALIZATION DEFINED

Scholars have referred to parents' communications to children about
ethnicity as "developmental processes by which children acquire the behaviors, perceptions, values, and attitudes of an ethnic group, and come
to see themselves and others as members of such a group" (Rotheram &
Phinney, 1987, p.11). Although the process as described here suggests
that racial socialization should not be restricted to communications
solely about race and suggests its relevance to all families (particularly
families of color), scholars have described its unique relevance for African American parents and families. In the African American community,
racial socialization has traditionally been considered a rearing practice
that is intended to promote psychologically and physically healthy children in a society where dark skin and/or African features may lead to
detrimental outcomes (Peters, 1985). Similarly, Thornton, and his colleagues conceptualize the process as including "specific messages and

practices that . . . provide information concerning the nature of race status as it relates to: (1) personal and group identity, (2) intergroup and interindividual relationships, and (3) position in the social hierarchy" (Thornton, Chatters, Taylor, & Allen, 1990, pp. 401–402). Stevenson (1994a, 1994b) extended this conceptualization by proposing that racial socialization involves parents' instruction to their children about racism in society, educational struggles, importance of extended family, spiritual and religious awareness, African American culture and pride, and transmission of childrearing values. The conceptualization of racial socialization is also informed by the work of Hill (1997) and his typology of African American family strengths that remain relevant today. This typology includes high achievement orientation, strong work ethic, flexible family roles, close kinship bonds, and strong religious orientation. Hill linked several positive aspects of African American family and child development (e.g., resiliency in low-income children, continuing influence of Black extended families) to African cultural legacies.

In this chapter we define racial socialization quite simply as the process by which messages are transmitted/communicated inter- and intragenerationally regarding the significance and meaning of race and ethnicity. Furthermore, racial socialization involves teaching children values and norms associated with race and ethnicity, and problem-solving skills that enable children to be flexible in their approach to race-related situations without losing a core sense of self. We view this communication as an important determinant of children's race-related attitudes and beliefs and their sense of efficacy in negotiating race-related barriers and experiences.

CONTENT OF MESSAGES

Given that socialization occurs within a societal environment that is frequently incompatible with attaining positive mental health (Thornton et al., 1990), racial socialization is one means by which African American parents address their concerns. The conceptual framework proposed by Boykin and Toms (1985) provides us with a basis for a deeper understanding of the multiplicity of racial socialization messages and practices African American parents use. Boykin and Toms argue that Blacks must simultaneously negotiate at least three distinctive realms of experience. They call this phenomenon the *triple quandary*—containing what they refer to as mainstream, minority, and cultural experiences. For Black parents these realms may guide childrearing practices. That is, Black parents must not only negotiate the three realms themselves but also socialize their children to navigate and successfully operate in each of them. To do so, parents draw from each of these realms, and each plays a valuable role in the racial socialization process.

Mainstream experiences focus on promoting the goals, values, and influences of the dominant culture (i.e., White, middle-class). All African American parents participate in some aspect of mainstream America culture and therefore prepare their children to negotiate this reality by conveying those things that transcend race. For instance, African American parents teach life skills and convey the importance of personal qualities such as honesty, confidence, ambition, and respect, independent of race. With the goal of raising happy and successful children in American society, African American parents often focus on universally human values in this society by emphasizing self-development, life skills, morality, equality, and peaceful coexistence (Spencer, 1983).

Minority experiences involve ways of promoting awareness of and preparation to cope with minority status. Highlighting the minority experience is associated with preparing children for an oppressive environment. African American parents recognize that being Black means that their children must prepare for a nonsupportive world and learn how to survive and cope with racial prejudice, racial discrimination, and racism. As a result, many African American parents will point to the need for their children to understand the social, economic, and political forces impinging on racial equality in order to enhance their ability to cope with the realities associated with being Black in America.

The *cultural experiences* realm refers to those cultural customs, values, and traditions (i.e., styles, motifs, and patterns of behavior) unique to being of African descent. The core character of these expressions is linked to a traditional West African cultural ethos through reciting proverbs and storytelling about historical events and figures (Nobles, 1974). The messages of Black cultural experiences can be both negative and positive. They can encompass pride in one's racial and cultural history, as well as shame as the result of internalized racism.

Boykin and Toms (1985) suggest that there is a range of socialization experiences across all three realms, and that some parts of all will be found in every family. They may be represented in one family by the extent to which mainstream goals and values are promoted or embraced. They may be seen in the extent to which African American cultural socialization goals have been overtly articulated. Furthermore, the meaning families give to oppression and racism and the display of responses to cope with such may vary within the same family. Thus, the degree to which parents employ one or some combination of socialization strategies varies greatly. Given the historical variability of African Americans in the United States, African American parents differ in their perceptions of their racial and ethnic group and even in their perceptions of society at large (Thornton, 1997). So, whereas all parents and families seek to orient their children to the external environment, the content of the messages they proffer to their children vary because of the unique contexts and circumstances of African American families.

Research to date has focused on the ways in which African American parents promote racial pride and commitment in their children, orient them to race-related barriers, and prepare them to succeed in mainstream endeavors (e.g., egalitarian virtues). A number of scholars have developed specific typologies that represent the various racial socialization messages that parents convey to their children. Bowman and Howard (1985) examined the content of racial socialization messages given by African American parents to their children by asking African Americans (ages 14 to 24) the most important messages their parents or caregivers people gave them about what it means to be Black. Bowman and Howard coded the open-ended responses in five categories: no race messages (38% of sample), racial pride (23%), self-development orientation (14%), racial barrier awareness (12%), and egalitarian views orientation (12%). Racial pride messages emphasized African American unity, teachings about heritage, and instilling positive feelings toward the group. Self-development messages emphasized individual excellence and positive character traits. Racial barrier messages emphasized an awareness of racial inequities and strategies for coping with them. Egalitarian messages emphasized interracial equality and coexistence. This categorization scheme for the content of race socialization messages has been adapted and used by a number of other authors (e.g., Sanders Thompson, 1994; Stevenson, 1994a, 1994b; Thornton et al., 1990).

Hughes and Chen (1997) conducted one of the few studies that directly asked African American parents what types of race messages they convey to their children. They found three themes in the race socialization messages that their sample of 157 African American parents reported relaying to their children (ages 4–14 years). These three themes consisted of (1) cultural socialization; (2) preparation for bias; and (3) promotion of mistrust. Cultural socialization was the most frequently endorsed dimension of race socialization, followed by preparation for bias, and, finally, the promotion of mistrust. In developing the Scale of Racial Socialization (SORS) for African American adolescents, Stevenson (1994a, 1994b) distinguished among four types of racial socialization messages in his measure: spiritual religious coping, extended family caring, cultural pride, and racial awareness teaching. Table 13.1 provides a summary of the racial socialization content areas that have emerged in the literature thus far. In sum, although there are consistent themes with regard to the content of racial socialization messages that have been assessed across studies, there is also considerable variation as well. Thus,

TABLE 13.1. Racial Socialization Themes Identified by Authors

Spencer (1983)	1. Concerns about educational success 2. Childrearing about race, racism, and discrimination 3. Childrearing about gender concerns 4. Knowledge of Black history for child and parent 5. Childrearing about civil rights
Boykin & Toms (1985)	1. Mainstream societal values 2. Minority status 3. Black cultural context
Peters (1985)	1. Teaching children to survive 2. Self-respect and pride 3. Nonreciprocality of fair play 4. Getting a good education 5. Expressing love
Bowman & Howard (1985)	1. Racial barriers 2. Self-development 3. Ethnic pride 4. Egalitarianism
Thornton (1997)	1. Racial pride 2. Black heritage 3. Good citizenship/moral virtues 4. Achievement/hard work 5. Acceptance of one's race 6. Presence of blocked opportunities 7. Religious principles 8. Peaceful coexistence with Whites 9. Acceptance of self (non-race-related)
Jeter (1994)	1. Pro-dominant culture socialization 2. Pro-ethnic culture socialization 3. Confounded culture socialization 4. Raceless culture socialization
Stevenson (1994b)	1. Spiritual and religious coping 2. Extended family caring 3. Cultural pride reinforcement 4. Racism awareness teaching
Hughes & Chen (1999)	1. Cultural socialization 2. Preparation for future bias 3. Promoting racial mistrust 4. Egalitarianism
Stevenson (2003)	1. Discrimination alertness 2. Antagonism coping 3. Cultural pride reinforcement 4. Cultural legacy appreciation 5. Mainstream fitting
Coard, Wallace, et al. (2004)	1. Racism preparation 2. Racial equality 3. Racial achievement 4. Racial pride

to date there is no consensus in regard to a taxonomy of racial socialization messages.

MODE OF TRANSMISSION

Although research confirms the use of a variety of racial socialization messages among Black parents, the mode by which these messages are taught varies. Parents' use of racial socialization takes many forms, and the messages are based on the experiences of both parent and child. Coard, Wallace, and colleagues (2004) provide additional insight into the methods by which parents transmit or communicate race-related messages. According to this study, the methods that parents and families use to teach their children take many forms. These forms include *verbal* communications (i.e., using reasoning, explaining, lecturing, storytelling about race). Parents initiate and promote a verbal exchange that provides clarification and knowledge. In their most common form, such exchanges occur when parents read culturally affirming books to their children or share their own childhood experiences for historical lessons. For example, in the Coard, Wallace, and colleagues study, parents reported, "We go through the inventors and the civil rights leaders to learn more about his [my son's] culture and feel good about it" and "I explain that she [my daughter] is African American. I try to talk to her a little bit about her history. . . . Every day I tell my daughter stories about what a black person did that day." *Exposure* is another tool Black parents use to racially socialize children. For example, parents may choose to provide their children with cultural experiences by exposing them to cultural stimuli (e.g., museums, African art, Kwanzaa festivals, foods). "You just don't see enough good things [on television] with black faces on it. But then when I do see something good, I try to, you know, tape it and show it a couple of times." Another parent stated, "I try to keep up on what is going on that is positive in our neighborhood . . . participate in the block parties and marches to further the cause, you know." Another form is *modeling*. *Modeling* refers to parents teaching children by demonstrating particular behaviors or actions and encouraging their children to imitate them. A common example may be the purposeful decision not to use derogatory, self-disparaging, or stereotypical remarks in front of their children or allow others to use them in their presence. "I don't want my child picking up bad language about Black people . . . Black this . . . Black that . . . why does everything Black have to be bad? I definitely don't use it and I don't allow it in my home, and my children see this." Or, "If I see people hanging out on the stoop and they start getting wild and cursing each other, I just shake my head and walk upstairs, and now sometimes my daughter will start walking up first. She doesn't need to see me involved in any nonsense on the block. Basically, I just try to set an example myself and show them [my children]."

FACTORS ASSOCIATED
WITH RACIAL SOCIALIZATION

Although African American parents have diverse viewpoints as to the importance of relaying race socialization messages to their children (Murray, Stokes, & Peacock, 1996; Spencer, 1983), research suggests that most African American families frequently engage in racial socialization practices with their children and consider these teachings unique, routine, and even critical aspects of Black childrearing (Biafora et al., 1993; Bowman & Howard, 1985; Coard, Wallace, et al., 2004; Sanders Thompson, 1994; Thornton, 1997). Studies consistently report that a majority of African Americans participate in some form of racial socialization (Caughy, O'Campo, Randolph, & Nickerson, 2002; Coard, Wallace, et al., 2004; Hughes, 2003; Hughes & Chen, 1997; Hughes & Johnson, 2001, Smith, Atkins, & Connell, 2003). Using data from the National Survey of Black Americans, Thornton and colleagues suggested that approximately 75% of African American parents actively provide their children with race socialization messages (Thornton et al., 1990). Similarly, Stevenson (1995) also found that roughly three fourths of his sample of African Americans reported receiving race socialization messages from their parents.

Although a vast majority of African American parents report engaging in racial socialization practices, research indicates that there are demographic and family factors that point to differences in the nature of those practices. Bowman and Howard (1985) reported that the racial socialization messages that African American parents transmit are influenced by the gender of their children, with girls receiving more messages geared toward developing racial pride, and boys receiving more messages emphasizing racial barriers and discrimination. Thornton and colleagues (1990) reported that marital status, age, education, and geographic location influenced both the approach to racial socialization and the strategies used. They found that parents who were married were more like to socialize their children according to racial concerns. This was also the case for parents who were older (as compared with younger) and parents who were more highly educated. African American parents living in the Northeast also engaged in racial socialization more than those in other regions of the country.

More recent studies have continued to document the familial and environmental factors that influence the use of racial socialization practices (Hughes, 2003; Hughes & Chen, 1997, 1999; Smith et al., 2003).

For example, Hughes and Chen (1997) found differences in parental racial socialization practices as a function of the child's age. In general, parents of older children used racial socialization practices more frequently than parents of younger children. In particular, parents of older children reported transmitting more messages that emphasize recognition of discrimination and bias than parents of younger children (Hughes & Chen, 1997). In addition to the gender of their children, parents' own experiences also influence how they socialize their children with respect to race. The messages that parents give their children regarding race are often influenced by the racial socialization messages that parents received from their parents when they were children (Hughes & Chen, 1997). Parents' experiences with racial discrimination in the workplace and other contexts outside the home also impact the messages that they send to their children (Hughes & Chen, 1997). This finding further reinforces the need for more studies to examine racial socialization beyond the family to include school and community factors.

RACIAL SOCIALIZATION AND CHILD OUTCOMES

There is growing evidence that parents' racial socialization practices have an impact on important child developmental and psychological outcomes (e.g., Biafora et al., 1993; Caughy et al., 2002; Constantine & Blackmon, 2002; Frabutt, Walker, & MacKinnon-Lewis, 2002; Johnson, 2001; Marshall, 1995; Oliver, 1989; Smith et al., 2003; McKay, Atkins, Hawkins, Brown, & Lynn, 2003; Stevenson, 2003; Stevenson, Herrero-Taylor, Cameron, & Davis, 2002). For example, studies have linked parents' racial socialization efforts to children's quality of life in terms of both behavioral competence and psychological health (Spencer, 1983). In particular, Spencer (1983) found that childrearing practices that emphasized the existence of racial discrimination were associated with more positive child outcomes, as well as evidence suggesting that childrearing practices that ignore race and racism may leave children ill prepared for the social injustices they are likely to face in the future. Providing messages to children that emphasize pride in one's race and one's racial heritage have been associated with a number of positive child outcomes, such as higher levels of self-esteem, well-developed racial identities, more positive socioemotional functioning, more adaptive anger expression, fewer externalizing and internalizing problems, and more effective racial coping skills (Caughy et al., 2002; Constantine & Blackmon, 2002; Demo & Hughes, 1990; Johnson, 2001; Marshall, 1995; McAdoo, 1985; Spencer, 1983, 1987; Stevenson, 1995, 2003; Stevenson et al., 2002; Stevenson, Reed, Bodison, & Bishop, 1995). In addition, racial socialization practices that emphasize racial pride have been associated with a variety of prosocial outcomes for children, including more positive and involved mother–child interactions (Frabutt et al., 2002) and prosocial bonding to other socialization agents (e.g., school, community), which may in turn counter potential interpersonal violence in their peer groups (Oliver, 1989; Smith et al., 2003).

Although the research literature consistently suggests the positive benefits of racial socialization practices that emphasize racial pride, the relationship between racial socialization practices that emphasize the existence of racism and racial barriers and child outcomes is more equivocal. There is some research that has provided evidence suggesting a positive link between parents' providing messages about racial barriers and child outcomes such as higher academic functioning and feelings of efficacy (Bowman & Howard, 1985) and decreased depression (Stevenson et al., 1995). Some researchers have argued that the absence of such socialization places the child at greater risk once he or she experiences racial discrimination (Bulhan, 1985; Fanon, 1962; Stevenson, 2003; Wilson, 1990). They argue that without a knowledge of the existence of racism, children who experience racial discrimination may be more likely to personalize such racist behavior and stereotypes, which may in turn lead to increases in antisocial behavior and the expression of anger toward others. At the same time, other researchers caution that an overemphasis on racial bias and discrimination may undermine children's development and cause isolation (Biafora et al., 1993; Marshall, 1995). They argue that too frequent or blatant messages about racial barriers may provide children (especially at younger ages) with a view of the world as a scary and threatening place. Such a view may increase anxiety and self-consciousness in children who may not have the cognitive and/or emotional skills to cope with such information. More research is needed to further explicate when, how, and for whom parents should transmit messages regarding the existence of racial barriers.

In sum, the research literature clearly suggests that parents' racial socialization practices have implications for the way in which African American children function in the world. Some of these relationships are consistent and straightforward, and others are more complex. Further research is needed before we have a complete understanding of the role of racial socialization in African American childrearing practices.

WHERE DO WE GO FROM HERE?

To date, the research literature on racial socialization has made great strides in helping to delineate the processes by which attitudes regarding

the significance and meaning of race are transmitted. The research literature has also made meaningful linkages between specific racial socialization practices and specific child outcomes. Nonetheless, racial socialization literature is in its infancy and there are several areas in which
improvement is necessary. These areas include focusing on a single person's perspective (parent or child) of racial socialization, modeling racial
socialization as a static process, viewing racial socialization as a unidirectional process, and focusing on only the independent impacts of types
of racial socialization messages. In the following pages, we briefly address these issues with suggestions on which future research on racial socialization in African American families can build. We conclude with a
discussion of the implications of the racial socialization process for policy directed at African Americans.

CRITIQUE OF THE RACIAL
SOCIALIZATION LITERATURE

Single Perspective

A significant limitation in the research literature is that most studies use
only one perspective (either the parent's or the child's) to assess both the
frequency and the content of the messages in the race socialization process. The current state of racial socialization research focuses on only
one facet of the socialization process. Few studies have utilized multiple
perspectives in assessing racial socialization. Research that assesses racial socialization from only one source implicitly assumes that both parents and children are experiencing the racial socialization process the
same way. Recent research suggests that such an assumption is untenable
(LeSane, 2002; Scottham, 2003). For instance, a parent may take his or
her children to Kwanzaa festivals in the hope of instilling racial and ethnic pride. Yet the children may perceive no message regarding race, but
instead experience the outing as only a fun trip. In addition to the possibilities of parents and children having different interpretations of the
same event, failure to assess racial socialization from the perspectives of
both the parent and the child prohibits researchers from examining how
the parent's and the child's perception of the racial socialization process
influence each other.

Static Nature

Another issue related to the unidirectional focus of the research literature on racial socialization is the static nature of most of the studies. Racial socialization unfolds over time. It is a cumulative process that builds

on previous experiences. Parents' messages about the significance and meaning of race are likely to change over time for a variety of reasons. Parents are likely to change their messages based on changes in their child's experiences. For instance, parents of teenagers are likely to use different messages and different modes of transmitting those messages than parents of preschoolers (Hughes & Chen, 1997). Parents are also likely to change their racial socialization practices, based on changes in their own attitudes of racial identity, because of new experiences in their own lives in regard to race. In addition, parents may change how they socialize their children based on their perceptions of the success and failure of previous racial socialization practices. Unfortunately, there is little research on the dynamic nature of the racial socialization process. Almost all of the existing studies have assessed racial socialization practices at a single point in time. The current literature is replete with studies that are either retrospective or cross-sectional in nature despite the obvious developmental significance of the race socialization and racial identity development processes. Our search of the existing literature failed to uncover a single published study that investigated the relationship between African American parents' race socialization messages and the development of their adolescent children's racial identity attitudes in a prospective manner.

Unidirectional Phenomenon

Racial socialization has been primarily operationalized as a unidirectional phenomenon. Most of the current research has focused exclusively on the messages that parents give their children regarding the meaning of being Black. Little attention has been paid to how children's experiences, behaviors, and attitudes influence parents' beliefs regarding what messages they should be transmitting to their children. A number of authors have pointed out that the relationship between parent variables and child variables is often reciprocal (e.g., Bell, 1968; Bronfenbrenner, 1979; Stattin & Kerr, 2000). Racial socialization does not just occur in a vacuum; it usually occurs within a situational context in which the events of the moment or day lead to a discussion of race. Parents often transmit racial socialization messages in order to provide their child with what he or she needs to be able to handle the event at hand. They are frequently given with little forethought or contemplation by the parents. Although parents are generally the ones who are transmitting the messages to their children regarding the significance and meaning of race, the process is often recursive. Parents are often forced to rethink their own attitudes regarding race as a result of their children's experiences in regard to race (Cross, 1991).

These changes in the parents' racial identity influence their subsequent racial socialization practices.

Independence

A final limitation of the research literature is its failure to capture the fact that parents' racial socialization messages are multifaceted and synergistic. In other words, the total content of the messages that parents send their children regarding race is often greater than the sum of individual messages. At present, most of our current conceptualizations of the content of racial socialization messages have focused on identifying a taxonomy of messages that parents transmit to children and have then looked at how each of these types of messages has been related to various outcomes independent of the other types of socialization messages. These messages not only have individual direct influences, but they interact with other messages that are sent to provide broader and deeper meaning. It is also true that parents provide messages that are seemingly incompatible, but which in reality are very nuanced and reasoned. Often it is the combination of these messages that has the greatest impact on child outcomes. For instance, two children whose parents similarly emphasize the prevalence of racial barriers for African Americans, but who differ in the extent to which their parents also emphasize messages suggesting that they should have pride in their race, are likely to interpret the meaning of the racial barriers differently. The parents who emphasize racial barriers without also emphasizing racial pride may be placing their child at greater risk for feelings of low self-efficacy and racial efficacy, whereas the parents of the other child may be providing their child with a more effective coping repertoire against racial discrimination.

RECOMMENDATIONS FOR FUTURE RESEARCH

Several methodological and analytic changes are needed in order for research literature on racial socialization to more accurately capture the multifaceted, bidirectional, dynamic, and synergistic nature of the racial socialization process in African American families. First, multiple sources are needed to comprehensively assess the racial socialization process. For instance, more research is needed that assesses both the parents' and the children's perceptions of the racial socialization messages that have been transmitted. Although it is likely that there is some relationship between the messages that parents report sending and the messages that children report receiving, it is unlikely that there is a one-to-one correspondence between the two (Slevin & Wingrove, 1983). Unfortunately, researchers' reliance on one point of view makes it impossible to assess the actual correspondence between the messages that parents send and the messages that adolescents receive. In addition, observational methods should be employed to assess the prevalence of racially and culturally relevant objects (including books and artwork) in the home, as well as the content of the messages that may be associated with such objects (see Caughy, Randolph, & O'Campo, 2002). For example, the Parent–Child Race-Related Observation Measure (PC-RROM) developed by Coard and Wallace (2001) is an observational measure designed to assess race-related communication between parent and child. Parent–child dyads are videotaped in 15-minute sessions consisting of three semistructured situations that vary in racial socialization strategies/techniques to illicit race related interactions. Observational methods of this sort (e.g., Coard, Foy-Watson, & Wallace, 2004) are able to assess racial socialization messages that are transmitted unintentionally as well as subliminally (such as the number of Black books in the family library).

To examine the dynamic nature of the racial socialization process, future research is needed that employs longitudinal designs. At present, most of the research has utilized single assessments that ask individuals to provide either a retrospective description of their racial socialization practices over a specified period of time or observations of a discrete racial socialization event. Such approaches are extremely limited in their ability to assess changes in racial socialization behavior over time. Future research needs to incorporate designs that include multiple assessments of racial socialization. These multiple assessments could be done across relatively long or short periods of time. For instance, yearly assessments of the parent's and child's experiences with the racial socialization process can impart information regarding how the process unfolds developmentally. At the same time, obtaining multiple assessments of parents' and children's racial socialization experiences over a shorter period of time can provide a more detailed picture of the actual racial socialization process. For instance, research designs utilizing daily diary methods may get more accurate information than retrospective reports regarding the frequency, type, and situational contexts in which racial socialization occurs (Yip & Fuligni, 2002). By including assessments of both parents' and children's perceptions of the racial socialization process in these longitudinal designs, researchers will also be in a position to examine the bidirectionality of the racial socialization process. Such a design will allow for the testing of both recursive and nonrecursive relationships between parents and children.

Finally, changes in analytic strategies may help to better capture the synergistic nature of the impact of various racial socialization messages on child outcomes. At present, the majority of studies examine only independent associations of certain types of racial socialization messages and child outcomes. These analyses usually consist of analyzing the direct associations between several racial socialization subscales and a child outcome using a multiple regression. Rarely are interactions among the subscales examined to assess the multiplicative nonlinear relationship among the variables. Even more promising is the use of more person-oriented approaches to operationalize racial socialization, such as the use of cluster analyses to create profiles of messages within individuals. Such an approach would provide information as to what combination of racial socialization messages are associated with the most positive or negative child outcomes. With this approach, we will not only be in a better position to identify synergistic relationships, but we will also be better able to provide information that would be useful in developing interventions.

POLICY IMPLICATIONS AND RECOMMENDATIONS

Although the research on racial socialization is still in its infancy and we have a way to go until its full potential is realized, there are a number of policy implications worth noting. First, we have enough evidence that racial socialization processes play an important role in child and family outcomes to warrant that racial socialization be viewed as a significant component to initiatives and policies directed at understanding the diversity of family processes along racial and ethnic lines. Understanding racial socialization processes as indigenous protective factors of individuals, families, and communities of color may play a key role in the elimination of racial and ethnic disparities in physical and mental health outcomes. As a result, we recommend as a policy that greater resources be dedicated to fund research that further explicates the racial socialization process in African American families. This increase in research funding should not only be directed toward research that seeks to understanding the underlying processes as well as the social ecological context in which racial socialization, but increased funding is also needed for extensive evaluation of existing and new interventions that address racial socialization as a focus of intervention. These evaluations need to be systematic across interventions and outcomes so as to identify what works and for whom. In addition, such evaluation research will help in the development and testing of conceptual models of racial socialization.

It is important that policies that do not have racial socialization as a focus of intervention also consider the impact that the heterogeneity of African Americans' attitudes regarding the significance and meaning of race may have on the effectiveness of the policy. For instance, busing poorer African American students to more affluent, predominately White schools seems to have obvious benefits regarding the educational opportunities of the African American students. However, the messages the student has received regarding what it means to be Black are also likely to play a part in how comfortable the student feels about the school, which, in turn, is likely to effect the student's academic performance. As a result, the effectiveness of busing as a strategy is likely to vary across students, in part as a result of the students' attitudes and beliefs regarding race. These attitudes and beliefs are likely to be reinforced by how a student is socialized about race. An understanding of the role of the racial socialization processes will help interventionists and policymakers to avoid the mistake of believing that one size fits all when it comes to developing remedies for the myriad of challenges that face African Americans. For example, interventions that explicitly promote an Afrocentric orientation are more likely to be successful in recruiting participants whose racial identity attitudes are consistent with such an orientation, than they will be in recruiting participants whose racial identity attitudes are inconsistent or in conflict with an Afrocentric orientation. As a result, in order for policies, interventions, policymakers, and interventionists to be truly culturally responsive to the African American community, they need to be informed by a thorough understanding of the complexity and variability of African Americans' attitudes regarding the role and meaning of race in their lives.

CONCLUSION

The transmission of messages regarding the meaning of race across generations is an important task for the African American family. The racial socialization process in African American families has grown out of their unique sociohistorical niche within American society. As a result, the racial socialization process has developed into a multifaceted, dynamic, and bidirectional racial and cultural imperative for African American families. The racial socialization process also occurs within a larger social-ecological context. The current research has implicated the importance of racial socialization in a number of important child outcomes. Current research has also begun to delineate predictors associated with the content of various racial socialization messages. Although the current research literature has made several important contributions, further advancements are needed with regard to both the development of conceptual models and the design of empirical studies. These advancements must better represent the complexity associated with both the nature of and the context in which racial socialization occurs. An enhanced understanding of the racial socialization process not only is important for the development of the research literature, but has important implications for the development of interventions and policies to address the myriad of challenges that many African American families face. Once we have a better understanding of these complexities, we will be in a better position to develop more effective interventions and policies that are responsive to the heterogeneity within the African American family.

NOTE

1. In this chapter we make a distinction between the terms "Black" and "African American." We view the term "Black" as being an ambiguous concept that is not necessarily inclusive of all persons of African descent, depending on the individual's viewpoint. We use the term "African American" to refer to those individuals of African descent who have received a significant portion of their socialization in the United States. As such, they share a heritage and a set of values that are related to their common historical experiences in this society. Thus, we use the term "Black" when referring to the individuals' own phenomenological view of the makeup of their reference group and the term "African American" when referring to the group of people on whom this chapter focuses.

REFERENCES

Abell, E., Clawson, M., Washington, W. N., Bost, K. K., & Vaughn, B. E. (1996). Parenting values, attitudes, behaviors, and goals of African American mothers from a low-income population in relation to social and societal contexts. *Journal of Family Issues, 17,* 593–612.

Barnet, D., & Kidwell, S. L. (1997, April). *Parenting correlates of attachment among inner city African American preschoolers.* Paper presented at the biennial meeting of the Society for Research in Child Development, Indianapolis, IN.

Bell, R. Q. (1968). A reinterpretation of the direction of effects in studies of socialization. *Psychological Review, 75,* 81–95.

Biafora, F. A., Warheit, G. J., Zimmerman, R. S., Gil, A. G., Apospori, E., Taylor, D., & Vega, W. A. (1993). Racial mistrust and deviant behaviors among ethnically diverse Black adolescent boys. *Journal of Applied Social Psychology, 23,* 891–910.

Bowman, P. J., & Howard, C. (1985). Race-related socialization, motivation, and academic achievement: A study of black youth in three-generation families. *Journal of the American Academy of Child Psychiatry, 24,* 143–141.

Boykin, A. W., & Toms, F. D. (1985). Black child socialization: A conceptual framework. In H. P. McAdoo & J. L. McAdoo (Eds.), *Black children: Social, educational, and parental environments* (pp. 33–52). Newbury Park, CA: Sage.

Bronfenbrenner, U. (1979). *The ecology of human development: Experiments by nature and design*. Cambridge, MA: Harvard University Press.

Bulhan, H. A. (1985). *Frantz Fanon and the psychology of oppression*. New York: Plenum Press.

Caughy, M. O., O'Campo, P. J., Randolph, S. M., & Nickerson, K. (2002). The influence of racial socialization practices on the cognitive and behavioral competence of African American children. *Child Development, 73*(5), 1611–1625.

Caughy, M. O., Randolph, S. M., & O'Campo, P. J. (2002). The Africentric Home Environment Inventory: An observational measure of racial socialization features of the home environment for African American preschool children. *Journal of Black Psychology, 28*, 37–52.

Coard, S. I., Foy-Watson, S., & Wallace, S. A. (2004). *The Parent–Child Race-Related Observational Measure (PC-RROM): A preliminary investigation of reliability and construct validity*. Manuscript in preparation.

Coard, S. I., & Wallace, S. A. (2001). *The parent child race-related observational measure (PC-RROM): An observational measure of racial socialization*. Unpublished measure.

Coard, S. I., Wallace, S. A., Stevenson, H. C., & Miller Brotman, L. (2004). Towards culturally relevant preventive interventions: The consideration of racial socialization in parent training with African American families. *Journal of Child and Family Studies, 13*(3), 277–293.

Constantine, M.G., & Blackmon, S. B. (2002). Black adolescents' racial socialization experiences: Their relations to home, school, and peer self-esteem. *Journal of Black Studies, 32*(2), 322–334.

Cross, W. E., Jr. (1991). *Shades of black: Diversity in African-American identity*. Philadelphia: Temple University Press.

Deater-Deckard, K., Dodge, K. A., Bates, J. E., & Pettit, G. S. (1996). Physical discipline among African American mothers: Links to children's externalizing behaviors. *Developmental Psychology, 12*, 1065–1072.

Demo, D., & Hughes, M. (1990). Socialization and racial identity among Black Americans. *Social Psychology Quarterly, 53*, 364–374.

Denby, R. W., & Alford, K. A. (1996). Understanding African American discipline styles: Suggestions for effective social work intervention. *Journal of Multicultural Social Work, 4*(3), 81–98.

Fanon, F. (1962). *Black skin, White masks*. New York: Grove Press.

Frabutt, J. M., Walker, A. M., & MacKinnon-Lewis, C. (2002). Racial socialization messages and the quality of mother/child interactions in African American families. *Journal of Early Adolescence, 22*(2), 200–217.

Franklin, A. J., Boyd-Franklin, N., & Draper, C. V. (2002). A psychological and educational perspective on Black parenting. In H. P. McAdoo (Ed.), *Black children: Social, educational, and parental environments* (2nd ed., pp. 119–140). Thousand Oaks, CA: Sage.

Hill, R. (1997). *The strengths of Black families*. New York: Emerson Hall.

Hughes, D. (2003). Correlates of African American and Latino parents' messages to children about ethnicity and race: A comparative study of racial socialization. *American Journal of Community Psychology, 31*(1/2), 15–33.

Hughes, D., & Chen, L. (1997). When and what parents tell children about race: An examination of race-related socialization among African American families. *Applied Developmental Science, 1,* 200–214.

Hughes, D., & Chen, L. (1999). The nature of parents' race-related communications to children: A developmental perspective. In L. Balter & C. S. Tamis-LeMonda (Eds.), *Child psychology: A handbook of contemporary issues* (pp. 467–490). Philadelphia: Psychology Press/Taylor & Francis.

Hughes, D., & Johnson, D. (2001). Correlates in children's experiences of parents' racial socialization behaviors. *Journal of Marriage and the Family, 63,* 981–995.

Jeter, R. F. (1994). *Racial socialization: The effectiveness of the transmission of messages about race by Black parents to their college-aged children.* Unpublished doctoral dissertation, University of Pennsylvania, Philadelphia.

Johnson, D. (2001). Parental characteristics, racial stress, and racial socialization processes as predictors of racial coping in middle childhood. In A. M. Neal-Barnett, J. M. Contreras, & K. A. Kerns (Eds.), *Forging links: African American children clinical developmental perspectives* (pp. 57–74). Westport, CT: Praeger.

Kelly, M. L., Power, T. G., & Wimbush, D. D. (1992). Determinants of disciplinary practices in low-income Black mothers. *Child Development, 63,* 573–582.

LeSane, C. L. (2002). Racial socialization in Black families: A selective review of the literature. *Perspectives, 8*(1), 27–34.

Marshall, S. (1995). Ethnic socialization of African American children: Implications for parenting, identity development, and academic achievement. *Journal of Youth and Adolescence, 24*(4), 377–396.

McAdoo, H. P. (1985). Racial attitude and self-concept in young Black children over time. In H. P. McAdoo & J. L. McAdoo (Eds.), *Black children: Social, educational, and parental environments* (pp. 213–242). Newbury Park, CA: Sage.

McGroder, S. M. (2000). Parenting among low-income African American single mothers with preschool-age children: Patterns, predictors, and developmental correlates. *Child Development, 71,* 752–771.

McKay, M. M., Atkins, M. S., Hawkins, T., Brown, C., & Lynn, C. J. (2003). Inner-city African American parental involvement in children's schooling: Racial socialization and social support from the parent community. *American Journal of Community Psychology, 32*(1/2), 107–114.

Murray, C. B., Stokes, J. E., & Peacock, M. J. (1996). Race socialization of African American children: A review. In R. L. Jones (Ed.), *African American children, youth, and parenting* (pp. 209–229). Hampton, VA: Cobb & Henry.

Nobles, W. (1974). Africanity: Its role in Black families. *The Black Scholar, 5,* 9.

Oliver, W. (1989). Black males and social problems: Prevention through Afro-centric socialization. *Journal of Black Studies, 20*(1), 1–19.

Peters, M. F. (1985). Racial socialization of young Black children. In H. P. McAdoo & J. L. McAdoo (Eds.), *Black children: Social, educational, and parental environments* (pp. 159–173). Newbury Park, CA: Sage.

Peters, M. F. (1988). Parenting in Black families with young children: A historical perspective. In H. P. McAdoo (Ed.), *Black families* (2nd ed., pp. 228–241). Beverly Hills, CA: Sage.

Richards, H. (1997). The teaching of Afrocentric values by African American parents. *Western Journal of Black Studies, 21*(1), 42–50.

Rotheram, M. J., & Phinney, J. S. (1987). Introduction: Definitions and perspectives in the study of children's ethnic socialization. In J. S. Phinney & M. J. Rotheram (Eds.), *Children's ethnic socialization: Pluralism and development* (pp. 10–28). Beverly Hills, CA: Sage.

Safyer, A. W. (1994). The impact of inner-city life on adolescent development: Implications for social work. *Smith College Studies in Social Work, 64*(2), 153–167.

Sanders Thompson, V. L. (1994). Socialization to race and its relationship to racial identification among African Americans. *Journal of Black Psychology, 20,* 175–188.

Scottham, K. (2003). *What we tell our sons and daughters: Parent–child race socialization among African American adolescents* [Dissertation abstract]. Ann Arbor: University of Michigan Press.

Slevin, K. E., & Wingrove, C. R. (1983). Similarities and differences among three generations of women in attitudes toward the female role in contemporary society. *Sex Roles, 9,* 609–624.

Smith, E. P., Atkins, J., & Connell, C. (2003). Family, school, and community factors and relationships to racial-ethnic attitudes and academic achievement. *American Journal of Community Psychology, 32*(1/2), 159–173.

Spencer, M. B. (1983). Children's cultural values and parental child rearing strategies. *Developmental Review, 3,* 351–370.

Spencer, M. B. (1987). Black children's ethnic identity formation: Risk and resilience in castelike minorities. In J. S. Phinney & M. J. Rotheram (Eds.), *Children's ethnic socialization* (pp. 103–116). Newbury Park, CA: Sage.

Stattin, H., & Kerr, M. (2000). Parental monitoring: A reinterpretation. *Child Development, 71,* 1072–1085.

Stevenson, H. C. (1994a). Racial socialization in African American families: Balancing intolerance and survival. *Counseling and Therapy for Couples and Families, 2,* 190–198.

Stevenson, H. C. (1994b). Validation of the scale of racial socialization for African American adolescents: Steps toward multidimensionality. *Journal of Black Psychology, 20,* 445–468.

Stevenson, H. C. (1995). Relationship of adolescent perceptions of racial socialization to racial identity. *Journal of Black Psychology, 21,* 49–70.

Stevenson, H. C. (2003). *Playing with anger: Engaging the coping emotions of African American boys through cultural socialization and athletic movement.* Westport, CT: Praeger.

Stevenson, H. C., Davis, G., & Abdul-Kabir, S. (2001). *Stickin' to, watchin' over, and gettin' with: An African American parent's guide to discipline.* San Francisco: Jossey-Bass.

Stevenson, H. C., Herrero-Taylor, T., Cameron, R., & Davis, G. Y. (2002). "Mitigating instigation": Cultural phenomenological influences of anger and fighting among "big-boned" and "baby-face" African American youth. *Journal of Youth and Adolescence, 31*(6), 473–485.

Stevenson, H. C., Reed, J., Bodison, P., & Bishop, A. (1995). *Silence is not always golden: Adolescent racial socialization attitudes and the experience of depression and anger.* Unpublished manuscript, University of Pennsylvania, Philadelphia.

Thornton, M. C. (1997). Strategies for racial socialization among Black parents: Mainstream, minority and cultural messages. In R. J. Taylor, J. S. Jackson, & L. M. Chatters (Eds.), *Family life in Black America* (pp. 201–215), Thousand Oaks, CA: Sage.

Thornton, M. C., Chatters, L. M., Taylor, R. J., & Allen, W. R. (1990). Sociodemographic and environmental correlates of racial socialization by Black parents. *Child Development, 61,* 401–409.

Ward, J. V. (2000). *The skin we're in: Teaching our teens to be emotionally strong, socially smart and spiritually connected.* New York: Simon & Schuster.

Wilson, M. N. (1990). Familial support in the Black community. *Journal of Clinical Child Psychology, 19* (4), 347–355.

Wright, M. A. (1998). *I'm chocolate, you're vanilla: Raising healthy Black and biracial children in a race-conscious world.* San Francisco: Jossey-Bass.

Yip, T., & Fuligni, A. J. (2002). Daily variation in ethnic identity, ethnic behaviors, and psychological well-being among American adolescents of Chinese descent. *Child Development, 73,* 1557–1572.

CHAPTER 14

Beyond the Birth Family

African American Children
Reared by Alternative Caregivers

Ellen E. Pinderhughes
and Brenda Jones Harden

African American children grow up in diverse family settings, ranging from "nuclear" families to households headed by single parents to a variety of extended family situations. A small but significant group of African American children do not reside with their birth parents, but are reared by kin (blood relatives), foster and adoptive families, as well as families united through legal guardianship. Across these diverse family arrangements there are common challenges or issues confronting parents and caregivers of African American children. As in all families, one set of challenges includes using a parenting style and engaging in parenting processes that will facilitate effective childrearing. Unique to families of color, another challenge is helping children develop with an appreciation of their cultural legacy and an understanding of the potential discrimination they will face. Because these themes are universal for families raising African American children, we leave further discussion of these themes to other chapters in this book. This chapter, instead, examines issues unique to African American children in the most common alternative caregiving arrangements—specifically, kinship care, foster care, and adoption.

Because these families are created by the removal of children from their biological parents, there are unique challenges with which caregiver, child, and biological parent must contend. Whether the removal is voluntary or involuntary, it signals the perspective that the child's needs are better met in another family setting. Whereas in some cases caregivers and birth parents privately or informally negotiate the kinship arrangement, many kinship, foster, and adoptive families are formed through the intervention of the child welfare system. Too often the intervention is prompted by a reported failure of the biological parents to ensure the safety and well-being of their children (Berrick, 1998). When this occurs, a judgment is made by child welfare and legal professionals that a child's needs for safety and protection cannot be met by his or her biological parents and the child must be placed with a family competent to meet these needs.

THE OVERREPRESENTATION OF AFRICAN AMERICAN CHILDREN IN ALTERNATIVE CAREGIVING ARRANGEMENTS

As compared with children in other racial/ethnic groups, African American children are more likely to live apart from their birth parents. Recent census data (U.S. Bureau of the Census, 2002) indicate that approximately 8% of African American children reside in households that do not include either of their birth parents. In contrast, approximately 3% of European American children live in such households. The proportion of American children living with their grandparents varies by race/ethnicity as well. Nine percent of African American children reside with their grandparents, as opposed to 4% of European American children, 6% of Hispanic children, and 3% of Asian American children (Fields, 2003). Evidence from empirical studies across the nation has confirmed the findings yielded by census data. Multiple studies of families in which children are being reared by relatives have suggested that these arrangements are more commonly found among the African American population (Berrick, Barth, & Needell, 1994; Chipungu, Everett, Verduik, & Jones, 1998; Scannapieco, Hegar, & McAlpine, 1997).

In addition, African American families are more likely to be involved in the child welfare system than would be expected, given their general numbers in the population. Although the evidence suggests that African American children are no more vulnerable to maltreatment than other children (particularly when socioeconomic factors are controlled for; e.g., Sedlak, & Broadhurst, 1996), the proportion of African American children in the foster care system far exceeds their proportion in the general population (Courtney et al., 1996; Lau et al., 2003; Needell, Brookhart, & Lee, 2003; U.S. Department of Health and Human Services [USDHHS], 2003b). Specifically, Adoption and Foster Care Analysis and Reporting System (AFCARS) data reveal that 38% of children in foster care are of African American descent, despite the fact that they represent only 15% of the U.S. child population (USDHHS, 2003a).

Once in the foster care system, African American children are less likely to be returned to their biological families (Courtney, 1994; Wells & Guo, 1999; Wulczyn et al., 2001). They also tend to remain in the foster care system longer than children of other racial groups (Barth, 1997; Courtney, 1994; Wulczyn, Hislop, & Goerge, 2001). There are also racial disparities in the number and quality of services foster children receive, with African American children faring the worst. African American children have fewer contacts with their caseworkers and have fewer written case plans (Courtney et al., 1996). They also are less likely to receive developmental and psychological assessments and mental health treatment while in care (Garland, Landsverk, & Lau, 2003). They have fewer parental visits, and their biological parents are less likely to receive family preservation and reunification services (Brown & Bailey-Etta, 1997; Lawrence-Webb, 1997).

In regard to the settings in which foster children are reared, African American children tend to be cared for by unrelated persons in traditional foster family homes. However, they are more likely to be placed temporarily or permanently with relatives than their European American counterparts (Ehrle & Geen, 2002). Thus, they are slightly less likely than European American children to be placed in traditional foster home settings. In specific urban areas, relative placements have exceeded foster home placements for African American children (e.g., Chicago; Testa, 2001). Although African American children are less likely to be placed in adoptive homes than their European American counterparts (Barth, 1997; USDHHS, 2003b), increasingly they are being adopted, sometimes by their own relatives (Testa, 2004). In fact, data from the Multistate Data Archive suggest that the adoption of African American infants may be closing the gap between the rates of foster care exits experienced by African American and European American children (Wulczyn, 2003).

In sum, African American children have a higher likelihood than European American children of residing in homes without the presence of their birth parents. This holds true across a variety of settings, including "informal" arrangements between their parents and relatives and placements that are facilitated by the child welfare system. These alternative arrangements have multiple implications for the experiences of African American children and their developmental outcomes. These issues are discussed in turn in the sections on the various family arrangements—non-kinship foster care, kinship care, and adoption.

NON-KINSHIP FOSTER CARE

Originating in the 1800s, and organized on a state-by-state basis, the foster care system is charged with ensuring the safety of, permanency for, and well-being of all children in the system (Berrick, 1998; Waldfogel, 2000). Traditional foster care has a long, complex history in the United States with respect to African American children and families. According to some scholars, this service sector basically ignored African American children prior to the 1960s (e.g., Roberts, 2001; Smith & Devore, 2004). For example, most public and private child welfare agencies did not provide foster and adoptive placement services for African American children (Billingsley & Giovannonni, 1972; Everett, Chipungu, & Leashore, 1991; Smith & Devore, 2004), During this era, some agencies were created specifically to serve African American children in vulnerable family situations, such as New York's Harlem-Dowling agency. With increased national attention in the ensuing decades given to the civil rights of African Americans across social institutions, African American children and families increasingly became consumers of child welfare services (Everett et al., 1991; Smith & Devore, 2004).

The child welfare system includes a complex array of services, including child protection, foster care, and adoption. Foster care is defined as the temporary placement of a child in a stable family setting, during which time a permanent home is sought for the child: a return to a "rehabilitated" biological parent, placement with a relative, or adoption (Berrick, 1998). Foster parents are licensed to care for children on a 24-hour basis. To be licensed, they must attend extensive preservice training and undergo a "home study," a process in which their individual, family, and home characteristics are examined to determine whether they meet the criteria for the license. African American families may be less likely to meet the licensing requirements than European American families (Chipungu & Bent-Goodley, 2004; Denby & Rindfleisch, 1996). For example, they may be less likely to complete the training and paperwork required for licensure or to have homes that meet the stringent safety and space mandates.

While caring for children, foster parents receive a monthly stipend to pay for the children's board and maintenance expenses. The limited data on foster care payments suggest that this financial assistance is critical for African American families (Fees et al., 1998). Foster parents must attend regular "booster" trainings and receive regular home visits while actively caring for children (Cuddeback & Orme, 2001). The cultural competence of both the preservice and in-service trainings that African American foster parents receive has been called into question (Chipungu & Bent-Goodley, 2004; Smith & Devore, 2004). Similarly, the cultural competence of the foster care social workers has been noted as crucial to maintaining a positive relationship between African American foster families and the child welfare agencies (McPhatter, 1997; Pinderhughes, 1991).

Non-Kin Foster Caregivers

Over the last few decades, the needs of the foster care system and the characteristics of foster families have changed appreciably. Regardless of race, child welfare systems are losing record numbers of foster parents as a result of foster parent adoptions, the demands of being a foster parent, and economic demands requiring more women in the workforce (Barbell & Freundlich, 2001; Chipungu & Bent-Goodley, 2004). Because of the dwindling supply of traditional foster parents and efforts at recruiting a new cadre of potential foster families, the population of foster parents has become considerably more diverse (Cox, Buehler, & Orme, 2002; Orme et al., 2004). Specifically, although caregivers are still predominately female, there is now a small but growing number of male foster care providers. In addition, many foster parents are single parents and are members of multigenerational households. There is greater age variability as well, with many traditional foster parents reaching their older years and many young persons being licensed as foster parents. Although most foster parents are of European American ancestry, expansion of the requirements for foster parent licensure has increased the proportion of African American foster parents over the last few decades. Some of this increase is attributable to the rising number of relatives who are approved as foster parents (Testa & Slack, 2002; USDHHS, 2000).

Perhaps related to the increasing racial and economic diversity of the foster parent population, current foster parents are a fairly vulnerable group of families. Findings from various studies indicate that foster parents have poorer physical health, higher rates of mental health difficulties, more compromised parenting, greater family dysfunction, and lower socioeconomic levels than their counterparts in the general population (Orme et al., 2004; Orme & Beuhler, 2001). These risk factors must be addressed in the context of the unique cultural characteristics of the African American foster family population (Dillon, 1994). African American foster caregivers tend to be older and in poorer health than their European American counterparts (USDHHS, 2000), thus experiencing more personal constraints on their ability to provide effective care and supervision. Despite these higher individual stressors, as well as the stress associated with minority status in the United States (McLoyd, 1990), one study of the quality of family functioning found more similarities than differences between African American and European American foster families (Seaberg & Harrigan, 1999). African American foster caregivers receive fewer supports than do their European American counterparts (e.g., Courtney et al., 1996).

African American Children in Non-Kinship Care

There are limited data on the functioning of children in foster care, and even less on African American children in such care. The National Survey of Child and Adolescent Well-Being (NSCAW, 2002) has brought the field closer to a solid knowledge base about the developmental functioning of foster children. This study examines the needs of foster children being reared in a variety of contexts, including foster family and kinship settings. Findings from this and other studies present a profile of foster children that suggests that they are more compromised than are children in the general population across developmental domains. Although most of the extant studies generally control for race and ethnicity, the available evidence is particularly germane to African American children, given their overrepresentation in the foster care system.

Before considering developmental outcomes in foster children, one must note an important caveat to the evidence. It is difficult to disentangle the multiple preplacement influences on foster child outcomes from the impact of foster care experience per se (e.g., Pinderhughes, Jones Harden, & Schweder, in press). Children in foster care are biologically vulnerable to many poor developmental outcomes because of genetic factors, prenatal drug exposure, and other physical health issues. The majority of these children have experienced maltreatment prior to foster care entry as well, which has been documented to have a major impact on children's outcomes across domains (e.g., Cicchetti & Toth, 1997; Hildeyard & Wolfe, 2001). Moreover, the child's experiences while in foster care have an impact on developmental outcome. For example, the placement instability while in care (e.g., number of foster homes) influences how the child adjusts (James, Landsverk, & Slymen, 2004; Newton, Litrownik, & Landsverk, 2000). Facilitating the integration of a foster child into the family is very risky (Pinderhughes, 1996); foster families may function with different boundaries, rules, and patterns of interactions than those with which foster children have experience. The quality of the parenting in foster families also contributes to the child's development (Jones Harden, 2004; Orme & Buehler, 2001). Such issues as subsequent experiences of maltreatment and the emotional commitment of the foster parent also have great effects on the child (Zuravin, Benedict, & Somerfield, 1993).

Despite the preceding caveat, many studies have pointed to the deleterious impact of foster care on children's physical health, cognitive and
academic functioning, and social-emotional well-being. In regard to
physical health, pediatric and public health scholars have documented
that foster children have a higher level of morbidity throughout childhood, higher rates of growth abnormalities, and more untreated health
problems than children not involved in the foster care system (Halfon,
Mendonca, & Berkowitz, 1995; Risley-Curtiss, Combs-Orme, Chernoff,
& Heisler, 1996). Data from the NSCAW study and smaller studies
point to cognitive developmental delays in this population of children as
well (e.g., Clyman & Harden, 2002; NSCAW Research Group, 2002). In
addressing academic achievement, some studies have found that foster
children perform more poorly on academic achievement tests, have
poorer grades, and have higher rates of grade retention and special education
placement (Konenkamp & Ehrle, 2002; Yu, Day, & Williams, 2002).

The social-emotional development of foster children is the domain
that has received the most empirical attention. Research has suggested
that foster children are more likely to have insecure or disordered attachments and the adverse long-term outcomes associated with such attachments (Dozier, Stovall, Albus, & Bates, 2001). Most studies have estimated that at least 50% of foster children also have mental health
difficulties, including higher rates of depression, poorer social skills,
lower adaptive functioning, and more externalizing behavior problems
such as aggression and impulsivity (e.g., Stein, Evans, Masumdar, &
Rae-Grant, 1996; USDHHS, 2003a). Research has also documented
high levels of mental health service utilization among foster children
(e.g., Garland et al., 2003; Garland, Landsverk, Hough, & Ellis-
MacLeod, 1996; Halfon et al., 1992).

Race/ethnicity is a salient factor in understanding the well-being of
children in the foster care system. The relation between race/ethnicity
and outcomes is fairly complex. Diverse studies point to the variability
in findings. In one investigation, few differences were found between European American, Latino, and African American youth in their levels of
psychosocial functioning and engagement in risk behaviors (Taussig &
Talmi, 2001). Another study found that African American foster children had death rates comparable to their peers in the general population, whereas the death rates for European American and Latino foster
youth were considerably higher than those of their counterparts in the
general population (Barth & Blackwell, 1998). In a study of preschool
foster children, African American children had significantly lower scores
on tests of cognitive and language functioning than a group of children
from a combination of other racial/ethnic groups (Jones Harden &
Clyman, 2004). As with African American foster parents, the psycho-

social needs of African American foster children do not translate into the receipt of higher levels of service. For example, Garland and colleagues (2000, 2003) have found that African American foster children consistently receive fewer mental health services than European American foster children.

Transracial Foster Placements

Some African American children experience transracial placements (i.e., are cared for by non–African American foster parents). With the insufficient availability of African American foster parents, children sometimes are placed with European American parents who have different cultural backgrounds and experiences. For all children who have been removed from their birth families and placed in foster care, the maintenance of links to their culture of origin is critical (Jones Harden, 2004; McRoy, 1996). When children are placed transracially, the maintenance of these links becomes more challenging. Transracial foster caregivers are engaged in learning about African American culture and normative practices simultaneously as they face incorporating the child into their family and their community and negotiating visits with birth parents. Birth parents may display resentment and hostility about the transracial placement, further constraining foster caregiver–birth parent relations. Racial socialization, parental messages designed to help children develop a healthy racial identity, and found to be linked to youth adjustment (e.g., Bowman & Howard, 1985; Stevenson, 1995), may also be challenging. The only known study on transracial foster placements suggests that foster caregivers receive insufficient support to racially socialize their children (Campbell, 2002).

KINSHIP ARRANGEMENTS

Kinship care has a rich history in the African American community, being viewed by some scholars as a vestige of African-based practices that survived the devastating effects of the middle passage and slavery (e.g., Hill, 1997), or by other scholars as an adaptive response to the destruction of families in slavery and the repressive welfare practices of the early to mid-20th century (e.g., Roberts, 2001). Irrespective of its actual origin, kinship care provides a family resource for birth parents who, for various reasons, are unable to care for and protect their children. There are three types of kinship care: (1) private kinship care, whereby the birth parent and kin caregiver informally agree that the caregiver will assume caregiving responsibility, (2) voluntary kinship care, in which a child is placed with a state-approved relative, but the relative is not licensed as a foster parent, and (3) kinship foster care, in which the state has placed the child with relatives who become licensed foster parents (Ehrle, Geen, & Clark, 2001).

Kinship foster care has emerged in the past 20 years as a critical strategy for the care and protection of African American children (Geen, 2004; Testa & Slack, 2002). Due in part to a dwindling foster family base and an increase in the number of children cared for by kin, the increase in state-recognized kinship placements has also reduced the racial disparity in numbers of children in foster care in some jurisdictions (e.g., Testa, 2004). Although the involvement of the child welfare system distinguishes kinship foster care from private or voluntary kinship care, there are many similar challenges for kin arrangements. There is some evidence that private kinship and voluntary kinship care providers, as well as the children for whom they care, are similarly vulnerable groups (Ehrle & Geen, 2002; Goodman, Potts, Pasztor, & Scorzo, 2004). In this section, we address common issues for kinship arrangements and note unique issues specific to each kinship arrangement.

Kinship Caregivers

Kinship caregivers tend to be older (Berrick et al., 1994; Chipungu et al., 1998; Gebel, 1996) and to have more physical health complications than do licensed foster caregivers (e.g., Minkler & Fuller-Thompson, 1999; USDHHS, 2000), thus facing more challenges to their ability to be effective caregivers. The literature on grandparents raising grandchildren points to the poor mental health of these caregivers and suggests that their health and mental health may worsen under the burden of caring for children (Minkler & Fuller-Thompson, 2000). Many studies have pointed to their socioeconomic vulnerability, including being more likely than non-kin foster parents to lack a high school diploma, to be single parents, and to live in poverty (see Cuddeback, 2004; Geen, 2004). Recent research has also suggested that their parenting and home environments may be more compromised than those of non-kin foster parents (Brooks & Barth, 1998; Clyman et al., in press; Jones Harden, Clyman, Kriebel, & Lyons, 2004).

Kinship caregivers not only face the numerous challenges that characterize foster caregiving, but also face these challenges with less support from the child welfare system. Although foster kin caregivers are licensed and eligible to receive services, they typically receive fewer services than do non-kin foster caregivers (Chipungu et al., 1998; Cuddeback, 2004). Some states do not provide subsidies to non-licensed private kin caregivers (Ehrle et al., 2001; Leos-Urbel, Bess, & Green, 2002). Lacking

state recognition for foster care status also excludes private kin caregivers from eligibility for social casework and other supports available
to foster caregivers. In the context of very limited systemic support, as
well as the external neighborhood and societal stressors that confront
African American caregivers (McLoyd, 1990), private kin caregivers
must provide concrete and psychological caregiving and obtain needed
services for the children in their homes.

African American Children in Kinship Care

Because African American children are more likely to be in kinship care
arrangements than are European American children, it is important to
consider the effects of kinship placement on children in any discussion of
African American children. Most African American children in kinship
settings live in private kinship arrangements (Geen, 2004). There is limited research on the developmental outcomes for children who are
reared by relatives, whether through informal arrangements or formal
placement through the child welfare system. Available evidence from
several strands of the literature, including foster care, custodial grandparents, and multigenerational families, indicates considerable variability in developmental outcomes. As with the research on foster children,
there is limited research that specifically addresses outcomes for African
American children in kinship care. Again, the significant overrepresentation of African American children in this population renders the
available evidence particularly relevant.

The data on the effects of kinship care on child outcomes yield a
complicated picture. Early research suggested that children in kinship
care were faring at least as well as other foster children (Benedict,
Zuravin, & Stallings, 1996; Dubowitz et al., 1994; Scannapieco et al.,
1997), whereas other studies found that children in kinship care had
more behavior problems (Berrick et al., 1994; Keller et al., 2001). Research on academic functioning suggests that these children are less
likely to repeat a grade or to be enrolled in special education (Brooks &
Barth, 1998; Goerge, Voorhis, Grant, Casey, & Robinson, 1992; Landsverk, Davis, Ganger, Newton, & Johnson, 1996). Retrospective research
of adults who were in foster care also yields contrasting findings: One
study found that women formerly in kinship care had more psychological vulnerabilities (Carpenter & Clyman, 2004), whereas another study
reported comparable functioning among those formerly in kinship care
and nonrelative care (Benedict et al., 1996). This complicated picture
suggests that the critical question is not whether kinship care is better
than nonrelative care, but rather for whom and under what circum-

stances is kinship care effective. In short, research should next cast its focus on moderators of kinship experiences.

In the NSCAW study, children in kinship care had fewer scores in the clinical range on a variety of developmental measures than children in non-kin foster care (Administration on Children and Families, 2003). However, the data in this study suggest that kinship caregivers may choose to care only for children who are functioning well, or that child welfare workers may elect to place less problematic children with kinship care providers. It has also been documented that kinship care providers tend to take younger children (Geen, 2004), who may have fewer problems. Thus, decisions by child welfare workers and kinship care providers may explain the better outcomes found among children in kinship homes.

The data on the children's experience of kinship placements are far less equivocal than those regarding their outcomes. Multiple studies have documented that kinship homes are more stable and permanent for children than non-kin foster homes (Altshuler, 1999; Berrick, Needell, & Barth, 1999; Cuddeback, 2004; Geen, 2004; USDHHS, 2000), although kinship placements "disrupt" as well (Testa, 2001). Children in these placements live in closer proximity to their neighborhoods of origin and are more able to maintain cultural linkages (Chipungu et al., 1998). Moreover, children in kinship placements do not experience the trauma of being separated from familiar social networks. Specifically, they are more likely to have contact with their birth parents and siblings, and to be placed with their siblings (Chipungu et al., 1998; Geen, 2004). In contrast, they are less likely to be reunified with their birth parents and less likely to be adopted (Geen, 2004; Goerge, 1990; Testa, 2001, 1997).

This evidence underscores the complex relationship dynamics created for children and their caregivers in kinship arrangements. The implications of these experiences for children remain unclear. For example, the impact of more frequent access to birth parents is not empirically known (USDHHS, 2000) and must be disentangled from the reason for the kin placement. In addition, the fewer financial and psychological resources of kinship caregivers certainly influences the caregiving environment their children experience, including how parents under such stress are able to relate to the children in their care. In fact, some studies have documented that the home environments of kinship caregivers are more compromised than those of foster care providers (Barth, 2001; Clyman et al., in press). Other evidence suggests that the kinship caregiving environment, although not optimal, is generally positive for children (USDHHS, 2000). For example, kinship caregivers demonstrate a higher level of commitment to and acceptance of the children in their care and are less likely to maltreat them (Benedict et al., 1996).

ADOPTIVE FAMILY ARRANGEMENTS

When parental rights are voluntarily or involuntarily terminated, children become eligible for adoption. In recent years, averages of 120,000 children have been adopted each year in the United States (National Information Adoption Clearinghouse, 2003). Although African American children in the child welfare system have lower rates of adoption than European American children (Barth, 1997; Brooks & James, 2003), adoptions of African American children have increased over the last decade largely as a result of the provisions of the Adoption and Safe Families Act and the federal Adoption 2002 initiative (Testa, 2004). In fact, African American children represented the largest share of children who were adopted from the foster care system in 2000 (Testa, 2004). Based on recent data from the Multistate Data Archive, African American infants appear to be moving much more quickly through the foster care system toward adoption, a trend that is reducing racial disparities in foster care length of stay in these states (Wulczyn, 2003). In addition, foster parents and relatives are increasingly becoming adoption resources for foster children (Testa, 2004). Although more long-term research is needed, it does not seem that the passage of the Multiethnic Placement Act of 1994 and the Interethnic Placement Act of 1996 (MEPA/IEPA) is the factor that is increasing the adoption of African American children (Testa, 2004).

Most placements involve adoptions of infants through licensed private adoption agencies, whereas about 15–18% involve placements of children over age 3, usually from foster care. Whereas international adoptions, involving placement of children from outside the United States are common for children from Asian, Eastern European, and Latin American countries, they are rare for children of African descent. Special needs adoptions involve placement of children who have a developmental, physical, or emotional disability, are members of a sibling group or a minority group, or meet a given state's criteria for being an older child. Transracial adoptions involve placement of an adoptee with a family of a different race.

There are several common issues facing all adoptive families: acknowledgment of similarities and differences in the adoptive and birth families' life cycles (e.g., Kirk, 1964), parenting adopted children (e.g., Brodzinsky & Pinderhughes, 2003), the adoptee's adjustment and identity development (e.g., Brodzinsky, 1990), and the degree of contact or openness (Grotevant & McRoy, 1998) between adoptive and birth families. Among the issues facing families adopting African American children, two stand out as particularly salient: openness and transracial adoption.

Openness in Adoption

Over the past few decades, adoptions have become increasingly more open, in large part due to the expectations of birth parents relinquishing their infants to know about, in some cases to choose, and in other cases to meet the adoptive parents (National Adoption Information Clearinghouse, 2003). Nowadays, adoptions vary in how much contact or information is shared, ranging from no contact at all (confidential adoption), to exchange of nonidentifying information through a third party (mediated adoption), to exchange of identifying information and, perhaps, face-to-face meeting (fully disclosed adoption) (Grotevant & McRoy, 1998). Estimates of placement characterized by these different levels of contact are extremely sketchy; one study found that 69% of adoptions involved some contact (Berry, 1991).

A highly controversial aspect of adoption, openness, became a research topic relatively recently (Frasch, Brooks, & Barth, 2000; Grotevant & McRoy, 1998; McRoy, Grotevant, & White, 1988). Findings from a respected longitudinal research program on infant adoptions (Grotevant & McRoy, 1998; Grotevant, Ross, Marchel, & McRoy, 1999; Wrobel, Ayers-Lopez, Grotevant, McRoy, & Friedrick, 1996) found that contrary to the concerns of those opposed to open adoption, birth parents are no more likely to seek to reclaim custody, adoptive parents' sense of entitlement to be parents is not jeopardized, and adoptees can experience a healthy adjustment. However, contrary to those extolling the benefits of open adoption, the resolution of grief for birth parents was not guaranteed. In sum, mutual agreement about the level of contact between adoptive and birth parents is the critical element. Another important element is flexibility for changing the arrangements over time—in either direction on the continuum.

This small and growing body of literature lacks the participation of African American families, so we know little about the numbers or experiences of African American families involved in mediated or fully disclosed adoptions. It is not easy to forecast the patterns of participation or outcomes for African American families, because of two competing historical patterns. Although African Americans have a rich and long tradition of private kinship placements (e.g., Hill, 1997), suggesting an inclination toward more openness in adoptions, these families also have a history of neglect by social service and child welfare agencies (Billingsley

& Giovannoni, 1972; Roberts, 2001), pointing to a wariness of agency mediation in or facilitation of adoption contact. However, socioeconomic differences in adoptions involving different levels of openness may emerge. A common pattern in adoption is that lower-income African American families tend to have more success adopting older children from foster care than do middle-income families (e.g., Rosenthal, 1993). Middle- to upper-income African Americans are more likely to have the resources to adopt infants through private agency placements. Older child foster placements present a mixed picture of openness: whereas parental rights have been permanently terminated, the adoptee intimately knows who his or her birth parents and family are. The adoptee also may have occasional contact with the extended birth family. Thus, lower-income families may experience more contact with birth families than do middle-income families. Clarification of these issues awaits the focus on African American families in research on openness.

Transracial Adoption

From the era of the civil rights movement through the nascence of the Black Power era, transracial adoption emerged as an option of choice for European American parents. In 1971, during the height of this period, 2,500 children were placed in transracial adoptions. Abruptly reduced by reactions to the National Association of Black Social Workers' dictum that transracial adoption was tantamount to cultural genocide, transracial adoption became rarer over the next 20–25 years. Recent federal policies supportive of transracial placements (i.e., MEPA, IEPA) have again placed transracial adoption on the adoption map. In this country, where the salience of race still occupies local, state, and national discourse, parents raising African American children face the challenge of preparing their children to succeed as adults of color. This may mean providing support and advocacy for a child's success in school and in the community, as well as active support for the child's development of his or her ethnic identity. However, parents in transracial adoptions must also anticipate the placement's impact on the family, for the perception of the family by the community and society may change.

Although African American parents vary as to the amount and content of race-related information they share with children, two important findings have emerged in the developing literature on racial socialization. First, African American children whose parents highlight their group's cultural history have higher self-esteem and more positive attitudes toward their cultural group (e.g., Stevenson, 1995). Second, messages about racial barriers are linked to higher grades and feelings of efficacy among children, as well as less depression (e.g., Bowman &

Howard, 1985; Stevenson, 1995). Thus, this literature suggests the importance of racial socialization messages for youth adjustment.

The literature on the impact of transracial placements on adoptee development yields some inconsistencies (Lee, 2003). On one hand, several studies suggest that individual and group identity do not suffer, despite great variation in adoptive parents' attention to racial socialization (e.g., Brooks & Barth, 1999; Simon, Alstein, & Melli, 1994). On the other hand, some studies report that group identity is negatively affected (e.g., Deberry, Scarr, & Weinberg, 1996; Hollingsworth, 1997). Deberry and colleagues noted a concerning pattern among a small sample of families in which parents' racial socialization practices decreased as the children moved into adolescence, with corresponding shifts in adoptees' Eurocentric and Afrocentric values. Recent case study accounts from adults raised in transracial placements highlight not only the love and appreciation of the adoptees for their families, but also the struggles they have encountered with their sense of self as African Americans (e.g., Pinderhughes, 1997; Simon & Rhoorda, 2000).

In sum, the complexities of transracial adoption highlight multiple levels of parenting challenges faced in these families: common child-rearing challenges faced by all parents, adoption-related challenges faced by all parents raising adopted children, challenges faced by parents raising children of color, and challenges faced by parents whose children are from a different cultural group. Despite these multiple layers of challenge in transracial placements, there is no systematic emphasis set forth in the MEPA, IEPA, or related regulations on assessing or training prospective transracial adoptive parents. This hole in adoption policy and practice must be addressed.

POLICY ISSUES

Family policy in the United States emanates from a complex set of laws, regulations, and procedures that lacks a cohesive philosophy and an interconnected funding stream (Jacobs & Davies, 1994; Kamerman, 1996). There are multiple national policies that may affect children in these alternative caregiving environments, including those addressing child maltreatment and income supports for low-income families. Table 14.1 provides brief summaries of the provisions of these major policies. The ensuing discussion addresses the policy landscape specific to African American children and families in these diverse caregiving situations.

The leading legislation affecting the families discussed in this chapter is the Adoption and Safe Families Act (ASFA). Proponents of ASFA assert that this legislation moves the field forward in meeting the devel-

TABLE 14.1. Brief Summaries of the Provisions of Major Family Policies

Policy	Provisions
Adoption and Safe Families Act (ASFA; 1997)	• Shortened the time frame for permanency decisions for foster children from 18 to 12 months after entry. • Mandated the initiation of termination of parental rights (TPR) for children in care for 15 of previous 22 months, for abandoned infants, and for children whose parents have committed specific felonies. • Emphasized the safety of children in foster care. • Excluded long-term foster care as permanency option. • Included kinship placement as a permanency option. • Identified unreasonable situations for reunification. • Promoted concurrent planning (permanency through reunification and adoption are concurrently addressed). • Provided monetary incentives to states for adoptions. • Created performance measures for assessing states' child welfare systems. • Established performance-based incentive system for child welfare payments to the states. • Allowed for more flexible use of Title IV-E funds.
Adoption Assistance and Child Welfare Act (1980)	• Mandated securing the least restrictive placement. • Established administrative and legal process for reviewing children's permanency status. • Emphasized "reasonable efforts" to prevent placement and reunify children with their families of origin.
Title IV-E of the Social Security Act of 1935	• Created largest source of funding for care of foster children. • Prevented use of funds for services to biological families.
Title IV-B of the Social Security Act of 1935 (currently named the Promoting Safe and Stable Families Act)	• Created federal funding for services to support families to maintain their children at home and to reunify children with their biological families. • Provided funding for biological family support/preservation services and adoption promotion and support programs. • Authorized Court Improvement Program.

TABLE 14.1. (*continued*)

Policy	Provisions
Multi-Ethnic Placement Act (MEPA; 1994); replaced by Interethnic Placement Act (IEPA; 1996)	• Prohibited federally funded agencies from discriminating against children of color by delaying or failing to pursue their permanent placement. • Prohibited consideration of race when it delays or denies permanent placement of a child. • Authorized significant monetary penalties for child welfare agencies out of compliance. • Allowed private parties to sue based on discrimination. • Mandated recruitment of minority foster/adoptive families.
Foster Care Independence Act ("Chafee Program"; 1999) (an expansion of the 1986 Independent Living Initiative)	• Addressed needs of adolescents transitioning out of the foster care system. • Provided funds to pay for the board and maintenance of 18- to 21-year-old youth in foster care. • Legislated funding for programs to facilitate independence in these youth. • Authorized use of funds for health care, housing, education, and other services. • Mandated state accountability for outcomes for this group. • Mandated preparation for foster parents caring for older adolescents.

opmental needs of children by mandating expeditious permanency decisions for them. However, other scholars (e.g., Roberts, 2001) suggest that the practices emanating from such legislation may sever the ties that African American families may have. These scholars argue that the supports to help families care for their children and rehabilitate themselves are not available, so the ultimate effect of such policies as ASFA is to achieve permanency for children outside their birth families.

There are other specific policies that support families, such as the Safe and Stable Families Act. In addition, currently there are funds available through child welfare "waivers," by which localities can divert funds saved through reductions of their numbers of children in foster care to other purposes, such as family support, preservation, and reunification. Despite these policies, the resources for such family-centered services are severely lacking (Wulczyn, 2004). The financial incentives states and counties may receive for adoption and the financial reimbursements they receive for foster care clearly outstrip the meager resources available for services to promote the stability and well-being of maltreating families (Bess, Andrews, Jantz, Russell, & Geen, 2003). The insufficiency of these latter resources compound the inequities in resources available for African American families involved with the child welfare system.

Policies for kinship care suffer from a lack of cohesion and direction from the national level. Thus, kinship care policies are quite variable across states (Ehrle et al., 2001; Geen, 2004). Some states routinely provide relative caregivers with foster care board rates and services, whereas others provide them only with public assistance allotments (i.e., Temporary Assistance for Needy Families [TANF] payments). Some states have created comprehensive service networks targeted specifically to relative caregivers who provide legal, family support, mental health, and other ancillary services. Relatedly, in some jurisdictions, relatives are encouraged to make informal arrangements to care for the vulnerable children in their midst, and therefore the children never become "cases" in the child welfare system. Other jurisdictions may require formal involvement with the child welfare system whenever a child is removed from a biological parent. Thus, what occurs in practice in regard to families in which a relative is caring for a minor child differs from jurisdiction to jurisdiction, from family to family.

Two race-specific policies, MEPA and its successor IEPA, grew out of the concern of some practitioners and policymakers that African American and other minority children were not being placed in permanent homes as expeditiously as possible. Adoption practices favoring in-race placements provided few options for majority families seeking to adopt. Indeed, national trends indicated that many European American families were waiting for children to adopt and many African American children were waiting for adoptive placement (Brooks & James, 2003). Although the data on the long-term impact of these policies are not yet available, preliminary evidence suggests that MEPA and IEPA have not had an appreciable impact on the adoption of African American children by European American families (Testa, 2004). However, the press of legislation such as this to secure permanency for African American children has led to more permanent relative placements and an increased emphasis and effort relative to the adoption of minority children.

CONCLUSION

Five critical surrogate arrangements for African American children include non-kinship foster care, three variations of kinship care—private kinship care, voluntary kinship care, and kinship foster care—and adoption. As this chapter has examined the issues facing caregivers, children, and birth parents in each of these placements, several themes have emerged. First, the knowledge base of the impact of these arrangements on the functioning of African American caregivers and children is woefully insufficient. Emerging research in this area, particularly regarding kinship arrangements, suggests that these placements warrant greater understanding. Although the new NSCAW study on children in foster care may contribute to rectifying the literature gap, other studies are needed as well. Second, consideration of issues associated with these placements, beyond the typical challenges confronting parents described elsewhere in this book, illustrates that surrogate arrangements complicate childrearing in ways that suggest the importance of additional services for families united through foster care, kinship care, or adoption. Although the developmental implications of these caregiving experiences are yet to be fully understood, it is certain that these alternative family arrangements provide a critical resource for African American children whose birth parents are unable to care for them.

REFERENCES

Administration on Children and Families. (2003). *National Survey of Child and Adolescent Well-Being, One Year in Foster Care, Wave 1 Data Analysis Report*. Washington, DC: Administration on Children and Families, U.S. Department of Health and Human Services.

Altshuler, S. (1999). Child well-being in kinship foster care: Similar to, or different from, non-related foster care? *Children and Youth Services Review, 20*(5), 369–388.

Barbell, K., & Freundlich, M. (2001). *Foster care today*. Washington, DC: Casey Family Programs.

Barth, R. (1997). Effects of age and race on the odds of adoption versus remaining in long-term out-of-home care. *Child Welfare, 76*(2), 285–308.

Barth, R. (2001). Policy implications of foster family characteristics. *Family Relations, 50*(1), 16–19.

Barth, R., & Blackwell, D. (1998). Death rates among California's foster care and former care populations. *Children and Youth Services Review, 20*(7), 577–604.

Benedict, M., Zuravin, S., & Stallings, R. (1996). Adult functioning of children who lived in kin vs. non-relative foster homes. *Child Welfare, 75*, 529–549.

Berrick, J., Needell, B., & Barth, R. (1999). Kin as a family and child welfare resource: The child welfare worker's perspective. In R. Hegar & M. Scannapieco (Eds.), *Kinship foster care: Practice, policy and research*. New York: Oxford University Press.

Berrick, J. D. (1998). When children cannot remain home: Foster family care and kinship care. *The Future of Children, 8*, 72–87.

Berrick, J. D., Barth, R., & Needell, B. (1994). A comparison of kinship foster homes and foster family homes: Implications for kinship foster care as family preservation. *Children and Youth Services Review, 16*(1–2), 33–63.

Berry, M. (1991). The practice of open adoption: Findings from a study of 1,396 families. *Children and Youth Services Review, 13*, 379–395.

Bess, R., Andrews, C., Jantz, A., Russell, V., & Geen, R. (2003). *The cost of protecting vulnerable children III* (Occasional Paper No. 61). Washington, DC: Urban Institute.

Billingsley, A., & Giovannoni, J. (1972). *Children of the storm: Black children and American child welfare.* New York: Harcourt, Brace Jovanovich.

Bowman, P. J., & Howard, C. (1985). Race-related socialization, motivation, and academic achievement: A study of Black youth in three-generation families. *Journal of the American Academy of Child Psychiatry, 24*, 134–141.

Brodzinsky, D. M. (1990). A stress and coping model of adoption adjustment. In D. Brodzinsky & M. Schechter (Eds.), *The psychology of adoption* (pp. 212–243). New York: Oxford University Press.

Brodzinsky, D. M., & Pinderhughes, E. E. (2003). Parenting and child development in adoptive families. In M. Bornstein (Ed.), *Handbook of parenting* (2nd ed., Vol. 1, pp. 279–312). Mahwah, NJ: Erlbaum.

Brooks, D., & Barth, R. (1998). Characteristics and outcomes of drug-exposed and non-drug-exposed children in kinship and non-relative foster care. *Children and Youth Services Review, 20*(6), 475–501.

Brooks, D., & Barth, R. P. (1999). Adult transracial and inracial adoptees: Effects of race, gender, adoptive family structure, and placement history on adjustment outcomes. *American Journal of Orthopsychiatry, 69*, 87–99.

Brooks, D., & James, S. (2003). Willingness to adopt black foster children: Implications for child welfare policy and recruitment of adoptive families. *Children and Youth Services Review, 25*, 463–487.

Brown, A., & Bailey-Etta, B. (1997). An out-of-home care system in crisis: Implications for African American children in the child welfare system. *Child Welfare, 46*, 65–84.

Campbell, H. M. (2002). Psychological adjustment of same race and transracially placed African American foster children and racial socialization practices of foster parents: An exploratory study. *Dissertation Abstracts International, 63*(1-B), 563.

Carpenter, S., & Clyman, R. (2004). The long-term emotional and physical well-being of women who have lived in kinship care. *Children and Youth Services Review, 26*(7), 673–686.

Chipungu, S., & Bent-Goodley, T. (2004). Challenges of contemporary foster care. *The Future of Children, 14*(1), 75–93.

Chipungu, S., Everett, J., Verduik, M., & Jones, J. (1998). *Children placed in foster care with relatives: A multi-state study.* Washington, DC: U.S. Department of Health and Human Services.

Cicchetti, D., & Toth, S. (Eds.). (1997). *Developmental perspectives on trauma: Theory, research, and intervention.* Rochester, NY: University of Rochester Press.

Clyman, R. B., & Harden, B. J. (2002) Infants in foster and kinship care. *Infant Mental Health Journal, 23*(5), 433–434.

Clyman, R., Jones Harden, B., Little, C., Spuhler, E. R., Chandramouli, V., & Loman, M. (in press). Family environments of family and kinship foster care. *Child Abuse and Neglect.*

Courtney, M. E., Barth, R. P., Duerr Berrick, J., Brooks, D., Needell, B., & Park, L. (1996). Race and child welfare services: Past research and future directions. *Child Welfare, 75,* 99–137.

Courtney, M. (1994). Factors associated with the reunification of foster children with their families. *Social Service Review, 68*(1), 82–108.

Cox, M., Buehler, C., & Orme, J. (2002). Recruitment and foster family service. *Journal of Sociology and Social Welfare, 29*(3), 151–177.

Cuddeback, G. (2004). Kinship family foster care: A methodological and substantive synthesis of research. *Children and Youth Services Review, 26*(7), 623–639.

Cuddeback, G., & Orme, J. (2001). Training and services for kinship and non-kinship foster families. *Child Welfare, 81*(6), 879–909.

Deberry, K., Scarr, S., & Weinberg, R. (1996). Family racial socialization and ecological competence: Longitudinal assessments of African-American transracial adoptees. *Child Development, 67,* 2375–2399.

Denby, R., & Rindfleisch, N. (1996). African Americans' foster parenting experiences: Research findings and implications for policy practice. *Children and Youth Services Review, 18*(6), 523–552.

Dillon, D. (1994). Understanding and assessment of intragroup dynamics in family foster care. *Child Welfare, 73*(2), 129–139.

Dozier, M., Stovall, K. C., Albus, K. E., & Bates, B. (2001). Attachment for infants in foster care: The role of caregiver state of mind. *Child Development, 72,* 1467–1477.

Dubowitz, H., Feigelman, S., Harrington, D., Starr, R., Zuravin, S., & Sawyer, R. (1994). Children in kinship care: How do they fare? *Children and Youth Services Review, 16,* 85–106.

Ehrle, J., & Geen, R. (2002). Kin and non-kin foster care: Findings from a National Survey. *Children and Youth Services Review, 24*(1–2), 15–35.

Ehrle, J., Geen, R., & Clark, R. (2001). Children cared for by relatives: Who are they and how are they faring? *New federalism: National survey of America's families.* Washington, DC: Urban Institute.

Everett, J., Chipungu, S., & Leashore, B. (Eds.). (1991). *Child welfare: An Africentric perspective.* New Brunswick, NJ: Rutgers University Press.

Fees, B., Stockdale, B., Crase, S., Riggins-Caspers, K., Yates, A., Lekies, K., & Gillis-Arnold, R. (1998). Satisfaction with foster parenting: Assessment one year after training. *Children and Youth Services Review, 20,* 347–363.

Fields, J. (2003). Children's living arrangements and characteristics: March 2002. (*Current Population Reports,* Series P20-547). Washington, DC: U.S. Bureau of the Census.

Frasch, K. M., Brooks, D., & Barth, R. P. (2000). Openness and contact in foster care adoptions: An eight-year follow-up. *Family Relations, 49*(4), 435–446.

Garland, A., Hough, R., Landsverk, J., McCabe, K., Yeh, M., Ganger, W., & Reynolds, B. (2000). Racial and ethnic variations in mental health care utilization among children in foster care. *Children's Services: Social Policy, Research and Practice, 3*(3), 133–146.

Garland, A., Landsverk, J., Hough, R., & Ellis-MacLeod, E. (1996). Type of maltreatment as a predictor of mental health service use in foster care. *Child Abuse and Neglect, 20*, 675–688.

Garland, A., Landsverk, J., & Lau, A. (2003). Racial/ethnic disparities in mental health service use among children in foster care. *Children and Youth Services Review, 25*, 489–505.

Gebel, T. (1996). Kinship care and nonrelative family foster care: A comparison of caregiver attributes and attitudes. *Child Welfare, 75*(1), 5–18.

Geen, R. (2004). The evolution of kinship care policy and practice. *The Future of Children, 14*(1), 131–150.

Goerge, R. (1990). The reunification process in substitute care. *Social Service Review, 64*, 422–457.

Goerge, R., Voorhis, J., Grant, S., Casey, K., & Robinson, M. (1992). Special-education experiences of foster children: An empirical study. *Child Welfare, 71*(5), 419–437.

Goodman, C., Potts, M., Pasztor, E., & Scorzo, D. (2004). Grandmothers as kinship caregivers: Private arrangements compared to public welfare oversight. *Children and Youth Services Review, 26*(3), 287–305.

Grotevant, H. D., & McRoy, R. G. (1998). *Openness in adoption: Connecting families of birth and adoption.* Thousand Oaks, CA: Sage.

Grotevant, H. D., Ross, H. M., Marchel, M. A., & McRoy, R. G. (1999). Adaptive behavior in adopted children: Predictors from early risk, collaboration in relationships within the adoptive kinship network, and openness arrangements. *Journal of Adolescent Research, 14*, 231–247.

Halfon, N., Berkowitz, G., & Klee, L. (1992). Mental health service utilization by children in foster care in California. *Pediatrics, 89*, 1238–1244.

Halfon, N., Mendonca, A., & Berkowitz, G. (1995). Health status of children in foster care. *Archives of Pediatric and Adolescent Medicine, 149*, 386–392.

Hildeyard, K., & Wolfe, D. (2001). Child neglect: Developmental issues and outcomes. *Child Abuse and Neglect, 26*(6-7), 679–695.

Hill, R. (1997). *The strengths of African American families: Twenty-five years later.* Washington, DC: R & B.

Hollingsworth, L. D. (1997). Effect of transracial/transethnic adoption on children's racial and ethnic identity and self-esteem: A meta-analytic review. *Marriage and Family Review, 25*, 99–130.

Jacobs, F., & Davies, M. (1994). *More than kissing babies?: Current child and family policy in the United States.* Westport, CT: Auburn House.

James, S., Landsverk, J., & Slymen, D. (2004). Placement movement in out-of-home care: Patterns and predictors. *Children and Youth Services Review, 26*(2), 185–206.

Jones Harden, B. (2004). Safety and stability for foster children: A developmental perspective. *Future of Children, 14*(1), 31–48.

Jones Harden, B., & Clyman, R. (2004). *The contribution of the home environment to cognitive-language functioning in young foster children.* Unpublished manuscript.

Jones Harden, B., Clyman, R., Kriebel, D., & Lyons, M. (2004). Kith and kin care: Parental characteristics and attitudes of foster and kinship caregivers. *Children and Youth Services Review, 26*(7), 657–671.

Kamerman, S. (1996). Child and family policies: An international review. In E. Zigler, S. L. Kagan, & N. Hall (Eds.), *Children, families and government* (pp. 31–50). New York: Cambridge University Press.

Keller, T., Wetherbee, K., LeProhn, N., Payne, V., Sim, K., & Lamont, E. (2001). Competencies and problem behaviors of children in family foster care: Variations by kinship placement status and race. *Children and Youth Services Review, 23*, 915–940.

Kirk, H. D. (1964). *Shared fate.* New York: Free Press.

Kortenkamp, K., & Ehrle, J. (2002). *Well-being of children involved in the child welfare system: A national overview.* Washington, DC: Urban Institute.

Landsverk, J., Davis, I., Ganger, W., Newton, R., & Johnson, I. (1996). Impact of psychosocial functioning on reunification from out-of-home placement. *Children and Youth Services Review, 18*(4–5), 447–462.

Lau, A., McCabe, K., Yeh, M., Garland, A., Hough, R., & Landsverk, J. (2003). Race/ethnicity and rates of self-reported maltreatment among high-risk youth in public sectors of care. *Child Maltreatment, 8*(3), 183–194.

Lawrence-Webb, C. (1997). African American children in the modern child welfare system: A legacy of the Flemming rule. *Child Welfare, 46*, 9–30.

Lee, R. (2003). The transracial adoption paradox: History, research, and counseling implications of cultural socialization. *Counseling Psychologist, 31*(6), 711–744.

Leos-Urbel, J., Bess, R., & Geen, R. (2002). The evolution of federal and state policies for assessing and supporting kinship caregivers. *Children and Youth Services Review, 24*, 37–52.

McLoyd, V. C. (1990). The impact of economic hardship on Black families and children: Psychological distress, parenting, and socioemotional development. *Child Development, 61*, 311–346.

McPhatter, A. (1997). Cultural competence in child welfare: What is it? How do we achieve it? What happens without it? *Child Welfare, 46*, 239–254.

McRoy, R. (1996). Racial identity issues for Black children in foster care. In S. Logan (Ed.), *Black family: Strengths, self-help and positive change.* Boulder, CO: Westview Press.

McRoy, R., Grotevant, H. D., & White, K. D. (1988). *Openness in adoption: New practices, new issues.* New York: Praeger.

Minkler, M., & Fuller-Thomson, E. (1999). The health of grandparents raising grandchildren: Results of a national study. *American Journal of Public Health, 89*(9), 1384–1389.

Minkler, M., & Fuller-Thomson, E. (2000). Second time around parenting: Factors predictive of grandparents becoming caregivers for their grandchildren. *International Journal of Aging and Human Development, 50*(3), 185–200.

National Information Adoption Clearinghouse. (2003). *Adoption: Numbers and trends.* Retrieved July 1, 2004, from http://naic.acf.hhs.gov/

Needell, B., Brookhart, M., & Lee, S. (2003). Black children and foster care placement in California. *Children and Youth Services Review, 25* 431–462.

Newton, R. R., Litrownik, A. J., & Landsverk, J. A. (2000). Children and youth in foster care: Disentangling the relationship between problem behaviors and number of placements. *Child Abuse and Neglect, 24,* 1363–1374.

NSCAW Research Group. (2002). Methodological lessons from the National Survey of Child and Adolescent Well-Being: The first three years of the USA's first national probability study of children and families investigated for abuse and neglect. *Children and Youth Services Review, 24,* 513–541.

Orme, J., Buehler, C., McSurdy, M., Rhodes, K., Cox, M., & Patterson, D. (2004). Parental and familial characteristics of family foster care applicants. *Children and Youth Services Review, 26*(3), 307–329.

Orme, J. G., & Buehler, C. (2001). Foster family characteristics and behavioral and emotional problems of foster children: A narrative review. *Family Relations: Journal of Applied Family and Child Studies, 50,* 3–15.

Pinderhughes, E. E. (1991). The delivery of child welfare services to African American clients. *American Journal of Orthopsychiatry, 61,* 599–605.

Pinderhughes, E. E. (1996). Toward understanding family readjustment following older child adoptions: The interplay between theory generation and empirical research. *Children and Youth Services Review, 18,* 115–138.

Pinderhughes, E. E., Jones Harden, B., & Schweder, A. (in press). Children in foster care: The long road from research to policy. In L. Aber, L. Allen, D. Phillips, & S. Jones (Eds.), *Child development and social policy: Knowledge for action.* Washington, DC: American Psychological Association.

Pinderhughes, R. B. (1997). *The experience of racial identity development for transracial adoptees.* Unpublished doctoral dissertation, Massachusetts School of Professional Psychology, Boston.

Risley-Curtiss, C., Combs-Orme, T., Chernoff, R., & Heisler, A. (1996). Health care utilization by children entering foster care. *Research on Social Work Practice, 6*(4), 442–461.

Roberts, D. (2002). *Shattered bonds: The color of child welfare.* New York: Basic Civitas Books.

Rosenthal, J. A. (1993). Outcomes of adoption of children with special needs. *The Future of Children, 3,* 77–88.

Scannapieco, M., Hegar, R., & McAlpine, C. (1997, September/October). Kinship care and foster care: A comparison of characteristics and outcomes. *Families in Society, 78*(5), 480–488.

Seaberg, J., & Harrigan, M. (1999). Foster families' functioning, experiences and views: Variations by race. *Children and Youth Services Review, 21*(1), 31–55.

Sedlak, A., & Broadhurst, D. (1996). *Third National Incidence Study of Child Abuse and Neglect.* Washington, DC: U.S. Department of Health and Human Services, National Center on Child Abuse and Neglect.

Simon, R. J,. Alstein, H., & Melli, M. S. (1994). *The case for transracial adoption.* Washington, DC: American University Press.

Simon, R. J., & Roorda, R. M. (2000). *In their own voices: Transracial adoptees tell their stories.* New York: Columbia University Press.

Smith, C., & Devore, W. (2004). African American children in the child welfare and kinship system: From exclusion to over inclusion. *Children and Youth Services Review, 26*(5), 427–446.

Stein, E., Evans, B., Masumdar, R., & Rae-Grant, N. (1996). The mental health of children in foster care: A comparison with community and clinical samples. *Canadian Journal of Psychiatry, 4*(6) 385–391.

Stevenson, H. C. (1995). Relationships of adolescent perceptions of racial socialization to racial identity. *Journal of Black Psychology, 21*(1), 49 - 70.

Taussig, H., & Talmi, A. (2001). Ethnic differences in risk behaviors and related psychosocial variables among a cohort of maltreated adolescents in foster care. *Child Maltreatment, 6*(2), 180–192.

Testa, M. (1997). Kinship foster care in Illinois. In R. Barth, J. Berrick, & N. Gilbert (Eds.), *Child welfare research review* (Vol. 2). New York: Columbia University.

Testa, M. (2001). *The changing significance of race and kinship for achieving permanency for foster children.* Paper presented at Race Matters: A Research Forum, Westat, Inc. and the Children and Family Research Center, UIUC, Washington, DC.

Testa, M. (2004). When children cannot return home: Adoption and guardianship. *The Future of Children, 14*(1), 115–130.

Testa, M., & Slack, K. (2002). The gift of kinship foster care. *Children and Youth Services Review, 24*(1-2), 79–108.

U.S. Bureau of the Census. (2002). *Current population survey report.* Washington, DC: Author.

U.S. Department of Health and Human Services, Administration on Children, Youth, and Families, Children's Bureau. (2000). *Report to the Congress on kinship foster care.* Washington DC: U.S. Government Printing Office.

U.S. Department of Health and Human Services (USDHHS). Administration on Children and Families. (2003a). *National survey of child and adolescent well-being: baseline report on one-year foster care sample.* Washington, DC: Author.

U.S. Department of Health and Human Services, Administration on Children, Youth, and Families, Children's Bureau. (2003b). *The adoption and foster care analysis and reporting system (AFCARS) report: Preliminary FY 2001 estimates as of March 2003.* Washington DC: U.S. Government Printing Office.

Waldfogel, J. (2000). Child welfare for the 21st century. *Children and Youth Services Review, 22*, 681–683.

Wells, K., & Guo, S. (1999). Reentry and reunification of foster children. *Children and Youth Services Review, 4*, 273–294.

Wrobel, G., Ayers-Lopez, S., Grotevant, H. D., McRoy, R. G., & Friedrick, M. (1996). Openness in adoption and the level of child participation. *Child Development, 67*, 2358–2374.

Wulczyn, F. (2003). Closing the gap: Are changing exit patterns reducing the time African American children spend in foster care relative to Caucasian children? *Children and Youth Services Review, 25*, 393–408.

Wulczyn, F. (2004). Family reunification. *Children, Families and Foster Care, 14*(1), 95–113.

Wulczyn, F., Hislop, K., & Goerge, R. (2001). *Foster care dynamics 1983–1998.* Chicago: Chapin Hall Center for Children.

Yu, E., Day, P., & Williams, M. (2002). *Improving educational outcomes for youth in care: A national collaboration.* Washington, DC: Child Welfare League of America.

Zuravin, S., Benedict, M., & Somerfield, M. (1993). Child maltreatment in family foster care. *American Journal of Orthopsychiatry, 63*(4), 589–596.

CHAPTER 15

Style Matters

Toward a Culturally Relevant Framework
for Interventions with African American Families

Howard C. Stevenson, Donna-Marie Winn,
Chanequa Walker-Barnes, *and* Stephanie I. Coard

Recent commissions and task forces on the reduction of mental health disparities for and the ethical treatment of ethnic minorities have consistently called for an increase in cultural competence in the application of psychological services (American Psychological Association, 2003; U.S. Department of Health and Human Services, 2001, 2003). Notably, the surgeon general has urged the mental health profession to pay more attention to how culture may influence the role of the clinician; the stigma and the prevalence of, expression of, and coping with mental illness (U.S. Department of Health and Human Services, 2001). Recent statistics reveal that as compared with the national rate of 33% of adults needing mental health care who actually receive it, the rate for African American[1] clients is much lower, and in most studies, is half of whatever rate is found for European Americans (Swartz et al., 1998). It is not clear whether this unmet need reflects inadequate opportunities for African Americans to access the mental health system or a culturally inappropriate service system that African Americans shun. Most likely, both factors play a role in the unmet mental health needs of African Americans.

The costs for such high rates of unmet mental health care needs among African Americans are substantial. Researchers have demonstrated that ethnic minorities have been found to bear the brunt of the burden of unmet mental health needs that lead to poorer health out-

comes (Myers, Lewis, & Parker-Dominguez, 2003; U. S. Department of
Health and Human Services, 2001). The facets of American society that
make life difficult for African Americans (e.g., social status, economic
status, discrimination, racism) are exacerbated by the lack of mental
health resources, particularly culturally relevant resources, to ameliorate
the emotional consequences of being an American of African descent.
The burden of unmet mental health needs coupled with psychological
practices bereft of cultural relevance makes for a woeful picture of the
current state of mental health care of African American families.

Documentation of the lack of cultural relevance in psychological
and educational interventions has spanned four decades and is more important than diagnostic clarity, therapeutic connection, or follow-up
treatment as a mandate for sustainable and effective psychological practice for African American youth and their families (Boyd-Franklin, 2003;
Stevenson & Renard, 1993; Sue & Sue, 1990; Vargas & Koss-Chioino,
1992). As practitioner-scholars, we assert that the relationship between
African American families and their psychological care providers must
be situated within a broader cultural context than traditional, mainstream clinical practice. Mainstream practice places a primacy on strategies of pathology-based diagnoses and classification, establishing distance between clinician and client, prohibiting or limiting therapist
disclosure, and focusing on ameliorating "dysfunctional" behaviors
(Potts & Watts, 2003). We argue that such strategies are less efficacious
with African Americans because of their failure to attend to the pervasive and omnipresent influence of culture and unique styles of expression.

Although at first glance the contention of the primacy of culture in
therapeutic effectiveness seems radical, one has only to look to the narratives of African Americans as they experience interventions that seek
to ameliorate their conditions, to find support for the primacy of incorporating cultural worldviews into psychological practice. The following
is a testimonial of a parent following the completion of a culturally relevant multifamily therapy group:

> "I thought this was another one of those programs that was going to
> try to get [my son's] behaviors in check. Y'all not like those thera-
> pists at [treatment facility]. Y'all hit it dead on, he's being beat down
> everyday by the system. These school people see him as black and big
> and bad. . . . When we got to talking about that, his anger come out.
> I didn't know he was holding all that in. Now, he's acting more and
> more like the son that I know he is. He's started to mind, but I still
> don't use that time out stuff on him. . . . Now that [taking away]
> privileges stuff, it works."

This and other "stories" represent a deep knowledge and unique vantage point of parents' experiences and constitute a perspective that is not traditionally incorporated into mainstream psychological practice (Denman, 1991; Dyson & Genishi, 1994; Sanders, 2002; Sue & Zane, 1990). Given the importance of cultural relevance as highlighted by national commissions, researchers, clinicians, and clients alike, the next logical question is, What does it mean to incorporate culture in the clinical context? What should be said or done differently to move traditional practice from a typically monocultural, mainstream framework toward a culturally relevant framework?

We believe one response to this question is the use of style or stylings. Stylings are actions and interactions that are designed to create, augment, and give meaning to and refer to the "conscious or unconscious manipulation of language or mannerisms to influence favorably the hearers of a message" (Asante, 1987, p. 39). In the context of therapy with African Americans, style refers to those crucial therapeutic moments when African Americans display and look for signs from the therapist that the therapeutic context provides a safe environment that allows for full cultural expression of emotions, thoughts, behaviors, and movements. It is therapists' ability to understand the significance of African American culture, history, and experience that provides meaning and context for clients' behaviors and experiences.

In this chapter, we attempt to define those elements of therapeutic style and context that maximize the potential healing of African Americans. We begin by discussing how the effectiveness of mainstream psychological practice with African Americans is hampered by therapists' ignorance of African American social experiences. Next, we describe five modes of behavioral expression or style that should be integrated into prevention and intervention efforts with African Americans in order to maximize their efficacy. We note the importance of the stylistic actions and expressions and their impact on how mainstream clinical services will need to shift to meet the emotional needs of African American families. Finally, we outline specific constructs, practices, and policies that are fundamental to a culturally relevant framework and suggest ways to integrate these notions of style into clinical practice.

However, there is an important caveat to be heeded: Although the transformation to a culturally relevant framework requires a paradigm shift in the landscape of current mainstream practice (Akbar, 1985; Myers, 1988), we do not mean to suggest that African Americans are aliens on the human landscape of functioning. Furthermore, Black families are not all alike, and investigation of each family's dependence on alternate cultural worldviews is an underlying premise of our within-race and cross-race diversity. We assert that African American families are *both* similar to *and* different from other families.

TO BE A PROBLEM: PSYCHOLOGY'S IGNORANCE OF OR ARROGANCE TOWARD CULTURAL RELEVANCE

To be African American is to be a problem in the eyes of some human service providers (Jones, 2003). The conceptualization, practice, research, and evaluation of human service is situated within the larger social and ecological politics that have a history of discrimination, misinterpretation, and ignorance of basic human functioning in different cultural contexts (Jones, 2003; Potts & Watts, 2003). In fact, traditional psychology may not know exactly what it does not know if the basic foundation of relevant conceptualization of problems is unquestioned. Asante's (1987) critique of Western scientific inquiry as being replete with "the arrogance of not knowing that they do not know what it is that they do not know, yet they speak as if they know what all of us need to know (p. 4)" is no small conundrum for African American families. We believe that our discussion on cultural relevance should begin with the problem of therapists' cultural ignorance rather than how to dismantle the malignant images of African Americans as "problems," inasmuch as the former is a prerequisite to the latter. Two types of cultural ignorance on the part of treatment providers, researchers, and educators of clinicians contribute to a lack of attention to culturally relevant intervention in traditional psychology. They include (1) ignorance of the impact of a history of discriminatory perceptions and experiences on African American psychological worldview and adjustment and (2) ignorance of the accurate meanings of diverse African American emotional expressions.

Ignorance of the Impact of Historical and Current Discrimination on Functioning

There should be no question that African American families have had and continue to endure significant emotional and physical hardship and trauma simply for being different in skin color, cultural values, worldview orientation, religious worship, and language style (Holliday & Holmes, 2003). The perniciousness of White supremacy, fortified by societally entrenched social intervention programs like enslavement and lynching, has been systemically widespread and has been significantly in-

fluenced by and has contributed to distorted and stereotyped perceptions of the emotional and physical attributes of African Americans
(Shapiro, 1988). This has led to bizarre and violent intervention efforts
based on psychological theories that are devoid of the conceptualizations of and knowledge generated from ethnic minorities and imbued
with elements whose very foundations rely on scientific racism (Holliday
& Holmes, 2003). The question remains as to how much knowledge of
these physical and psychological atrocities are present in the interdisciplinary clinical training programs across the country.

The question remains as to how much knowledge of Thomas and Sillen (1991) identified unique ways that 19th-century
psychiatry misdiagnosed African American behavior and emotional ex-
pressions. One misdiagnosis involved the classification of enslaved Afri-
cans' running away behavior or excursions for freedom from slavery as
drapetomania or *flight from home madness*. The very idea that social
science and helping professionals developed a diagnostic term to classify
a desire for freedom from enslavement as psychopathological says something about the context that surrounded African American clients or victims of early helping systems. Certainly, widespread knowledge about
the government-sanctioned Tuskegee Syphilis Study justifies collective
distrust of American helping systems (Jones, 1981). African American
families distrust traditional clinical practice for reasons related to this
misassignment of pathology to their healthy reactions and to societally
sanctioned discrimination and murder delivered at the hands of helpers.
This mistrust is typically not communicated openly by clients to their
therapists, but rather manifests as refusal to participate in treatment,
silence during sessions, or early dropout. These actions are often misin-
terpreted by therapists as further signs of psychopathology rather than
mistrust, thus exacerbating the wide gulf between therapist and client.
An example of the emergence of healthy cultural paranoia follows:

A Caucasian school-based counselor sought consultation from her
African American supervisor when families during her first multifamily group were deafeningly silent. These same families had been
very talkative when she initially recruited them. Even the first few
families to arrive to the group session were initially very talkative.
The supervisor encouraged the interventionist to probe families re-
spectfully in the comfort of their own homes to understand if group
dynamics around race, culture, and class had emerged. Indeed, the
families' collective silence was emblematic of their healthy distrust
of a recruitment process that had apparently resulted in the homog-
enous (all minority) student "leadership" group, despite the school's
significant Caucasian student population. Despite families' initial
affinity for their Caucasian interventionist, her happiness at their

arrival seemed to portend a cluelessness or racial insensitivity. When
the interventionist proactively talked with the families about their
previous experiences with discrimination in school, the families became more animated and engaged. The interventionist was able to
support parents' suspiciousness and vigilance upon seeing the group
composition and help the parents and the students learn many ways
to confront situations that appear inequitable.

In spite of evidence of Black social progress, most mainstream treatment providers are deeply ignorant of their own culture's role in African
America's mistrust of the majority culture (Whaley, 2001). The therapist–
client alliance can be jeopardized by a therapist who, ignorant of the
cultural meaning of behavioral expressions by African Americans, demonstrates inappropriate engagement with the cultural style of the participants. The following anecdote provides a vivid example of the therapist's
failure to apprehend his own historical-cultural role as White subjugator
of African American males with his use of the name "Boy":

A mother who was attending her weekly parenting group grew frus-
trated with her son's noncompliance with her directions for him to
stop touching a bookcase and return to participate in the group activities. "Boy, I told you to stop touching those books and come sit
down." The impact of a Caucasian male interventionist paraphras-
ing the mother's directions to her child was fairly predictable. When
the group leader said, "Boy, didn't you hear your mother tell you to
stop touching that!" the room grew silent and came to a standstill.

Traditional behavioral science researchers stand beside clinicians in
their blatant, though perhaps naive, cultural biases. Historical ignorance
aside, the fact that most psychology researchers fail to include discrimination as a key explanatory variable in African American family functioning reflects the biased context of traditional clinical psychology.
Fisher, Jackson, and Villaruel (1997) report that despite discriminations
against various ethnic minorities, the greater housing discrimination experienced by African Americans and Latinos who were barred from living in White neighborhoods yielded far more negative educational outcomes for their youth as compared with those of many Asian groups,
owing to the better schooling opportunities in those neighborhoods.
How systemic racism has blocked the educational and economic opportunities of African Americans for generations through employment,
housing, and health care discrimination may be more detrimental to
their emotional outcomes than researchers may be able to assess (Clark,
Anderson, Clark, & Williams, 1999; Darity, 2003; Harrell, 2000). The

biggest challenge here may not be just the omission of discrimination as a construct in intervention research and practice, but the very denial among researchers that prevents the broadening of research questions to include discrimination as a variable to study for African Americans. Holliday and Holmes (2003) warn that because the history and teaching of psychology is full of racism denial, generations of students of psychology are both ignorant of other ways of knowing and unable to ask culturally relevant questions.

Ignorance of the Meanings of African American Behavioral and Emotional Expression

Style matters. Style is one of many characteristics found in models of unique cultural expressions of African Americans that have been developed by multiple scholars (Asante, 1987; Boykin & Toms, 1985; Dixon, 1976; Dixon & Foster, 1971; Jones, 1991; Kochman, 1981; Myers, 1988; Pasteur & Toldson, 1982; Rose, 1982; White & Parham, 1990). Unfortunately, traditional psychology in America has focused primarily on an exclusive self-contained individualism often to the neglect of appreciating culturally different expressions of personality and emotion that can be found in ensembled or embedded perspectives on individualism (Sampson, 1988). Reliance on cultural deficit and culturally inferior models by traditional psychology in research and practice has led to misinterpretation of the emotional expressions of African Americans (Potts & Watts, 2003). Unintentional racism, lack of isomorphic attribution, and limited exposure to and practice of cultural competence by clinical professionals are major obstacles to effective cross-cultural communication (Bochner, 1986; Ridley, Chih, & Olivera, 2000; Ridley, Hill, & Weise, 2001; Triandis, 1976). Ignorance and lack of exposure to cultural difference contributes to the failure of clinicians and researchers to attribute accurate meanings to the verbal and nonverbal communications and behaviors by African Americans.

Across three decades, African Americans have been overdiagnosed with schizophrenia and underdiagnosed with affective and anxiety disorders (Adebimpe, 1981; Baker & Bell, 1999; Delahanty et al., 2001; Fellin, 1989; Paradis, Hatch, & Friedman, 1994; Wright, Scott, Pierre-Paul, & Gore, 1984). Wright and colleagues (1984) report that misdiagnosis has occurred since the 18th century, and Baker and Bell (1999) confirm that it continues to plague contemporary mental health practices with African Americans. Misdiagnosis masks the ignorance and underskilled abilities of psychological professionals to interpret Black stylistic expressions as being functional and not merely fear-generating.

We are most concerned about those moments when mental health professionals fearfully react to the behaviors of African Americans without being responsive to the meanings or feelings embedded in those behaviors.

Does ignorance of the meaning of history, discrimination reality, and emotional expressions of African Americans fully explain the lack of cultural relevance in our conceptualization, implementation, and interpretation of intervention and research models? No. Nor does the identification of these levels of peculiar ignorance presuppose an inherent, immutable disability in the therapist or the therapists' system. But we propose these concerns as starting points that can lead to defining cultural relevance as foundational for sound intervention and research frameworks.

STYLE MATTERS: ELEMENTS OF A CULTURALLY RELEVANT FRAMEWORK

Traditional therapeutic approaches are "arm's-length" models that rely heavily on highly verbal and intellectualized forms of communication. Although models of psychotherapy have evolved over time, there still seems to be an unquestioning acceptance of the basic assumptions inherent in early models of practice. Therapeutic exchanges are characterized by a hierarchical relationship between therapist and client, with clients revealing their private thoughts, feelings, and experiences to a therapist who discloses very little, if any, personal information. Therapists in training are cautioned to maintain emotional and physical distance from clients in order to avoid problems arising from transference and countertransference. Although such practices are intended to protect both therapists and clients, they may be a reflection of the cultural and personality backgrounds of the pioneers of psychotherapy rather than the result of scientific research documenting their effectiveness (Morawski, 1997). Indeed, evidence supports the proposition that some degree of therapist self-disclosure results in a stronger therapeutic alliance as well as better treatment outcome (Barrett & Berman, 2001). Moreover, European American therapists are not likely to address race with clients of color, in contrast to African American therapists who routinely do so, even though both groups see the benefits of such discussions (Knox, Burkard, Johnson, Suzuki, & Ponterotto, 2003).

Based on our collective clinical experience with this population, we outline five categories of cultural relevance that have been absent from traditional methods of treatment delivery and that should be infused into clinical training: (1) the dynamic use of language, (2) spirituality and religion, (3) human connection, (4) movement, and (5) racial socialization. Some of these categories reflect cultural values and traditions that should undergird therapeutic efforts with African Americans, and others are specific tools to be incorporated into prevention and intervention strategies.

The Dynamic Use of Language

The delivery of mainstream therapeutic intervention relies heavily on the verbal interchange between therapist and client. However, this interchange is often restricted by the use of language that reflects the cultural background of the therapist rather than the client. That is, the language of therapy is imbued with a culture that is White, middle or upper class, highly educated, and male. This practice occurs not only because the majority of therapists, particularly the pioneers of psychotherapy, have themselves fit this cultural description, but also because the vast majority of therapists, including women and people of color, continue to be trained in contexts that support this cultural frame.

In the context of intervention with African Americans, this cultural difference is manifested not as a difference in language, but rather a difference in linguistic style. Most prominent are the use of rhythm, styling, lyrical balance, and melodious voice to convey meaning. Asante (1987) remarks that this linguistic style, termed "tonal semantics" by Smitherman (1977), is the hallmark of Black rhetorical expression. Words and phrases may have different, even opposite, connotations depending on the speaker's vocal tone and rhythm. For ex ample, the word "bad" means "good" if said in a certain way. Ignorance of such linguistic nuances on the part of therapists can result in potentially serious misunderstandings about clients' intents and experiences. Traditional African American communication is further distinguished from typical American English by three additional culturally specific modes of discourse: call-response, signification, and narrative sequencing (Smitherman, 1977).

Call-Response

Call-response is the "spontaneous verbal and nonverbal interaction between speaker and listener in which all of the speaker's statements ('calls') are punctuated by expressions ('responses') from the listener" (Smitherman, 1977, p. 104). Responses may be subtle (e.g., a slight head nod) or emphatic (e.g., a shout, banging on a table). Although most carefully preserved in the church, it also pervades aspects of everyday communication and emphasizes traditional West African values of group cohesiveness, cooperation, and the collective common good. The functional value of call-response is similar to the family systems concept of resonance in that it serves to synthesize speaker and listener in a dynamic interchange in which the listener communicates to the speaker, "I hear you." This mode of discourse has significant implications for the therapeutic alliance with African American clients, who may interpret therapist silence (verbal and nonverbal) as a lack of an affective connection at best, and a confirmation of the therapist's "me expert, you crazy" mentality at worst.

Signification

Signification is "the verbal art of insult in which a speaker humorously puts down, talks about, needles—that is, signifies on—the listener" (Smitherman, 1977, p. 118). Examples of signification are perhaps the most common anecdotes reported by observational researchers who conduct research with African American families. For example, Cauce (personal communication, June 21, 2002) cites "playful aggression" as a form of communication in which African Americans jokingly threaten each other with physical harm. This form of communication, like most forms of signification, is usually viewed negatively when taken at face value by a coder who is unfamiliar with African American cultural patterns and who believes that the statement implies a real physical or emotional threat. However, the fundamental aspect of signification is that the target is not supposed to "take it personally." Indeed, signification, which often includes elements of sarcasm, can often be used as an effective method of behavioral control in that it communicates displeasure in a culturally sanctioned manner. The use of humor is deliberate in that it provides the target with two options: (1) to "come back" with a signification of his or her own or (2) to laugh along with the joke. Thus, rather than shutting down dialogue, signification can create an opening for interaction.

Narrative Sequencing

Narrative sequencing refers to the use of storytelling and concrete narratives about real or hypothetical events to explain a point or to persuade listeners to one's own point of view. Rather than objective reporting, events are dramatically acted out and narrated. Narrative sequencing, which "though highly applauded by blacks, . . . is exasperating to whites who wish you'd be direct and hurry up and get to the point" (Smitherman, 1977, p. 148), can be used to teach a lesson or to recreate the emotional and spiritual experience of an event so that it can be better understood by the listener.

Implicit in this discussion is the assumption that African American linguistic styles—call-response, tonal semantics, signification, and narrative sequencing—are fundamental methods of social-affective communication among African Americans. Consequently, a therapeutic setting that hinders the utilization of these modes of discourse also hinders full emotional expression by African American clients. Clinicians who are unfamiliar with African American linguistic styles may misinterpret client communication, attribute pathology where there is none, and overlook cultural resources and strengths that might aid in treatment. Such ignorance impedes the therapeutic alliance, limits client self-disclosure, and contributes to early dropout and unsuccessful treatment.

Spirituality and Religion

Spirituality and religion[2] are central organizing principles within African American culture and encompass both private and public practices, including membership at a local religious institution, attendance at formal worship services, prayer, and belief in the value of instinct and intuition (Brodsky, 2000; Mattis, 2002; Mattis, Fontenot, & Hatcher-Kay, 2003; Mattis, Hearn, & Jagers, 2002; Mattis & Jagers, 2001). There is growing evidence that the use of religious and spiritual practices such as prayer, meditation, and attendance at religious services improves health behaviors and is associated with a reduced risk of mental and physical health problems, including hypertension, substance use disorders, and depression (George, Larson, Koenig, & McCullough, 2000; Hackney & Sanders, 2003; Koenig & Larson, 2001; Seybold & Hill, 2001). Spiritual practices and church-based religious support have also been found to moderate the relation between stress and health outcomes (Bowen-Reid & Harrell, 2002; Maton, 1989). Parental religious involvement has been found to predict positive parent–child relationships, marital quality, and child behavioral and emotional outcomes (Brody, Stoneman, Flor, & McCrary, 1994).

Despite such findings, there has been little systematic attempt to integrate spirituality and religion into current prevention and intervention efforts, and, historically, these phenomena have been labeled by social scientists and practitioners as avoidant coping strategies (e.g., Ellis, 1960; Freud, 1949; Pruyser, 1977). By confusing spiritual faith with avoidance coping, clinicians may undermine the therapeutic alliance by framing the client as one who "does not want to be helped," underestimate the vast internal resources and resilience of such clients, and misdiagnose "inactive" faith decisions as avoiding engagement with emotional pain and life struggle. The task of the therapist is to distinguish between those clients for whom faith is an active choice and those for whom it is an avoidance strategy, a process that would require the therapist to help clients engage their faith in problem resolution. Indeed, although clients and clinicians alike often perceive a dichotomy between the therapeutic and spiritual domains, acknowledging the importance of a spiritual reality could aid the culturally relevant delivery of interventions.

Human Connection

Transitioning to a culturally relevant framework positions one's view of clients as human in the center of the framework. A large part of successfully implementing therapeutic interventions with client families hinges on the establishment of a positive relationship between the families and the treating professionals (Norcross, 2002), especially for families whose cultural realities are persistently invalidated or denigrated by others (Boyd-Franklin, 2003). A new term, "cultural attunement," indicates the practice of continuous accurate interpretations, validations, and affirmations of the meanings of African American functioning, which is a central prerequisite to human connection. This is the meaning of isomorphic attribution—that African American families feel and know that their helpers are attaching the same meaning that they would ascribe to their own behavior and emotional expressions (Hoskins, 1999; Zamel & Stevenson, 2003). According to Hoskins (1999), the influence of cultural attunement on therapist development assumes a fundamental reliance on five major principles, which include (1) acknowledging the pain of oppression, (2) engaging in acts of humility, (3) acting with reverence, (4) engaging in mutuality, and (5) maintaining a position of "not knowing." Zamel and Stevenson (2003) add to this list the appreciation of a "same, but different" or "both–and" reality orientation. To be culturally attuning, interventionists must consider how Black families, their functioning, and their worldviews are both the same as and different from other families'. Nevertheless, this value of human connection presupposes that helpers must get closer to, rather than distant from, the cultural expressions of Black clients.

The Psychology of Movement

Movement is more than the displacement of personal space. It also reveals who a person is and how he or she thinks (Boykin & Toms, 1985; Gardner, 1993; Gardner, Kornhaber, & Wake, 1996). Different cultural traditions prioritize different human functions, with some cultures thinking that movement style matters little in personality functioning. Boykin and Toms (1985) have identified movement as one of nine characteristics of African American cultural expression. Gardner (1993) has described how movement is often considered to be a "less refined" skill as compared with cognitive processing. We believe a thematic style issue for Black families is to prioritize movement as a personality statement. Family members move in unison and in opposition to each other, and these physical and psychological dynamics are revealing. This advanced understanding of the psychology of humans can be thwarted if therapists persist in devaluing movement in the understanding of functioning. After all, the body does not express physicality only, but is "also the vessel of the individual's sense of self, his most personal feelings and aspirations, as well as that entity to which others respond in a special way because of their uniquely human qualities" (Gardner, 1993, pp. 235–236).

Ironically, therapists can reduce their capacity to learn and know humanity by how they limit the amount of psychological knowledge they expect to gain from watching individuals in movement. However, if one operates as if humans reveal something about their personality strengths, weaknesses, and style when engaged in movement that cannot be screened and edited, the stage for understanding the individual at a deeper psychological level is set. Stevenson (2003) described the Preventing Long-Term Anger and Aggression in Youth (PLAAY) project, in which *in vivo* intervention during the athletic movement of basketball and martial arts proved essential in developing intense emotional connections with Black male youth with histories of aggression. The utility of movement as a diagnostic aid and intervention strategy is not limited to the activity of clients, as noted by Coard on facilitating parenting workshops with African American families:

> When I am teaching a skill or intervening with a parent on a particular point I will move physically forward in an attempt to engage them and suggest that I am saying some thing of importance. But when I am done making my point, I purposely step or sit back to let them know that one, I am done and two, that I am willing to let them contemplate what I have said and three, that I am open to hearing their feedback. I use movement to let them know that they "have the floor." I make these movements purposefully to get parents to engage and it increases their willingness to give their testimony. The parents respond to this and I see it as a respectful "move" on my part that increases my connection with them. African Americans like immediate feedback and expression, although not necessarily verbal. It is not just allowing for the expression but the immediate expression. If I didn't use the non-verbal [communication], I think I would "lose" my [African American] parents. (personal communication, February 11, 2004)

Racial and Cultural Socialization

African American parents routinely engage in racial socialization practices as part of their parenting repertoire (Caughy, O'Campo, Randolph, & Nickerson, 2002), and growing research evidence indicates that these practices are related to better socioemotional, behavioral, and academic outcomes for children. Correlational studies provide evidence of relations between perceived and actual parental racial socialization practices and positive child outcomes, including well-developed racial identity development (Demo & Hughes, 1990, Stevenson, 1995), socioemotional functioning (McAdoo, 1985; Spencer, 1983, 1987), higher academic functioning (Bowman & Howard, 1985; Sanders, 1997), better behavioral competence (Caughy et al., 2002), heightened self-esteem (Constantine & Blackmon, 2002), positive and involved mother–child interactions (Frabutt, Walker, & MacKinnon-Lewis, 2002), decrease in depression and anger (Stevenson, Reed, Bodison, & Bishop, 1995), racial coping and competence (Johnson, 2001), and prosocial bonding to other socialization agents (e.g., school, community) (Oliver, 1989).

Racial socialization is a process that encompasses a legacy of skills, including awareness of the scope and prevalence of discrimination, preparation for coping with racism, appreciation of one's cultural legacy, commitment to and pride in one's racial identity, belief in racial equality, and an orientation toward individual and academic achievement (Coard, Wallace, Stevenson, & Brotman, 2004; Stevenson, 2003). These skills may be consciously or unconsciously communicated to African American children by their parents or extended family members and used to deflect and negotiate a hostile environment. This process may require an ability to be different people at different times, a duality of socialization, without losing a core sense of self. Some believe it is required that African Americans be aware of and able to "fit in" with the mainstream, whether they accept its values or not. Although diversity exists among Blacks, most must make common psychological sense of the dominant culture's openly disparaging view of them. Teaching their children to deflect negative messages about themselves and negotiate racial barriers, as well as reinforcing positive attributes of being Black, are all necessary but unique parenting tasks that lead to the development of healthy racial identities and the prevention of maladjustment (Allen & Majidi-Ahi, 1989). It is a balancing act for Black parents to find ways to warn Black children about racial dangers and disappointments without overwhelming them. Either extreme can lead to the development of defensive styles that may leave a child inadequately prepared to negotiate the world with a realistic perspective. Understanding these conflicts, how they may be manifested, and how they are or may be successfully negotiated are talents that should fall well within the skills of culturally relevant helpers.

Summary

We argue that culturally relevant practice must (1) take into account the historical and current realities of African Americans that shape current psychosocial functioning and attitudes toward treatment, (2) be imbued with knowledge of and appreciation for culturally specific modes of emotional and personality expression, and (3) move beyond distance-based, sedentary methods of treatment delivery to reflect the ensembled individualism that is deemed vital to optimal functioning among African Americans, including spirituality and religion, human connectedness, movement, and racial socialization. This framework is not intended to be exhaustive, nor is it intended to be applied indiscriminately to all African American families. As noted by Hill, Murry, and Anderson (Chapter 2 in this book), the African American population is becoming increasingly diverse with respect to income, education, religion, regionality, and country of origin. Although the effectiveness of clinical interventions with many African Americans may be improved with the application of this framework, there are also those who would be better served by more traditional approaches. Likewise, whereas we would argue that the proposed framework is particularly applicable in work with African Americans, it is also likely to be useful for other ethnic minority groups as well as for some individuals from the majority culture. Consequently, as with any other intervention strategy, therapists should not adhere to this framework based simply on a client's racial background, but should assess its goodness-of-fit with the client's worldview. We assert that incorporating and fostering this framework in prevention and intervention efforts will increase retention and successful treatment rates of African Americans. In the following section, we provide recommendations as to how clinicians move toward delivering culturally relevant treatment to African American families.

RECOMMENDATIONS FOR MOVING TOWARD A CULTURALLY RELEVANT FRAMEWORK FOR INTERVENTIONS WITH AFRICAN AMERICAN FAMILIES

Development of Therapist Self-Knowledge

We recommend that therapists self-critique their personal racial and cultural identity history and countertransference and enhance their knowledge of their identity in relation to the clients they serve (Burton, Winn, Stevenson, & Clark, 2004). Therapists must learn to analyze consciously the power dynamics, the style and worldview differences, and the limitations/benefits of cultural understanding present in the therapeutic encounter for self, clients, and context (Stevenson & Renard, 1993). When working with African American families, clinicians should make note of verbal/nonverbal, direct/indirect, and conscious/unconscious cultural moments of confluence, conflict, and silence.

Development of Knowledge of and Appreciation for African American Cultural Style

To work effectively with African American families, clinicians must experience intense and meaningful engagement in and understanding of the cultural context, legacies, and styles of these families. This includes developing awareness of the current and historical realities of discrimination and racism that impact the socioemotional functioning of African American families and contribute to their current mistrust of the majority culture and mental health professionals. Moreover, it means learning to appreciate the linguistic stylings, spiritual/religious realities, collectivist identities, and movement expressions of African Americans with the goal of igniting the individual- and extended-self passions for health and healing in clients.

Assessment of the Meaning of Culturally Relevant Strategies for Change

We argue that for all African American clients, there should be an assessment, whether structured or informal, of the degree to which a culturally relevant framework is appropriate. At a minimum, clinicians working with African American families, regardless of the clinicians' ethnic backgrounds, must continuously ascertain whether clients feel that the therapeutic relationship is congruent with their cultural reality and beliefs. Moreover, clinicians should determine the emotional intensity, developmental appropriateness, and amount of racial socialization needed for families. Therapists should also assess the role and meaning of clients' spiritual beliefs and practices and their utility in affecting clients' emotional well-being.

Integration of Culturally Relevant Treatment Strategies into Practice

Following the appropriate assessment and determination of the utility of this framework with a particular client or family, clinicians should take steps to integrate culturally relevant treatment strategies into practice. Therapeutic strategies may include (1) actively talking to families and youth about racism, examining how to combat the prevalence and psychosocial impact of racism on their lives and the lives of others; (2) helping clients set priorities about which situations call for a direct or indirect response and learn why some strategies are more effective than others, given the context; and (3) helping clients to determine which situations might be dangerous to respond to directly, as well as helping them to explore alternative methods of expressing or managing angry feelings.

POLICY IMPLICATIONS OF CULTURALLY RELEVANT INTERVENTION

We see the policy implications of developing a culturally relevant framework for interventions with African Americans as threefold. First, practitioners and the agencies they work in should provide, to children, youth, and families, psychological services that integrate the cultural competence ethical guidelines and recommendations made by nationally accredited organizations (American Psychological Association, 2003; the President's New Freedom Commission on Mental Health, 2003; U.S. Department of Health and Human Services, 2003). Such cultural competence guidelines promote the acquisition of cultural knowledge through formal training, guided mentorship, and supervision. The ability of service providers to understand and affirm the unique stylistic behaviors and expressions of the African Americans they serve is critical. To do so involves, first, acquiring knowledge about and an understanding of the historical, political, and racial context of the communities in which these agencies and their families reside. In addition to training practitioners, we recommend providing this same training to auxiliary staff who interact with African American clients as they enter, engage, and leave the agency. This may include staff members responsible for receiving and greeting families, serving families food, and giving directions, as well those who are in charge of agency maintenance.

Second, African Americans must know that they have a right to obtain culturally competent intervention, even if this means that their health insurers pay for service providers who are "outside their networks." As it currently stands, insurers rarely inform their insureds of their rights to be treated by someone who is culturally competent. Third, we recommend that local and national funding agencies incorporate culturally relevant guidelines and recommendations into RFPs (Requests for Proposals) for family programming. These RFPs should stipulate guidelines that mandate training and a level of cultural competence when proposing to deliver services or conduct research with African Americans. This training and competence should become a requirement for researchers, practitioners, and supervisors alike. Moreover, funding sources should begin initiatives to evaluate cultural relevance and the role of cultural competence in promoting and sustaining efficacious treatment outcomes.

As we stated earlier, it is not our intention to oversimplify African American people, their behaviors, or their expressions, because African Americans are as diverse and complex as the many bodies of water on the earth. The stylistic themes or elements we have presented constitute the "water" of Black cultural expression, water that is appropriated and expressed differently and to varying degrees among different Black families. The culturally relevant categories proposed in this chapter are meant as guides to direct helpers toward interventions that are more proximal to the water and stylings of the African American families they serve. The culturally relevant framework presented herein suggests not only that the unwieldy and often amorphous waters and stylings of culturally different individuals and families provide an opportunity for therapists to come to understand their clients' unique vantage point and deep knowledge of their experiences, but that the understanding and utilization of these waters and stylings constitute the missing context in traditional psychological practice and research (Stevenson, 2003). Certainly, although individuality exists and the meaning-making processes of individuality will vary, cultural boundaries of sameness also exist. Central to this chapter is the knowing of what meaning clients are trying to convey through style. Style matters.

NOTES

1. In this chapter "African American" and "Black" are used interchangeably throughout to represent families and individuals of African descent. However, we acknowledge the distinctions in terms as noted by Coard and Sellers (Chapter 13, this volume).
2. For the sake of simplicity, we use the terms "religion" and "spirituality" interchangeably in this chapter. However, we note that theologians as well as several psychologists distinguish between the terms (e.g., Mattis & Jagers, 2001).

REFERENCES

Adebimpe, V. R. (1981). Overview: White norms and psychiatric diagnosis of Black patients. *American Journal of Psychiatry, 138,* 279–285.
Akbar, N. (1985). Our Destiny: Authors of a scientific revolution. In H. P. McAdoo

& J. L. McAdoo (Eds.), *Black children: Social, educational, and parental environments* (pp. 17–31). Thousand Oaks, CA: Sage.

Allen, L., & Majidi-Ahi, S.(1989). Black American children. In J. T. Gibbs & L. N. Huang (Eds.), *Children of color* (pp. 148–178). San Francisco: Jossey-Bass.

American Psychological Association (2003). Guidelines on multicultural education, training, research, practice, and organizational change for psychologists. *American Psychologist, 58*(5), 377–402.

Asante, M. K. (1987). *The Afrocentric idea*. Philadelphia: Temple University Press.

Baker, F. M., & Bell, C. (1999). Issues in the psychiatric treatment of African Americans. *Psychiatric Services, 50*(3), 362–368.

Barrett, M. S., & Berman, J. S. (2001). Is psychotherapy more effective when therapists disclose information about themselves? *Journal of Consulting and Clinical Psychology, 69*, 597–603.

Bochner, S. (1986). Coping with unfamiliar cultures: Adjustment or culture learning? *Australian Journal of Psychology, 38*(3), 347–358.

Bowen-Reid, T. L., & Harrell, J. P. (2002). Racist experiences and health outcomes: An examination of spirituality as a buffer. *Journal of Black Psychology, 28*, 18–36.

Bowman, P. J., & Howard, C. (1985). Race-related socialization, motivation, and academic achievement: A study of black youth in three-generation families. *Journal of the American Academy of Child Psychiatry, 24*, 143–141.

Boyd-Franklin, N. (2003). *Black families in therapy: Understanding the African American experience* (2nd ed.). New York: Guilford Press.

Boykin, A. W., & Toms, F. D. (1985). Black child socialization: A conceptual framework. In H. P. McAdoo & J. L. McAdoo (Eds.), *Black children: Social, educational, and parental environments* (pp. 33–52). Newbury Park, CA: Sage.

Brodsky, A. E. (2000). The role of religion in the lives of resilient, urban, African American, single mothers. *Journal of Community Psychology, 28*, 199–219.

Brody, G. H., Stoneman, Z., Flor, D., & McCrary, C. (1994). Religion's role in organizing family relationships: Family process in rural, two-parent African American families. *Journal of Marriage and the Family, 56*, 878–888.

Burton, L. M., Winn, D., Stevenson, H., & Clark, S. L. (2004). Working with African American clients: Considering the "homeplace" in marriage and family therapy practices. *Journal of Marital and Family Therapy, 30*(4), 113–129.

Caughy, M. O., Campo, P. J., Randolph, S. M., & Nickerson, K. (2002). The influence of racial socialization practices on the cognitive and behavioral competence of African American children. *Child Development, 73*(5), 1611–1625.

Clark, R., Anderson, N. B., Clark, V. R., & Williams, D. R. (1999). Racism as a stressor for African Americans: A biopsychosocial model. *American Psychologist, 54*, 805–816.

Coard, S. I., Wallace, S. A., Stevenson, H. C., & Brotma, L. M. (2004). Towards culturally relevant preventive interventions: The consideration of racial socialization in parent training with African American families. *Journal of Child and Family Studies, 13*(3), 277–293.

Constantine, M. G., & Blackmon, S. B. (2002). Black adolescents' racial socializa-

330   SOCIALIZATION PROCESSES

tion experiences: Their relations to home, school, and peer self-esteem. *Journal of Black Studies, 32(2),* 322–334.

Darity, W. A. (2003). Employment discrimination, segregation, and health. *American Journal of Public Health, 93(2),* 226–231.

Delahanty, J., Ram, R., Postrado, L., Balis, T., Green-Paden, L., & Dixon, L. (2001). Differences in rates of depression in schizophrenia by race. *Schizophrenia Bulletin, 27(1),* 29–38.

Demo, D., & Hughes, M. (1990). Socialization and racial identity among Black Americans. *Social Psychology Quarterly, 53,* 364–374.

Denman, G. A. (1991). *Sit tight and I'll swing you a tale . . . using and writing stories with young people.* Portsmouth, NH: Heineman.

Dixon, V. (1976). Worldviews and research methodology. In L. King (Ed.), *African philosophy: Assumptions and paradigms for research on black persons.* Los Angeles: Fanon Research and Development Center.

Dixon, V., & Foster, B. (1971). *Beyond black or white.* Boston: Little, Brown.

Dyson A. H., & Genishi, C. (1994). *The need for story. Cultural diversity in classroom and community.* Urbana, IL: National Council of Teachers of English.

Ellis, A. (1960). There is no place for the concept of sin in psychotherapy. *Journal of Counseling Psychology, 7,* 188–192.

Fellin, P. (1989). Perspectives on depression among Black Americans. *Health and Social Work, 14(4),* 245–252.

Fisher, C. B., Jackson, J., & Villarruel, F. (1997). The study of African American and Latin American children and youth. In W. Damon (Series Ed.), & R. M. Lerner (Vol. Ed.), *Handbook of child psychology: Vol. 1. Theoretical models of human development.* (5th ed., pp. 1145–1207). New York: Wiley.

Frabutt, J. M., Walker, A.M., & MacKinnon-Lewis, C. (2002). Racial socialization messages and the quality of mother/child interactions in African American families. *Journal of Early Adolescence, 22(2),* 200–217.

Freud, S. (1949). *The future of an illusion.* New York: Liveright.

Gardner, H. (1993). *Multiple intelligences: The theory in practice.* New York: Basic Books.

Gardner, H., Kornhaber, M. L., & Wake, W. K. (1996). *Intelligence: Multiple perspectives.* Orlando, FL: Harcourt Brace.

George, L. K., Larson, D. B., Koenig, H. G., & McCullough, M. E. (2000). Spirituality and health: What we know, what we need to know. *Journal of Social and Clinical Psychology, 19,* 102–116.

Hackney, C. H., & Sanders, G. S. (2003). Religiosity and mental health: A meta-analysis of recent studies. *Journal for the Scientific Study of Religion, 42,* 43–56.

Harrell, S. P. (2000). A multidimensional conceptualization of racism-related stress: Implications for the well-being of people of color. *American Journal of Orthopsychiatry, 70(1),* 42–57.

Holliday, B. G., & Holmes, A. L. (2003). A tale of challenge and change: A history and chronology of ethnic minorities in the United States. In G. Bernal, J. E. Trimble, A. K. Burlew, & F. T. L. Leong (Eds.), *Handbook of racial and ethnic minority psychology* (pp. 15–64). Thousand Oaks, CA: Sage.

Hoskins, M . L. (1999). Worlds and lives together: Developing cultural attunement. *Child and Youth Care Forum, 28,* 73–85.

Johnson, D. (2001). Parental characteristics, racial stress, and racial socialization processes as predictors of racial coping in middle childhood. In A. M. Neal-Barnett, J. M. Contreras, & K. A. Kerns (Eds.), *Forging links: African American children clinical developmental perspectives* (pp. 57–74). Westport, CT: Prager.

Jones, J. (1991). The politics of personality: Being Black in America. In R. L. Jones (Ed.), *Black psychology* (pp. 305–318). Hampton, VA: Cobb & Henry.

Jones, J. (2003). Constructing race and deconstructing racism: A cultural psychology approach. In G. Bernal, J. E. Trimble, A. K. Burlew, & F. T. L. Leong (Eds.), *Handbook of racial and ethnic minority psychology* (pp 65–76). Thousand Oaks, CA: Sage.

Jones, J. H. (1981). *Bad blood.* New York: Free Press.

Knox, S., Burkhard, A. W., Johnson, A. J., Suzuki, L. A., & Ponterotto, J. G. (2003). African-American and European-American therapists' experiences of addressing race in cross-racial psychotherapy dyads. *Journal of Counseling Psychology, 50,* 466–481.

Kochman, T. (1981). *Black and White styles in conflict.* Chicago: University of Chicago Press.

Koenig, H. G., & Larson, D. B. (2001). Religion and mental health: Evidence for an association. *International Review of Psychiatry, 13,* 67–78.

Maton, K. I. (1989). The stress-buffering role of spiritual support: Cross-sectional and prospective investigations. *Journal for the Scientific Study of Religion, 28,* 310–323.

Mattis, J. S. (2002). Religion and spirituality in the meaning making and coping experiences of African American women: A qualitative analysis. *Psychology of Women Quarterly, 26,* 308–320.

Mattis, J. S., Fontenot, D., & Hatcher-Kay, C. (2003). Religiosity, racism and dispositional optimism among African Americans. *Personality and Individual Differences, 34,* 1025–1038.

Mattis, J. S., Hearn, K., & Jagers, R. (2002). Factors predicting communal attitudes among African American men. *Journal of Black Psychology, 28*(3), 197–214.

Mattis, J. S., & Jagers, R. J. (2001). A relational framework for the study of religiosity and spirituality in the lives of African Americans. *Journal of Community Psychology, 29,* 519–539.

McAdoo, H. P. (1985). Racial attitude and self concept in young Black children over time. In H. P. McAdoo & J. L. McAdoo (Eds.), *Black children: Social, educational, and parental environments* (pp. 213–242). Newbury Park, CA: Sage.

Morawski, J. G. (1997). White experimenters, white blood, and other white conditions: Locating the psychologist's race. In M. Fine, L. Weis, L. C. Powell, & L. M. Wong (Eds.), *Off white: Readings on race, power, and society.* New York: Routledge.

Myers, H., Lewis, T., & Parker-Dominguez, T. (2003). Stress, coping, and minority health: A biopsychosocial perspective on ethnic health disparities. In G. Bernal, J. Trimble, K. Burlew, & F. Leong (Eds.), *Handbook of racial and ethnic minority psychology.* Thousand Oaks, CA: Sage.

Myers, L. J. (1988). *Understanding an African-centered world view: Introduction to an optimal psychology.* Dubuque, IA: Kendall/Hunt.

Norcross, J. (2002). *Psychotherapy relationships that work.* New York: Oxford University Press.

Oliver, W. (1989). Black males and social problems: Prevention through Afrocentric socialization. *Journal of Black Studies, 20*(1), 1–19.

Paradis, C. M., Hatch, M., & Friedman, S. (1994). Anxiety disorders in African Americans: An update. *Journal of the National Medical Association, 86*(8), 609–612.

Pasteur, A. B., & Toldson, I. L. (1982). *Roots of soul: The psychology of Black expressiveness.* New York: Anchor/Doubleday.

Potts, R. G., & Watts, R. J. (2003). Conceptualization and models: The meanings of difference in racial and ethnic minority psychology. In G. Bernal, J. E. Trimble, A. K. Burlew, & F. T. L. Leong (Eds.), *Handbook of racial and ethnic minority psychology* (pp 65–75). Thousand Oaks, CA: Sage.

Pruyser, P. W. (1977). The seamy side of current religious beliefs. *Bulletin of the Menninger Clinic, 41,* 329–348.

Ridley, C. R., Chih, D. W., & Olivera, R. J. (2000). Training in cultural schemas: An antidote to unintentional racism in clinical practice. *American Journal of Orthopsychiatry, 70*(1), 65–72.

Ridley, C. R, Hill, C. L., & Wiese, D. L. (2001). Ethics in multicultural assessment: A model of reasoned application. In L. Suzuki, J. G. Ponterotto, & P. J. Meller (Eds.), *Handbook of multicultural assessment: Clinical, psychological, and educational applications* (2nd ed., pp. 29–45). San Francisco: Jossey-Bass.

Rose, L. F. R. (1982). Theoretical and methodological issues in the study of Black culture and personality. *Humboldt Journal of Social Relations, 10,* 320–338.

Sampson, R. J. (1988). Local friendship ties and community attachment in mass society: A multi-level systemic model. *American Sociological Review, 53,* 766–779.

Sanders, J. L. (2002). Racial socialization. In J. L. Sanders & C. Bradley (Eds.), *Counseling African American families: The family psychology and counseling series* (pp. 41–57). Alexandria, VA: American Counseling Association.

Sanders, M. G. (1997). Overcoming obstacles: Academic achievement as a response to racism and discrimination. *Journal of Negro Education, 66*(1), 83–93.

Seybold, K. S., & Hill, P. C. (2001). The role of religion and spirituality in mental and physical health. *Current Directions in Psychological Science, 10,* 21–24.

Shapiro, H. (1988). *White violence and black response: From Reconstruction to Montgomery.* Amherst: University of Massachusetts Press.

Smitherman, G. (1977). *Talkin and testifyin: The language of Black America.* Detroit, MI: Wayne State University Press.

Spencer, M. B. (1983). Children's cultural values and parental child rearing strategies. *Developmental Review, 3,* 351–370.

Spencer, M. B. (1987). Black children's ethnic identity formation: Risk and resilience in castelike minorities. In J.S. Phinney & M.E. Rotheram (Eds.), *Children's ethnic socialization* (pp. 103–116). Newbury Park, CA: Sage.

Stevenson, H. C. (1995). Relationship of adolescent perceptions of racial socialization to racial identity. *Journal of Black Psychology, 21*, 49–70.

Stevenson, H. C. (2003). The conspicuous invisibility of black ways of being: Missing data in new models of children's mental health. *School Psychology Review, 32*(4), 520–524.

Stevenson, H. C., Reed, J., Bodison, P., & Bishop, A. (1995). *Silence is not always golden: Adolescent racial socialization attitudes and the experience of depression and anger.* Unpublished manuscript, University of Pennsylvania, Philadelphia.

Stevenson, H. C., & Renard, G. (1993). Trusting ole' wise owls: Therapeutic utilization of cultural strengths in African American families. *Professional Psychology: Research and Practice, 24*(4), 433–442.

Stevenson, H. C., Jr. (2003). *Playing with anger: Teaching coping skills to African American boys through athletics and culture.* Westport, CT: Praeger.

Sue, D. W., & Sue, D. (1990). *Counseling the culturally different: Theory and practice* (2nd ed.). New York: Wiley.

Sue, S., & Zane, N. (1987). The role of culture and cultural techniques in psychotherapy: A critique and reformulation. *American Psychologist, 42*, 37–45.

Swartz, M. S., Wagner, H. R., Swanson, J. W., Burns, B. J., George, L. K., & Padgett, D. K. (1998). Comparing use of public and private mental health services: The enduring barriers of race and age. *Community Mental Health Journal, 34*(2), 133–144.

President's New Freedom Commission on Mental Health. (2003). *Achieving the Promise: Transforming mental health care in America.* Rockville, MD: U.S. Department of Health and Human Services, New Freedom Commission on Mental Health.

Thomas, A., & Sillen, S. (1991). *Racism and psychiatry.* New York: Citadel.

Triandis H. (1976). *Variations on Black and White perceptions of the social environment.* Urbana: University of Illinois Press.

U.S. Department of Health and Human Services. (2001). *Mental health: Culture, race, and ethnicity—A supplement to mental health: A report of the Surgeon General.* Rockville, MD: U.S. Department of Health and Human Services, Substance Abuse and Mental Health Services Administration, Center for Mental Health Services.

Vargas, L. A., & Koss-Chioino, J. D. (1992). Through the cultural looking glass: A model for understanding culturally responsive psychotherapies. In L. A. Vargas & J. D. Koss-Chioino (Eds.), *Working with culture: Psychotherapeutic interventions with ethnic minority children and adolescents* (pp. 1–24). San Francisco: Jossey-Bass.

Whaley, A. L. (2001). Cultural mistrust: An important psychological construct for diagnosis and treatment of African Americans. *Professional Psychology: Research and Practice, 32,* 555–562.

White, J. L., & Parham, T. A. (1990). *The psychology of Blacks: An African-American perspective* (2nd ed.). Englewood Cliffs, NJ: Prentice-Hall.

Wright, H. H., Scott, H., Randolph, P.-P., Raymond, G., & Tony, A. (1984). Psychiatric diagnosis and the Black patient. *Psychiatric Forum, 12*(2), 65–71.

Zamel, P. C., & Stevenson, H. C. (2003). *Towards a cultural attunement approach in psychological interventions with Black youth.* Unpublished manuscript, University of Pennsylvania.

Index

Children/adolescents (*continued*)
family socialization of, 264
in foster care
  mental health care provided to, 292
  social-emotional development of, 291
  transracial placements, 292
  vulnerability of, 290–291
in grandparent-headed households, 6. *See also* Grandparents, parenting by
insulating from racism, 265
living with biological parents, 88
racial socialization of. *See* Racial socialization
religious socialization of, 194–197
school performance of. *See* Academic achievement; School performance
special needs, church support of, 203
two-home, 89–90
well-being of. *See* Child well-being
Church
role in elder care, 220
separation from state, 205
See also Religious institutions
Civil War, social conditions following, 82–83
Class
diversity in, 28
religious affiliation and, 193
Clinical practice
corporal punishment and, 257–258
cultural worldviews in, 16–17
Cohabitation, prevalence of, 91
Community
African American sense of, 27
definition/manifestation of, 30
ethnic diversity of, marital happiness and, 126–129
experiences/perceptions of, measuring, 122–125
influence on marriage, 112
  family characteristics and, 119–120
minorities in, psychological/behavioral outcomes and, 117–118
perceived adversity of, 118–119, 124, 128

social control as function of, 115–116
social integration in, 122
social support of, 122, 127–128
structural variables in, 121–122
Community context, 13–14
characteristics of, 14
Conflict Tactics Scale, 246
Context
adaptation to, 4
See also Community context; Sociocultural context
Contraception, attitudes toward, religion and, 197
Coping strategies, spirituality/religion as, 202, 321
Corporal punishment
in African American versus European American families, 15–16
anger and, 249
children's interpretations of, 256, 259
context of, 248–251
controversy over, 255
cultural attitudes toward, 207
cultural context of, 245–263
development of attitudes about, 256–257
effects of
  causal mechanisms in, 255–257
  on child outcomes, 251–255
  externalizing problem outcomes and, 251–253
  parental emotional support and, 253–254
  parental goals and, 251
policy implications, 258–259
practice implications, 257–258
religious affiliation and, 248
in single- versus two-parent families, 247–248
Swedish ban on, 258
Crack cocaine, youth violence and, 56
Crime victimization, rate of, 55–56
Cultural bias, in behavioral sciences, 315–317
Cultural disadvantage theory, 11
Cultural issues, in clinical practice, 16–17
Cultural values
about race/ethnicity, 266
African, preservation of, 34

Income
  African American, 67, 146–147
    historical factors affecting, 80
  data on, 46
  family, child development and, 6
  family structure and, 5
  racial disparities in, 7, 84
Infant mortality rate
  African American, 46
  racial disparities in, 54–55
Infants, African American, adoption of, 287
Institutional practice, critiques of, 4
Institutionalized racism, 136
  historical impacts of, 316–317
  socioeconomic legacies of, 7–8
Interactional-situational approach, 14
Interethnic Placement Act, 301*t*, 302
Interventions
  culturally relevant framework for, 311–334
    human connection in, 322
    movement in, 322–323
    policy implications, 327–328
    racial/cultural socialization in, 324–325
    recommendations for, 325–327
    spirituality/religion in, 321–322
    style matters in, 318–325
    treatment strategies in, 326–327
  ignorance of cultural relevance in, 314–318
  lack of cultural relevance in, 312
  movement as, 323
  safe context for, 313
  stylings in. *See* Style/styling
Isomorphic attribution, 322

J

Jim Crow laws, 82
Job opportunities. *See* Employment
Jobless rate. *See* Unemployment

K

Kwanzaa, 34

L

Language
  African, in African American English, 32
  African American use of, 319–321

call-response in, 319–320
  narrative sequencing in, 320–321
  signification in, 320
  See also African American English
Language environment, academic achievement and, 229–230
Living arrangements
  single, 92
  See also Homeplace; Housing
Low birth weight, racial disparities in, 55
Low-income families
  after-school programs and, 152–153
  goals of, 35–36
  and importance of homeplace, 169–177
  research on, 37
  See also Poverty
Lynching, 82–83
  legacies of, 314–315

M

Malaysia, wealth redistribution in, 84
Marital relationships, 111–134
  community disorganization perspective of, 113–114, 113*f*
  community poverty and, 114
  community support of, 118
  emotional/physical health and, 111
  percentage African Americans in, 111
  residential stability and, 114–117
  socioeconomic disadvantage and, 112
  workplace discrimination and, 150–151
Marriage
  African American male versus female pattern of, 121
  mate availability and, 112
  public policy and, 99
  walking, 88
Massacres, post–Civil War, 82–83
Medicaid, 52–53
Medicare, 52–53
Mental health
  nonstandard work schedules and, 143–144
  racial inequities and, 119
Mental health care, for African Americans, 311–312
Ministries, outreach, 204–205
Minority groups, commonalities/distinctions among, 32–35